Michael Chamberlain focuses on medieval Damascus to develop a new approach to the relationship between the society and culture of the Middle East. The author argues that historians have long imposed European strictures onto societies to which they were alien. Western concepts of legitimate order were inappropriate to medieval Muslim society where social advancement was dependent upon the production of knowledge and religious patronage, and it was the household, rather than the state agency or the corporation, that held political and social power. An interesting parallel is drawn between the learned elite and the warriors of Damascus who, through similar strategies, acquired status and power and passed them on in their households. By examining material from the Latin West, Sung China, and the Sinicized empires of Inner Asia, the author addresses the nature of political power in the period and places the Middle East within the context of medieval Eurasia.

Cambridge Studies in Islamic Civilization

Knowledge and social practice in medieval Damascus, 1190–1350

Cambridge Studies in Islamic Civilization

Titles in the series

B. F. MUSALLAM. *Sex and society in Islam: birth control before the nineteenth century*
SURAIYA FAROQHI. *Towns and townsmen of Ottoman Anatolia: trade, crafts and food production in an urban setting, 1520–1650*
PATRICIA CRONE. *Roman, provincial and Islamic law: the origins of the Islamic patronate*
STEFAN SPERL. *Mannerism in Arabic poetry: a structural analysis of selected texts, 3rd century AH/9th century AD–5th century AH/11th century AD*
BEATRICE FORBES MANZ. *The rise and rule of Tamerlane*
AMNON COHEN. *Economic life in Ottoman Jerusalem*
PAUL E. WALKER. *Early philosophical Shiism: the Ismaili Neoplatonism of Abū Yaʿqūb al-Sijistānī*
BOAZ SHOSHAN. *Popular culture in medieval Cairo*
STEPHEN FREDERIC DALE. *Indian merchants and Eurasian trade, 1600–1750*
AMY SINGER. *Palestinian peasants and Ottoman officials: rural administration around sixteenth-century Jerusalem*

Knowledge and social practice in medieval Damascus, 1190–1350

MICHAEL CHAMBERLAIN
University of Wisconsin

CAMBRIDGE
UNIVERSITY PRESS

Published by the Press Syndicate of the University of Cambridge
The Pitt Building, Trumpington Street, Cambridge CB2 1RP
40 West 20th Street, New York, NY 10011-4211, USA
10 Stamford Road, Oakleigh, Melbourne 3166, Australia

First published 1994

Printed in Great Britain at the University Press, Cambridge

A catalogue record for this book is available from the British Library

Library of Congress cataloguing in publication data

Chamberlain, Michael
Knowledge and social practice in medieval Damascus, 1190–1350 /
Michael Chamberlain.
p. cm.–(Cambridge studies in Islamic civilization)
Includes bibliographical references.
ISBN 0-521-45406-9
1. Damascus (Syria)–Politics and government. 2. Damascus
(Syria–Intellectual life. 3. Elite (Social science)–Syria–
Damascus–History. I. Title. II. Series.
DS99.D3C48 1994
956.91′4402–dc20 93-46181 CIP

ISBN 0 521 454069 hardback

SE

To my family

Contents

Preface

It is sad but unavoidable that a single book can never pay off all the debts its production has incurred. This study began as an attempt to understand the social uses of knowledge by the learned elite of Damascus, and took me in directions I originally had no intention of pursuing. The book is aimed at a number of audiences, in part to acknowledge that it could never have been completed without borrowing from other disciplines. Having taken much from anthropologists, sociologists, comparative historians, and historians of China and the Latin West, I hope they will find something here to interest them in turn.

The notes are at the bottom of the page, not to give an impression of scholarly formidableness, but to allow the book to be read in two ways. Scholars of medieval Islamic history will notice that the notes not only are intended to support the argument, but in many cases to advance it. Scholars of other fields may read the narrative without reference to the notes.

This book, not to mention the greater part of my education, would not have been possible without my teacher Ira Lapidus. Without his example, I would have not tried to become a historian; without his guidance and support, I would never have made it thus far. I am also grateful to my teachers, William Brinner, Eugene Irschick, Hamid Algar, André Ferré, and others.

I must also thank the history departments at Berkeley, Stanford, and Wisconsin. This book would not have been possible without the support and good conversation I found in these three places. I am especially indebted to Peter Duus, Richard Roberts, and Joel Beinin for their support and encouragement at Stanford. I am also very grateful to André Wink, whose ideas entered the dissertation upon which this book is based before either of us knew we would find ourselves in Madison, and who has given me much advice and support since my arrival here.

As much as anything else, this book is a product of talks with friends, the support of friends, and thoughts about friends, so I would like to thank Rikki Allanna Zrimsek, Irène Keller, Margaret O'Brien, Lisa Saper, Margaret Malamud, Wendy Verlaine, Mia Fuller, James Ketelaar, David McDonald, Mary Conn, Peter Flood, Holly Huprich, and Brendan Phipps. To Krystyna von Henneberg, who helped me through the dissertation upon which this book is based, I owe more than space allows me to express.

I would also like to thank readers of various versions of the manuscript, who pointed out errors and infelicities and suggested new ways of thinking about these problems and presenting them: Richard Bulliet, William Courtenay, Patricia Crone, Dale Eickelman, Jan Heesterman, Krystyna von Henneberg, Anatoly Khazanov, David McDonald, Margaret Sommerville, André Wink, Lynne Withey, and the readers for the Press whose names are unknown to me. I am much appreciative of the efforts my editors, Marigold Acland and Mary Starkey, have put into the production of the book. It goes without saying that all errors are my own. Also many thanks to the École des hautes études en sciences sociales, where some of these ideas were first presented.

The libraries in which I have worked, and where I have always been happy, include the University of California, Stanford University, the Hoover Institution, the University of Wisconsin, Cambridge University, the British Library, the Bibliothèque Nationale, the Vatican Library, and the Süleymaniye, Köprülü, and Topkapi libraries in Istanbul. To the staff of the Köprülü, where often I worked long periods alone, I am especially grateful for many small kindnesses. To the people in Damascus and Aleppo who have helped me with this project, and shown me so much kindness, I have not the words to express my gratitude. I am also grateful to Donald Little for supplying me with microfilms of manuscripts that have been withdrawn from circulation in Istanbul. Finally, I can hardly express enough my thanks to Jacqueline Sublet and the Institut pour l'histoire et la recherche des textes, both for their kindly reception and their incomparable collection of microfilmed manuscripts.

For the money that supported this project I thank the US taxpayer (trebly), the Mellon Foundation (doubly), the Graduate School at Berkeley, The Wisconsin Alumni Research Foundation (doubly), and the Middle East Study Center of the University of California and the history department at Stanford (both multiply).

Abbreviations

Annales: ESC	*Annales: économies, sociétés, civilisations*
BEO	*Bulletin d'études orientales*
BSOAS	*Bulletin of the School of Oriental and African Studies, University of London*
CSSH	*Comparative Studies in Society and History*
EI (1)	*Encyclopedia of Islam*, 1st edn. (Leiden, 1913–38)
EI (2)	*Encyclopedia of Islam*, 2nd edn. (Leiden, 1954–)
IC	*Islamic Culture*
IJMES	*International Journal of Middle East Studies*
JA	*Journal Asiatique*
JARCE	*Journal of the American Research Institute in Egypt*
JAOS	*Journal of the American Oriental Society*
JESHO	*Journal of the Economic and Social History of the Orient*
JSS	*Journal of Semitic Studies*
MIFD	*Mélanges de l'Institut Français de Damas*
MW	*The Muslim World*
RAA	*Revue des Arts Asiatiques*
REI	*Revue des études Islamiques*
REMMM	*Revue du monde musulman et de la Méditerranée*
RSO	*Revista degli studi orientale*
SI	*Studia Islamica*
ZDMG	*Zeitschrift der Deutschen Morgenländischen Gesellschaft*

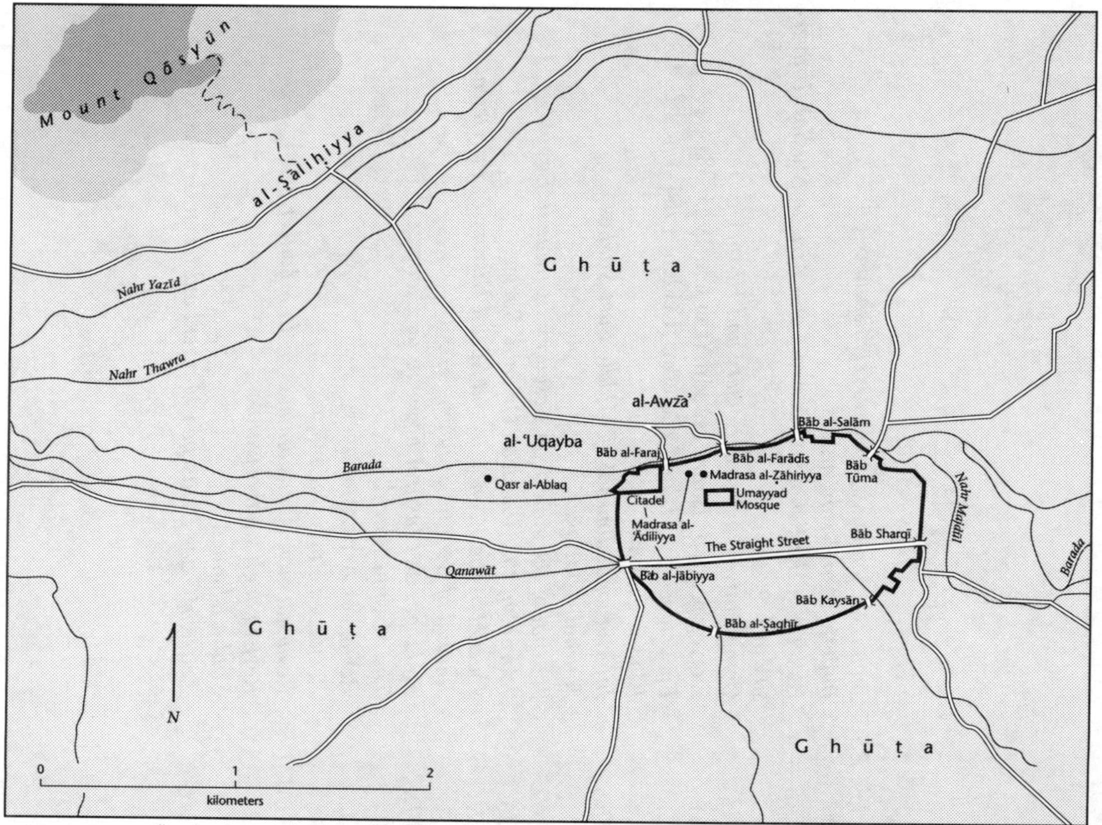

Compiled by Sara Arscott, from N Elisséeff, *La Description de Damas d'Ibn 'Asākir* (Damascus, 1959).

1 Damascus and its surrounding region

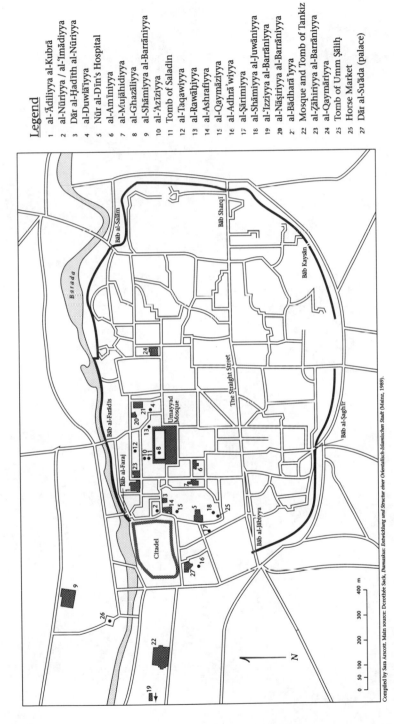

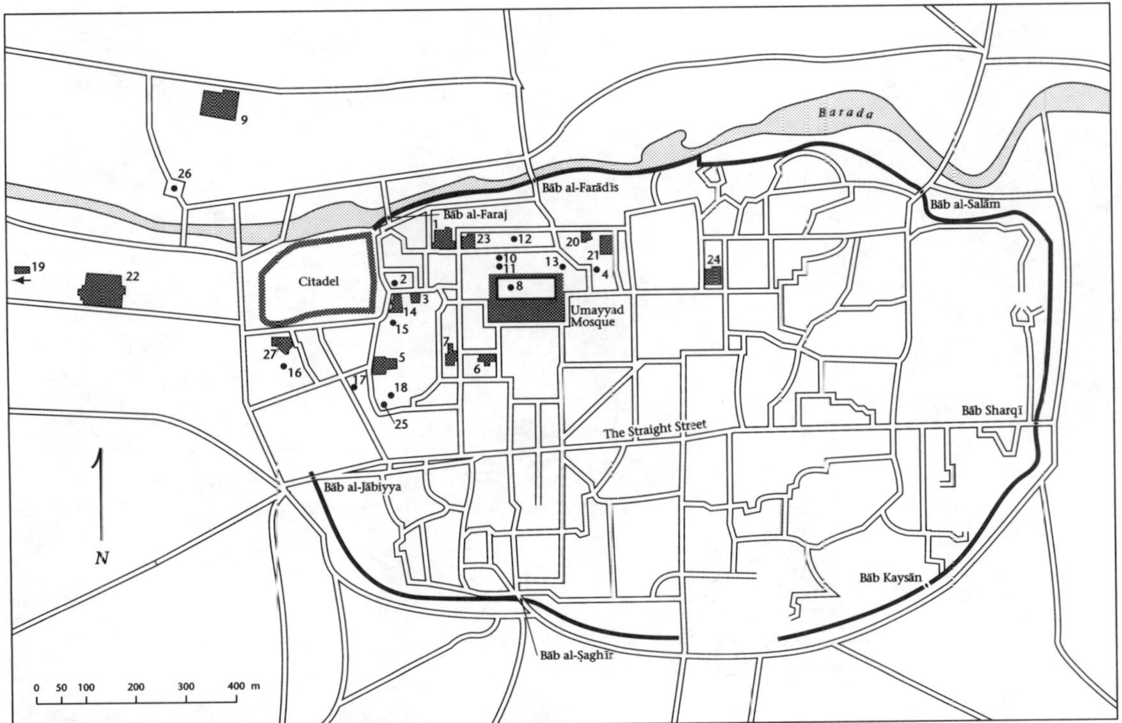

Compiled by Sara Arscott. Main source: Dorothée Sack, *Damaskus: Entwicklung und Structur einer Orientalisch-Islamischen Stadt* (Mainz, 1989).

2 Damascus in the thirteenth century

Legend

1 al-ʿĀdiliyya al-Kubrā
2 al-Nūriyya / al-ʿImādiyya
3 Dār al-Ḥadīth al-Nūriyya
4 al-Duwlāʿiyya
5 Nūr al-Dīn's Hospital
6 al-Amīniyya
7 al-Mujāhidiyya
8 al-Ghazāliyya
9 al-Shāmiyya al-Barrāniyya
10 al-ʿAzīziyya
11 Tomb of Saladin
12 al-Taqawiyya
13 al-Rawāḥiyya
14 al-Ashrafiyya
15 al-Qaymāziyya
16 al-Adhrāʾwiyya
17 al-Ṣārimiyya
18 al-Shāmiyya al-Juwāniyya
19 al-ʿIzziyya al-Barrāniyya
20 al-Nāṣiriyya al-Barrāniyya
21 al-Bādharāʾiyya
22 Mosque and Tomb of Tankiz
23 al-Ẓāhiriyya al-Barrāniyya
24 al-Qaymāriyya
26 Tomb of Umm Ṣāliḥ
25 Horse Market
27 Dār al-Suʿāda (palace)

Introduction

General statement of the problem

This book is about the social uses of learning in high medieval Damascus. The topic offers an opportunity to address two problems that historians of the period have puzzled over but not resolved.

The first arises out of the methodologies Western historians have applied to high medieval Islamic societies. Over the last two generations a number of historians have applied various methodologies of European social and institutional history to the period. The medieval Middle East would appear to be a suitable object of these approaches. The apparently undivided sovereignty of its rulers, the role of law in the regulation of its social life, the relatively high monetization of its economies, the existence of bureaucracies and large urban garrisons of standing armies – collectively these give the high medieval Middle East the characteristics of a highly complex and urban society on a par with early modern Europe. It should be not surprising perhaps that appearing frequently in studies of the period are familiar entities such as "government," "the state," "higher education," "the army," "bureaucracy," and "administration." Notions such as "dynastic legitimacy" and the distinction between the private and public spheres also find their way into the field. Historians often employ these concepts casually, but uncritical use has often put the field in danger of anachronism and confusion. Another problem with this approach is that it often leads historians to use "corruption," "usurpation," and "illegitimacy" as explanatory devices when the entities and institutions they study do not function as expected.

Several recent historians have acknowledged that the formal objects of social and institutional history have often eluded us. The most sensitive accounts of the period have stressed the informality of social practices and groups, while others have described informal analogues to the permanent hierarchical institutions and social bodies characteristic of other medieval societies. This notion of informality is useful to the extent that it distinguishes the high medieval Middle East from societies that had permanent hierarchical institutions and groups. But the observation is largely negative. It does little but reiterate that the high medieval Middle East was not characterized by some of the structural characteristics of some other Eurasian societies of the period. Also, in its implicit comparison to Europe, the focus on informality has often concentrated less on what was there than what was not. This first problem led to the principal issue that this book seeks to address. In looking for the defining possibilities and constraints on culture, social life, and politics, can we be satisfied with describing either the "corruption" of the formal institutions of other societies or their "informal" analogues?

The second problem concerns the evidence that has come down to us from the high medieval Middle East. The period is rich in sources. It also had abundant supplies of cheap paper, a dry climate, and administrative traditions stretching back to late antiquity. However, in spite of conditions conducive to the production and preservation of document collections comparable to those of the Latin West, the period is surprisingly poor in original document collections. George Duby's memoirs might tempt medieval Islamic historians to lament the past's unfairness to the field.[1] To the ten thousand original documents Duby exploited from the archive of the Abbey of Cluny alone a historian of the high medieval Middle East might counterpoise a much smaller number from some very large empires.

Given the small number of original documents that have survived from the high medieval Middle East, and the inadequacy of concepts derived from European historiography, it might seem reasonable to question whether a social history of the period is possible at all. The point of departure of this study is the similarity between the historiographical and conceptual problems. Where the sociological emphasis has been on the "lack" of formal institutions and group structures, the historiographical problem has been to grapple with the "scarcity" of original document collections. Given that in both cases the somewhat artificial standard of comparison is Europe, a reexamination of the methods of social history as applied to the Middle East might lead to new perspectives on these lasting problems.

The line of inquiry that this study proposes is to examine the practices by which power and status were acquired, exerted, and asserted. In the high medieval Middle East, this study will argue, it was the elite household (*bayt*, pl. *buyūt*), and not the state, the agency, or the autonomous corporate or religious body, that held power, and that exercised it in most of its social, political, cultural, and economic aspects. When we compare the medieval Middle East with other Eurasian societies of the period, a more productive approach is to examine the practices by which powerful households acquired power and prestige and passed them on to their descendants. Studying the practices of the patriarchal household – "economy" in the Aristotelian sense – also brings together various fields that historians have dealt with as separate conceptual

[1] G. Duby, *L'histoire continue* (Paris, 1991), 37.

unities.[2] Attention to the strategies of households rather than the taxonomy of formal institutions also helps us compare the Middle East with other societies without treating Europe as a privileged standard. It also helps us to understand how the exercise of power in the period formed the inescapable environment of elite households, both civilian and military, and shaped their strategies within it in similar ways.

This approach in turn allows us to examine the surviving "literary" sources in a new light. If we ask how elite strategies of survival made use of writing, we can exploit in a new way those written materials that were preserved in large numbers. Is the relative scarcity of collections of original documents due to accidental (and therefore unproblematic) loss, or to another reason that we have overlooked? If archival administrative, household, or corporate documents survived only in small numbers, what accounts for the preservation of the large number of sources, especially the biographical dictionaries, that social historians have seen as "literary" and "formulaic"? Why were these sources composed, stored, and preserved? What ends did the effort and money invested in these materials serve?

This book is an exploratory essay that works out these two problems together. It ceases lamenting the absence of original documents, or squeezing what can be got out of the small number that have survived. Rather, this study interprets the surviving "literary" sources as a means of understanding the cultural practices by which households attempted to survive in time. By reading these sources in this way, we come to understand issues that have long eluded medieval Islamic historians. How did our subjects imagine the nature of the social universe and maneuver within it? How did households acquire status and power and hold onto them over time? In the absence of stable and hierarchical institutions, how are we to understand the exercise of power in the period? The interior of the household was defined by the silence that respected its sacred and untouchable character. However, our sources, often written by members of these households, and many more describing the careers of their members in some detail, give us a unique if oblique view into how households survived in the larger world. This study will attempt to show that these elusive, "formulaic," and literary sources were not merely spared the accidents that somehow befell other more "serious" sources, but rather that they should be interpreted as repositories of the practices by which households survived over generations.

By using these sources to understand how elite households made use of cultural practices for social ends, we accomplish three things. First, we begin to exploit the sources that are available to us in a more critical and productive manner. Second, we may compare the medieval Middle East to other agrarian

[2] See O. Brunner, *Neue Wege der Sozialgeschichte* (Göttingen, 1956), 7–32 for the development of the Aristotelian concept of "economics" out of household management.

civilizations of medieval Eurasia with greater sensitivity – though this study will suggest more than it settles in this respect. And finally we can reach a more precise understanding of the accurate though non-specific notion of the "informality" of high medieval Islamic societies.

Social survival in the high medieval Middle East

European observers of the medieval Middle East have long been interested in, and often horrified by, the precarious conditions of social survival of its elites. Beginning in the early modern period, and continuing into the present, European writers have searched the Middle East for the mechanisms which reproduced European feudal, aristocratic, or bourgeois society. Failing to find what they expected, many have experienced the Middle East as the nightmarish reversal of the European social order.[3]

In a subjective sense these writers were correct. There is no doubting the rarity in the Middle East of the formal mechanisms of transmitting status that Europeans have prized.[4] Civilian elite (aᶜyān) households could not make use of such European institutions as inherited rights, immunities, franchises, charters, deeds, titles or patents of nobility or office, or hereditary privileges. Nor could the aᶜyān restrict their status to small groups through the cultural strategies of elite groups elsewhere. They had little of the "natural" taste and "good breeding" of hereditary aristocracies, nor the ideology of bureaucrats and professional associations. Moreover, unlike elites in the Ottoman empire or Sung China, to mention just two examples, they were unable to insert themselves into state agencies to acquire or transmit elite status. As the aᶜyān "lacked" these legal, corporate, or state mechanisms of household survival, there seems little reason to reject the traditional European perception of them as the "servants" or "slaves" of despots, and of the social order generally as either "despotic," "disorderly," or "corrupt."

[3] See for a classic example de Montesquieu, who believed that the absence of private property and a hereditary nobility in the Middle East were the determining characteristics of "Oriental despotism," C.-L. de Montesquieu, *L'esprit des Lois*, vol. I (Paris, 1867), 64–5. Also N. Daniel, *Islam, Europe, and Empire* (Edinburgh, 1966), 3–18, 30; A. Grosrichard, *Les Structures du sérail, la fiction du despotisme asiatique dans l'Occident classique* (Paris, 1979); P. S. Springborg, "The Contractual State. Reflections on Oriental Despotism," *History of Political Thought*, 8, no. 3 (Winter, 1987), esp. 414–31; Springborg, *Western Republicanism and Oriental Despotism* (Austin, TX, 1992); L. Valensi, *Venise et la Sublime Porte. La Naissance du despot* (Paris, 1987).

[4] As it has become common scholarly usage, I use the term *aᶜyān* to refer to civilian elites, and in the case of Damascus in the period those civilians who were capable of competing for stipendiary posts (*manṣabs*) through their acquired learning and manners. The use of the term should be qualified, however, even as it retains its descriptive utility. The sources for Damascus and elsewhere could refer to both civilians and warriors as aᶜyān (the *aᶜyān al-umarāᶜ* for example); and civilian elites had a number of other terms denoting their conviction of their superiority over others: *khāṣṣa* ("elect"), *akābir* ("great"), *ashrāf*, and many others. The absence of a single and specific term for elite status is another indication that Damascus was not a society with estates or formal grades of rank. But with these reservations I will use the term for simplicity's sake and to conform to standard usage.

However, what this perception fails to account for is the successful survival of aᶜyān households throughout the high medieval Middle East. In Damascus (which added to these apparent impediments to social reproduction a number of its own) some households transmitted their status from the early sixth/twelfth century to well beyond the middle of the eighth/fourteenth. Many others passed on their status more modestly but just as certainly for two or three generations. This book asks how these households, living in a turbulent period, able to control property only with difficulty, made use of cultural practices associated with knowledge (*ᶜilm*) in their strategies of social survival.

Knowledge, cultural capital, and social survival

Long before contemporary scholars began to look at knowledge as the "cultural capital" of elites, medieval Muslim writers associated knowledge with social survival. "The capital of the student," wrote Ibn Jamāᶜa, "is his thoughts."[5] Ibn al-Ḥājj also linked money and knowledge as forms of social capital: "knowledge (ᶜilm) will protect you, while you have to protect your money. Knowledge judges others while money is adjudicated. Money decreases when it is spent, while knowledge is accounted as alms when it is dispensed."[6] As much as their "treasures of knowledge, not of gold" the words by which they represented themselves – *ᶜulamāᵓ* ("learned"), *ahl al-ᶜilm* ("people of knowledge") – affirmed their association of status with knowledge.[7]

Yet, as critical as understanding the social uses of knowledge is, how aᶜyān households made use of learning in their strategies of social survival remains an open question. This is not due to any lack of interest in the subject of learning broadly defined. Since the Middle Ages, European scholars have studied Islamic scholastic, philosophical, scientific, and legal literatures, and a large and ever-growing body of scholarship on these subjects has appeared since. More recently intellectual historians have studied the lives and works of

5 Ibn Jamāᶜa, *Tadhkira al-sāmiᶜ wa al-mutakallim* (Beirut, 1974), 72. Metaphors associating learning with capital or money are a commonplace in the sources. See for example the shaykh who "spent all he had in the coffers of his knowledge" (mā ᶜindahu min khazāna ᶜilmihi), Ṣafadī, *Aᶜyān al-ᶜAṣr*, Süleymaniye Kütüphanesi, Atif Effendi MS 1809, 623b; also ibid., 57b; Abū Shāma, *Tarājim rijāl al-qarnayn al-sādis wa al-sābiᶜ al-maᶜrūf bi al-dhayl ᶜalā al-rawḍatayn* (Beirut, 1974), 41. Knowledge was prized as the "inheritance of the prophets," in ḥadīth, ditties, and commonplaces: Subkī, Staatsbibliothek, Berlin, preuss. Kulturbesitz Or. 8, no. 1440, fol. 33: "wa-lā irth ilā shirᶜa Aḥmad." Ignorance was occasionally referred to as being "short of merchandise in ᶜilm" (qalīl al-biḍāᶜa fī ᶜilm): Ibn Kathīr, *al-Bidāya wa al-nihāya fī al-tāᵓrīkh* (repr., Beirut, 1982), 14/123; for similar metaphors see Subkī, Staatsbibliothek MS, 14; Ṣafadī, *al-Wāfī bi-al-wāfayāt*, H. Ritter et al. eds., *Das Bibliographische Lexicon* (Istanbul, 1931-), 18/396. See also Zarnūjī, *Kitāb taᶜlīm al-mutaᶜallam ṭarīq al-taᶜallum* (Beirut, 1981), 39; Ibn al-Ḥājj, *Madkhal al-sharᶜ al-sharīf,* 4 vols. in 2 (Cairo, 1929), 1/87; Ibn Nāṣir al-Dīn, *Tarājim Ibn Taymiyya*, British Library Or. MS 7714, fol. 11.

6 Ibn al-Ḥājj, *Madkhal*, 1/69.

7 For "treasures of knowledge, not of gold" (kunūz al-ᶜilm lā adh-dhahab) see Ṣafadī, *al-Wāfī*, 21/342.

exemplary scholars or important movements. They have been joined by institutional historians, who have traced the origins and diffusion of institutions related to the transmission of knowledge.

Social historians have also been interested in the aʿyān, for a variety of reasons. The aʿyān were the authors of our sources, which reflect their lives and concerns. The learned elite were also judges (*qāḍīs*), teachers, and communal leaders. Ira Lapidus has analyzed the social roles of the learned elite to criticize the notion that "Oriental despotism" atomized cities into isolated groups incapable of cooperating with one another.[8] Historians following Lapidus have looked to the ʿulamāʾ to explain how a precarious social equilibrium was maintained in the face of ethnic and religious diversity and contradictory interests.[9] Lapidus, Joan Gilbert, and Carl Petry have analyzed how the ʿulamāʾ mediated among military and ruling elites, merchants, artisans, and the common people; how they carried out administrative and judicial functions in the absence of bureaucratic state agencies; and how they ensured continuity from generation to generation in unsettled societies.[10]

However, even though a large body of literature has appeared on Islamic intellectual, legal, and institutional history, and a smaller one on the social functions of the learned elite in cities, these approaches have been less concerned with understanding how the aʿyān used knowledge for social and political ends. Legal and intellectual historians have considered social–historical questions to be on the margins of their central concerns. When they have studied the social aspects of knowledge, they have wanted to understand the contexts or origins of important ideas, and not the social and political uses of knowledge in historical time in specific places. Institutional historians, I will argue below, have often mistaken practices of social competition for institutional structures. Both groups have also seen the ʿulamāʾ as a natural and unproblematic social category throughout Islamic history, and have often been insensitive to local and temporal variations.

Social historians have been more alert to the specific character of the groups that referred to themselves as the aʿyān or ʿulamāʾ. However, because these historians have been largely concerned with the ʿulamāʾ's social roles, they have emphasized the learned elite's relational characteristics vis-à-vis other groups. The aʿyān's intrinsic properties, their struggles with one another, how they made use of their learning and cultivation in social competition, all remain open issues.

Even though historians have long been interested in the study of learning

[8] I. Lapidus, *Muslim Cities in the Later Middle Ages* (Cambridge, MA, 1967), 1–8, 185–91.

[9] R. Bulliet, *The Patricians of Nishapur* (Cambridge, MA, 1972); Lapidus, *Muslim Cities*; C. Petry, *The Civilian Elite of Cairo in the Later Middle Ages* (Princeton, 1981); C. Cahen, *Pre-Ottoman Turkey*, J. Jones-Williams trans. (London, 1968); R. Mottahedeh, *Loyalty and Leadership in an Early Islamic Society* (Princeton, 1980).

[10] Lapidus, *Muslim Cities*, 107–15, 130–42, 189–90; Petry, *The Civilian Elite*, 321–3; J. Gilbert, "The ʿUlamaʾ of Medieval Damascus and the International World of Islamic Scholarship," Ph.D. Dissertation (University of California, Berkeley, 1977), 144.

and in the social functions of the ʿulamāʾ, we have yet to investigate relations between universal cultural practices and particular social strategies. This book is an inquiry into how the aʿyān of Damascus, over a 160-year period in the high Middle Ages, acquired and made use of knowledge in their strategies of social survival. By studying the social uses of knowledge, my aim is to raise and address a number of central problems in the social and cultural history of the high medieval Middle East. How did aʿyān households reproduce themselves in time? How did they defend themselves from predation by warriors? By what means did the aʿyān gain their useful loyalties and cultural distinction? What were the practices by which they competed with one another? How did they imagine the nature of the social universe and plot their trajectories within it? The answers to these questions, this study will suggest, lie not in the social, legal, and institutional structures and processes that have long attracted scholarly attention.[11] Nor can they be described satisfactorily as "informal" or "personal" without draining them of their particularity and complexity. Rather, these problems are better addressed by interpreting the social uses in historical time of cultural practices that scholars have often seen as universally "Islamic," and without particular social uses.

Much of this study will cover what may appear to be well-trodden territory. The cultural practices that this book will examine are nearly universal in pre-modern Islamic socictics, indeed in literate agrarian societies in general. Lecturing, reading, writing, reproducing texts, debating, discipleship, and scholarly friendship seem so widespread as to be marginal to the interests of social historians. These practices and relationships were similar to, and often influenced by, ancient rhetorical education, medieval scholasticism, and medieval Jewish education. It is not surprising therefore that scholars have studied the production of knowledge in the context of the history of education: in other places, it is where practices related to the production of knowledge often converge. However, in the case of Damascus I hope to show that we have often misinterpreted these practices precisely by studying them as "educational." In Damascus, cultural practices associated with the production of knowledge had different meanings and uses. Placing these practices in their correct context reveals much about broader and unresolved issues concerning power, culture, and social relations.

This study focuses on the aʿyān in part because the sources on them are better than on the social history of other groups such as the warrior elite and (to a much greater extent) the common people. However, aʿyān households can be studied not only to advance our understanding of medieval Islamic scholarship, or the ʿulamāʾ as a social category, but also to address relations among power, culture, and social life on a more general level. Modern scholars

[11] See I. Lapidus, *Muslim Cities in the Later Middle Ages*, 2nd. edn. (Cambridge, 1984), xiv–xv; Mottahedeh, *Loyalty and Leadership*, 1–7 for two social historians who have turned to the study of culture and manners broadly defined as critical not only in themselves, but also as a means of understanding these other domains.

have generally drawn a hard and fast distinction between warrior elites (*amīrs*) and the aʿyān, and have seen their relationships to one another as a division of social and political labor.[12] However, this book will show how both amīrs and aʿyān had similar relations to rulers, similar forms of social and political competition, and imagined the social and political universes in similar ways. In particular, as I shall show in the following chapters, many of the cultural practices we have taken to be "educational" in the case of the aʿyān had much wider uses, and often characterized military households as well. We will also see, to the extent possible, how the common people made use of these practices. By using the limited information available on the common people, I hope both to question the extent to which these cultural practices were monopolized by the elite and to ask how universal practices were contested by particular groups.

In order to arrive at this argument the book will first devote a number of pages to discussing the nature of political power in Damascus, in the Middle East as a whole, and in the wider context of Eurasian history in the period. Two central concepts of the argument are what may be termed the "maladroit patrimonialism" of high medieval Middle Eastern rulers; and its relationship to "*fitna*," or struggle, sometimes violent and sometimes not, carried out without reference to the "state" or interference from it. Fitna is a term with so many meanings that it should be discussed at the outset. Its meanings in the classical Arabic lexicons and in the Qurʾān and ḥadīth include "disorder," "civil war," "factional competition," "sedition," "madness," "temptation," and the sexual attractiveness of women, in all cases implying either a threat to legitimate order or a collapse into social, political, psychological, or sexual disorder. What this study hopes to accomplish is to demonstrate that while fitna was indeed feared as dangerously divisive and destructive, in concert with maladroit patrimonialism it remained nonetheless the inescapable environment and indeed the fundamental dynamic of politics and social life.

By examining the relationship of maladroit patrimonialism to fitna we can understand the distinctive and often misunderstood character of high medieval Middle Eastern politics. Rulers lived in cities and recognized few impediments to seizing the wealth of others. Rulers also had the power to redistribute status and revenue sources continuously. However, we cannot consider them "despots" in any real sense of the term. Rulers had no monopoly of coercive force. Throughout the period under consideration, rulers never had the knowledge, the agencies, and the independent coercive power to coordinate and control the subordinate elites upon whom they depended to rule. Rather, power was diffused among the households of powerful amīrs and aʿyān. Rulers were dependent on the same households – of

[12] The most influential study in this respect is M.G.S. Hodgson's discussion of the "dividing up of power," in the "aʿyān-amīr system," *The Venture of Islam. Conscience and History in a World Civilization*, vol. II: *The Expansion of Islam in the Middle Periods* (Chicago, 1974), 64–9, 91–4, esp. 64.

both aʿyān and amīrs – whom they regularly subjugated to predation. Thus the peculiar character of high medieval Middle Eastern politics. The dynamic tension in high medieval Middle Eastern cities such as Damascus was between the diffusion of power and revenue sources among elite households on the one hand; and the physical propinquity of rulers, their ability to reassign revenue sources, and the relative absence of restraints on their seizure of property on the other. This tension is what gives fitna its explanatory utility.

Two major spheres of aʿyān social life – what we have formalized as "higher education" and the "suppression of heresy" – were both experienced by our subjects as arenas of fitna. In both cases they experienced fitna within the domain of knowledge much as amīrs did within the domain of war. This study will suggest that we look beyond the formal, public, and legalistic aspects of power and social life, and try instead to understand their abiding possibilities and constraints. By studying the competitive practices of fitna as exercised by both amīrs and aʿyān, we come to understand on a more general level what historians have formalized as the distinct spheres of "society," "culture," and the "state." We can also undermine the anachronistic notion of the existence of "state" and "society" as distinct entities, and of political and social competition as the separate domains of amīrs and aʿyān respectively. Fitna, as we shall see in the course of this study, was not the temporary breakdown of a preexisting legitimate order, but in concert with maladroit patrimonialism formed the central dynamic of all elite social and political life. It imposed its logic on most of their political and social relationships.

Approaches to culture and society in the medieval Middle East

When Western scholars have studied medieval Middle Eastern peoples, they have brought with them an implicit theory, often a deterministic one, of relations between culture and social life. Europeans have long taken Islam as a historically transcendent object of inquiry. The constitution of Islam as a historical object began with the earliest European descriptions of the Middle East. Beginning with the crusades, and continuing into the present, it has often been Islam that "explains" the terrifying, pathetic, or exemplary otherness of Middle Eastern peoples.[13] When we think about the "feudal" Latin West or "imperial" China it is an attribute of their political organization that we seize upon as emblematic of what is most important about them. But the words by which scholars represent the medieval Middle East – the Islamic World, Islam, Islamdom, the Muslim World – reveal how Western scholars have continued to take religious culture to represent the Middle East. Even today, a glance at journal or course titles will reveal the degree to which this concentration on religion continues to dominate the field.

[13] See M. Rodinson, *Europe and the Mystique of Islam*, R. Veinus trans. (Seattle, 1987), 3–48, 60–71.

Like many generalizations, this focus on Islam both hides and reveals a truth. There is no doubt that many people in the pre-modern Middle East understood power and collective life with reference to the sacred, more so perhaps than is true of some other pre-modern societies. The aᶜyān of medieval Middle Eastern societies styled themselves – and in our period supported themselves – as a religious elite. Rulers and warriors explained their strategies and sometimes understood them in religious terms. Moreover, the sources were shaped by a religious sensibility when they were not religious in intent, and cannot be interpreted without an understanding of their religious content.

However, having registered the importance of religion as an object of study, giving Islam the priority it has had brings with it several drawbacks. First, this approach has often obliterated differences among Middle Eastern societies that are distinct in other respects. Islamicists have looked for continuities among societies as different as the seventh-century Ḥijāz, ninth-century Baghdād, and fourteenth-century Damascus, and have often enshrined correspondences among them as truths about a single historical object. In addition, the Islamicist approach has tended to focus attention on origins (of ideas, groups, religious practices, etc.) as a category of historical explanation. Finally, by failing to situate relations between culture and society in specific historical contexts, the Islamicist approach has occasionally lapsed into an essentialism, one that seeks to explain all behavior with reference to a single cultural construct. Ignoring what it dismisses as local or pathological variations on a universal theme, or taking local practices as evidence for universal structures, this approach has regularly effaced the specific character of the societies it examines. It rarely asks how culture becomes a stake or a weapon in specific struggles. In short, Islamicist studies of the pre-modern Middle East have often erased differences among Middle Eastern societies, while constructing artificial and often misleading differences with Europe.

Recent studies of relations between society and culture have tried to escape the occasional universalism and essentialism of this approach. One strategy has been to bring to the study of the medieval Middle East some of the concepts and methods of European social and institutional history. A number of monographs have examined cities, bureaucracies, institutions of justice and social control, cultural institutions such as *madrasas* ("law colleges") and *khanqāhs* (*ṣūfī* "convents"), groups such as sectarian communities, men's associations (*futuwwas* and *aḥdāth*), legal schools (*madhhabs*), ṣūfī orders, and legal and administrative phenomena such as *waqf* (charitable foundation) and *iqṭāᶜ* (temporary land grant). These studies have put the historiography of the high medieval Middle East on a more self-conscious and comparative basis.

However, as promising as such approaches seemed at the outset, they have not worked as well as their proponents expected. The most sensitive studies of the period have realized that formal entities, agencies, institutions, and groups did not determine social relations in the medieval Middle East to the extent they did in the Latin West. Studies of formal entities have advanced only partial explanations of the nature of political and social power, of how aʿyān households reproduced the conditions of their elite status, how they passed on their status and wealth to their descendants, how they constructed and imagined their social ties, and how they competed among themselves and against others. Where social historians began by calling into question some of the anachronistic assumptions of earlier Islamicist scholarship, some of their most important conclusions have been largely negative: formal entities and institutions did not determine social life in the expected manner. By lamenting the "corruption" or positing "informal" analogues to "formal" European practices and entities, we have yet to disengage from ideas we have learned to distrust.

The problem for historians is that after having taken terminology, methods, and concepts from European social history, we have often failed to question their applicability to societies outside Europe. When we attempt to describe a society so distant in time, the first task is to understand Europe's historiographical practices in relation to Europe's own practices of domination and social reproduction. When it has failed to take these fundamental differences into consideration, the modern historiography of the medieval Middle East has often imposed European social ideals on societies that cannot sustain them.

The problem of evidence

A similar problem arises when we look at the application of European methods of exploiting historical evidence to Islamic social history. If there is any medieval Middle Eastern city that seems open to the practices of social history, it is Damascus. There is perhaps more literary, epigraphic, and material evidence on Damascus in the Ayyūbid and Mamlūk periods than on any other city of the high medieval Middle East, with the possible exception of Cairo. Travelers' accounts, chronicles, biographical dictionaries, buildings, street plans, inscriptions, coins, manuals for clerks and secretaries, and treatises on every aspect of intellectual life exist in large numbers. Damascus was also fortunate, from the perspective of historians, in having several generations of local historians and biographers. It would seem that the abundance, variety, and detail of the sources make Damascus an ideal subject for social historians.

Yet in the midst of apparent plenty, social and cultural historians of Damascus – together with historians of other cities of the medieval Middle East – have found the sources impoverished on many of the questions they most wanted to answer. The chronicles and biographical dictionaries convey little information on several of the critical problems that historians have tried to address, while these sources carry masses of information that historians have seen as marginal to their interests. Failing to find the desired information on the social functions of structures and groups, and deluged by what seem to be anomalous or useless anecdotes, scholars of the period have often concluded with some reluctance that these sources are "austere," "stereotypical," or "formulaic."[14] Given the deficiencies of the sources with respect to the critical questions of social history, some scholars have doubted whether a social history of the high medieval Middle East is possible at all. Damascus, although it possesses sources in greater quantity than most other cities, has posed many of the same intractable problems as other cities of the period.

There are several possible strategies that historians might adopt in the face of the difficult nature of the evidence for high medieval Islamic societies. One, already long essayed, has been to sift through the standard sources for their information on social, political, cultural, or economic groups and institutions. While much important work remains to be done, few surprises are to be expected from this approach, and crucial questions remain that it cannot address.

A second strategy is that adopted most notably and successfully by Joan Gilbert for high medieval Damascus and Carl Petry for late medieval Cairo.[15] Gilbert and Petry tabulated the quantifiable information in the biographical dictionaries to address a number of questions about the social origins and composition of civilian elite groups. These scholars have shown that patient handling and sensitive interpretation of serial data can produce important conclusions regarding the affiliations, composition, and social origins of the civilian elite. They have also argued persuasively that accurate prosopographical data can be extracted from the ever-problematic biographical dictionaries. However, in addressing several critical issues, this approach has pointed to others which by its nature it cannot settle. How did the aᶜyān understand their relationship to the social world? What were their strategies for reproducing the conditions of their elite status? By what institutions, codes, and practices did they struggle for power, wealth, and prestige among themselves and against others? These are questions that elude study by quantitative methods even though they may benefit from them.

A final strategy has been the intensive exploitation of the few original documents that have survived from the period. We know that in this highly literate period large numbers of petitions, decrees, contracts, qāḍī-records (records of judges' opinions), wills, estate inventories, and administrative documents were drawn up. However, few of these have survived in the original.

14 On the biographical dictionaries see R. Bulliet, "A Quantitative Approach to Medieval Muslim Biographical Dictionaries," *JESHO* 13 (1970), 195–211; Bulliet, *Patricians of Nishapur*, xi–xiii; H.A.R. Gibb, "Islamic Biographical Literature," in B. Lewis and P.M. Holt eds., *Historians of the Middle East* (Oxford, 1962), 54–8; I. Hafsi, "Recherches sur le genre 'Ṭabaqāt' dans la littérature arabe," *Arabica* 23 (1976), 228–65; 24 (1977), 1–41, 150–86; R.S. Humphreys, *Islamic History: a Framework for Inquiry* (Princeton, 1991), 188–92.

15 C. Petry, *The Civilian Elite*; Gilbert, "The ᶜUlamaʾ." See also R.W. Bulliet, *Conversion to Islam in the Middle Period. An Essay in Quantitative History* (Cambridge, MA, 1979), for a wide-ranging discussion of quantitative approaches to the biographical dictionaries.

Scholars have long regretted this absence of major document collections from the high medieval Middle East. Many scholars, it is fair to say, believe that it is the rarity of documentary evidence that is responsible for the wide gaps in our knowledge of the social history of the period.[16] Some scholars have also lamented that medieval Middle Eastern historiography has lagged behind other fields because of the small number of original documents that have survived from the period. In part because of the rarity of original documents, historians of the high medieval period have given those documents that have been found ever-growing attention, and have placed ever-growing hopes in them.[17] Exploiting original documents, however few in number they may be, has several apparent advantages. Countering the charge that historians of the medieval Middle East privilege literary sources, the study of documents has promised to put the field on the road to historiographical legitimacy. It also has promised to shed new light on issues that other sources obscure or ignore.

Yet as obvious as it might seem for historians to privilege collections of original documents, here too the results have been mixed. Even the most active proponents of original documents have recognized that the number of surviving documents is much smaller than is the case for the high and late medieval Latin West, Sung China, or the Ottoman empire, to take just three examples, and that the uses historians may put them to are more limited still. But one question we have yet to ask is whether document collections had uses in the high medieval Middle East comparable to their uses in these other societies. Is accidental loss the reason that historians have so few original document collections from the high medieval Middle East?

One way to address this problem is to compare the uses of collections of original documents in the high medieval Middle East with other societies in which documents have survived in larger numbers. The collection of original documents has a privileged status in European historiography in part because it has a privileged status in European social and political competition. In the Latin West documents were unmistakable proofs of privilege, exemption, competence, precedent, honor, or possession. As nations, classes, corporations, religious bodies, families, status groups, and factions fought out their struggles with documents, they took measures to preserve them. This accounts in part for the survival of a large number of collections of original documents from high medieval Europe compared to the high medieval Middle East. The critical position of the document within European social and political competition also shaped the development of modern European historiography. When European historians began to exploit original documents, it was often to examine such symbolic charters to subvert or assert inherited rights,

[16] See for examples E. Ashtor, *The Medieval Near East: Social and Economic History* (London, 1978), esp. 1; C. Cahen, *Introduction à l'histoire du monde musulman médiéval, VIIe-XVe siècle: méthodologie et éléments de bibliographie* (Paris, 1983), 51.

[17] As Humphreys, *Islamic History*, 40, puts it, "documentary materials are quickly moving from the periphery to the center of historical thinking in the Islamic field." See also Cahen, *Introduction*, 51–82.

autonomy, sovereignty, titles, and ownership. Collections of documents therefore survived in greater numbers not by accident, but because elite groups exerted themselves to preserve them. And the crucial role of documents in European historiography is in like manner grounded in European practices of social and political competition.

In the high medieval Middle East, however, rulers maintained patrimonial if not absolutist claims, considered most of the wealth of their subjects their own, and permitted other social bodies none of the formal autonomies they had in Europe. Individuals, households, religious bodies, and groups did not brandish documents as proofs of hereditary status, privilege, or property to the extent they did in the Latin West. Nor were their strategies of social reproduction recorded, sanctified, or fought out through documents to the extent they were in Europe.

There were several partial and occasional exceptions to this general observation. First, subject religious communities (*dhimmīs*) preserved two categories of documents over time. As dhimmīs had a defined legal status and a contractual relationship to the dominant community, some preserved documents that asserted specific exemptions or privileges. The Geniza records, which stored the written materials of the Jewish community of Cairo, are the other form of document collection preserved by a subject religious community.[18] The Geniza's importance to the study of Mediterranean and Indian Ocean economic history is incomparable, and it has made the Jewish communities of Cairo and others with which they were in contact some of the best-studied communities in the medieval Mediterranean world. However, the Geniza was not an archive but a closed storehouse, and the papers that were preserved there were kept because of religious restrictions that forbade the destruction of written materials. It also is more valuable on the history of Jewish and merchant communities than on the dominant elite.[19]

A second exception is the trove of documents from the Ḥaram al-Sharīf in Jerusalem that Donald Little has studied with laudable tenacity, thoroughness, and precision. As valuable and rare as this find is, it appears to be composed for the most part of the records of a single qāḍī that survived by

[18] See esp. S. D. Goitein, *A Mediterranean Society: the Jewish Communities of the Arab World as Portrayed in the Documents of the Cairo Geniza*, 4 vols. (Berkeley and Los Angeles, 1967–84).

[19] For Mamlūk-period documents attesting to dhimmī exemptions or privileges see A.S. Atiya, *The Arabic Manuscripts of Mount Sinai* (Baltimore, 1955); Atiya, "An Unpublished XIVth Century Fatwā on the Status of Foreigners in Mamluk Egypt and Syria," in *Paul Kahle Festschrift, Studien zur Geschichte und Kultur des Nahen und Fernen Ostens* (Leiden, 1953), 55–68; H. Ernst, *Die mamlukischen Sultansurkunden des Sinai-Klosters* (Wiesbaden, 1960); S.M. Stern, "Two Ayyūbid Documents from Sinai," in S.M. Stern ed., *Documents from Islamic Chanceries* (Oxford, 1965), 9–38, 207–16; N. Risciani, *Documenti e firmani* (Jerusalem, 1931). On one occasion part of the Jewish community of Damascus produced a document, supposedly drawn up by the Prophet, releasing them from paying the tax imposed on non-Muslims (*jizya*). The document was denounced as a forgery by Ibn Taymiyya and others: Ibn Kathīr, 14/19.

lucky accident.[20] At the same time as these sources demonstrate the extent to which a single individual could make use of documents, their casual storage shows how their importance was relatively minor in the long-term control of power, property, or status. A third exception are documents such as the permission granted by one individual to another to represent a text or a body of knowledge (*ijāzas*) and certificates of pilgrimage or study that attested to the learning or piety of single individuals. These were in the normal course of events kept by their recipients, although in at least one case a book of transmitters of *ḥadīth* (accounts of the Prophet's words and deeds) was preserved in the mosque in the Ḥanbalī neighborhood of al-Ṣāliḥiyya on Mount Qāsyūn.[21] Although these categories of documents provide useful information on a number of subjects, none is directly comparable in size or importance to the collections of original documents of the high or late medieval Latin West.

The fourth exception to this general observation is the *waqfiyya*, the foundation deed of the household charitable endowment (*waqf ahlī* or *waqf ahliyya*). The foundation of waqfs was one of the critical social and political practices of the period, as has been demonstrated most notably by one of the finest historians of medieval Cairo, Muḥammad Muḥammad Amīn, and put into application in a recent excellent study by Jonathan Berkey.[22] As the waqf was perhaps the sole secure and readily available means of controlling property over time, waqfiyyas were without doubt a means by which the control of property was associated with documents.

Individual waqfiyyas were kept in various places. Although the registry of waqfs (*diwān al-awqāf*) may have kept some records of individual waqfs, one indication of the lack of faith individuals placed in document collections was the inscription of the stipulations of the waqf on the lintel or around the dome of the building the waqf supported. The beneficiaries of lesser waqfs often kept

[20] For the Ḥaram al-Sharīf collection see L. Northrup and A.A. Abul-Ḥājj, "A Collection of Medieval Arabic Documents in the Islamic Museum at the Ḥaram al-Šarīf," *Arabica* 25 (1978), 282–91; D. Little, *A Catalogue of the Islamic Documents from al-Ḥaram aš-Šarīf in Jerusalem* (Beirut, 1984), 7–21, 59, 60. Little estimates that between one-half to two-thirds of the documents belonged one way or another to a single Shāfiʿī qāḍī and administrator (nāẓir) of endowments. Others are largely royal decrees, appointments to manṣabs, estate inventories, and petitions (*qiṣṣa*), the latter two categories of documents drawn up in the course of a qāḍī's regular duties; also H. Luṭfi, *Al-Quds al-Mamlukiyya: a History of Mamluk Jerusalem based on the Ḥaram documents* (Berlin, 1985).

[21] J. Sourdel-Thomine and D. Sourdel, "Nouveaux documents sur l'histoire religieuse et sociale de Damas au Moyen-Age," *REI* 32, no. 1 (1964), 1–25, for certificates of pilgrimage from the Saljūkid and Ayyūbid periods kept in the Umayyad Mosque. On the "booklet of auditors" (kurrāsa al-sāmiʿūn), see chapter 4, note 209.

[22] M.M. Amīn, *al-Awqāf wa al-ḥayā al-ijtimāʿiyya fī miṣr* (Cairo, 1980); Amin, *Catalogue des documents d'archives du Caire, de 239/853 à 922/1516* (Cairo, 1981); J. Berkey, *The Transmission of Knowledge in Medieval Cairo* (Princeton, 1992); for another fine study see U. Haarmann, "Mamluk Endowment Deeds as a Source for the History of Education in Late Medieval Egypt," *al-Abḥāth* 28 (1980), 31–47. Waqfiyyas in Syria have not inspired a level of scholarship comparable to Cairo.

(or concealed) the original deed themselves. Moreover, waqfiyyas have to be used with care, as they refer to the intentions of the founder of a waqf. While these documents are without question informative on a variety of issues, we often do not have independent confirmation that the provisions of waqfiyyas were actually enacted. In fact, numerous reforms of waqfs and accusations of the "corruption" of waqfs and the usurpation of their income are fair though not conclusive indications that often they were not. In any case, waqfiyyas are most convincing as sources on the social uses of waqfs when their provisions are confirmed by other sources, rather than refuted as is often the case. The waqfiyyas that have survived also say more about a small section of the ruling (especially warrior) elite's temporary control of property than they do about the aᶜyān. In Damascus, at least, a number of aᶜyān families controlled household waqfs over time, but most protected property with some difficulty and without the sanctification of possession through waqf.

With these occasional and partial exceptions the high medieval Middle East had few collections of original documents comparable to those preserved by the corporate bodies of the Latin West. As a general and necessarily loose principle, where in the high and late medieval Latin West collections of documents were on occasion lost by accident, in the Middle East it was by accident that they survived.

Moreover, in spite of the patrimonial practices of ruling groups in the Middle East, state archives and imperial literature would be of less use to urban social history, even had they survived, than such sources elsewhere. Scholars have turned up the occasional petition or handful of administrative documents, but in spite of the magisterial scholarship that these documents have inspired, they are valuable precisely because they are rare.[23] Even at the time, although registers and archives of various types existed, neither the bureaucracy nor recipients of these documents preserved them over long periods in major document collections comparable to those of the Latin West, the Ottoman empire, or Sung China. Nor was there any imperial literature in the medieval Middle East comparable to that of Sung China.[24]

Documents were important to the functioning of the regime, especially in recording who (temporarily) controlled what (temporary) revenue source.

[23] S.M. Stern, "Petitions from the Ayyūbid Period," *BSOAS* 27 (1964), 1–32; 29 (1966), 233–76. Major decrees in Syria have not survived except in inscriptions and as models for secretaries and clerks in administrative manuals: see G.L. Wiet, "Répertoire des décrets mamlouks de Syrie," *Mélanges René Dussaud*, 2 vols. (Paris, 1939), 521–37.

[24] On the predominance of imperial historiography in the Sung period see H. Franke, "Some Aspects of Chinese Private Historiography in the Thirteenth and Fourteenth Centuries," in W.G. Beasley and P.G. Pulleyblank eds., *Historians of China and Japan* (London, 1961), 115–34, esp. 118 for the possibility that the Sung forbade all private historical writing; D.C. Twitchett, "Chinese Biographical Writing," in Beasley and Pulleyblank, *Historians*, 95–114, esp. 110–12 for how biographies, intriguingly similar in some respects to the biographical dictionaries of the Islamic world, were compiled by imperial officials to record the careers of officials, exemplify the values of the civil service, and validate the Confucian sensibility professed by officialdom.

Middle Eastern *diwāns* (registries) carried out cadastral surveys, kept detailed records of land and land grants, and were charged with the provision of money, grain, and goods to the ruler's household and his military formations. Rulers also wrote (with the aid of the chancellory) decrees for a variety of purposes. However, the document collections that existed appear not to have had the critical role in political or social competition characteristic of state, corporate, or household archives elsewhere. The chronicles rarely mention document collections in the context of social or political competition. This is not entirely due to neglect. Commercial contracts never extended to the political arena, and political relations were not generally understood as contractual. Nor did the decree produce elite status over generations, though there were a few exceptions. While petitions and their ensuing decrees were drawn up, these dealt with ephemeral problems. They rarely provided a basis for a notion of precedent, either in common law or in state practice, and there was little need to preserve them over long periods.[25] It is significant that in terms of decrees that produced temporary elite status we have models of decrees in manuals for secretaries rather than the decrees themselves. Otherwise state or administrative documents do not provide information on many of the crucial questions of urban political or social history to the extent they do elsewhere.

Here again the absence of surviving document collections is not entirely reducible to accidental loss, as scholars have often assumed.[26] A more satisfying explanation can be found in the nature of state power. If high medieval Middle Eastern rulers claimed a more undivided sovereignty than was the case with states in the Latin West, in common with other horse-warrior states of medieval Eurasia they had neither the knowledge nor the skills to administer the societies they dominated. Together with other such regimes they had a functional dependence on their subjects. Rulers in general did not penetrate the cities they dominated through intrusive state agencies, but by fitting themselves into existing social and cultural practices and turning them to political use. The formal state agencies of the high medieval Middle East were rudimentary compared to those of the Ottoman empire or Sung China, to take just two examples, and the agencies that existed preserved few documents (with the exception of land registries) over long periods. Even regions such as Egypt whose secretarial traditions stretched unbroken from Antiquity did not have a powerful or intrusive bureaucracy compared to states in other times and places. The Sung use of documents in the administration of the economy, in keeping detailed censuses, and in controlling subordinate elite institutions generally had few analogues in the medieval Middle East. In consequence, just as there were few large collections of original documents from notable and magnate households, cities, guilds, courts, or religious entities such as social

[25] For this observation see G. Leiser, review of S.M. Stern, *Coins in Documents from the Medieval Middle East*, in *JSS* 33 (1988), 144–5. [26] Cf. Cahen, *Introduction*, 55–7.

historians of Europe have exploited, there were also few state archives (and little imperial literature) comparable to the Ottoman empire or Sung China.

The scarcity of original documents thus represents a fundamental difference in the social uses of writing from the other societies we have been considering. Groups in the high medieval Middle East did not incorporate, acquire formal autonomy or liberty, or reproduce themselves in time through documents in the manner of groups elsewhere. With the partial exception of the waqfiyyas, the few documents that have survived from the period convey less information about social relations than documents elsewhere. In most cases the possession over time of offices, status, property, and autonomy was neither claimed nor contested with reference to document collections. The antagonisms that Europeans fought out with decrees, titles, charters, patents, and deeds were contested in other domains.

There is no question that medieval Islamic historians should continue to search out documents and cherish those that they find. However, rather than privilege collections of original documents, we should return to a more fundamental question: how did the aʿyān make use of their control over writing to advance their social and political strategies? If the aʿyān of the high medieval Islamic Middle East did not generally preserve document collections as a means of transmitting status, did they make no social use of preserved written materials? One solution to this problem is to try to make better use of the evidence we do possess. If we stop asking what collections of original documents are available from this society or that, we can try to understand relationships among the storage of written materials, the contestation of the past, and the strategies of elites. This study suggests that it is the very "literary" information that has frustrated scholars in their search for more respectable sources that carries the most revealing information on relations between social strategies and cultural practices. Biographical literature in particular had many of the same uses in high medieval Damascus as collections of original documents had elsewhere and in other periods. The stereotypical material in these literary sources is not irrelevant to social history. On the contrary, it exists in such abundance because it had social uses that motivated our subjects to compose and preserve it.

The difficulty remains how to approach these problematic sources. Some were written later than the period they describe, all are filled with unverifiable anecdotes and shaped by literary conventions that are difficult to interpret. An obstacle that all social historians face is that our view of our subjects' practices is inevitably obscured by our subjects' own practices of representation. The sources from the high medieval Middle East include thousands of often idealized descriptions of individuals, accounts shaped by long-enduring literary conventions. When we read chronicles and biographical dictionaries we face the inevitable problem of distinguishing reliable accounts from literary commonplaces. While it is clear that dates, places, and names were generally correct, it is harder to demonstrate the accuracy of the anecdotes that were told of individuals or the honorifics that were applied to them. This is why scholars have often hesitated to accept information on single individuals from these sources.

However, anecdotes such as those found in chronicles and biographical dictionaries also had social uses that can be interpreted. If we use these sources to understand the meanings and uses of the language in the biographies, we need not be hindered by the possibility that a specific anecdote or honorific may not have applied to a single individual. Whether these anecdotes were true or false is in some respects less important than that to those who told them and listened to them they made sense. It is their plausibility – how these memorialized accounts of individual lives fit into a social logic that our sources and their subjects shared – that we need to understand. To the extent that such language was formulaic it is something of an advantage, as through it we can glimpse at how our subjects imagined the social universe and plotted their movements within it. Rather than get bogged down determining the veracity of single anecdotes, historians should learn to listen to these stories, to understand how the aᶜyān made use of the past and contested it. For this purpose the biographical dictionaries and chronicles of Damascus have some positive advantages over the collections of original documents preserved by groups in some other contemporary societies. To the aᶜyān these accounts constituted the useful past, a past that was intended to secure their futures. As such these sources can be interpreted to understand how they perceived the social world and learned to survive in it.

Moreover, historiographical suspicion can be carried too far in the case of the high medieval period. This material poses fewer problems of interpretation than the biographical dictionaries of earlier periods of the Islamic Middle East, of Sung biographical literature, of saints' lives in Europe, or of late antique hagiography. Some of these biographies are quite lengthy, were written and read by their contemporaries, and included information that their subjects themselves provided.[27] We also have a number of accounts that scholars wrote about themselves, though to call this material autobiographical would be an overstatement. Because of the large amounts of material written by individuals about their contemporaries, associates, and intimates, we have in the case of high medieval Damascus a less obstructed view of our subjects than similar literature from other periods provides. So where we may never know whether particular people in fact had the "honor" or "piety" that a particular source attributed to them, these anecdotes are likely to have been "true" in the sense that these stories were believed by their contemporaries. To dismiss this information would be like claiming that the concept of "honor" is unimportant for the cultural history of medieval Europe because we know that

[27] For examples of shaykhs who wrote out their own biographies (*tarjama*) for other shaykhs see Subkī, Staatsbibliothek MS, 36–8. Tāj al-Dīn Subkī's biography of his father is 132 manuscript pages, and other exemplary shaykhs of the period benefited from similar lengthy attention.

some men called honorable were not, or might not have been, or that even if they were we can never be sure because honor was an expected topos. To ignore this information because it may be "untrue" is to ignore what are perhaps the most productive sources on some of the critical questions of the social and cultural history of the period.

There are other sources that can help us interpret some of the difficult material – especially the ubiquitous but unspecific words and phrases encountered at every turn – in the biographical dictionaries. *Fatwās* (legal opinions of individual jurists) and epistles (*rasāʾil*) provide invaluable and relatively unproblematic supplements. Waqfiyyas and decrees are also useful, but must be used with care, since, as mentioned already, these documents mandated a result that often was not realized. Other sources such as the treatises written by jurists such as Ibn Jamāʿa, al-Subkī, and Ibn al-Ḥājj pose more difficult problems of interpretation. These sources have been described as "pedagogical manuals," or descriptions of the functioning of educational institutions, or angry denunciations of the corruptions of their times. In most cases the intent of these authors in writing remains either unclear or misunderstood by contemporary historians. Another problem is that some of these writers were from cities other than Damascus, though many passed through the city at one time or another. In all cases we have to read these sources critically, and we must be especially concerned to take into account the motives of their authors in writing them. But as these sources provide detailed descriptions of cultural practices that the biographers refer to obliquely if ubiquitously, they are invaluable as a supplement to the major sources of this study.

Less of a problem is the late date of some but by no means all of the chronicles and biographical dictionaries examined here. Ṣafadī, the author of the largest and most detailed biographical dictionaries of the period, died in 764/1363, and Nuʿaymī more than a century after that. However, even though the great *ṭabaqāt* or biographical dictionaries have survived better than smaller works, many other scholars wrote biographies of their contemporaries in their lifetimes, and all indications are that later scholars copied their predecessors' work with care. Moreover, several sources "written" by later authors such as Ibn ʿAbd al-Hādī or Nuʿaymī were in large part compilations of earlier texts. The selection and rearrangement of this material was common among these writers, and is an interesting topic in itself; but the vast amount of common material in earlier and later works confirms that later writers in most cases copied their predecessors as faithfully as they could. Moreover, we should ask whether accounts copied by later writers in their "own" works are any less reliable than the "original" sources copied by later (occasionally much later) copyists. As I shall show below, the search for "authorial intentionality" or "individuality" in the production and reproduction of these texts imposes modern expectations concerning how texts are composed and transmitted on a very different period. In any case, the large quantity of material written by high medieval Damascenes about themselves and their contemporaries is possibly unequaled in medieval Middle Eastern historiography.

The gap between the literary commonplace and the social reality need not be a barrier to historians. One suggestion of this study is that none of this "literary" material is meaningless or without social uses. That we possess these biographies and personal anecdotes at all is a tribute to the money, labor, and knowledge invested in composing and preserving them. If we square our strategies for exploiting historical sources with our subjects' practices of representation and their uses of written material, these sources present some positive advantages over the collections of original documents preserved by some other contemporary Eurasian societies. If we learn to read these sources carefully, we can begin to understand the specific character of high medieval Middle Eastern social and cultural history with greater sensitivity and without an ever-implicit comparison to Europe.

Knowledge and social practice

When the methodologies of European social and institutional history are applied to the high medieval Middle East, and it emerges that formal groups and institutions in the Middle East had different forms and uses, we should pose the question: why has the study of formal institutions and group structures occupied such a central place in European social history? Perhaps the most important reason is that European practices of domination and social reproduction were expressed through differentiated institutions and well-defined social bodies, much more than was the case of the medieval Middle East. Comparisons of the formal institutions and groups of the Middle East and Europe have undoubted heuristic value. However, if historians are to avoid forever conjuring up an image of Europe in the world outside it, we should be alert less to structural differences than to differences in social practice.

A question social historians of the medieval Middle East should ask is what were the practices that produced and reproduced elite status, rather than whether its institutional and group structures were similar to those of the Latin West. Attention to social practice can help historians understand (and avoid) the imposition of concepts derived from European experience on societies outside Europe. Europeans have long imposed notions of legitimate order on their subjects through metaphors of functioning structures and bodies. Such notions of order have long shaped the "scientific" description of societies through metaphors taken from machines, buildings, cell structures, and texts.[28] One point of this study is to suggest that the social life of the medieval Islamic world (at the very least) cannot be diagrammed on a chart or a map, interpreted as a "text," or represented through metaphors derived from functioning bodies. Nor can it be analyzed juridically as a system of rules. Rather, it is best approached by examining the practices by which groups oriented their actions to the future. It is in understanding such practices –

[28] Cf. M. Douglas, *Natural Symbols. Explorations in Cosmology* (New York, 1982), xii.

rather than the structural forms that these practices took in Europe and a number of other societies – that social historians may find new approaches to old problems.

Interest in the practices by which households transmit their status has a long history in European social thought. Although attention to the uses of culture within the social strategies of groups goes back to Durkheim, Weber, and Fustel de Coulanges, among recent writers it is Elias and Bourdieu who have opened up new fields of reflection for historians.[29] Elias and Bourdieu studied practices of social reproduction out of a rejection both of the objectivist claims of mid-twentieth-century social science and the subjective or phenomenological hermeneutics proposed as alternatives to it. Bourdieu in particular has tried to understand how his subjects plot out their movements within the social world's possibilities and constraints. To Bourdieu, the critical practices of a society are to be found not in the "rules," but rather in the "practical sense" or "practical logic" by which people seek to understand the world and shape their futures in it.[30] Some of the most crucial of these practices are those by which lineages invest time, labor, and experience to acquire the symbolic and social "capital" that becomes expendable currency in the struggle for household survival.[31] To Bourdieu, attention to the strategy rather than the rule is not a "replacement of structure by consciousness" as a subject of interpretation, but rather is a means of understanding how the structural and the individual interact.

This rethinking of the practices of sociological analysis has opened up new possibilities for social history. Examining practices of social reproduction enables us to establish interrelations between domains that historians have considered distinct. By examining household strategies, we can better consider relations among sex, property, the family, power, culture, and social

[29] P. Bourdieu, *La Distinction: Critique sociale du jugement* (Paris, 1979), trans. by R. Nice as *Distinction: a Social Critique of the Judgement of Taste* (Cambridge, MA, 1984); Bourdieu, *Le Sens Pratique* (Paris, 1980), translated by R. Nice as *The Logic of Practice* (London and New York, 1990); Bourdieu, *Esquisse d'une théorie de la pratique précédée de trois études d'ethnologie kabyle* (Geneva, 1972), trans. by R. Nice as *Outline of a Theory of Practice* (Cambridge, 1977); Bourdieu, *Choses Dites* (Paris, 1987); Bourdieu, *Homo academicus* (Paris, 1984); Bourdieu with J.-C. Passeron, *Les Héritiers* (Paris, 1964), trans. by R. Nice as *The Inheritors: French Students and their Relation to Culture* (Chicago, 1979); N. Elias, *Über den Prozess der Zivilisation*, 2 vols. (Basel, 1939; Suhrkamp, 1976), translated by E. Jephcott as *The Civilizing Process* in 3 vols.: *The History of Manners* (New York, 1978), *Power and Civility* (New York, 1982), *The Court Society* (New York, 1983).

[30] See P. Bourdieu, *In Other Words: Essays towards a Reflective Sociology*, M. Adamson trans. (Stanford, 1990), 59–75; Bourdieu, *Esquisse d'une théorie de la pratique*; Bourdieu, *The Logic of Practice*, 52–65. See especially his comparison of the "rules of marriage" and the "elementary structures of kinship" with matrimonial strategies within practices of social reproduction in ibid., 187–99. Bourdieu reprises these themes in a critique of "juridisme" in *Choses Dites*, 94–105.

[31] On symbolic capital see Bourdieu, *Outline of a Theory of Practice*, 178–9, and Bourdieu, *The Logic of Practice*, 108–12, on how symbolic capital is used to transmute the private "egoistic" interests of its possessors into "'disinterested' collective, publicly avowable, legitimate interests."

relations simultaneously. We also widen the phenomena that social historians study to include manners, deportment, conduct, ritual, the presentation of the body, and the imitation of the old by the young.[32] We can also use evidence that social and cultural historians have seen as anomalous or elusive. Accounts of dreams, gestes, gestures, and *bons mots*, the tall tales, cover stories, and hagiographic commonplaces of biographical anecdotes all provide useful information on relations between cultural practices and social strategies. Such an approach will help us understand better where the modern conceptual unities of politics, culture, economy, and society merged in Damascus and in other areas of the high medieval Middle East – in the household.

This study seeks to interpret practices that social historians of the high medieval Middle East have largely ignored in their search for the "deeper structures" of social life, and that cultural historians have seen as universally Islamic, largely without particular social meanings and uses. In particular, this study shows how the aʿyān acquired and used the rare symbolic capital by which they claimed power, resources, and social honor and passed them on within lineages. The aʿyān of Damascus advanced their strategies of social survival through cultural practices associated with knowledge. Scholars have studied these practices as aspects of higher education. However, the analysis of what follows is not a contribution to the study of education. Its aim is quite different. Lecturing, reading, writing, friendship among scholars, and the imitation of cultural exemplars can address some larger and long-unsettled questions, not just to approach institutional history or the history of education. By studying such practices we can begin to understand how elite households constructed their fundamental social bonds, competed among themselves and with others, and passed on their status in time.

In order to compare the social history of the high medieval Middle East to that of other medieval societies, we should examine these practices, rather than the structures and institutions that in Europe were one way such practices were articulated. Although this is not a comparative study in the sense that it compares two societies systematically on any given problem, and still less contributes to a universal model, it nonetheless makes comparisons throughout. The reason for this is three-fold. First, from the earliest European descriptions of Islamic societies, disentangling European projections from Middle Eastern realities has been difficult at best. Since the medieval period, most European descriptions of the Middle East have been at least implicitly comparative, and contemporary historians can only benefit by trying to make these comparisons explicit. Second, when studying practices as elusive and universal as those related to the production of knowledge, situating them against similar practices elsewhere can elicit some of their particular meanings and uses. Finally, by putting the place and period in the widest possible

[32] See the introduction to the 1968 edition of Elias, *The History of Manners*, 221–63.

historical context, we can alert ourselves to the contingent nature of our own practices of analysis and description. Perhaps only by the systematic suspicion that attention to wider contexts induces can we try to avoid inscribing an image of ourselves in the past.

The two areas most often brought into comparison are the Latin West, especially high medieval France, and Southern Sung China (1127–1279). These of course are large and varied regions, and can be used for comparative purposes only in broad strokes and with numerous reservations. But there are defensible reasons for bringing them into a study of the high medieval Middle East. One is that both regions experienced larger developments in Eurasian history that also affected the high medieval Middle East, and can be studied to understand the peculiarities of the Middle Eastern experience. A second reason is that in several of the crucial questions of the study – the nature of medieval sources, the problematic issue of state power, the study of medieval education, among others – the Latin West and Sung China provide well-studied and familiar points of comparison. But the most important reason for bringing in these two regions is that it enables us to criticize the mistaken imposition of European notions of order on the high medieval Middle East. The Latin West and Sung China have been seen as societies that correspond reasonably well to European notions of legitimate order. One of the principal arguments of this book is that scholars have long imposed preconceived ideals of order on the medieval Middle East, and have seen departures from these ideals in the Middle East as "corruption," "despotism," or "disorder." By studying societies that fit (however problematically) modern European notions of legitimate order we come to understand the different character of social life in the high medieval Middle East generally, and more specifically in the case examined here, Damascus.

Each of the chapters that follow will try to understand how the aʿyān households of Damascus made use of knowledge in their strategies of social survival. Chapter 1 examines how changing forms of domination in seventh/twelfth- and eighth/thirteenth-century Damascus transformed the recruitment, relations to power, and conditions of social reproduction of the civilian elite. It places these developments in the wider context of Eurasian history in the period to bring out the peculiarities of the high medieval Middle East, and to introduce the concepts of maladroit patrimonialism and fitna as they shaped the social history of Damascus. Chapter 2 looks at madrasas and dār al-ḥadīths to understand how the household charitable foundation (waqf ahlī) and the transmission of knowledge intersected in the social life of the city. This chapter addresses previous scholarship more than the others, both to show how the problem has been misconstrued and to set up the arguments in the following chapters.

The central argument of the book begins with chapter 3. This chapter argues that the proliferation of household charitable institutions transformed the arena of elite social life by establishing a large number of stipendiary posts called *manṣab*s, not by providing the aʿyān with a new and specialized form of "higher education." The chapter shows that manṣabs became objects of social struggle among the aʿyān in the same manner as iqṭāʿs (temporary land grants) became prizes of competition among amīrs. The chapter argues that in both cases it is only by studying competitive practices of fitna that can we understand the distinctive character of politics and social life in the city. Chapter 4 examines how the aʿyān gained their cultural distinction, advanced their social strategies by it, and passed it on within their households. Its purpose is to examine the ritual, mimetic, and performative practices that underlay what in the modern world (and in much scholarship about the medieval Islamic world) are conceived of as separate cultural and social domains. By looking at how both warrior and aʿyān households made use of these practices, this chapter also proposes to demonstrate that they cannot be trimmed down to fit a discussion of "higher education," as they have usually been conceived. Chapter 5 examines how the aʿyān made use of their control over the production of knowledge in their larger social strategies. In this chapter I hope to show that the domains of "law," "education," and the "suppression of heresy," were conceived as arenas of fitna in which social prizes were contested by similar practices and represented in nearly identical language. The chapter argues that just as civilians and warriors maneuvered in a similar environment, the arena of fitna, their practices within it further blur the distinction between the "political" domain of warriors and the "social" domain of civilians.

Geographical limitations, chronology, transliteration, and citations

Specific geographical and chronological designations remain unresolved problems in the history of the medieval Islamic world. The term "Middle East" is of course anachronistic, but it is useful to the extent that it defines one region of the larger Islamic world that has posed similar conceptual and historiographical problems. In this book the term refers to those areas that were subjected directly or indirectly to Saljūk forms of political power, legitimation, and social control, especially Egypt, Syria, Anatolia, al-ʿIrāq, and Iran. These regions were so distinctive that this study does not presume to pronounce on all of them, but rather to address students of the period, who face similar problems in each of them. Chronology poses a similar difficulty. For the purposes of this work the somewhat artificial notion of a "high medieval" period resolves a number of problems. The high medieval period in Syria and Egypt begins with the arrival of the "military patronage" Saljūk-successor states of the Nūrids and Ayyūbids in the mid-twelfth century. Forms and practices of political power, patterns of military recruitment, the support and way of life of urban elites, and relations between cities and villages all changed in this period throughout Syria and Egypt. The period is one in which Syria and Egypt maintained a strong and fairly stable position within

Mediterranean and Indian Ocean patterns of trade, and in which Syria and Egypt experienced the arrival of large numbers of outsiders such as Franks, Kurds, Turks, and Mongols. The terminus is more difficult to define, but the Black Death of 748/1347–749/1348–9 was, if not the end of the period, the beginning of the end. The epidemic not only had a devastating effect on the region demographically, with the economic, social, and political consequences that followed, but also transformed the Mediterranean economy. In any case, a transitional period between the Black Death and Tamerlane's invasion of Syria in 803/1400 inaugurated the marked changes that gave the late medieval period its distinctive characteristics.

Transliteration: I have followed a modified *International Journal of Middle East Studies* format, with several differences. Titles and proper nouns are spelled as they are in data bases and research resources, i.e. without assimilation of the definite article or elision of the hamza al-waṣl. In the transliteration of texts, nouns are largely unvoweled except when necessary to avoid solecisms such as the placement of three consonants in a row, to convey the correct reading, or in the case of poetry, where I have given a transliteration of sound rather than script in order to permit easier verification of my readings. Well-known persons and places are referred to by their standard English name, when there is no possibility of confusion: Saladin for Ṣalāḥ al-Dīn Ayyūbī, Mecca for al-Makka, but al-ᶜIrāq rather than Iraq to call attention to differences between medieval and modern usage. The term Syria refers to the region bounded by the Tarsus to the north and al-ᶜArīsh to the south.

Citations: in citing Arabic sources I have followed the practice of Arab historians of separating the volume from the page number with a slash. For example, Ṣafadī, *al-Wāfī*, 22/101 refers to volume 22, page 101. In citing Arabic manuscripts I have generally followed the pagination of the texts as written in by later scholars or librarians, with *a* referring to the left page and *b* to the right, when appropriate, that is to say when it is impossible to verify foliation or when the letters are written in the text. In manuscripts with multiple pagination, I have cited the number on the page that seems to fit the dominant scheme, even though in one or two cases the dominant scheme shifts in mid-text. Until these manuscripts are reliably edited and published there will always be room for confusion and debate, and I hope that others who have used these texts will bear with me if our citations do not agree exactly. Citations of unpaginated chronicles are by the year.

CHAPTER 1

The aᶜyān of Damascus, 590/1193–750/1350

In the high medieval period, Damascus was larger and richer than most other cities in the Middle East, and its inhabitants exploited a variety of sources of wealth. Outside the walls, and watered by the Barada river, was the agricultural plain of the Ghūṭa, which produced cash crops for landlords.[1] Damascus was one of the wealthiest trading cities of the region, and straddled trade routes connecting the Mediterranean, Central Asia, Arabia, and the Indian Ocean. The city was also a political and administrative center, and at times an imperial capital. It attracted clerks and secretaries, poets, holy men, scholars, and soldiers from many parts of the Islamic world. It was a shrine center itself and benefited from the traffic in pilgrims to other holy places such as the Ḥijāz and Jerusalem. Yet, while Damascus supported landowners, merchants, holy men, bureaucrats, soldiers, and scholars, one of the striking continuities of the high medieval period is that elites of such varied types transmitted their status over generations by their control over property only with difficulty. Although it is clear that some households controlled property better than others, secure control of property over time never provided the *stabilitas loci* that it did in Europe.

There were several reasons for the disjunction between the long-term control of property and the power and status of aᶜyān households. First, Islamic inheritance law, to the extent that it determined practice, obstructed the transmission of property intact through descent groups.[2] Gifts *inter vivos*, benefices, and charitable foundations provided only partial expedients by which individuals could limit the large number of their heirs. A second related reason was the structure of authority within families. Senior male members of extended families, and not single lines of descent within them, tended to hold power and control property. Although cooperation among descent groups

[1] On the Ghūṭa and the agricultural wealth of the city see N. Elisséeff, "Dimashḳ," *EI* (2), 278; Elisséeff, "Ghūṭa," *EI* (2); Ibn Shākir (al-Kutubī), *ᶜUyūn al-tawārīkh*, Nabīla ᶜAbd al-Munᶜim Dāwūd and Fayṣal al-Sāmir eds. (Baghdad, 1984), 21/299; Abū Shāma, *Dhayl*, 222; R.S. Humphreys, *From Saladin to the Mongols: The Ayyubids of Damascus* (Albany, 1977), 12–13.

[2] J. Schacht, *An Introduction to Islamic Law* (Oxford, 1964), 169–74; N. J. Coulson, *Succession in the Muslim Family* (Cambridge, 1971).

provided a partial corrective to this, property generally tended to be parceled out over time rather than preserved intact under the control of a single line of descent. A third reason was the absence of intermediate social structures such as formal estates or corporate bodies between ruling groups and the general population.[3] Aᶜyān households could not reliably turn corporate social practices or entities to their benefit.

While we have no reliable statistics on elite control over property in the period, what most confirms the precariousness of property is the high level of predation on civilians by ruling warriors and outside conquerors. As the sources make clear again and again, warriors mulcted wealthy city people frequently, and often confiscated large sums of cash from them, even if they sometimes left cash-producing properties in the control of individuals. Although individuals often had the political connections and social capital to control property in their lifetimes, few large fortunes survived their deaths for long. While historians often refer to the civilian elites of high medieval Muslim cities as "urban notables," the aᶜyān of Damascus do not fit well Weber's definition of urban notables as a group that controls property with confidence, values a leisurely lifestyle, and participates by birthright in politics.[4]

To understand how changing forms of domination transformed the social universe of the city's aᶜyān and conditioned their social strategies within it, it will be useful first to examine some of the wider changes that Damascenes found themselves living through. Damascus during this period was subjected to a number of political forms and practices that became widespread throughout medieval Eurasia. To see more clearly the distinctiveness of the social and cultural history of Damascus, and of the Middle East more broadly, we turn first to a consideration of the wider medieval Eurasian context.

The unity of the medieval Eurasian world

The Middle East in the thirteenth and fourteenth centuries shared a number of characteristics with other Eurasian agrarian societies of the period. Historians have long stressed the integrity and uniqueness of Islamic civilization as a historical unity. However, in spite of the features that mark off the Islamic world – its characteristic forms of trade, religion, high culture, and political and social organization – the region resembled in some important respects other areas of contemporary Eurasia.

The reason for these similarities was the medieval integration of the Eurasian continent, a phenomenon that long preceded European expansion within it. A series of interrelated developments – growing trade networks,

[3] See especially Lapidus, *Muslim Cities*, 185–91.

[4] M. Weber, *Economy and Society*, G. Roth and C. Wittich eds. (Berkeley and Los Angeles, 1978), 950; for an illuminating discussion of the "notable" in the Weberian sense see P. Veyne, *Bread and Circuses: Historical Sociology and Political Pluralism*, B. Pearce trans. (London, 1990), 42–54.

large-scale movements of currency and technology, the diffusion of similar forms of state power, religion, and ideology, pressures from steppe and desert peoples, and exposure to common disease pathogens – exposed many areas of the continent to similar influences.

Possibly the most crucial reason for the increasing integration of the continent was the diffusion of new military technologies.[5] Beginning in Late Antiquity, new weapons and equipment, including horse and camel saddles, the stirrup, and horse-warrior equipment and hand-weapons, upset the balance of foot-soldiers and horsemen characteristic of antiquity. Horse-warriors throughout the continent broke up older forms of empire and established new forms of political organization. Even Vikings and Arabs, arriving in agrarian regions on ships or camels, adopted the horse and techniques of horse warfare in order to conquer rather than raid.[6] By around 1100 (and in many places much earlier), from Japan to the Atlantic, most regions capable of supporting horses also supported a socially and politically dominant horse-riding elite.

The major exception – though a partial and temporary one – was China in the Southern Sung period. What accounted for the Southern Sung's relative immunity to the horse-warrior revolution occurring elsewhere was its salutary combination of terrain unsuited to horses, the world's first permanently stationed navy, excellent fortifications, gunpowder weapons, and cast-iron technology that allowed for the mass production of effective weapons and equipment, especially crossbows.[7] Even so the Southern Sung put an expensive and bureaucratically organized effort into acquiring its own horses, and guarded one of its frontiers by giving a hereditary group of horse-warriors its independence and autonomy.[8] Each of these factors contributed to its temporary immunity to developments occurring elsewhere.

With the partial exception of China, there were two major consequences of the dominance of horse-warriors in agrarian Eurasia. One was to narrow the

5 W. McNeill, *The Pursuit of Power: Technology, Armed Force, and Society since A.D. 1000* (Chicago, 1982), 15–23, for a suggestive synthesis of scholarship on the role of the horse in Eurasian history. Lynn White Jr. has done more than any other scholar to study the diffusion of military technology throughout the continent: L. White, *Medieval Technology and Social Change* (Oxford, 1962); White, "The Crusades and the Technological Thrust of the West," in V.J. Parry and M. E. Yapp eds., *War, Technology, and Society in the Middle East* (London, 1975), 97–112; see also J. Beeler, *Warfare in Feudal Europe, 730–1200* (Ithaca, 1971), 9–10; P. Contamine, *La Guerre au moyen âge* (Paris, 1980), trans. by M. Jones as *War in the Middle Ages* (Oxford, 1984), 28, 58, 67.

6 See D.R. Hill, "The Role of the Camel and the Horse in the Early Arab Conquests," in Parry and Yapp, *War, Technology and Society*, 32–43; Contamine, *War in the Middle Ages*, 28ff.

7 See P.J. Smith, *Taxing Heaven's Storehouse: Horses, Bureaucrats, and the Destruction of the Sichuan Tea Industry, 1074–1224* (Cambridge, MA, 1991), 14; H. Franke, "Siege and Defense of Towns in Medieval China," in F. Kierman and J.K. Fairbank eds., *Chinese Ways of Warfare* (Cambridge, MA, 1974); Lo Jung-Pang, "The Emergence of China as a Sea Power during the Late Sung and Early Yuan Periods," *Far Eastern Quarterly* 14 (1955), 489–503; Lo Jung-Pang, "Maritime Commerce and its Relationship to the Song Navy," *JESHO* 12 (1969), 57–107; McNeill, *The Pursuit of Power*, 32–9.

8 Smith, *Taxing Heaven's Storehouse*, 248–306.

range of political economies throughout the continent. Many regions now supported expensive horse-riding warriors, their weapons and equipment, and their animals from agriculture, plunder, and trade revenues. As these regions were now subjected to similar imperatives and constraints, they came to resemble one another in some crucial respects, even when they had no direct contact among themselves.

Another consequence was the fragmentation of political power throughout the agrarian regions of the continent. From the perspective of rulers of centralized states, small groups of horsemen were difficult either to dominate directly or to defeat on the battlefield. In many regions of agrarian Eurasia, horse-warriors either controlled power and resources or disputed them with the ruling groups of central states. When horse-warriors tried to monopolize the agricultural surplus and military power, ruling establishments found it difficult to subject them to their control. Even where rulers claimed sovereignty over large areas, and had supporters to advance their claims, they allowed warrior elites a fair degree of privilege and autonomy, and political power if not sovereignty itself tended to be parcelized. The memory of universal empire survived in Japan, the Middle East, and the Latin West, and in each of these places horse-warriors derived their legitimacy in part from a surviving symbol of a one-time imperial unity. Emperors, caliphs, or popes all filled sacral roles that rulers could not. But centralized administration and imperial ideology were incipient if not incidental characteristics of central states. Where rulers had some control over horse-warriors, they most often ruled by playing off the dynamic tension of rival interests. Though they may have tried, rulers could rarely command their military support through an impersonal hierarchical leadership, or overawe them with an imperial ideology. Instead, power was often diffused among groups that were rarely leveled beneath an effective apparatus of government.[9]

How power, sovereignty, and resources were parceled out among rulers and horse-warriors differed from region to region. Although some scholars have portrayed the Latin West as paradigmatic of "feudal" medieval societies, compared to the Middle East its politics were exceptionally fragmented.[10]

[9] For Europe there is a large literature on these topics. See especially O. Brunner, *Land und Herrschaft: Grundfagen der territorialen Verfassungsgeschichte Österreiches im Mittelalter* (Vienna, 1965) for an account of how practices of the "feud," and not the structures of the "state," were at the basis of the social and political orders of medieval Austria. Brunner's account should be of interest to medieval Islamic historians, as it is an important and controversial critique of nineteenth-century liberal historiography's emphasis of law and the distinction between the public and private spheres as the foundation of legitimate social order. For India see J.C. Heesterman, *India and the Inner Conflict of Tradition* (Chicago, 1988), 16ff. for an acute and wide-ranging discussion of medieval politics that addresses issues of interest to medieval Islamic historians.

[10] On medieval relations among control of land, sovereignty, and military power see Contamine, *War in the Middle Ages*, 238–49; J.S. Critchley, *Feudalism* (London, 1978); P. Crone, *Pre-Industrial Societies* (Oxford, 1989), 147–75; N. Elias, *Power and Civility*, 3–201; M. Mann, *The Sources of Social Power*, vol. I (Cambridge, 1986); P. Anderson, *Lineages of the Absolutist State* (London, 1980); Brunner, *Land und Herrschaft*; P. Duus, *Feudalism in Japan*, 2nd edn.

Rulers in both the high medieval Latin West and the Middle East balanced land-holding horse-warrior lineages with manpower recruited with cash and dependent on rulers. But the relative proportions of these two groups in terms of power and control over revenue were reversed. In the Latin West *stipendiarii, mercenarii milites, ministeriales*, and others attached to rulers and paid in cash did not hold the preponderance of social or political power.[11] Well into the late fourteenth century they were overshadowed by a feudal hereditary aristocracy.[12] In the Middle East military lineages existed, but they were few in number.[13] Decisive military power and the social status that went with it were held by warriors in urban garrisons replenished frequently by fresh troops recruited with cash, not by a territorially dispersed aristocracy.

Even though relationships among land, sovereignty, and military power in the two civilizations were similar, there were clear differences as well. In the Latin West – rivaled (but not equaled) only by Japan in this respect – aristocrats had formal autonomies, derived sovereignties, seignorial jurisdiction, and effective control over land.[14] The power and autonomy of the aristocracy derived from an earlier period, when rulers had few resources other than land and booty to reward their military supporters, but in the high medieval period rulers rarely tried to abolish the formal rights of the nobility. On the contrary, the control of the feudal aristocracy over land and hereditary status solidified in the period.[15]

Where by the thirteenth century some kings in the Latin West began to benefit from techniques of centralized administration, a cult of royalty, garrisons of royal troops, the resources of cities, and monetized economies, these rulers still had fewer political resources than ruling groups in the Middle East. Relative to Middle Eastern rulers they generally had fewer resources in precious metals. Moreover, even when some rulers had more money than their rivals, they had fewer sources of recruitment of unattached manpower. The

(New York, 1976); M. Bloch, *Feudal Society*, L. Manyon trans. (London, 1961); F.L. Ganshof, *Feudalism* (New York, 1951); E.A.R. Brown, "The Tyranny of a Construct: Feudalism and the Historians of Medieval Europe," *American Historical Review* 79 (1974), 1063–88; R. Irwin, *The Middle East in the Middle Ages: the Early Mamluk Sultanate 1250–1382* (London, 1986).

11 See especially Contamine, *War in the Middle Ages*, 65–99. Also for an interesting account of a European situation that appeared much like a Middle Eastern one, see Frederick II's garrisoned company of mounted "Saracen" archers in Apulia in P. Piere, "I Saraceni di Lucera nella storia militare medievale," *Archivio Storico Pugliese* 6 (1953), 94–101.

12 Contamine, *War in the Middle Ages*, 99.

13 For one example see the Banū Ḥijjī, a military lineage at least three generations in length; see Jazarī, *Ḥawādith al-zamān*, Bibliothèque Nationale, fonds arabes MS 6739, 236. For a short episode of hereditary control over property in Baybar's reign see Irwin, *The Middle East*, 50; Irwin, "ʾIqṭāʿ and the End of the Crusader States," in P. M. Holt ed., *The Eastern Mediterranean Lands in the Period of the Crusades* (Warminster, 1977), 62–77.

14 On similarities between European and Japanese relations among land, sovereignty, local administration, and politics, see Duus, *Feudalism in Japan* , esp. 12–13.

15 For one view of how centralizing royal power in France was counterbalanced by the aristocracy's continuing claims to autonomy in thirteenth-century France, see M. Bourin-Derruau, *Temps d'équilibres temps de ruptures. XIIIe siècle* (Paris, 1990), 199–204, 256–9.

Latin West had no internal barbarians, and even if there were barbarian peoples on its frontiers, rulers seldom if ever recruited them.[16] Rulers in the Latin West also had, in general, fewer and smaller cities than the ruling groups of some regions in the Middle East.

In part because the political resources of kings in the Latin West were relatively meager (though undoubtedly increasing) a feudal aristocracy continued to appropriate a large share of surplus production and usually resided on the land, over whose inhabitants they retained jurisdiction. Europeans have often regarded in retrospect this parcelization of sovereignty as a "consensual" political system, the absence of which elsewhere is taken as symptomatic of a "failure" to develop a hereditary aristocracy, one with formal "rights." Viewing the Latin West from a wider Eurasian perspective, a high medieval observer might have been troubled by just the opposite: the Latin West appears to have "failed" to forestall the appearance of a territorial aristocracy and the spatial parcelization of sovereignty.

One consequence of the relative isolation of the Latin West and Japan was that more than in several other agrarian areas of Eurasia, hereditary aristocracies held local leadership and controlled local revenues. While feudal aristocrats cooperated on the basis of common interests and values with royal or imperial authorities, they were jealous of their prerogatives. Kings and emperors, with some exceptions, accommodated themselves to a fractious and independent military elite, one conscious of its "rights." The power of monarchies and their agents grew throughout the period. The heavily armored knight was first joined and then supplanted by massed infantry and archers; the local nobility found its jurisdictional authority circumscribed. But the business of the aristocracy continued to be war; and their way of life rural. It was only beginning around 1500 in Europe and 1600 in Japan that monarchies had the money, administrative agencies, and gunpowder weapons to undercut decisively the derived sovereignties and seignorial authority of feudal aristocrats.

By contrast, in several other areas of agrarian Eurasia, ruling groups throughout the medieval period had greater resources in cash, goods, and unattached manpower. Ruling groups of agrarian states on the periphery of Central and Inner Asia gained revenues from a variety of sources, including trade, tribute, plunder, and agriculture. With these revenues, rulers recruited and supported barbarian manpower to a greater extent than rulers in the medieval Latin West. Agrarian empires on the frontier arc of Central and Inner Asia enticed troops from among pastoral and mountain peoples into their service. Some also purchased slaves as imperial guards, or, as happened

[16] See P. Crone, *Pre-Industrial Societies*, 150ff. for the relative absence in Europe of internal or external barbarians as sources of military recruitment. Italian cities, for long an exception, did rely for their defense on mercenaries and the use of more sophisticated weaponry (especially crossbows and pikes) and fortifications; but this was to defend small cities rather than to dominate large areas.

in the Middle East, as whole commands.[17] The formal autonomies, derived sovereignties, and "rights" to property of the Latin West were rare or non-existent in other areas of the continent.

Another critical difference between the Latin West and Japan on the one hand and the Middle East (together with a number of other areas of Eurasia) on the other was that in the Latin West and Japan pastoralists were rarely if ever integrated into state apparatuses. Elsewhere pastoralists were often a critical source of military manpower. To the regular misery of Sung generals, and the approval of Mamlūk writers, pastoralists were hardier on campaign than peasants or city people, and were often good horsemen and archers, skills best learned in childhood.[18] Moreover, in agrarian regions pastoralists were usually outsiders, and where they had no local ties they could be played as trumps in local political conflicts. Recruitment of pastoralists widened the gap between warriors and the city people among whom they lived. The warrior elite of many agrarian societies across Eurasia was separated by language, culture, and way of life from the agriculturists and city people they ruled.

Another difference was that in the Middle East the political power of the ruling elite was exercised from cities. When rulers recruited manpower with cash and settled decisive elements of it in urban garrisons, they blocked horse-warriors from controlling the surplus and leadership in rural areas. Urban settlement also gave ruling groups the administrative and ideological services of literate city people. Scribes recorded revenue sources and oversaw the income and expenditures of ruling households, necessary services to outside conquerors. Rulers also made use of scholars to translate tribal conquest into legitimate rule in the eyes of their subjects. Moreover, scholars provided rulers with truths which could be directed against their own kin, boon-companions, and tribal supporters. The ideological services of scholars elevated the authority of rulers over warriors and insulated ruling houses from their kin and tribal supporters. Rulers found these ideas especially useful in countering pastoral ideas of clan solidarity and sovereignty, as well as the egalitarianism of the war band.[19] By associating themselves with scholars, priests, and religious leaders, rulers made claims to power unthinkable in pastoral or war-band society.

All of these resources – cash revenues, recruitment of unattached military manpower, cities, and the services of urban elites – counterbalanced the tendency of horse-warriors to autonomy. When Middle Eastern rulers had the

[17] This was a long-term development. In the ʿAbbāsid period, the caliphate reduced its dependence on its own soldiers by recruiting outsiders until it had entire regiments composed of slaves: D. Ayalon, "The Muslim City and the Mamlūk Military Aristocracy," *Proceedings of the Israel Academy of Sciences and the Arts*, 2, no. 14 (1967), 313; Ayalon, "The Euro-Asiatic Steppe – a Major Reservoir of Power for the Islamic World," *Proceedings of the 25th Congress of Orientalists* (Moscow, 1960); P. Crone, *Slaves on Horses: the Evolution of the Islamic Polity* (Cambridge, 1980), 74–80. [18] Ayalon, "Mamlūk," 314.

[19] On Central Asian concepts of clan sovereignty see Humphreys, *From Saladin to the Mongols*, 67–9, 84, 240.

cash to recruit military manpower, garrisons in which to concentrate warriors, and cities that provided the services of literate civilians, they prevented warrior lineages from taking direct control of land. This was also largely true of a number of other states on the frontier arc of Central and Inner Asia. It was peripheral areas of Eurasia, such as the Latin West and later Japan, that were exceptions to this more general pattern. Only in such places were the political resources of ruling groups in money and unattached manpower so weak that warriors were able to settle on the land, exploit it directly, and claim shared sovereignties and seignorial jurisdiction.

To gain an idea of the continental extent of these practices, we may consider the common features of several contemporary empires on the rim of Central and Inner Asia, though others might be brought into the discussion as well. The "Islamic" empires of the Ghaznavids (999–1140) and Saljūks (1038–1194), and the "Sinicized" empires of the Jürchen Jin Dynasty (1115–1234) and Khitan Liao empire (907–1125) might seem at first glance to have little in common. However, in spite of evident differences among these empires, their similarities are striking enough to suggest a convergence of political constraints and possibilities around the frontier arc of Central and Inner Asia.

These four empires were ruled by horse-riding warriors of recent pastoral or semi-pastoral origin, though how Central and Inner Asian peoples came to control agrarian populations differed in each case.[20] These states all adjoined and often usurped territories of agrarian empires, and gained cash revenues (directly or indirectly) from trade. They also used revenues from trade, plunder, and tribute as political and military assets, in particular to procure sophisticated military technology and equipment and to support military manpower.[21] The political problematic of these states in ruling agrarian areas and controlling their own followers was similar in some general respects.

[20] On the Ghaznavids and Saljūks see below, note 23. On the similar characteristics and problematics of the "Sinicized kingdoms" see T. Barfield, *The Perilous Frontier. Nomadic Empires and China* (Oxford, 1989), 164–84; H. Franke, "Jurchen Customary Law and Chinese Law of the Chin Dynasty," in D. Eikemeir and H. Franke eds., *State and Law in East Asia* (Wiesbaden, 1981), 215–33; Franke, "The Forest Peoples of Manchuria: Kitans and Jurchens," in D. Sinor ed., *The Cambridge History of Early Inner Asia* (Cambridge, 1990), 400–23, esp. 408–10, 421–2; J. Gernet, *A History of Chinese Civilization* (Cambridge, 1982), 186–94, 350–9; R. Grousset, *L'Empire des steppes* (Paris, 1939), 180–222; Hok-lam Chan, *Legitimation in Imperial China: Discussions under the Jurchen-Chin Dynasty (1125–1234)* (Seattle and London, 1984), 20, 51–72, 75–81; 117–23; O. Lattimore, *Inner Asian Frontiers of China* (Boston, 1962), 128, 513–51; W. Rodzinski, *A History of China*, vol. I (Oxford, 1979), 145–52, 163–4; J.J. Saunders, *The History of the Mongol Conquests* (New York, 1971), 17–23; Jing-shen Tao, *The Jürchen in Twelfth Century China: a Study of Sinicization* (Seattle, 1976); Jing-shen Tao, "Liao," art. *Encyclopedia of Asian History*, A.T. Embree ed. (New York and London, 1988), 424–6; K. Wittfogel and Feng, Chia-Sheng, *History of Chinese Society: Liao (907–1125)* (Philadelphia, 1949); R. von Glan, *The Country of Streams and Grottoes. Expansion, Settlement, and the Civilizing of the Sichuan Frontier in Song Times* (Cambridge, MA, 1987), 173.

[21] See Fu Lo-Huan, "Natpat and Ordo. A Study of the Way of Life and Military Organization of the Khitan Emperors and their People," Ph.D. Thesis (University of London, 1950) for how the least "sinicized" of these empires in fact made substantial use of Chinese administrative techniques, ideas, and personnel. The Khitans largely lived outside China, and this fact and the

Although the troops of these empires were for the most part of tribal origin, the rulers of these states abolished or modified the tribal ties of their most crucial military formations, organized them in disciplined formations, and often stationed elements of their armies in fortified cities. In cities they also found efficient producers of weapons and equipment and in some cases experts in siege warfare.

Another common characteristic of these regimes was that they made use of literate city-dwellers for religious, ideological, and administrative services. Scholars and bureaucrats advanced the sustaining pretenses of these regimes' dominance to the world at large and helped them to exploit the resources of cities and villages. Mandarins, priests, or ᶜulamāᵓ, scholars often modified or rationalized the law codes, religious beliefs and practices, and ideas of sovereignty of pastoral conquerors. Scholars have usually studied pastoralist rule over agrarian areas by investigating the "Islamicization," or "Sinicization" of these empires; but a more important question, and a less idealist one, is to ask how rulers made selective use of pastoral manpower and agrarian resources for specific ends.

The fusion of nomad manpower, cash revenues, and imperial forms of political organization and ideology made these states powerful incubators of empires. They took military, political, ideological, and administrative practices from empires that preceded or bordered them; and their patterns of relations among pastoralist warriors and agrarian peoples became models for the empires that succeeded them. The Liao empire formulated several of the political practices the Mongols carried with them later and elsewhere.[22] In the case of South-West Asia, patterns of relations among ruling houses, barbarian manpower, and urban elites first worked out by the Ghaznavids and adopted by the Saljūks radiated throughout the Islamic world, including Iran, al-ᶜIrāq, Syria, Anatolia, al-Jibāl, and al-Hind, and in time their successors applied them throughout Egypt and North Africa as well.[23]

absence of the adoption of Chinese manners by the emperor led Fu to describe the empire as consisting of "two states." This seems to confuse the cultural problem of acculturation with the political problem of empire-building, one that in spite of some obvious differences seems similar to the Saljūk case. The Khitan emperor, through the system of the "dual administrations," exploited his Chinese domains and controlled his own supporters by making use of Chinese offices and administrators: 73–5, 78, and esp. 79; for the modification of tribal ties by the emperor see 99, 102, and esp. 111. Also, Fu's assertion that the Khitan emperor retained a pastoral mode of life is supported by evidence that seems to demonstrate that the emperor maintained something like a peripatetic imperial hunt, a very different thing, and one that again resembles, though in an exaggerated form, the Middle Eastern case.

22 See esp. P.B. Buell, "Sino-Khitan Administration in Mongol Bukhara," *Journal of Asian History* 13 (1979), 121–47, esp. 137 ff.

23 On the Ghaznavids see C.E. Bosworth, *The Ghaznavids: their Empire in Afghanistan and Eastern Iran* (Edinburgh, 1963); R.N. Frye ed., *Cambridge History of Iran*, vol. IV: *The Period from the Arab Invasion to the Saljuqs* (Cambridge, 1975); on the Saljūks see J.A Boyle ed., *The Cambridge History of Iran*, vol. V: *The Saljuk and Mongol Periods* (Cambridge, 1968); C. Cahen, "The Turkish Invasion: the Selchükids," in K. Setton gen. ed., *A History of the Crusades*, 2nd edn. (Madison, 1969). On the dissemination of these practices in al-Hind, see C.E. Bosworth, *The Later Ghaznavids. Splendour and Decay: the Dynasty in Afghanistan and Northern India, 1040–1186* (Edinburgh, 1977); A. Wink, *Al-Hind: the Making of the Indo-Islamic World* vol. I (Leiden, 1990), 21–3, 62, 127, 166.

The Saljūks especially combined Central Asian manpower and imperial ideology and organization more successfully than their rivals. Because they straddled both lucrative trade routes (although the exact amount of money they gained from trade is unknown) and the border between pastoral areas of Central Asia and agrarian areas of South-West Asia, Saljūk rulers had several advantages over their competitors. They had more nomad manpower than states in the center of the Islamic world. They also had more money from plunder and their control over trading cities. Finally, against both their nomad rivals and their own military supporters, they had the inestimable political services of cities and the artisans, clerks, intellectuals, and religious leaders who lived in them. The combination of horse-warrior military power, cash revenues, imperial organization, and the services of urban elites put a temporary end to the territorial fragmentation and the social and cultural diversity of the elites of the early medieval period. As the Saljūks conquered territories to the west, their version of more general Eurasian political practices spread throughout the high medieval Middle East. While the political structure of the empire fragmented within a generation of its greatest extent, these practices were generally adopted by the warrior states that followed it. As was the case of the Jin and Liao empires, the central problem of the Saljūk state was to learn to exploit agrarian societies by ruling through local elites; and to make use of agrarian resources for personal benefits and to dominate and organize the horse-warriors upon whose military power they depended.

These larger developments defined the possibilities and constraints of the strategies of many local groups. This study will show how the elite households of one of the largest and most complex cities in the Islamic world experienced these larger changes and tried to survive through them. This approach is not an attempt to contribute to the formulation of a universal model of Islamic societies in this period or any other. If anything, one should expect that the specific nature of the cultural, political, and social struggles in Damascus would demolish any attempt to create such a model. Studies of other cities of the period would undoubtedly do the same. The era in which a single monograph can "explain Islam" to the West has ended. As the diffusion of Saljūk practices cannot be explained in religious terms such as the "Sunnī Revival," the social and cultural history of cities in the heart of the Islamic world cannot be seen in purely religious terms. We must start from the bottom up and the inside out.

Even as we reject the study of cities and the groups that lived in them as local examples of larger religious developments, Damascus can be seen as an exceptionally well-documented example of relations among power, cultural practices, and social strategies characteristic of other cities in the Middle East in the period. Ancient Islamic scholarly, political, and social practices survived in Damascus as they did throughout the region. Damascus was also subjected to Saljūk forms of power, social control, and exploitation in a manner similar to other cities throughout the Middle East. Damascus can thus be studied as a particular example of wider developments, even as it can never be set up as a model either for "Islam" or for a universal history of Muslim cities.

Damascus from Nūr al-Dīn through the Mamlūks

Beginning his career as ruler of a fragment of the Saljūk empire, when Nūr al-Dīn Zangī (511/1118–569/1174) entered Damascus in 549/1154, he established the city as an imperial capital for the first time in four centuries. In the Marwānid period Damascus had been an imperial capital when it straddled the frontier between a reservoir of pastoral manpower and the agrarian–imperial regions of the Middle East. Its Arab rulers maintained an empire through a fusion of horse-warrior military power, imperial political practices, cash and land revenues, and monotheistic ideology. But their hegemony did not last long.

When Arabia was succeeded by Central Asia and Africa as sources of military manpower, Damascus lost its geopolitical importance. By the middle of the twelfth century the city had not been a major capital for many centuries. When empires formed over its horizons, in Fāṭimid Egypt and Saljūk Iran and al-ᶜIrāq, Damascus became a distant object of contention between them, its politics oscillating between rule by its leading households and rule by an imperial governor and his garrison. At the center of the Islamic world, the city's rulers were without the sources of manpower, the allure of plunder, and the ideological appeal of the border empires. Given the importance of warfare to Middle Eastern empire-building, for 400 years Damascus' geographical centrality ensured its political marginality.[24]

With the arrival of the crusaders in Syria beginning in 490/1097, Syria became once again a frontier region, now between the Latin West and South-West Asia. As the latest border region in the Muslim world, competition between Muslims and Crusaders (and later between Muslims and Mongols) set off the same empire-building process that had occurred on other frontiers. Nūr al-Dīn and the Ayyūbids and Mamlūks following him capitalized better than their rivals on the disorder caused by invasions of outsiders.[25] By fighting or promising to fight invaders, they gained a number of military and ideological advantages. The free-floating military resources of the Muslim world, including Arabs, Kurds, Turks, Mongols, border warriors, and

24 The fundamental study of Syria in the Fāṭimid period is T. Bianquis, *Damas et la Syrie sous la domination fatimide (359–468/969–1076). Essai d'intérpretation de chroniques arabes médiévales*, 2 vols. (Damascus, 1986–1989). For further references to the history of Syria in the tenth and eleventh centuries see M.D. Yusuf, *Economic Survey of Syria during the Tenth and Eleventh Centuries*, in *Islamkundliche Untersuchungen*, Band 114 (Berlin, 1985), 12–23. See also E. Sivan, *Interpretations of Islam, Past and Present* (Princeton, 1985), 112–22.

25 On Nūr al-Dīn see N. Elisséeff, *Nūr al-Dīn: un grand prince musulman de Syrie au temps des croisades (511–569 AH/1118–1174)*, 3 vols. (Damascus, 1967); H.A.R. Gibb, "The Career of Nūr al-Dīn," in Setton, *A History of the Crusades*; H.E. Mayer, *The Crusades*, J. Gillingham trans. (Oxford, 1972).

freebooters, drifted to states that promised war. Booty and an increase in trade during the crusades also gave more cash to rulers. Ideologically, Zangīds, Ayyūbids, and Mamlūks claimed the loyalties and resources of the cities as leaders of *jihād* (holy war), agents of the caliph, and supporters of Islam.

The strengthening of ruling institutions and solidarities through warfare brought into Syria political resources and practices that had previously existed on other frontiers. Syria beginning in the middle of the sixth/eleventh century was not subject to a distant capital, nor was it a collection of principalities or semi-autonomous governorships. It now became the core province of an empire, dominated by a collection of ruling households that recruited and balanced pastoralists, professional and slave troops, and urban elites. It held the central position in the empire only for a short time, and was eventually subordinated to Cairo, but throughout the period in question the city was the undoubted military and administrative center of Syria, and the second city of the empire.

Although Nūr al-Dīn, the Ayyūbids, and Mamlūks were all patrimonial rulers, they were nonetheless remote from the cities and villages they dominated. The warriors settled in Damascus' garrisons were for the most part slaves or pastoralists in origin. Alien to the city, their languages were unintelligible to civilians and their manners were often abhorrent to them.[26] Furthermore, because political power was vested in warrior households, not in state agencies, ruling groups only partially at best integrated the aʿyān into a state apparatus.[27] In any case, no bureaucratic form of recruitment such as occurred in Sung China bridged the gap between ruling groups and subordinate elites.

Moreover, none of these regimes had a bureaucracy with a high organizational capacity. They could not rely on the diwāns for political tasks, either to control and coordinate their own followers or to administer the city.[28] In spite of the large number and specialized functions of the secretarial offices described by such authors as Nuwayrī and Qalqashandī, these offices did not constitute a bureaucracy in the Ottoman or even less the Sung meanings of the term. As scholars have long recognized, the affiliations of both writers to the sultanate should be kept in mind when we read their often idealistic descriptions of either the organizational power of the diwāns or the ability of the

[26] However, there was a group of amīrs who were known as faqīhs (al-fuqahāʾ minaʾl-umarāʾ): Ibn Kathīr, 14/46. For a fine discussion of the attitudes of the ʿulamāʾ towards Turks in the fourteenth century see U. Haarmann, "Arabic in Speech, Turkish in Lineage: Mamlūks and their Sons in the Intellectual Life of Fourteenth-Century Egypt and Syria," *JSS* 33 (1988), 82–5. There were many soldiers who were local Syrians, but they appear not to have been well integrated into the regime, and little will be known of them until a study of the Syrian army is undertaken.

[27] On the administrative and economic functions of amīral households see Lapidus, *Muslim Cities*, 48–52. On the relative absence of specialized bureaucratic and administrative forms of administration see *ibid.*, 187.

[28] See Lapidus, *Muslim Cities*, 44–52 on the bureaucracy in Mamlūk Egypt and Syria, and Humphreys, *From Saladin to the Mongols*, 18–20 on the bureaucracy under Saladin.

sulṭān to administer his domains through them. The secretaries in the diwāns did not constitute a distinct social type comparable to the mandarin or the bureaucrat. As the chronicles and biographical dictionaries make abundantly clear, most holders of the highest positions in the diwāns in Damascus were recruited in this period from among existing learned or military elites.[29] The holders of these posts were not in this period a type of person noticeably different from the groups from which they were recruited. Secretaries, wazīrs, and the heads of other offices generally struggled for appointments by appealing to the major political and social households and networks of the city. There was no meritocratic recruitment, nor promotion from within the bureaucracy as professionals. They held these positions temporarily, with nothing approaching an ideology of bureaucratic tenure. They also had little if any notion of the independent and specialized nature of bureaucratic power as distinct from other forms of power.

Throughout the Ayyūbid and Mamlūk periods, clerks and secretaries financed and provisioned ruling and amīral households and their military dependants, oversaw the distribution of iqṭāᶜs and other revenue sources, and paid themselves. They provided specialized services to military households in a complex society, especially in regular record-keeping and occasional cadastral surveys, both of which they apparently accomplished with precision. However, they were incapable of monopolizing either the acquisition of revenue or its distribution in pursuit of political goals. They were also socially unintrusive, and the cultural institutions of the city were neither linked to them nor under their control.[30] There were no bureaucratically organized state courts or registers of private property, and the day-to-day administration of justice in cities was generally left to qāḍīs – who were neither recruited nor supported by a bureaucratic structure of offices. The drawing up of contracts, the registry of land ownership, and the inspection of the markets were additional functions that the diwāns did not control. Finally, the diwāns did not work as a group to their own advantage in the manner of the Sung or Ottoman bureaucracies. They did not struggle collectively against other social groups, and Damascus experienced nothing like the bureaucratic usurpation of the income of religious groups, merchants, and charitable foundations characteristic of Sung China, and still less the Sung bureaucratic control over large sectors of

29 There were some exceptions, such as the merchant who acquired the office of the kātib al-inshāʾ, Safadī, *Aᶜyān*, 52b. For the development of a civilian bureaucratic elite as a distinct social category in fifteenth-century Egypt, see Petry, *The Civilian Elite*, 200–20.

30 For how patronage rather than bureaucracy defined Ayyūbid policies in Egypt, see I. Lapidus, "Ayyūbid Religious Policy and the Development of the Schools of Law in Cairo," in *Colloque International sur l'histoire du Caire* (Cairo, 1974), 279–85; Lapidus, *Muslim Cities*, 186–8 for a more general statement. Cf. the Chinese bureaucracy under the Sung, which was capable of usurping revenues from charitable foundations and using them for its own purposes: Gernet, *Chinese Civilization*, 308. For a comparison with the Ottoman empire, where cultural institutions were supervised by a religious bureaucracy, see A. Ugur, *The Ottoman ᶜUlemā in the mid-17th Century: an Analysis of the Vakāʾīʿül-Fuzala of Mehmed Seyhi Eff*, in *Islamkundliche Untersuchungen*, Band 131 (Berlin, 1986), xxxvii–lxxiv.

the economy. Only in the Ottoman period were the ᶜulamāʾ integrated into a religious hierarchy under the partial supervision and control of the state. In Damascus, the combination of a monetized economy and a weak bureaucracy meant that ruling establishments could not command their soldiers or administer their cities through state agencies, but principally through the assignment of revenue sources.

Political power in the period was not exercised by agencies that held specific and differentiated functions. It was rather diffused in whole packages among the amīral households of the city, each of which had a similar structure and exercised power through similar practices. The relative power of these households fluctuated, at times quite rapidly, and the numbers of dependants any one of them could support for specialized services differed. But even sulṭāns were never capable of leveling down the amīrs, specializing their functions into purely military ones, and placing an effective administrative machinery over them. The aᶜyān supported rulers by giving them a channel of influence into cities, and by providing them with a notion of just rule. But the aᶜyān could not give rulers a bureaucratic state structure or social order. Among the aᶜyān the specialized powers and functions characteristic of bureaucracies later and elsewhere were more often held by single individuals and their households for short periods. In the cases of the aᶜyān and amīrs alike, it was the diffusion of power among their households that made fitna an ever-present reality.[31] One consequence of this diffusion of power among elite households was the ever-present possibility of fitna. To rulers the "quelling" or "quieting" (ikhmād or taskīn) of fitna – among amīrs and aᶜyān alike – became one of the principal arts of ruling.[32]

"Public" and "private" power

The politics of the high medieval period were shaped by two partly contradictory imperatives. Ayyūbid and Mamlūk rulers in principle denied their military supporters any autonomy or derived sovereignty. Rulers also considered most wealth their own. Because they could make political use of troops recruited from among pastoral peoples, of cities, officials, and money, rulers prevented amīrs from controlling the agricultural surplus directly.[33] At the same time, however, as was true of horse-warrior regimes elsewhere, rulers could not dominate their military supporters through *force majeure*, in spite of

[31] For Mamlūk military factionalism see Irwin, *The Middle East*, ii.

[32] For the sulṭān's "quelling" (ikhmād) of fitna among amīrs in 693/1294 see Jazarī, BN MS, 221, 230; for the quelling of civilian fitna over the use of the Umayyad Mosque in 694/ 1294–5 see *ibid.*, 302–3. Qalqashandī, *Subḥ al-aᶜshā* (Cairo, 1914–28), 12/43 listed the quelling of outbreaks of fitna (*burūq al-fitna*) as one of the four duties of the chief qāḍī. See also chapter 5, note 127.

[33] See Humphreys, *From Saladin to the Mongols*, 15–18, on the absence of subinfeudation and Saladin's assertion of control over the iqṭāᶜ.

the training and resources of royal troops. Instead, they negotiated, adjudicated, and played military commands (*imra*) and factions (*ṭāʾifa*; pl. *ṭawāʾif*) off against one another. While under a strong ruler the subordinate amīrs were kept in check, the ruling household's dominance was usually precarious.[34] The ruling household, composed of the ruler, his family and dependants, his mamlūks and military supporters, and a few dependent but not administratively subordinate amīrs and civilians, was itself one player in the political competition of the city. Moreover, all ruling households of the period began as households of amīrs, and never lost their original character entirely.

This tension – between the claims to sovereignty of ruling groups and their practical dependence on their clients and supporters – was the defining problem of politics in the Latin West as well. The various regions of the Latin West and the Ayyūbid and Mamlūk empires were ruled by small and exclusive horse-warrior elites. In both cases bureaucracies were weak compared with early modern states or imperial China. Rulers in both areas governed indirectly, often through religious leaders or military magnates. In both cases, because horse-warriors controlled land, political power was fragmented. However, the form political fragmentation took differed between the two.

In the Latin West, more than in many other Eurasian societies, military service was associated with land tenure and a host of other social and political functions: "fief et justice sont tout un." The aristocracy had titles to their land holdings, hereditary privileges, the legal status of nobility, territorial supremacy, and judicial rights over peasants. Beginning in the eleventh and twelfth centuries in Europe, they became a self-reproducing elite by their control over property within patrilineal lines of descent. Much of this was also true of Japan between the fourteenth and sixteenth centuries.[35]

In high medieval Syria, by contrast, sulṭāns and governors had the political resources to frustrate other social bodies' independent possession of power or wealth. Rulers made claims that rulers in the Latin West did not and generally could not. Ayyūbids and Mamlūks prevented their military supporters from appropriating the surplus directly, partly by paying them in cash, and mainly through the iqṭāʿ, or the revocable land grant, in return for service. In Syria, from 1190 onward, service was associated with temporary control of the usufruct of the land.[36] Amīrs with few exceptions had no hereditary rights to

[34] Irwin, *The Middle East*, 85–94, 152–9. [35] Duus, *Feudalism in Japan*, 61–84.

[36] Syria under Nūr al-Dīn and Saladin was an exception to the usual forms of iqṭāʿ, as these rulers allowed iqṭāʿs to become hereditary: Humphreys, *From Saladin to the Mongols*, 42–3, 371–5; C. Cahen, "L'évolution de l'Iqṭaʿ du IXe au XIIIe siècle: Contribution à une histoire comparée des sociétés médiévales," *Annales E.S.C.* 8, no. 1 (1953), 44–5; A.K.S. Lambton, "Reflections on the Iqṭaʿ," in G. Makdisi ed., *Arabic and Islamic Studies in Honor of Hamilton A. R. Gibb* (Leiden, 1965), 372. But this generally ended during the reign of al-ʿĀdil, who made eliminating the autonomy of his father's commanders the central policy of his regime: Humphreys, *From Saladin to the Mongols*, 141–5. There remained a few exceptions, such as the military family known as the Amīr al-Gharb settled near Beirut. They held their territories until the mid-fourteenth century, even increasing them following the cadastral survey (*rawk*) of Tankiz: see Ṣafadī, *al-Wāfī*, 12/362–4; Ibn Ḥajar, 2/54.

property. Instead, they had temporary franchises to collect revenue at its source.[37]

Property was not generally controlled by lineages, but by the military entourage of a powerful amīr or ruler (*ḥalqa* or *khāṣṣikiyya*), important amīrs, and military factions. Although in the early Ayyūbid period some iqṭāᶜs were hereditary, military lineages rarely acquired "rights" of possession of property. The beneficiaries of iqṭāᶜs formed within and around the households of amīrs and sulṭāns, and often survived long after the death of the founder himself.[38] Because iqṭāᶜs were given to individuals, these groups often became factions when their patron died and his iqṭāᶜs were redistributed. Amīrs had limited and temporary roles in local leadership and the administration of justice, no legal status or hereditary privileges, and no title deeds to the properties from which they derived their income. Instead, many were stationed in garrisons in fortified cities. Although amīrs sometimes spent time in their iqṭāᶜs, to oversee the harvest or pasture their horses, the Syrian warrior elite claimed nothing like the "rights" of a feudal nobility, nor do they seem to have sentimentalized country life. Syria in the Ayyūbid and Mamlūk periods had none of the parcelized sovereignty, subinfeudation, or vassal hierarchies characteristic of feudalism in the Latin West. In short, in medieval Syria, warrior elites were generally not hereditary, landed, or aristocratic.[39]

Thus, where horse-warriors in the high medieval Latin West parcelized power spatially, in the Middle East horse-warriors fragmented power factionally. In neither case did ruling establishments possess a monopoly of coercive power. Rulers in the Middle East wielded the political resources to garrison critical fractions of their military support in cities. Yet in spite of their apparent dominance Middle Eastern rulers could neither recruit nor support warriors and their horses through an administrative apparatus comparable to that of Sung China. Rulers stayed on top, and "usurpers" got there, by

37 On the iqṭāᶜ see D. Ayalon, "The System of Payment in Mamlūk Military Society," *JESHO* 1 (1957–8), 61; Humphreys, *From Saladin to the Mongols*, 371–5; Irwin, "ᶜIqṭāᶜ and the End of the Crusader States," 62–77; Irwin, *The Middle East*, 11, 109–11, 137–47; A.N. Poliak, *Feudalism in Egypt, Syria, Palestine, and the Lebanon, 1250–1900* (London, 1939); Lapidus, *Muslim Cities* , 46; H. Rabie, *The Financial System of Egypt, A.H. 564–741/A.D. 1169–1341* (London, 1972); H. Rabie, " The Size and Value of the Iqṭāᶜ in Egypt 564–741 A.H./1169–1341 A.D.," in M.A. Cook ed., *Studies in the Economic History of the Middle East From the Rise of Islam to the Present Day* (London, 1970), 129–38; for the distinction between the iqṭāᶜ al-imra and the iqṭāᶜ al-ḥalqa see Ṣafadī, *Aᶜyān*, 141a. For a failed attempt by an amīr's sons to inherit his iqṭāᶜ, claiming to be *fī bīkār* – a Persian word meaning that they were combatants – see Jazarī, BN MS, 445; also *ibid.*, 450 on the importance of bīkār.

38 See Irwin, *The Middle East*, 28, for examples of "factions" (in war they could just as easily be rendered as "regiments") – the Ṣāliḥīs, ᶜAzīzīs, Nāṣirīs, Qaymarīs, among others – that originated in (and took their names from) households of amīrs. The royal mamlūks, as Ayalon's many articles show, were attached directly to the sulṭān and can be considered as a larger and more complex version of the military households of amīrs.

39 On comparisons of the iqṭāᶜ with European feudalism, see Cahen, "L'évolution de l'Iqṭaᶜ," 50–1; Cahen, "Réflexions sur l'usage du mot 'Féodalité'," *JESHO* 3 (1960), 7–20; Lambton, "Reflections on the Iqṭāᶜ," 358–76. For European notions of "rights of possession," see J.P. Lévy, *Histoire de la Propriété* (Paris, 1972).

manipulating commands and factions that were neither wholly autonomous nor wholly dominated.[40]

This difference between the two civilizations also appears in the character of social bonds. Warriors in the Latin West and high medieval Syria both traded "service" (Arabic: *khidma*) for "benefit" (Latin: *beneficium*; Arabic: *niʿma* or *fāʾida*). Both tied themselves to their patrons through oaths, and through a language of personal affection taken from the household.[41] But these groups conceived of their loyalties differently. In the Latin West these bonds were private, contractual, and hereditary legal ties of vassalage. In high medieval Syria and Egypt, amīrs were settled in urban garrisons and attached to one another through acquired ties of affective intimacy. The bonds of loyalty within groups of ethnic outsiders, among mamlūks of the same cohort (*khushdāshiyya*), and between mamlūks and their masters and manumitters (*ustādhs*) were proverbial for their intimacy.[42] A mamlūk to his master was said to be like an "indivisible particle," as a sulṭān could say of an old comrade, "he is of my cohort (*khushdāshī*); he and I are a single thing."[43] However, although these ties were politically useful, they were at the same time unpredictable. The open social space that made such personal ties possible to establish also made them easier to break, and in practice the first task of an individual upon rising was to eliminate his possible rivals, which often meant precisely his cohort.[44] The rulers of the period, from Zangī through Saladin to many of the Ayyūbids and Mamlūks, including all founders of "dynasties," were amīrs, temporary commanders of loose and shifting formations. Their ties to their military supporters were not contractual so much as affectual. Where the relationship of the slave to his master was formalized as clientage or *walāʾ*, their mutual obligations were not enforceable through law. Rulers and amīrs had no legal status or complex of rights comparable to lordship or *dominium* in the Latin West.

40 The politics of the military faction was characteristic of many other regimes in the pre-Ottoman Middle East, and had social and cultural consequences that went well beyond politics. From the garrisons of post-conquest ʿIrāq, Syria, and Khurasān, to ʿAbbāsid Baghdād and Mamlūk Damascus and Cairo, a defining characteristic of the Islamic period was rivalry between military commands in urban garrisons on the one hand and ruling groups on the other. This rivalry had effects that went beyond politics. A subject that cannot be considered here, but one that deserves further investigation, is the emergence of the important religious and sectarian movements of the Islamic world out of social and political struggles in garrisons. Shīʿism, the Marwānid ghulāt, Khārijism, the ʿAbbāsid movement, and Ḥanbalism all seem to have appeared in garrisons within the context of competition between ruling groups and warriors.

41 For oaths (*taḥlīf*) among mamlūk amīrs renewed in a political crisis see for example Jazarī, BN MS, 394–5. Cf. Mottahedeh, *Loyalty and Leadership*, 42–62.

42 On khushdāshiyya see D. Ayalon, "L'Esclavage du Mamlouk," *Oriental Notes and Studies* 1 (Jerusalem, 1951), 29–31; Humphreys, *From Saladin to the Mongols*, 34.

43 Ṣafadī, *al-Wāfī*, 4/208: al-juzʾ alladhi lā yatajazāʾ; Ibn Kathīr, 13/348; for another example of the political mobilization of ties of khushdāshiyya see Jazarī, BN MS, 481.

44 See Irwin, *The Middle East*, 88–90; P.M. Holt, "Mamlūks," *EI* (2), 326. Cf. Mottahedeh, *Loyalty and Leadership*, 84–5.

Warrior households and outsiders in high medieval Syria

Rule by warrior households and competition among them characterized both the Ayyūbid and Mamlūk periods. Modern historians have generally drawn a sharp division between the two periods, and have treated them separately as distinct dynastic eras.[45] One reason for this division is that leadership tainted by slavery so appalled European sensibilities that to many writers it was self-evident that Mamlūk rule constituted a new and distinct form of state power.[46] This perception has a long history in European accounts of the medieval Middle East. As one eighteenth-century writer put it, "I could not say much of the Mamalucs, of whom I know no author that has written in particular; neither did they deserve that any should. For they were a base sort of people, a Colluvies of slaves, the scum of all the East, who, having treacherously destroyed the Jobidae, their Masters, reigned in their stead."[47] Gibbon had a similar horror of rule by slave soldiers, though he expressed it in slightly more measured language: "a more unjust and absurd constitution cannot be devised than that which condemns the natives of a country to perpetual servitude, under the arbitrary domination of strangers and slaves."[48] Abhorrence of slave rule has characterized much European scholarship since.[49]

Correspondingly, it is Western scholars who have been simultaneously confused over the nature of legitimate sovereignty and the strongest advocates

[45] See P.M. Holt, *The Age of the Crusades. The Near East from the Eleventh Century to 1517* (London and New York, 1986), 138, for an recent example of a scholar who stresses the break between the two. He contrasts an Ayyūbid dynastic principle to an "elective" Mamlūk sulṭanate, the Mamlūk amīrs "constituting an informal electoral college," *ibid.*, 141. See also Berkey, *The Transmission of Knowledge*, 11, for another recent scholar who has discerned a "dynastic principle" governing the Ayyūbid succession. Cf. Irwin, *The Middle East*, 26.

[46] On recruitment of mamlūk troops and Mamlūk relations between state and society in general see Holt, *The Age of the Crusades*, and "The Structure of Government in the Mamlūk Sultanate," in Holt, *The Eastern Mediterranean Lands*; D. Ayalon, "Studies on the structure of the Mamluk Army," *BSOAS* 15 (1953), 203–28, 448–76; 16 (1954); Ayalon, "The Muslim City and the Mamlūk Military Aristocracy," 311–28; Ayalon, *The Mamlūk Military Society* (London, 1979); Ayalon, "The Euro-Asiatic Steppe"; Ayalon, "The Wāfidiyya in the Mamlūk Kingdom," *IC* 25 (1951); Ayalon, "The System of Payment in Mamlūk Military Society," 37–65, 257–96; Ayalon, "Aspects of the Mamlūk Phenomenon: Ayyūbids, Kurds, and Turks," *Der Islam* 54 (1974), 1–32; Irwin, *The Middle East*, 1–18; Lapidus, *Muslim Cities*, 44–79. On domination by military slaves in the Middle East in the imperial and medieval periods see Crone, *Slaves on Horses*, 74–91; D. Pipes, *Slave Soldiers and Islam: the Genesis of a Military System* (New Haven and London, 1981). For medieval Latin reactions to military slavery see N. Daniel, *The Arabs and Medieval Europe* (London, 1975), 221–2.

[47] Anon., *The Life of the Reverend Humphrey Prideaux, D.D., Dean of Norwich* (London, 1748), quoted in P. M. Holt, "The Position and Power of the Mamlūk Sulṭān," *BSOAS* 37, no. 2 (1975), 327.

[48] E. Gibbon, *Decline and Fall of the Roman Empire* (New York, 1907), vol. X, 322–3.

[49] See for a typical example Lane-Poole's description of Baybars' success: "The slave had risen (by a twofold murder of his leaders, it is true) to become the greatest sultan of his century," S. Lane-Poole, *A History of Egypt: the Middle Ages* (London, 1901), 272; also Critchley, *Feudalism*, 48.

of an Ayyūbid legitimism.[50] However, the legal status of the mamlūk as opposed to the "free" Kurdish, Arab, "Turkish," or Mongol warrior or ruler does not attract much attention in the sources, though some grumbling about the slave origins of Mamlūk rulers was recorded.[51] What troubled medieval writers was perhaps less the "ignoble" and illegitimate origins of mamlūk rulers than the rupturing of patron–client bonds that was an inescapable possibility in the politics of fitna. In both the Mamlūk and Ayyūbid periods the most militarily powerful and politically important soldiers were outsiders recruited with cash, and in both periods the heads of ruling households balanced slave soldiers and free-born troops. Even in the Mamlūk period, the various "free" Kurds, Turks, and Mongols who migrated to Mamlūk domains (and were integrated into Mamlūk politics in groups) tended to be as politically and militarily effective as mamlūk troops and amīrs.[52] In both periods the loyalties of warriors were to their comrades and patrons, though the nature of the bond of the free-born warrior to his patron differed somewhat from that of the manumitted slave to his master.[53]

With the exception of some differences in the manner by which ties of loyalty were expressed, mamlūks resembled free troops in that they were one more military resource brought in by ruling groups who had the cash to recruit them. The difference between the political–military organization of the Middle East and the Latin West was not so much the employment of slave soldiers that scholars have seen as emblematic of high medieval Middle Eastern politics. It lay rather in the relatively greater preponderance in the Middle East of garrisoned commands of ethnic outsiders who were recruited with cash.[54] The

50 For examples see the account of the "usurpation of supreme power" by the Mamlūks in *Encyclopaedia Britannica*, 11th edn. (1911), s.v. "Mameluke"; H. Massé, *Islam*, H. Edib trans. (New York, 1938), 232, in which, discussing Atabeks, Seljûkids, and Ayyūbids he wrote, "Strangely enough, all these dynasties died of the same disease: the Praetorian Disease." Perry Anderson also stresses slave troops as one of the major distinguishing characteristics of medieval Islamic societies: *Lineages of the Absolutist State*, 505–6. Medieval Latin writers had a different view of Ayyūbid legitimacy: they rejected it, seeing al-Malik al-ʿĀdil ("Saphadin") as the "disinheritor of his cousins and usurper of the kingdoms of Asia," because he was the brother of Saladin and not his lineal descendant: Oliver of Damietta, *The Capture of Damietta*, J.J. Gavigan trans. in E. Peters, *Christian Society and the Crusades, 1198–1229* (Philadelphia, 1948), 70. A final example of the confusion that the search for dynastic legitimacy has produced is a rejection of Saladin himself as a "usurper": *Encyclopaedia Britannica*, 7th edn. (1842), vol. VIII, 483.

51 Irwin, *The Middle East*, 27, for a bedouin "rebellion" in Upper Egypt in 1250, defended as a refusal to accept rule by slaves.

52 On these groups – the wāfidiyya – and their importance see Irwin, *The Middle East*, 51–3, 71, 90–1, 94, 100, and esp. 108, in which Irwin makes the intriguing suggestion that it was the dwindling of immigrants in the first quarter of the thirteenth century that was responsible for a greater need to purchase mamlūks. See *ibid.*, 18, on how the Mamlūks (like the Ayyūbids before them) balanced both slave-born and free-born troops. Cf. D. Ayalon's pioneering study, "The Wāfidiyya," 81–104.

53 On similarities between Ayyūbid and Mamlūk military structures, see Humphreys, *From Saladin to the Mongols*, 7.

54 For another example of a state that lost control of land and came increasingly to rely on ethnic outsiders see S. Vyronis Jr., "Manpower in Byzantine and Turkish Societies," in Parry and Yapp, *War, Technology, and Society*, 126–8.

recruitment of slaves as soldiers in large numbers – as original and distinctive as it is – may thus be a special case of a wider phenomenon. The long history of Europeans' horror at slave rule may have reflected an even greater terror – the uncoupling of descent and status in a society more monetized than their own.

As recruitment and the organization of military power were not drastically different in the Ayyūbid and Mamlūk periods, neither was leadership. In both periods it was amīrs who established ruling households, and who made irregular and usually feeble ventures to establish their sons as their successors. This was largely true of the Ayyūbid and Qalāwūnid ruling households, both of which were short-lived alliances of powerful amīrs and the sons, households, and dependants of the leaders of one of the dominant commands. Sulṭāns were dependent to a large degree on one warrior faction or another, and they rarely if ever enjoyed universal assent to their legitimacy. When amīrs became rulers, other amīrs continued to look upon them as one among equals. In fitnas, ruling households often found themselves one faction among several.[55] In both the Ayyūbid and Mamlūk periods, the ruling household's lack of transcendent legitimacy, or of decisive power, meant that the death of the ruler often resulted in fitna. Warfare ended only when one amīr or another was able to mobilize political capital and military solidarities to confirm the previous household or establish a new one.

European historiography, by taking the personal status of the soldier and the pattern of succession to be main points of difference between Ayyūbids and Mamlūks, has overemphasized the "dynastic" aspect of differences between the two. Ayyūbid rulers and Mamlūk governors had the prestige and resources of the sulṭanate behind them, but in both periods it was rule by warrior households and competition among them that defined the political arena. In spite of the obvious differences between these regimes, in neither period did rulers have the decisive power or uncontested legitimacy to impose a "system of government" that would level the competing amīral households beneath an effective administrative apparatus. Rather, in both periods domination was a prize that was continuously contested.

Western scholars may no longer see sulṭāns and amīrs as kings and barons, as did earlier travelers; however, we continue to impute European political practices and mentalities to high medieval Middle Eastern peoples.[56] The continuous reshuffling of power and resources is one reason why Europeans have seen the politics of the period to be a disorderly and corrupt "tormented

[55] For one example see Humphreys, *From Saladin to the Mongols*, 32, for Saladin's political position as a co-equal among a group of amīrs.

[56] For a fourteenth-century traveler who recast Mamlūk politics into such European concepts and language, see L. Frescobaldi, *Viaggi in Terra Santa* (Florence, 1862), 25. See also Lord Kinross, *Portrait of Egypt* (London, 1966), 86, for the survival of such concepts. One should point out that as Europeans have dropped "kings" and "barons" from their vocabulary, a recent scholar found "feudalism," "feudal knights," "bourgeoisie," "lumpenproletariat," "mayors," "town militias," "consuls," and "urban republics" in the medieval Middle East: E. Ashtor, *A Social and Economic History of the Near East in the Middle Ages* (London, 1976).

recital of intrigues."[57] When ruling groups composed of horse-warriors had resources in cash and outside manpower, most wealth, power, and prestige became objects of unending competition. In the Ayyūbid and early Mamlūk periods, amīrs and members of ruling households jostled for power and resources. When they acquired them they could not contrive a permanent legal, divine, or natural "right" to them. Legitimacy in this setting was a prize like all other objects of competition. Fitna was less a temporary breakdown of legitimate political or social order than the inescapable environment, and even the very substance, of elite social life – both military and civilian. It imposed its logic on their social and political relationships and ways of seeing the world.[58]

Rulers, soldiers, and cities

Composed largely of outsiders, the warriors who ruled the city administered it indirectly. Scholars now agree that the notion of "oriental despotism" exaggerated both the power of ruling groups and the helplessness of urban elites before them.[59] Dominant but maladroit, the ruling groups of Damascus neither developed intrusive state agencies nor ruled by contracting with autonomous corporate groups – these they did not allow to exist. Warriors could not administer the city themselves. Yet they not only barred urban elites from securing corporate autonomies, but following Nūr al-Dīn they actively set out to reduce the power of aʿyān households. In consequence, ruling groups "administered" by learning to make use of the city's existing social and political practices.[60]

One way of understanding how the ruling elite inserted itself into the city is by examining their building programs. Rulers of the city did not assimilate its topography to a preexisting image of power. Throughout the period, in spite of an active patronage that brought about an "architectural florescence," there were few projects on an imperial scale.[61] Rather, households of ruling elites colonized existing space by building on open lots, by establishing

57 G. Wiet, *L'Egypte arabe*, 337, quoted by Humphreys in *From Saladin to the Mongols*, 414, note 12.

58 For a discussion of fitna within the monetized political context of the medieval Middle East and Mughal India, a discussion from which I have benefited greatly, and one which deserves the widest possible audience among historians of the medieval Islamic world, see A. Wink, *Land and Sovereignty in India. Agrarian Society and Politics under the Eighteenth-century Maratha Svarājya* (Cambridge, 1986), 21–34, 379–88. For the military factionalism of the Mamlūk period see Irwin, *The Middle East*, 152–9. For armed struggle between Venetians and Genoese seen by a contemporary author as fitna see Jazarī, BN MS, 241–2.

59 On Oriental Despotism see Anderson, *Lineages of the Absolutist State*, 463–5, 503–6; Lapidus, *Muslim Cities*, 1–8, 185.

60 See Lapidus, *Muslim Cities*, 44–78, for the roles of the Mamlūk elite in the administration of the city.

61 R. S. Humphreys, "Politics and Architectural Patronage in Ayyūbid Damascus," in C.E. Bosworth et al. eds., *The Islamic World from Classical to Modern Times. Essays in Honor of Bernard Lewis* (Princeton, 1989), 151–74; Humphreys, "The Expressive Intent of Mamlūk Architecture in Cairo," *SI* 35 (1972), 79, 83, 85.

household charitable foundations in palaces and houses, and by restoring the important religious buildings of the city, such as the Umayyad Mosque.[62] When the ruling household or powerful amīrs altered the street plan of the city, it was usually for military or religious purposes – to build fortifications, level dens of iniquity, and clear the right of way, often to make it easier to walk to the mosque. Rarely did they integrate a street plan and major buildings with an image of power. Ayyūbid and Mamlūk urbanism was largely an intrusive and opportunistic architecture of single buildings.[63]

Rulers' political theater and use of sacred objects was also rarely on a grand scale. As they had cleared out no new imperial spaces, and built more often for the civilian elite than for themselves, the rulers of Damascus rarely put on large-scale ritual ceremonies.[64] In contrast to other Middle Eastern imperial rulers before and since, Ayyūbids and Mamlūks rarely cast themselves as actors in sacralized imperial performances. They were more often a privileged audience for ritual performances enacted by others. The rulers of the city fit themselves into its existing ceremonial geography and ritual idioms. They made appearances at the major religious festivals, especially the *maḥmal*, the inauguration of religious foundations, and the funerals of scholars and ṣūfīs.[65]

[62] On such works see for examples Ibn Kathīr, 13/64, 75; 14/143, 144, 148, 154; Jazarī, *Tāʾrīkh*, Köprülü Kütüphanesi MS 1037, fol. 145; Ibn Shākir, Biblioteca Apostolica Vaticana, Vaticano Arabo MS, fol. 121; Ibn Shākir, *Fawāt al-wafayāt*, Muhī al-Dīn ʿAbd al-Hamīd ed., 2 vols. (Cairo, 1951), 1/242–5; Ṣafadī, *al-Wāfī*, 10/339–42; 13/423–4.

[63] The only attempt to undertake an even vaguely imperial urbanism in the period was Nūr al-Dīn's. The dār al-ḥadīth al-Nūriyya was a major project, involving the destruction of many houses, a bath, and a bakery: Nuʿaymī, *al-Dāris fī tāʾrīkh al-mudāris* (Damascus, 1367–70/1948–51), 1/99–100. The Ḥanafī madrasa founded by Nūr al-Dīn was built on the remains of the Umayyad Caliph Hishām's palace, the "last Caliph," as Ibn Shaddād, *al-Aʿlāq al-Khaṭīra*, S. Dahān ed. (Damascus, 1956), 2/203–4 put it, and as some Syrians must have seen it; Nuʿaymī, 1/610; Ibn Jubayr, *Riḥla* (Beirut, 1964), 286; Ibn Baṭṭūṭa, *Riḥla Ibn Baṭṭūṭa al-masammā tuḥfa al-nuẓẓār wa ʿajāʾib al-ʾasfār*, vol. I (Beirut, 1981), 1/221; Ibn al-Athīr, *al-Kāmil fī al-tāʾrīkh*, C.J. Thornberg ed. (Beirut, 1965), 11/264; N. Elisséeff, "Les Monuments de Nur al-Din," *BEO* 13 (1949–51), 5–43; J. Sauvaget and M. Ecochard, *Les monuments Ayyoubides de Damas*, (Paris, 1938–1950), vol. 2, p. 88. For another reference to Hishām's palace see Jazarī, BN MS, 242–3. Nūr al-Dīn, perhaps more than his predecessors, tried to demonstrate his reliance on civilians, explicitly eliminating many of the signs of power of other imperial rulers, such as the use of door-keepers and chamberlains. See Nuʿaymī, 1/611; Y. al-Tabba, "The Architectural Patronage of Nūr al-Dīn (1146–1174)," Ph.D. Dissertation (New York University, 1982).

[64] Fāṭimid Cairo and ʿAbbāsid Baghdād present instructive contrasts. See R.S. Humphreys, "Mamlūk Architecture," 85–6; M. Canard, "Le cérémonial fatimide et le cérémonial byzantin: essai de comparaison," *Byzantion* 21 (1951), 355–420; P. Sanders, "From Court Ceremony to Urban Language: Ceremonial in Fātimid Cairo and Fustāt," in Bosworth et al., *The Islamic World*, 311–21; Sanders, "The Court Ceremonial of the Fātimid Caliphate in Egypt," Ph.D. Dissertation (Princeton University, 1984). For ceremonial in the ʿAbbāsid period see D. Sourdel, "Questions de cérémonial ʿabbaside," *REI* 28 (1960), 121–48; al-Jāhiz, *Kitāb al-tāj*, trans. by C. Pellat as *Livre de la couronne* (Paris, 1954).

[65] Jazarī, Köp. MS, 297, 455, 500, 522, 530, 593. On the maḥmal or maḥmil generally see J. Jomier, *Le Maḥmal et la caravane des pèlerins de la Mecque XIII–XX siècles* (Cairo, 1953). For the funeral in 708/1308–9 of a fairly obscure ṣūfī ascetic (lā yāʾkul al-khubz) who lived in a village outside of the city that was nonetheless attended by the governor, the qāḍīs, and a group of the aʿyān see Ibn Kathīr, 14/48. For another see Jazarī, BN MS, 196.

They also supported and visited the sacred points in the religious geography of the city, such as the major shrines and the important holy men and scholars.[66] What might be termed the audience state of Damascus derived its legitimacy by observing, supporting, and applauding others' performances, but rarely by enacting themselves the sacred dramas characteristic of a number of other pre-modern states.[67]

Sulṭāns had few if any of the attributes of sacred kingship. They had few ritual functions or duties, no numinous properties, no sacral powers of healing or rule-making, nor any privileged relation to the divine. Unable to assert control over the sacred, rulers had rather to negotiate the use of it from others who were its arbiters. Al-Ashraf's purchase of a sandal said to have belonged to the Prophet is one illustration of the ideological dependence of rulers upon the learned elite. Al-Ashraf bought the relic from the family who owned it, intending to wear it around his neck for its grace or *baraka*. But in the end he could not exploit such sacred objects himself. Instead, the ʿulamāʾ prevailed upon him to establish the dār al-ḥadīth al-Ashrafiyya as a setting for the object.[68]

Scholars have often drawn a fairly strict division between civilians and warriors. The dependence of warriors on the aʿyān, however, induced many soldiers to adopt their culture and participate in it as best they could. When Baybars styled himself a scholar (*ʿālim*) this was just one obvious example of the cultural dependence of amīrs.[69] Princes, rulers, governors, amīrs and members of their households associated themselves with ṣūfīs and learned men and women. Many ruling elites not only patronized learning, but tried to acquire it themselves. They studied with learned people, wrote books, held audiences for the transmission of ʿilm (*majlis al-ʿilm*), and gave ijāzas.[70] Great

[66] Ibn Kathīr, 13/52, 346.

[67] For the classic study of the "theater state" see C. Geertz, *Negara: the Theater State in Nineteenth-Century Bali* (Princeton, 1980).

[68] Ibn Shākir, Vat. Ar. MS, 106, 134; Ibn Kathīr, 13/135, 147; Yūnīnī, *Dhayl mirʾāt al-zamān*, 4 vols. (Hyderabad, 1374–80/1954–61), 2/45, 46; Ṣafadī, *al-Wāfī*, 7/177; Sibṭ Ibn al-Jawzī, *Mirʾāt al-zamān fī tāʾrīkh al-aʿyān* (Hyderabad, 1370/1952), 8/713.

[69] Ibn Kathīr, 13/238. For other amīrs and rulers who styled themselves "ʿālim," see Ṣafadī, *Aʿyān*, 81a. See also al-Malik al-Kāmil, described as one who "loved" the learned, and who "was among them as one of them" (wa-hwa maʿahum ka-wāḥid minhum): Ibn Khallikān, *Wafayāt al-aʿyān wa anbā abnāʾ al-zamān*, 6 vols. M. ʿAbd al-Hamīd ed. (Cairo, 1948), 4/172. For an excellent exploratory study of Mamlūk culture in the fourteenth century, see Haarmann, "Arabic in Speech, Turkish in Lineage," 86–101.

[70] For examples see the amīr who held a majlis which was attended by ʿulamāʾ, poets, and notables: Nuʿaymī, 1/66. Many Ayyūbid princes represented themselves as learned. Ayyūbid princes attended ḥadīth sessions and studied various fields, including theology (*kalām*) and Hellenistic sciences (*al-ʿulūm al-awāʾil*: "sciences of the ancients"): Abū Shāma, *Dhayl*, 179, 195; Ibn Kathīr, 13/198; Nuʿaymī, 1/317, 318, 531; Ibn Shākir, *Fawāt*, 1/419. For princes and amīrs who composed or copied books see Ibn Wāṣil, *Mufarrij al-kurūb fī akhbār banī ayyūb* (Cairo, 1953), 4/78, 210–11; Nuʿaymī, 1/65; Sibṭ Ibn al-Jawzī, *Mirʾāt*, 8/577. For a prince who gave an ijāza to a scholar see Ibn Kathīr, 13/274. For a learned Turkish amīr who held sessions of ḥadīth see Nuʿaymī, 1/67. For the cultivation of religious learning among mamlūks see Berkey, *The Transmission of Knowledge*, 146–60; Haarmann, "Arabic in Speech, Turkish in Lineage," 85–96, 103–14.

warriors also liked to be seen giving deference to great scholars, sitting, "like students," before them.[71]

Ruling households also fit themselves into existing practices of political domination and social control. In spite of their political dominance in the city, Nūr al-Dīn, the Ayyūbids, and the Mamlūks only occasionally introduced intrusive state agencies. The diwāns rarely penetrated or coordinated even the ruling elite, much less the lower orders. Instead, rulers tried to gain control over the semi-autonomous offices (*waẓīfa*, pl. *waẓāʾif* or *manṣab*, pl. *manāṣib*) hitherto in the hands of the aʿyān.[72] These included, in addition to the manṣabs of the shaykh (mashyakha) of a dār al-ḥadīth or the *mudarris* (lecturer) of a *madrasa* (place of reading or lecture), such offices as the various judges or qāḍīs, the market inspector or *muḥtasib*, the administrators of charitable foundations, the supervisor of the treasury, and later included the administrator of the holy cities of the Ḥijāz.[73] Few of these offices in Syria were integrated into the diwāns, though the heads of the diwāns were also known as holders of manṣabs or waẓīfas. The social power of the manṣab-holder was not derived from the impersonal authority of the office, but from the prestige of the office-holder. When rulers made appointments to them it was not from within the bureaucracy but from among civilian elites who had religious prestige or political capital.

In the early Mamlūk period the aʿyān faced a number of attempts to place the city's religious office under the control of Cairo. Appointments were made directly from Cairo, bypassing the local aʿyān and amīrs. The chief qāḍīship was taken away from the sole control of the Shāfiʿī chief qāḍī, and each of the four madhhabs was given its own chief qāḍī. The justification advanced in Cairo for this reform was that the Shāfiʿī qāḍī had become lazy. However, there are several reasons to interpret it as an attempt to increase control over the city. First, it was applied to several cities in the empire. Second, the measure was resisted in Damascus by some of the religious elite, which it likely would not have been had it had no political aim. It was also popularly ridiculed in a ditty composed for the occasion: "The people of Damascus are sceptical/ of the number of judges; They are all suns [the honorific of each qāḍī was Shams al-Dīn, Sun of Religion]/ but their true state (ḥāl) is in the shadows; Whenever a sun is named qāḍī/ the shadows increase; Though our qāḍīs are all suns/ we remain in the darkest shadow." This measure also took place in the context of other policies intended to give the Mamlūks greater leverage over the aʿyān. Around the same time there were

[71] Jazarī, Gotha Ducale MS 1560, year 680.

[72] In other periods of Islamic history the terms manṣab and waẓīfa seem to have had distinct meanings. In Damascus in this period it was possible for any monetized honor or office to be referred to by either term. This study will generally use the term manṣab for clarity.

[73] For offices in Damascus in the Mamlūk period see Qalqashandī, esp. vol. XII of the eighteen-volume set; Subkī, *Muʿīd al-niʿam wa mubīd al-niqam*, D. Myhrman ed. (London, 1908); W. Popper, *Egypt and Syria under the Circassian Sultans 1382–1468 A.D. Systematic Notes to Ibn Taghrī Birdī's Chronicles of Egypt* (Berkeley and Los Angeles, 1955–8); M. Gaudefroy-Demombynes, *La Syrie à l'époque des mamelouks* (Paris, 1923); Nuwayrī, *Nihāya al-arab fī funūn al-adab*, vol. VIII (Cairo, 1931).

offices established to oversee religious foundations and office-holders, and the local garrison commander (*wālī al-shurṭa*) reduced the stipends of all religious manṣab-holders save those who supported him. However, these attempts to install an intermediate level of organization (if that is what they were) between Cairo and Damascus died out, and there is little mention of them in the sources later.[74]

Waqf and the household

Rulers and amīrs rewarded civilians through various means, including stipends and prizes, but it was principally through the waqf ahlī (or waqf ahliyya) or household religious foundation that they supported the aᶜyān whom they needed to rule.[75] Waqf in Islamic law means immobilization of property for religious ends.[76] It was the sole relatively secure means of protecting property from seizure. It also provided a legal fiction by which property could at least temporarily be passed on through single lines of descent.[77] Because property could be safeguarded best by tying it to a religious purpose, waqf became one of the major tools in the political and social strategies of the aᶜyān and warriors alike. It was not a mechanism of administration, but ruling elite households made use of it for political ends.

The principal waqfs founded by sulṭānal and amīral households in high medieval Damascus were madrasas, usually thought of as "law colleges," and occasionally as "universities." An earlier generation of scholars, including the great Islamicists Berchem and Goldziher, saw madrasas as instruments of state power. They associated a number of developments, including the triumph of Ashᶜarite Sunnism, the ideological defeat of Shīᶜism, and the restoration of the caliphate during the "Sunnī Revival," with the foundation of madrasas. While this explanation seemed to work reasonably well, George Makdisi and a number of modern scholars have discredited much of it.[78]

[74] Abū Shāma, *Dhayl*, 218, 226, 236; Ibn Kathīr, 13/245, 246; Lapidus, *Muslim Cities*, 136; Lapidus, "Ayyūbid Religious Policy," 282.

[75] For examples of stipends granted directly, see Ibn Abī Uṣaybiᶜa, *ᶜUyūn al-anbāʾ fī ṭabaqāt al-aṭṭibāʾ* (Beirut, 1965), 660, 661; Ṣafadī, *al-Wāfī*, 10/264 recorded a stipend granted by the sulṭān to an Egyptian scholar that went to "his sons, and the sons of his sons, forever (li-awlādihi wa-li-awlād awlādihi abadān)," but such a hereditary stipend was rare.

[76] On waqf see H.A.R. Gibb and J.H. Kramers eds., *Shorter Encyclopedia of Islam* (Leiden, 1953), s.v. waqf, 627; E. Clavel, *Le Wakf ou Habous*, 2 vols. (Cairo, 1896); G. Baer, "The Evolution of Private Landownership in Egypt and the Fertile Crescent," in C. Issawi ed., *The Economic History of the Middle East, 1800–1914* (Chicago, 1966).

[77] However, the protections of waqf were not absolute, as during fitnas or following disgrace notables could have their waqfs taken away from them. For one example of waqf properties taken from an individual during his exposure to the muṣādara see Yūnīnī, 2/392. See also Lapidus, *Muslim Cities*, 60–2. Again, this presents an intriguing contrast to Sung China, which also had a large number of religious charitable endowments. These, however, were usurped by the bureaucracy, which engaged in regular suppression of religious groups and the appropriation of their revenue sources: Gernet, *Chinese Civilization*, 301, 308.

[78] G. Makdisi, "Muslim Institutions of Learning in Eleventh-Century Baghdad," *BSOAS* 24 (1961); Makdisi, "La corporation à l'époque classique de l'Islam," in Bosworth et al. eds., *The Islamic World*, 196.

Emphasizing the legal status of madrasas as private acts of charity, these scholars have stressed the pietistic motives of their founders and the socially desirable project of supporting higher education.[79]

These later scholars have rendered an important service in demonstrating that madrasas were not founded as acts of state but rather as "private" waqfs. However, by correcting (or over-correcting) earlier views, they have bypassed several large issues. It is true that there is no evidence that madrasas were ever intended to advance an ideological program or train state cadres. It is also undeniable that in terms of Islamic law madrasas were pious foundations – which could be established only by individuals. However, waqfs often had political and social uses irrespective of their legal status. In overemphasizing the legal status of madrasas as charitable foundations, these scholars have stripped them of many of their social, ideological, and political uses.

The debate over whether madrasas were established out of private religious motives or whether they were state institutions has generally failed to take into account the peculiarities of high medieval Middle Eastern politics. The division between "private" and "public" acts on the part of powerful people distorts how the military elite dominated the city. As we have seen, ruling groups in medieval Damascus did not administer the city by contracting with autonomous civilian or religious entities; neither did they have a socially intrusive apparatus of state. Rather, rulers supported the elites upon whom they depended indirectly. With waqf as with iqṭāʿ, warrior households gave the men upon whom they depended temporary control over revenue sources. In neither case did the recipient of the revenue source acquire ownership in the later European sense – the right to abuse a thing or to alienate it.[80] By founding madrasas, powerful households could insert themselves into the cultural, political, and social life of the city, and turn existing practices and relationships to their own benefit. This was how charitable foundations became instruments of politics.

The political utility of madrasas also accounts for the preponderance of members of warrior and ruling households in madrasa foundations. From Nūr al-Dīn's arrival in the city in 549/1154 until 750/1350, the great majority of the madrasas in the city were founded by members of households of rulers or amīrs.[81] The role women played in foundations reveals the extent to which

[79] For example, "the chief motive for founding a waqf was qurba, drawing near to God, the desire to perform good works and to leave a legacy of such good works pleasing in the eyes of God who would not fail to reward the giver": G. Makdisi, *The Rise of Colleges: Institutions of Learning in Islam and the West* (Edinburgh, 1981), 39. Makdisi has done the fundamental study of the madrasa as a waqf. See *The Rise of Colleges*, 35–74, and Makdisi, "The Madrasa as a Charitable Trust and the University as a Corporation in the Middle Ages," in *Correspondance d'Orient* 2 (Actes du Vᵉ Congrès International d'Arabisants et d'Islamisants, Brussels, 1970); See also Amīn, *al-Awqāf*, for the best documented and thoughtful study of waqf to date.

[80] For the definition of ownership in Europe see Critchley, *Feudalism*, 16–17.

[81] Between 549/1154–5 and 620/1223–4 almost all madrasas and dār al-ḥadīths were founded by members of households of rulers and amīrs. Of the twenty-nine madrasas and dār al-ḥadīths founded in that period listed by Nuʿaymī, twelve were established by rulers, four by wives of

it was the household, and not amīrs or rulers themselves, who founded waqfs on a large scale. It also gives us a rare glimpse into the complexity of relations within households. Between 554/1159–60 and 620/1223–4, according to Nuʿaymī, five of the major foundations were established by women from military households, all but one from the ruler's household, and from 620 to 658/1259–60 another five foundations were founded by women from within ruling households or the households of important amīrs. The reasons given for these foundations are varied, but all show that these women acted as powerful members of warrior households.[82] If it is true that foundations were not acts of state, neither were their founders concerned with "private" religious merit. Rather, the foundation of madrasas is perhaps best seen as an example of the

rulers, and five by their intimates, dependants, servants, and retainers. Outside the ruling household, six were established by amīrs and their households. At least one of these, the Qaymāziyya, was established by an amīr so close to the ruling household that he might well be considered a member of it: Nuʿaymī, 1/572–4. The period between the arrival of Nūr al-Dīn in 554/1159 and the Mongol conquest of the city in 658/1260 had two distinct divisions. Between the arrival of Nūr al-Dīn and the year 620, only three madrasas or dār al-ḥadīths were founded by civilians outside the ruling establishment, and it is possible that in fact none of these was entirely a civilian foundation. Some sources hold that the ʿAṣrūniyya was founded by Nūr al-Dīn, and others by the wealthy scholar Ibn Abī ʿAṣrūn. The attribution of the madrasa to Nūr al-Dīn seems likely. Because the madrasa was named after its first lecturer, and because his progeny continued to control the position, it is possible that the memory of Nūr al-Dīn's foundation of the madrasa was forgotten: Ṣafadī, *al-Wāfī*, 17/572; Ibn Shaddād, 2/238; Nuʿaymī, 1/398–406. The second, al-ʿUmariyya, was originally founded in 554 by the Banū Qudāma, immigrants from Palestine who had fled the crusaders. This madrasa became the core of the Ḥanbalī neighborhood of al-Ṣāliḥiyya. But the sources agree it was founded as a zāwiya for holy men, not as a madrasa, which it became only later; in any case, it relied on the patronage of amīrs and rulers to be completed: Abū Shāma, *Dhayl*, 69–71; Ibn Kathīr, 13/38–9, 58, 59; D. Sack, *Damaskus. Entwicklung und Struktur einer Orientalisch-Islamischen Stadt* (Mainz, 1989), 82–3; Ibn Shaddād, 2/259; Ibn Ṭūlūn, *al-Qalā'id al-jawhariyya fī tāʾrīkh al-Ṣāliḥiyya* (Damascus, 1980), 1/4, 5; Nuʿaymī, 2/100; Ibn Kathīr, 13/58, 59. The third was the dār al-ḥadīth al-Fāḍiliyya, founded by an Egyptian secretary long in the employ of Syrian rulers, who might plausibly be considered a member of the ruling household: Nuʿaymī, 1/90–2. With the possible exception of these three foundations, then, all major foundations were creations of military households. Beginning around 620, the foundation of madrasas changed in two respects. First, the pace of foundation quickened. From 620 to the Mongol invasion of 658, forty-one major madrasas and dār al-ḥadīths were founded, of which sixteen were founded in the six years 623–8. Second, it was only after 620 that civilians without any recorded association to the ruling household began to found madrasas in appreciable numbers: between 620 and 658 civilians established at least eleven madrasas and dār al-ḥadīths. Following an eighteen-year hiatus after the Mongol invasion of 658, these trends picked up at a reduced rate. Between 676/1277–8 and 750, of those madrasas whose founders are known, three were founded by amīrs, one by a daughter of the Ayyūbid al-ʿĀdil, and four by civilians.

82 A powerful woman within the ruling Ayyūbid household, Rabīʿa Khātūn (d. 643/1245–6), a sister of Saladin and al-Malik al-ʿĀdil, founded a Ḥanbalī madrasa, although she herself was almost certainly Shāfiʿī, as were all the Ayyūbids but one. The reason was that she was prevailed upon by a Ḥanbalī woman scholar, al-Shaykha al-ʿĀlima Umma al-Laṭīf Bint al-Nāsiḥ al-Ḥanbalī. After Rabīʿa's death, Umma al-Laṭīf was exposed to the muṣādara almost immediately: Nuʿaymī, 2/80; Ibn Kathīr, 13/171, 128, 146, 333; Ibn Ṭūlūn, *al-Qalāʾid al-jawhariyya*, 1/158, 163; Ibn Shaddād, 2/257; Sibṭ Ibn al-Jawzī, *Mirʾāt*, 8/756. Sitt al-Shām, for another example, deeded her house as a madrasa at the instigation of the chief qāḍī. Her nephew al-Malik al-Muʿaẓẓam was angry that the qāḍī took her oath without his permission, and had him beaten and publicly humiliated: Abū Shāma, *Dhayl*, 117–18. See also Berkey, *The Transmission of Knowledge*, 161–7 for a different interpretation of the roles of women in the foundation of waqfs.

diffuse and irregular manner in which military households inserted themselves into the social life of the city.

Waqf and the warrior household

There were several social and political uses to which waqfs could be put. Beginning with Nūr al-Dīn, all rulers of Damascus faced the dilemma of rulers of external origin: they had simultaneously to co-opt part of the local elite and to bring in new men as alternatives to them. By founding madrasas, and by controlling manṣabs in them, rulers and amīrs could do both. Founders of madrasas brought in new men whose fortunes were tied to the success of their households, men whose religious prestige protected them somewhat from the resentment of the existing civilian elites.[83] Some scholars were lured to the city and given stipends because they were from important centers of military recruitment. This was especially true of the Kurdish scholars enticed to the city during the Ayyūbid period, when Kurds comprised an important portion of the army.[84]

A second reason that amīrs and others founded madrasas was to hold on to part of their property for their lifetimes, and to pass on a portion of it to their descendants. Amīrs, mamlūks, and wealthy civilians had a weak and temporary hold on property. In the event of death, disgrace, or temporary weakness, their fortunes were often confiscated.[85] To hold on to some of their property, and to pass it on to their intimates, they often deeded it as a waqf.[86] One immediate and personal advantage in deeding their houses as madrasas was that they could continue to live in them until their deaths.[87] Even a governor of

[83] J. Gilbert, "Institutionalization of Muslim Scholarship and the Professionalization of the ᶜUlamāᵓ in Medieval Damascus," *SI* 52 (1980), 105–35; Gilbert, "The ᶜUlamaᵓ"; Humphreys, "Politics and Architectural Patronage," 166–7.

[84] Humphreys, "Politics and Architectural Patronage," 166; Gilbert, "The ᶜUlamaᵓ," 40–2. Gilbert estimated that half of the resident ᶜulamāᵓ in the city during the period she covered were originally outsiders, and one-fifth to one-quarter were transients.

[85] This was true even of very high-ranking amīrs: the amīr Qaymāz, who had been the ustādh of Saladin, saw his property confiscated after the death of his patron: Ibn Kathīr, 13/23. See Amīn, *al-Awqāf*, 69–130 for the political uses of waqf in Cairo by amīrs and sulṭāns.

[86] The social and political uses of waqf have been studied more thoroughly for Egypt than for Syria. The fundamental study of the social uses of waqf is Amīn, *al-Awqāf*; see also his *Catalogue des documents d'archives du Caire de 239/853 à 922/1516* (Cairo, 1981). Other studies include H. Cattan, "The Law of Waqf," in M. Khadduri and H.J. Leibesny eds., *Law in the Middle East* vol. I (Washington, 1955); W. Heffening, "Waqf," art. *EI* (1); Makdisi, *The Rise of Colleges*, 35–74; C. Petry, "A Paradox of Patronage," *MW* 73 (1983), 190–5.

[87] See for example, the foundation deed dated 623 of the madrasa al-Ṣārimiyya, founded by Ṣārim al-Dīn Uzbak, a freedman of al-Sitt al-Adhrāᵓ. His waqf was intended first for himself and then for the use of Shāfiᶜī students. The waqf inscription, reportedly inscribed on the threshold or on the dome, read: "basmala, hadhāᵓl-makānuᵓl-mubārak ansha'āᵓṭ-ṭawāshīᵓl-ajal Ṣārim ad-Dīn Jawhar Ibn ᶜAbd Allah al-ḥurr ᶜatīq as-sitt al-kabīra al-jalīla ᶜIṣmat al-Dīn ᶜAdhrā' Ibna Shāhanshāh raḥimahā Allah taᶜālā; wahwa waqf maḥram wa-ḥabs mu'abbad ᶜalāᵓṭ-ṭawāshīᵓl-musammā ᶜalāhu muddata ḥayātihi thumma min baᶜdihi ᶜalāᵓl-mutafaqqiha min aṣḥābiᵓl-imāmiᵓsh-Shāfiᶜī raḍiya Allahu ᶜanhu w'an-naẓru fī hadhāᵓl-makān w'al-waqf ᶜalayhi liᵓṭ-ṭawāshī jawhar al-musammā ᶜalāhu muddata ḥayātihi ᶜalā mā dawwana fī kitābiᵓl-waqf": Abū Shāma, *Dhayl*, 11, 171; Ibn Kathīr, 13/156; Nuᶜaymī, 1/326.

the city made use of waqf in this way. In 700/1300–1 the governor, released from imprisonment after his dismissal, donned a scholar's turban and took up residence in "his madrasa," in which he was eventually buried.[88] Founding a madrasa was also a means of turning wealth seized in political competition into a long-term political or personal asset. This was the case of the Shāfiʿī madrasa al-Bādharāʾiyya, which was constructed from a house seized from an amīr in fitna.[89]

A third reason was to provide for their own tombs, which occasionally became household tombs, in which their intimates and dependants were buried. Scholars have long noted that if looked at from a purely formal or functional point of view, Syrian madrasas were tombs at least as much as they were anything else.[90] Damascenes, like many other medieval Middle Eastern peoples, felt a strong connection to the dead, and tombs – together with dreams, visions, and objects – had a vital role in linking the living and the dead. Finding suitable tombs in their lifetimes was one of the principal preoccupations of the city's amīrs and aʿyān, and those with the means tried not to die without one.[91] The preeminent families of the city also established their own family or individual tombs as waqfs.[92]

Amīral households seem to have established madrasas as tombs out of a mix of status and religious concerns. A ruler or amīr or one of their intimates, buried in a madrasa-tomb, was assured of having attendants in the form of Qurʾān-reciters, often on one of the prime pieces of real estate in the city, the tomb chamber window overlooking a main street.[93] Powerful men and

88 Dhahabī, *Kitāb al-ʿibar fī khabar man ʿabar,* Köprülü Kütüphanesi MS 1052, fol. 340.

89 Ibn Kathīr, 13/63. For the use of the waqf on a very large scale to turn wealth seized into political and household assets, see Saladin's seizure in Cairo of the wealth (including the palace) of the Fāṭimid caliph, the treasury, and the amīrs and wazīrs of the city, all of which he immobilized as waqf: Amīn, *al-Awqāf*, 66–8.

90 See R. Hillenbrand, "Madrasa," *EI* (2), 1139–40 for the inclusion of a mausoleum as the distinguishing feature of Syrian madrasas: "If . . . analyzed from the purely formal point of view, with no backward glance at their eastern origins, the obvious conclusion would be that a major, if not indeed the primary, purpose of the institution was to contain a monumental mausoleum." See also J. Sauvaget, "L'architecture musulmane en Syrie," in *RAA* 8 (1934), 36; D. Sourdel, "Réflexions sur la diffusion de la madrasa en orient du xie au xiiie siècle," *REI* 44 (1976), 165–84.

91 See for example Fakhr al-Dīn Ibn ʿAsākir, who while dying of cholera exerted himself to acquire a tomb: Abū Shāma, *Dhayl*, 39. Another shaykh while dying gave instructions for his tomb to be built: Ṣafadī, *al-Wāfī*, 10/270. A tomb was important for any man with distinction: the ruler of Mardīn was broken by al-Ashraf when visiting Damascus, and his host built a tomb for him that cost 1,000 dirhams: Abū Shāma, *Dhayl*, 134. For an amīr buried in his ustādh's (al-Malik al-Nāṣir) tomb in 664/1264–5 see Ibn Kathīr, 13/248; Nuʿaymī 1/122.

92 See Nuʿaymī 2/223–301 for a list and description of such family tombs. For an example of a shaykh who was buried in a madrasa he founded next door to his house see Jazarī, BN MS, 328. See also K. Moaz, "Le Mausolée d'Ibn al-Muqaddam," in *MIFD* (1929); A.R. Moaz, "Note sur le mausolée de Saladin à Damas: son fondateur et les circonstances de sa fondation," *BEO* 39–40 (1987–8).

93 J. Sauvaget, *Les Monuments Historiques de Damas* (Beirut, 1932); Sauvaget, "L'architecture musulmane en Syrie"; Sauvaget, "Notes sur quelques monuments musulmans de Syrie: à propos d'une étude récente," *Syria*, 24–5 (1944–8); Sauvaget, "Le cénotaphe de Saladin," *RAA* (1930), 168–75; Sauvaget and Ecochard, *Les Monuments Ayyoubides*; D. Herzfeld, "Damascus: Studies in Architecture," *Ars Islamica* 9–14 (1942–8); Hillenbrand, "Madrasa"; Abū Shāma, *Dhayl*, 132; Ibn Khallikān, 4/170.

women could also be more certain of permanent burial in their houses if they immobilized them as waqfs. By founding waqfs they could also look after their spiritual interests in the afterlife. As the establishment of a madrasa protected the security and prestige of amīral households in life, it could do so after death.

Madrasa-tombs had political as well as personal uses for powerful men, their households, and their supporters. Symbolic politics were played out through honoring and desecrating the power of tombs.[94] Ceremonies held at tombs also allowed the intimates and clients of the household of a powerful man – and such groupings were the basis of power in the city – to maintain their coherence as a group. On such occasions they recited the entire Qurʾān – a *khatma* – at a tomb at specific times following the death of a powerful man. The Ayyūbids, for example, used the madrasa-tomb of Saladin for their Friday prayer.[95] These events and others like it allowed a group held together by ties to a single individual to renew its bonds after his death, as his relatives, associates, clients, and intimates met to honor the individual who had been at the center of their political and social relationships.[96] Households and those attached to them – especially their military supporters – had an interest in ensuring that their patrons occupied an imposing tomb, as they hoped that some of the patron's power would survive his demise. One illustration of this was the large tomb that Qaymāz built for al-Malik al-Masʿūd in Cairo, after the latter had specifically ordered that he be buried in a simple grave in Mecca.[97] Tombs were not just for the dead, any more than patriarchal households were just for patriarchs.

Finally, amīral households established madrasas as a means of inserting themselves into the ritual and ceremonial geography of the city. Inaugural lectures, foundations, and ceremonies held in madrasas were major events. Such occasions were particularly important to amīral and ruling households, who had no charismatic qualification for their leadership, and were dependent on civilians for their legitimation. The establishment of foundations supported by waqfs was also a marker of status for the most powerful amīrs, and is in some respects comparable to the eugertism of notables in Antiquity.[98]

Although madrasas had all of these uses, they were generally not conceived as ideological projects, built to impress the population of the city with the power of ruling groups. The design of the madrasas was rarely monumental or purpose built.[99] After Nūr al-Dīn, who was the only ruler of the city to

94 For confiscation of the power of a tomb, see the case of the tomb of the hero of ʿAyn Jālūt, Kutuz, which became an object of pilgrimage. Baybars, responsible for his death, had the tomb sealed: Ibn Kathīr, 13/225–6. For the desecration of a tomb see Ibn Kathīr, 13/163, 269.

95 Abū Shāma, *Dhayl*, 151; Ibn Kathīr, 13/121; Nuʿaymi, 1/580.

96 See for example a khatma held in 732/1331–2: Jazarī, Köp. MS, 296.

97 Ibn Khallikān, 4/177.

98 See Amīn, *al-Awqāf*, 94–5 for a sensitive interpretation of an especially revealing quotation from Ibn Taghrībirdī that would seem to apply to amīrs in Damascus as well. For eugertism in Antiquity see Veyne, *Bread and Circuses*, esp. 5–59.

99 See Hillenbrand, "Madrasas," 1140, for the "loose boundaries" among building types. Even though some madrasas had numbers of rooms for students, the provision of rooms for

integrate a street plan with monumental buildings, few if any madrasas formed part of a larger project.[100] Most were built by owners of existing buildings or by others who acquired existing structures. In either case founders added a domed hall for a tomb in the main room and often a residence for the lecturer.[101] Many major buildings, including the dār al-ḥadīth al-Ashrafiyya, the tomb of Saladin, and the Ẓāhiriyya, were reworked houses. The surviving buildings show additions and decorations typical of religious buildings used for prayer, including muqarnas and miḥrābs. It is difficult to discern an imperial building program, even in household foundations constructed from original plans.[102] These buildings were not integrated with any street plan, and most were quite small. Thus, although madrasas were founded by members of military households, they did not represent an imperial building program. They were rather a household urbanism of small inserts into the existing geography of the city.

Other uses of household endowments

Amīrs and rulers made use of madrasas and dār al-ḥadīths for purposes that had little to do with education. Warriors and rulers supported the civilians they depended on partly by paying them directly with stipends (*jāmikiyya*) and partly by giving them manṣabs in madrasas.[103] Many of the important

students was an incidental rather than necessary aspect of madrasa foundation: see *ibid.* and D. Herzfeld, "Damascus: Studies in Architecture," 44–5. Some madrasas may have had a distinctive architecture intended to convey some message or image of power. The design of some madrasas was Iranian or Iraqi: see N. Elisséeff, "Dimashḳ," *EI* (2), 283; D. Herzfeld, "Damascus: Studies in Architecture," 16. The Ribāṭ al-Nāṣirī, founded by al-Malik al-Nāṣir, was said to be "one of the strangest buildings ever built," but there is no evidence that it was intended to convey an idea of power: Nuʿaymī, 1/117. The Nūriyya dār al-ḥadīth was also noted for its difference from local buildings, but this may have been the result of a mismatch between a plan by an ʿIrāqī architect and local building materials: Sauvaget and Ecochard, *Les Monuments Ayyoubides*, 24, 25.

100 On the urbanism of Nūr al-Dīn see: Elisséeff, "Les Monuments de Nur al-Din"; D. Herzfeld, "Damascus: Studies in Architecture"; Sauvaget, *Les Monuments Historiques*; Sauvaget, "Notes," *Syria*, 24 (1944–5), 21, 219; Sauvaget and Ecochard, *Les Monuments Ayyoubides*, vol. II, 88; Y. al-Tabba, "The Architectural Patronage of Nūr al-Dīn (1146–1174)." On Ayyūbid and Mamlūk madrasa architecture see Humphreys, "Mamlūk Architecture," 109–10.

101 For examples of madrasas established from existing buildings see Nuʿaymī, 1/55, 80, 97, 98, 114, 159, 169–73, 236, 237, 265, 274, 301–2, 368–9, 374, 431, 474, 518, 519, 530–2, 541–2, 555–6, 569–71, 573; Abū Shāma, *Dhayl*, 33, 59, 81, 86, 117–18, 119, 136–7, 148, 149, 169, 177; Abū Shāma, *al-Rawḍatayn*, 2/231, 239; Ibn Shākir, Vat. Ar. MS, 106, 134; Ibn Shākir, 21/134–9; Ibn Kathīr, 13/22, 23, 34, 46, 78, 84, 135, 181, 221; Ibn Shaddād, 2/207, 215, 227, 233, 236, 239, 241, 243, 262; Sibṭ Ibn al-Jawzī, *Mirʾāt*, 8/442, 642; Ibn Wāṣil, 3/60, 63; Ibn Ṭūlūn, *al-Qalāʾid al-jawhariyya*, 1/131; Yūnīnī, 3/247–8. Medical madrasas were also established from existing houses: Ibn Kathīr, 13/130; Ibn Shākir, Vat. Ar. MS, 101. For examples of the construction of the tomb-chamber and the residence for the lecturer see Nuʿaymī, 1/374; Yūnīnī, 3/236; Dhahabī, *Mukhtaṣar al-Jazarī*, Köp. MS, 26.

102 See Ibn Kathīr, 13/23; Nuʿaymī, 1/573 on the dār al-ḥadīth, and Ibn Kathīr, 13/3 on the tomb of Saladin. On the Ẓāhiriyya see Yūnīnī, 3/236; G. Leiser, "The Endowment of the al-Ẓāhiriyya in Damascus," *JESHO* 27 (1983), 33–55.

103 For the use of the term jāmikiyya for a stipend for a qāḍī see Abū Shāma, *Dhayl*, 236.

manṣabs were supported in part with income from madrasas. Madrasas supported the preacher of the Umayyad Mosque, and a group of madrasas known as the "qāḍīs' madrasas" supported the chief judges in the later Mamlūk period.[104] The sources occasionally called the madrasas that supported clients of powerful people "worldly manṣabs" (*manāṣib dunyāwiyya*).[105]

Moreover, as ruling groups relied on the aʿyān for services that rulers elsewhere obtained from bureaucracies and autonomous corporate or religious bodies, madrasas had many uses that we associate with such institutions and groups. They were residences for the chief qāḍīs, and seats from which they delivered judgment.[106] Notaries also sat in front of madrasas.[107] Sulṭāns and amīrs also made use of madrasas for specific tasks. Madrasas were residences for amīrs, collecting points for booty, and housing for ransomed prisoners.[108] Amīrs and governors also jailed civilians in madrasas.[109] In response to Mongol threats to the city, madrasas became storehouses for arms and centers for the training of civilians in military skills.[110] When an emissary from the Mongol conqueror Ghazān met with the aʿyān of the city, it was in a madrasa.[111]

Such were the benefits that household waqfs such as madrasas and dār al-ḥadīths provided to ruling elites. In a city in which ruling households were socially distant yet physically close to the groups they exploited, charitable foundations gave them the services we find in formal entities and practices elsewhere. Rulers, amīrs, and members of their households were politically and socially aloof. The diwāns lacked the intrusive purpose, the knowledge, and the specialized agencies to administer the city. Moreover, there were few if any corporate groups with which warrior households could contract to pursue their own objectives. Instead, such households administered the city, advanced a claim to domination, and looked after their own interests through

104 These included the two Shāmiyyas and the Ẓāhiriyya al-Juwāniyya: "wa jaʿalaʾsh-shaykh shams al-dīn al-barmāwī nāʾibahu fiʾl-khiṭāba wʾal-madāris al-mutaʿallaqa bihi [sic] ghayr madāris al-quḍāʾ [or possibly al-qaḍāʾ] wa-hyaʾsh-shāmiyyatayn wʾaẓ-ẓāhiriyyaʾl-juwāniyya": Nuʿaymī, 1/289.

105 These included especially the manṣab of the lecturer of the ʿĀdiliyya, Ghazāliyya, and Atābakiyya, and the manṣab of shaykh ash-shuyūkh: Ibn Kathīr, 14/106–7.

106 The Shāfiʿī chief qāḍī held the tadrīs of the ʿĀdiliyya, which was also his residence: Jazarī, Köp. MS, 421, 594; BN MS, 302, 334; Ibn Kathīr, 13/14; 14/111, 148, 165; Yūnīnī, 3/64, 65; Ibn Abī Uṣaybiʿa, 646. The Ḥanbalī chief qāḍī resided and gave judgment at the Jawziyya: Jazarī, Köp. MS, 225, 255; Ibn Kathīr, 14/76. The Ḥanafī qāḍī used the Nūriyya al-Ḥanafiyya: Ibn Kathīr, 14/42, 76. Another madrasa used as a seat and residence by chief qāḍīs was the Mujāhidiyya: Ibn Kathīr, 13/69. The Shāfiʿī deputy (*nāʾib*) qāḍī also gave judgment at the ʿĀdiliyya: Ibn Kathīr, 14/144.

107 Jazarī, Köp. MS, 429.

108 For two amīrs who resided in the Ashrafiyya see Jazarī, BN MS, 348. For madrasas used as collecting points for booty see Ibn Kathīr, 14/7. The ʿĀdiliyya al-Kubrā housed ransomed prisoners when they arrived with Frankish merchants in 727: Ibn Kathīr, 14/129.

109 For one example see Jazarī, BN MS, 237–9.

110 In the face of the Mongol threat of 680/1281 the sulṭān ordered each mosque and madrasa to set up an archery range so civilians could practice: Ibn Kathīr, 13/281; Ibn Shākir, 21/281. In the aftermath of the siege of 699/1299–1300 civilians began to store weapons in the markets and turned the madrasas into workshops: Ibn Kathīr, 14/12.

111 Ibn al-Dawādārī, Munajjid ed., 22.

the political use of legal devices such as waqf. The political use of waqfs on a large scale gave rulers and amīrs the mix of what we would call "private" and "public" benefits necessary to successful politics.

Exploitation of the aʿyān

As warriors used indirect means of recruiting and supporting the civilian elite, they also used indirect means of exploiting them. Taxes condemned as contrary to Islam provided some revenues. However, one consequence of the absence of a politically and fiscally effective bureaucracy was that amīrs often had no effective means of raising revenue, especially in fitnas or wars against outsiders. Instead, they made widespread use of temporary taxes, monopolies, forced loans and purchases, and especially the *muṣādara* or "mulcting" as it is somewhat misleadingly translated.[112]

The muṣādara imprisoned and tortured individuals or their families to compel the surrender of their fortunes.[113] It was historically an administrative device to appropriate the fortunes of office-holders after their dismissal, and throughout the Ayyūbid and Mamlūk periods this use of the muṣādara continued. The muṣādara was also used to confiscate the fortunes of men who died unexpectedly or who had no males in the family to protect their property, and in these instances the ruin of a house could be complete.[114] In addition to these lasting uses of the muṣādara, it also became a political and revenue-raising instrument of warrior households. So many of the merchants mentioned in the chronicles and biographical dictionaries were subjected to it that it is clear that few large merchant fortunes survived in families for long.[115]

Amīrs and rulers regularly made use of the muṣādara on a large scale. Several such muṣādaras were established in madrasas. After the Mamlūk seizure of the city, an expropriation board (*diwān al-istikhlāṣ*) was set up in a madrasa.[116] Another muṣādara was set up in 687/1288 in the tomb (*turba*) of

112 For the forced sale and forced loan, see Lapidus, *Muslim Cities*, 56–9.

113 For a few examples among many that could be cited, see Ibn Kathīr, 13/290 for the mulcting of a lecturer after his dismissal during a fitna caused by a contest between the governor and the sulṭān; *ibid.*, 14/165, for the torture of one of the Banū al-Qalānisī for 100,000 dirhams; Ṣafadī, *al-Wāfī*, 13/190 for another wealthy Banū al-Qalānisī exposed to the muṣādara by the governor of the city; *ibid.*, 6/39, for the torture of a merchant for 500,000 dirhams; Jazarī, Köp. MS, 450, for the torture of two qāḍīs, including a chief qāḍī.

114 See for example the fate of the family of a chief qāḍī who died without sons in 738/1337–8. The governor expelled his family and sealed his house. His money was confiscated from his sons-in-law, his daughters, and his wife; and his clothes, books, and riding animals were sold: Jazarī, Köp. MS, 602. When in 713/1313–14 a wazīr died without sons, his wives were married off, his houses occupied, and his money confiscated: Ibn Kathīr, 14/109. For the similar fate of an amīr who died without sons see Jazarī, BN MS, 559–60. See also Ibn Kathīr, 13/146 and Ṣafadī, *al-Wāfī*, 18/220 for examples of merchants whose fortunes were confiscated after their untimely deaths.

115 For two typical examples of the hundreds that could be cited see Ibn al-Ṣuqāʿī, 7; Ṣafadī, *Aʿyān*, 66a.

116 The Qaymāriyya was the seat of the diwān al-istikhlāṣ: Ibn Kathīr, 14/7. The muṣādara of 695/1295–6 was established in the ʿAzīziyya: Jazarī, BN MS, 349–50.

Umm Ṣāliḥ, one of the larger madrasas of the city. This muṣādara was conducted by an amīr and an ᶜālim who came to Damascus from Egypt with the specific aim of mulcting the wealthy aᶜyān.[117] Another instance was the visit of the sulṭān to Cairo in 695/1295–6, in which he demanded and received 80,000 dirhams from aᶜyān and amīrs alike. The sulṭān also set up a board at the ᶜAzīziyya madrasa in Damascus at which the entire yearly income (jāmikiyya) of the secretaries of the diwāns was taken.[118]

The muṣādara on a wide scale could also be used as a political tool in fitna. When a powerful individual fell from favor, his supporters could be exposed to the muṣādara en masse, as was the case with the supporters of al-Ṣāliḥ ᶜIsmāᶜīl.[119] Collective exactions were also used by conquerors to exploit the wealth of the city, and to extract money from old elites to give it to new men. One example was the Mongol seizure of the city in 699/1299–1300, during which the aᶜyān of the city were said to have lost 3,600,000 dirhams, in addition to what secretaries and amīrs lost.[120]

Thus, Ayyūbid and Mamlūk warrior households brought few new political or administrative practices to Damascus. They never imposed permanent, hierarchical, and impersonal institutions on the city to administer it. Instead, through a kind of maladroit patrimonialism they made political use of existing social, cultural, and administrative practices. The state in this period was not an impersonal entity, possessing specialized agencies, capable of formulating long-term strategies to pursue political goals. The politics of the city consisted of continuously renegotiated relationships among the ruling household, the important amīrs and their households, and civilian elites with specialized knowledge or religious prestige. If we are to speak of the state at all, it is as an abstraction of the personal ties of alliance, dependence, and dominance among these three groups. Rather than look for the mechanisms by which the state, as the primary embodiment and agent of power, diffused power from the top down, we need to understand a more complex situation. Studies of the bureaucracy, of such entities as the sultanate and the caliphate, of the legal and "public" aspects of power, are undeniably useful in themselves. These, however, do not cover the entirety, or even perhaps the most important part, of relations among power, cultural practices, and the social strategies of groups. Such approaches have been useful in medieval Islamic history only with so much qualification that they lose the very precision they are intended to introduce.

117 Ibn Kathīr, 13/311.

118 Jazarī, BN MS, 349–50. For other examples see the contender in a fitna who in 740/1242–3 demanded 1,000,000 dirhams from the merchants of the city: Ibn Kathīr, 14/195; in 636/1238–9 al-Jawād subjected Damascenes to the muṣādara until they came up with 600,000 dinars: *ibid.*, 13/152. See also *ibid.*, 14/79.

119 Ṣafadī, *al-Wāfī*, 18/525.

120 This sum is especially high in light of the fact that most of the aᶜyān had already decamped in the exodus or *jafla* to Cairo. Much of this money was redistributed to men the Mongols sponsored. The son of the preeminent Mongol intellectual, Naṣīr al-Dīn al-Ṭūṣī, received 100,000 dirhams from one such redistribution, and the ṣūfī chief shaykh received 600,000: Ibn Kathīr, 14/8, 9.

The aᶜyān and the new order

As Ayyūbids and Mamlūks learned to make use of existing practices for their own benefit, the aᶜyān of the city accommodated themselves to the military patronage state. In the long run, the recruitment and conditions of social reproduction of the aᶜyān were transformed, and the city's defanged pre-Nūrīd aᶜyān recast themselves as a cultural elite that competed for manṣabs. In the short term, however, what is striking about the culture and social practices of the aᶜyān is not a break with the pre-Nūrīd past, but rather continuity with it. The aᶜyān did not accommodate themselves to the military patronage state by any radical transformation of their social and cultural practices, but by making different uses of existing ones.

In the fifty years before the arrival of Nūr al-Dīn, the aᶜyān of the city disputed control of the city with imperial governors and garrisons. The aᶜyān defended their status through their control of city offices and their influence with associations of young men (aḥdāth and similar groups) that wielded violence in several forms.[121] Aᶜyān families survived partly because they could use young men's organized violence to protect property. While never formally autonomous, the city's aᶜyān disputed control of the city, often successfully, with Fāṭimid and Saljūkid governors and garrisons.[122] In this period they fit loosely (but still not well) Weber's definition of urban notables as a group that controls property and participates in politics autonomously.

With the new military patronage state, the aᶜyān's hold on property, its control over offices, and its command of organized violence all weakened. Beginning with Nūr al-Dīn, the aᶜyān lost control of the aḥdāth. The aᶜyān did not lose their military roles entirely, and some continued to participate in military campaigns. However, they were restricted to fighting external enemies, and were largely prohibited from taking part in the political struggles of the amīrs.[123] They never used military training or arms to defend themselves against amīrs. A few wealthy civilians established waqfs to protect property and pass on a portion of it to their descendants. One of the few merchants to establish a madrasa was a man named Ibn Rawāḥa. In spite of his interests all over Syria and a substantial fortune, he thought it prudent to deed his house as a madrasa and to reside in it until his death.[124]

121 C. Cahen, "Mouvements populaires et autonomisme urbain dans l'Asie Musulmane du moyen âge," *Arabica* 5 (1958), 225–50; 6 (1959), 25–56, 233–65; Cahen, "Aḥdāth," *EI* (2); E. Ashtor, "L'administration urbaine en Syrie médiévale," *RSO* 31 (1956), 73–128; Lapidus, *Muslim Cities*, 154.

122 See Ashtor, "L'administration urbaine," 118–22, and *A Social and Economic History*, 225–31 for an account of the struggles between "urban militias" and governors, which unfortunately suffers from uncritical use of terms such as "feudal" and "bourgeois."

123 For one extreme example of a lecturer who took part in Baybar's campaigns as a horse-archer see Jazarī, BN MS, 8.

124 Dhahabī, *Mukhtaṣar al-Jazarī*, Köp. MS, 26; Ibn Kathīr, 13/116; Nuᶜaymī, 1/265, 266, 274; Abū Shāma, *Dhayl*, 136–7, 149, 187, 189.

The descendants of aᶜyān founders could control the waqf as its administrators, and in a few cases they held the lecturer's manṣab at the madrasa.[125] But the protections of large-scale waqfs were less available to the aᶜyān than to amīrs.

Moreover, Nūr al-Dīn and his successors, by establishing a fairly large number of manṣabs in religious institutions, and by making appointments to existing or new offices, brought in their own new men while they recruited established households.[126] As the great aᶜyān households lost control over property and instruments of violence as vehicles of social reproduction, more and more they looked to manṣabs as a means of maintaining their status and social power. Some notable families, including the hitherto preeminent Banū al-Ṣūfī, lost their standing in the city.[127] Others benefited from the new order by accommodating themselves to patronage as practiced by Nūr al-Dīn and his successors. They now made use of their learning to compete for the "monetized honors" of the manṣabs, not to acquire the cultural distinction of a notability.[128] These were no longer (if in fact they ever were) "urban notables" in the Weberian sense; rather they were a cultural elite that maintained its social standing through competing for social prizes in the gift of others.

Some of the old families, together with descendants of scholars patronized by Nūr al-Dīn and Saladin, took advantage of the new opportunities provided by the military patronage state. Competing successfully for manṣabs over generations, the longevity of some of these families is striking.[129] The Banū al-Zakī had seven chief qāḍīs between the beginning of the sixth/twelfth century and the end of the seventh/thirteenth.[130] They claimed descent from the Umayyads, were tied by blood and marriage to other aᶜyān households, and had a large family tomb in which they interred themselves and their clients – including Ibn ᶜArabī. Many of this lineage had manṣabs in religious founda-

[125] See for examples Yūnīnī, 2/10, 337; Nuᶜaymī, 1/398–406.

[126] Gilbert, "The ᶜUlamaᵓ"; Gilbert, "Institutionalization of Muslim Scholarship." Secretaries in Syria were also of mixed origins under Saladin: Humphreys, *From Saladin to the Mongols*, 26. This process continued throughout the Ayyūbid and Mamlūk periods, as new rulers introduced into the city scholars beholden to them, for example, Ṣafadī, *al-Wāfī*, 21/341.

[127] Cahen, "Mouvements populaires," vol. I, 239; Ibn al-Qalānisī, 314–25; Ashtor, "L'administration urbaine," 122–6.

[128] On the concept of the monetized honor see Wink, *Land and Sovereignty*, 33, 294, 304, 321, 379; Wink, *al-Hind*, vol. I, p. 13.

[129] Several of these families have been studied. See W.M. Brinner, "The Banū Ṣaṣrā: a Study on the Transmission of a Scholarly Tradition," *Arabica* 7 (May, 1960), 167–95; F. Wüstenfeld, "Stammtafel der Familie Banū Asākir," *Orientalia* (Amsterdam, 1846); L. Pouzet, "La descendance de l'historien ᶜAli Ibn ᶜAsākir et ses alliances à Damas au viie/XIIIe siècle," in *Mélanges M. Allard et Nwyia* (1984), 515–29; K.S. Salibi, "The Banū Jamāᶜa: A Dynasty of Shāfiᶜī Jurists in the Mamlūk Period," *SI* 9 (1958); Salibi, "Ibn Jamāᶜa," *EI* (2). Gilbert covered the major aᶜyān lineages in "The ᶜUlamaᵓ," 154–86. The most detailed and sensitive study of a Syrian elite lineage is A.-M. Eddé, "Une Grande Famille de Shafiites Alépins. Les Banū l-ᶜAgamī aux XIIᵉ–XIIIᵉ siècles," *REMMM* 62 (1991), 61–71.

[130] L. Pouzet, *Damas au VIIe/XIIIe siècle. Vie et structures religieuses d'une métropole islamique* (Beirut, 1988), 121.

tions.[131] The Banū Sanī al-Dawla and the Banū al-Qalānisī also served Saljukids, Zangids, Ayyūbids, Mongols, and Mamlūks, and had waqfs in their lines of descent.[132] The Banū Abī ᶜAṣrūn held manṣabs in the city for 200 years, beginning before Nūr al-Dīn's reign. They were related by marriage to Saladin, and held the manṣab of the ᶜAṣrūniyya, a madrasa which served as the tomb of the lineage's founder, for three generations.[133] The Banū ᶜAsākir were related by both marriage and student–teacher ties to the Banū al-Zakī, the Banū al-Sulamī, and a number of scholars newly arrived in the city. They also controlled many city offices.[134] These families, and a number of others, were the *buyūtāt*, the aᶜyān lineages most successful at translating religious prestige into the social reproduction of status. They were known as "bayt al-ᶜilm," "bayt al-ḥadīth," or by other honorifics referring to the transmission of ᶜilm through lineages.[135] Characteristic of all was their use of religious prestige, political connections, and social distinction to protect wealth, to struggle for manṣabs, and to a lesser extent to control waqfs.

Once the aᶜyān aimed at manṣabs as a prime target of social competition, the recruitment of the elite opened up. Following Nūr al-Dīn and the proliferation of manṣabs in the city, established elites made room for immigrants and self-made men.[136] Wandering scholars, provincial elites, and immigrants fleeing Mongols and Crusaders joined scholars recruited by warrior households.[137] At the same time, aᶜyān families joined international networks of scholars, and Damascenes often departed the city to take up positions or seek their fortunes elsewhere.[138] Brought together in study-circles, tied to one another through marriage and discipleship, these men of disparate origins coalesced into a new elite whose recruitment remained fluid.[139] The aᶜyān did not form a closed

131 Ibn Kathīr, 13/32, 101, 156, 308; Abū Shāma, *Dhayl*, 136–7.

132 On the Banū al-Qalānisī see Ashtor, "L'administration urbaine," 106–7; on the waqfs of Ibn al-Qalānisī (lahu min awqāf wālidihi mā yakfīhī) see Ibn al-Ṣuqāᶜī, 176. On the Banū Sanī al-Dawla, and the waqfs in their line of descent from 520/1126–7 onwards, see Ṣafadī, *al-Wāfī*, 8/250; Yūnīnī, 2/10. They were also given the madrasa al-Qilījiyya by its founder: Nuᶜaymī, 1/569.

133 See Ibn Shaddād, 2/238; Nuᶜaymī, 1/398–406; Ṣafadī, *al-Wāfī*, 17/572.

134 Nuᶜaymī, 1/180–2; Ibn Kathīr, 13/101.

135 See for a few examples of the hundreds that could be cited: Ṣafadī, *al-Wāfī*, 7/177, 18/134; Ṣafadī, *Aᶜyān*, 5b; Ibn Shākir, 21/29; Yūnīnī, 1/333; 2/354–5, 487; 3/39; Ibn Kathīr, 13/66, 264, 314.

136 Gilbert estimated that approximately half of the senior ᶜulamāʾ in the period up to 1260 were immigrants, and one-quarter to one-fifth were transients: "The ᶜUlamāʾ," 40–2. The number of artisans who made their way into the ranks of the learned was not large, but it was still significant. See Ibn Abī Uṣaybiᶜa, 670–1, for a carpenter and stone cutter who began studying Euclid to learn the "secrets" of carpentry, and then learned more of the Greek sciences until he became an engineer, mathematician, and physician, noted for his edition of Galen and for maintaining the water clock in the Umayyad Mosque. He had stipends for keeping the clock in running order and for his service in a hospital (*bimāristān*). He was also known for his books on medicines, on war and administration (*siyāsa*), and for his abridgement of Isbahānī's *al-Aghānī*.

137 For one account of how an immigrant from Baghdād encountered others from his home city see Ibn Abī Uṣaybiᶜa, 686.

138 See Gilbert, "The ᶜUlamāʾ," 6.

139 See *ibid.*, 19, on marriage relations between scholars from outside the city and established elites.

group or caste, and throughout the period under consideration we cannot consider them anything like a monolithic "establishment." In income, relations to rulers, and status, the aᶜyān covered a wide range; it was social trajectory more than origin or even position that defined most aᶜyān households.

Although the recruitment of the learned elite was relatively open, and the circulation of individuals if not of households was rapid, the aᶜyān constituted nonetheless a self-conscious group. The aᶜyān had their own characteristic cultural style, conviction of superiority, and tactics of exclusion. Many inhabited certain neighborhoods such as al-Ṣāliḥiyya or Darb al-ᶜAjamī.[140] The learned also had a syndic called the *naqīb al-mutaᶜammamīn* or the "syndic of those who wear the turban." The functions of this syndic are unclear, but he may have checked the claims to learning of new arrivals on the model of the "syndic of the descendants of ᶜAlī Ibn Abī Ṭālib," who verified the claims of newcomers to Ṭālibid descent.[141] But what defined the new elite, and what advanced their strategies of social reproduction, was less money, land, title, certified competence, or office than the exemplary possession of ᶜilm.

By acquiring ᶜilm, the aᶜyān expected two things, and it was these common expectations – rather than income, land, or office – that defined them as a social category. First, through learning they made themselves eligible to compete for manṣabs. The jurists never elaborated a concept of the "right" to a manṣab, nor were manṣabs acquired through any formal qualification comparable to the Sung examination. However, acquiring a manṣab required *istiḥqāq*, a quality which combined notions of "suitability," "adequacy," and "eligibility." The precise definition of istiḥqāq was debated by the sources, but the consensus seems to be that with respect to civilians it referred to the piety and learning appropriate to a recipient of waqf income.[142] Both teachers and students were described as holding manṣabs, and both were collectively known as "the eligible" (*al-mustaḥiqīn*).

Istiḥqāq was a quality expected of recipients of monetized honors. All recipients of waqf income in madrasas – including shaykhs and students – had to be seen as "eligible" to hold on to their manṣabs, as did soldiers for their pay (jāmikiyya) and amīrs for their iqṭāᶜs. One indication of the relationship of istiḥqāq to income was a review of the army held in 711/1310–11. The secretary of the army (*kātib al-jaysh*) according to Nuwayrī was expected to register

140 On al-Ṣāliḥiyya see Ibn Ṭūlūn, *al-Qalāʾid al-jawhariyya*; Sack, *Damaskus*, 82–3. On the residence of many among the learned in the Darb al-ᶜAjamī, see Abū Shāma, *Dhayl*, 95.

141 Ṣafadī, *al-Wāfī*, 8/304. For a "naqīb al-ṭālibiyīn" who died in 689/1290 see Jazarī, BN MS, 5a. Whatever these offices were, they were seldom cited in the sources, and rarely in the context of social and political competition.

142 Subkī, *Muᶜīd*, 28. For suitability (istiḥqāq lʾil-manāṣib), which referred to ability, correct belief, and morality, see Nuᶜaymī, 1/305; an example of "suitability" (istiḥqāq) in a document appointing a lecturer to a manṣab: Ṣafadī, *al-Wāfī*, 13/415. For the "moment of eligibility" ("waqt al-istiḥqāq") as a stage a young person had to reach before obtaining a manṣab see Subkī, *Ṭabaqāt*, 6/253; for an appointment to a manṣab described as "by istiḥqāq," see Subkī, Staadtsbibliothek MS, 16; also chapter 2, note 110.

recipients of iqṭāᶜs, cash, and measures of grain according to their various categories, in order to verify their istiḥqāq.[143] However, formal reviews of the military were fairly rare, in this one the army registry (*diwān al-jaysh*) proved itself incompetent: "They could not tell a good soldier from a bad one, nor a new arrival from one whose migration (*hijra*) to the gates of the sulṭān was early. They were incapable of recognizing the eligible (*mustaḥiq*)." In the event a qāḍī able to "determine the mustaḥiq from the interloper (*dakhīl*)" took over the review.[144] Another indication of the universal nature of revenue sources was the opposite of istiḥqāq – ᶜ*ajz*, (also ᶜ*ajaz*) or "incapacity." To aᶜyān and warriors both, ᶜajz when demonstrated could cost a shaykh, amīr, student, or soldier his manṣab, iqṭāᶜ stipend, or soldier's pay.[145]

Second, the aᶜyān made use of their learning to acquire a form of social honor known as *ḥurma*.[146] Ḥurma was a quasi-sacred combination of honor and inviolability that referred to cities, women, and sacred objects as well as families and individuals.[147] Both civilians and warriors acquired ḥurma, though the ḥurma of civilians referred to learning and piety rather than the honor of the warrior.[148] Among civilians, ḥurma earned them both respect and a certain inviolability among rulers and the common people.[149] The aᶜyān

143 Nuwayrī, 8/201. 144 Ibn al-Dawādārī, 9/238–9.

145 See the individual whose stipend was cut off by an amīr because of his "incapacity": "qaṭaᶜa khubzahu liʾannahu ẓahara ᶜajzahu" Safadī, *Aᶜyān*, fol. 27b. Also Ibn al-Dawādārī, 9/244.

146 Ḥurma was defined by Lane (*An Arabic–English Lexicon*) as "the state of being sacred, or inviolable; sacredness and inviolability; reverence, respect, honor." Lane quoted one use of the term: "When a man has a relationship to us, and we regard him with bashfulness, we say, lahu ḥurma."

147 Yūnīnī, 2/400. Damascus was said to have ḥurma when it was under the leadership of a wise governor: Abū Shāma, *Dhayl*, 150. For the preservation of the ḥurma of Aleppo when the city surrendered honorably during a siege see Ibn al-ᶜAdīm, *Zubda al-ḥalab fī tāʾrīkh ḥalab*, S. Dahān ed. (Damascus, 1968), 65. In a debate whether it was permissible for a Muslim to be cursed, one protagonist produced a ḥadīth (not in Wensinck) : "The ḥurma of the Muslim is greater than the ḥurma of the kaᶜba," Ibn Khallikān, 2/447. Sacred texts also had ḥurma. Paper makers were admonished not reuse paper with quotations from the Qurʾān, ḥadīth, or the names of prophets or angels on it, because it had ḥurma: Ibn al-Ḥājj, 4/89. Ḥurma could also be challenged. A shaykh was praised for never challenging anyone's ḥurma (lāʾsqaṭa li-aḥad ḥurma): Yūnīnī, 4/61. Although as far as this writer knows there have been no studies of ḥurma in the pre-modern Middle East, the association of ḥurma with the sexual honor of the family in some modern Middle Eastern societies is suggestive of other meanings that may have existed in our period: see D. Eickelman, *The Middle East: an Anthropological Approach*, 2nd edn. (Englewood Cliffs, NJ, 1989), 204–5.

148 For sulṭāns, amīrs, and members of ruling households who had ḥurma, see Ibn Shākir, 21/128; Ibn Kathīr, 13/321; Ibn Khallikān, 1/162–3; Sibṭ Ibn al-Jawzī, *Mirʾāt*, 8/642; Yūnīnī, 3/230, 238. For the revolt of some of al-Nāṣir Qalāwūn's mamlūks against him as a violation of his ḥurma (kharaqū ḥurma as-sulṭān) see Ibn Kathīr, 13/338. For the ḥurma of shaykhs see for example the story of the Qurʾān-reciter who lost his ḥurma because he drank wine with al-Malik al-Ashraf, and became a wanderer in shame: Abū Shāma, *Dhayl*, 134; Sibṭ Ibn al-Jawzī, *Mirʾāt*, 8/632. A shaykh could be apparently impious but still possess ḥurma: see for example the shaykh known for his unbelief, who held study sessions for Samaritans, Muslims, Jews, and Christians, and cultivated the Hellenistic sciences, who nonetheless was known for the widespread recognition of his ḥurma: Yūnīnī, 2/165.

149 Some variation of "lahu ḥurma wāfara ᶜindaʾl-mulūk wʾal-aᶜyān" was very common in death-notices of shaykhs. See for examples Ṣafadī, *al-Wāfī*, 1/179, 18/397; Ibn Shākir, 21/120; Yūnīnī, 4/131.

also struggled to acquire ḥurma for use in competition over manṣabs. When Ibn Sāᶜīd al-Dawla (d. 709/1309–10) was lobbying for the post of wazīr, he went to a holy man outside the city and won from his encounter a ḥurma greater than that of the sitting wazīr.[150] Among the military ḥurma was also associated with advancement, as in the case of the man who acquired ḥurma in the eyes of al-Malik al-Manṣūr, and was made an amīr and given large iqṭāᶜs.[151] Ḥurma was also imagined as a quantity that could increase or decrease; once lessened, its holder's shame made his wealth more vulnerable to plunder.[152]

Men generally did not acquire learning in order to gain professional knowledge or qualifications. The object of learning was the prestige of the cultivated personality, which produced ḥurma and istiḥqāq. The eligibility of warriors and the learned alike for monetized honors was represented in virtually identical language. This is the first of many points of comparison between amīrs and aᶜyān. These two groups made use of similar cultural practices for similar social and political ends. In spite of the diversified nature of elites – composed of warriors and shaykhs from often distant origins – they also maneuvered within a similar environment. Most faced a central set of core problems of survival and success.

Household survival in the Latin West, the Middle East, and Sung China

To situate the distinctiveness of the arena of social and political competition in Damascus within the wider context of Eurasia in the period, it will be useful to compare elite strategies of survival in several areas of the continent. Urban elites in the Latin West had two broad strategies of social reproduction. First, families in cities of the Latin West occasionally adopted the titles and way of life of the aristocracy. They bought land in the countryside, had themselves ennobled, and transmitted their status to their descendants through the same mechanisms by which the feudal nobility kept prestige and property within lineages.[153] Urban elites in the Latin West could also make use of corporations and religious groups. The greater guilds, religious orders, the church, universities, militias, and other associations allowed notables to use some of the mechanisms that produced and reproduced elite status.

In China, on the other hand, it was by inserting some of their members into

150 "Fa-lamā ṭalaba lʾil-wizāra iltajāʾa ilā zāwiyati-sh-shaykh Naṣr fa-li-dhālika kānat ḥurmatuhu awfar min ḥurmati-l-wazīr wʾaᶜẓam": Ṣafadī, *Aᶜyān*, 141b. For another example of an appointment to the wizāra made because of the ḥurma of an individual see Jazarī, BN MS, 574. For a poet whose great ḥurma in the eyes of the ruling Ayyūbid households (*al-mulūk*) helped him get appointed wazīr, see Ibn Khallikān, 4/110.

151 Jazarī, BN MS, 5a: "qad zāda (al-Malik al-Manṣūr) fī ḥurmatihi wa-ammarahu waᶜaṭāhu iqṭāᶜ sitīn fāris."

152 See Ṣafadī, *Aᶜyān*, 31a, for the loss of ḥurma leading to the plunder of an individual's wealth.

153 On the adoption by urban elites of the way of life of the aristocracy see Bloch, *Feudal Society*, vol. I, 322–4.

the civil service that elite lineages in the Sung period sought to reproduce their status, and merchants and others sought to advance it.[154] Sung officials prevented merchants from controlling property securely or achieving legal invulnerability. The merchant families of the Sung period may have had a more secure hold on property than was the case with merchants in the Middle East, but they were still subject to predation by imperial officials as long as they lived in cities.[155] Nor could they turn autonomous corporate or religious groups and practices to their own benefit. The bureaucracy regularly seized the income and revenue sources of religious groups and foundations, although family foundations provided some security of property. Merchant families had two broad strategies of advancing their status, one through "bribery" and the other by introducing their sons into the civil service. Although the bureaucracy subjected merchants to an array of disabilities, not the least of which was disdain and social inferiority, merchant families struggled to place their sons in it through the educational system. The upper-class status of the gentry was based on land more than membership in the civil service, but the gentry used their control over land and their kinship connections to acquire education and office for their sons.[156] From the perspective of both groups, the "ladder of success" was to tilt the examination system in favor of their sons.[157]

Because of the peculiarities of Middle Eastern politics, none of these possibilities was open to Damascenes. As we have seen, in the Middle East there were few aristocracies, corporate bodies, or state apparatuses into which

[154] See J. Chafee, *The Thorny Gates of Learning: a Social History of Examinations* (Cambridge, 1985) on the use of the examination in household survival and mobility strategies; E. Balazs, *Chinese Civilization and Bureaucracy* (New Haven, 1964), 6–33; Smith, *Taxing Heaven's Storehouse*, 4, 5, 78–108; M. Weber, "The Chinese Literati," in H. Gerth and C. W. Mills eds., *From Max Weber: Essays in Sociology* (New York, 1958); T. H. C. Lee, "Sung Education Before Chu Hsi," in W. T. de Bary and J.W. Chafee eds., *Neo-Confucian Education: the Formative Stage* (Berkeley and Los Angeles, 1989), 126–7; W. Chan, "Chu Hsi and the Academies," in Bary and Chafee, *Neo-Confucian Education*, 389–413.

[155] E. Balazs, "Urban Developments," in J. Liu ed., *Change in Sung China, Innovation or Reconstruction?* (Lexington, MA, 1969), 14; Balazs, "The Birth of Capitalism in China," *JESHO* 3 (1960), 201–3.

[156] See Chafee, *The Thorny Gates of Learning*, 10; Cf. Balazs, "The Birth of Capitalism in China," 202; E.O. Reischauer and J.K. Fairbank, "China's Early Modern Society," in Liu, *Change in Sung China*, 2, 3.

[157] On the Sung period use by elites of the examination system, and on alternative paths of recruitment into the bureaucracy, see B. McKnight, "Mandarins as Legal Experts: Professional Learning in Sung China," in Bary and Chafee, *Neo-Confucian Education*, 493–516; McKnight, *Village and Bureaucracy in Southern Sung China* (Chicago, 1972); Chafee, *The Thorny Gates of Learning*, 10, 98–115; Chafee, "Education and Examinations in Sung Society," Ph.D. Dissertation (University of Chicago, 1979), 176–208; E.A. Kracke, Jr., *The Civil Service in Early Sung China* (Cambridge, MA, 1953); T.H.C. Lee, *Government, Education, and Examinations in Sung China* (Hong Kong, 1975); Lee, "Sung Education," 121–2. See Chafee, *The Thorny Gates of Learning*, 23, 24; W. W. Lo, *An Introduction to the Civil Service of Sung China, with Emphasis on its Personnel Administration* (Honolulu, 1987), esp. 79–111 for the *yin* privilege or "imperial grace of protection" that gave elite families a safety net in introducing their progeny into the bureaucracy – but even here their sons had to take an examination, and half failed.

urban elites could insert themselves. Rulers were powerful enough – and physically close enough – to prevent the elite from establishing autonomous social bodies. Nor could the aʿyān transmit status through the meticulous maintenance of group boundaries, because group affiliations were fluid and the social circulation of the city was rapid. Aʿyān households maneuvered within a form of domination in which rulers prevented the emergence of autonomous bodies, yet did not penetrate the city by effective state institutions.

We thus face a peculiar problem in trying to understand household strategies of social survival, a problem that mirrors the singular character of political power in the period. How did the aʿyān reproduce their status in a social environment that both medieval Europeans and Sung Chinese would have seen as lethal, one without the protections of permanent wealth, office, or corporation? As we have seen, in high medieval Damascus the social goal of the aʿyān was the manṣab, which had to be won by individuals. Yet the acquisition of manṣabs was not "meritocratic" in any useful sense of the term. In understanding household strategies of survival, the question is how the aʿyān inculcated into their young the disposition to acquire the social and cultural "capital" that allowed them to participate in the struggle for manṣabs. Before considering how they acquired their cultural capital (as they themselves conceived of it) we should first examine in greater detail the dominant approach to relations between society and culture in the period – the madrasa.

CHAPTER 2

Madrasas, the production of knowledge, and the reproduction of elites

The study of madrasas would seem an ideal way of analyzing an institution that articulated relations among politics, cultural practices, and the strategies of social elites.[1] Scholars have generally believed that the appearance of madrasas in the high medieval Middle East transformed higher education. They have also often agreed that madrasas had structures and uses similar to the specialized institutions of higher education in other societies, especially in educating jurists and bureaucrats by providing them an advanced legal curriculum. This chapter examines the madrasas of high medieval Damascus to address two major questions. What was the relationship between the transmission of knowledge and the proliferation of household waqfs such as madrasas in the city? How did madrasas serve elite social and political strategies?

[1] Literature on madrasas includes: Bulliet, *Patricians of Nishapūr*, 47–60; M. van Berchem, "Origine de la madrasa," *Matériaux pour un corpus Inscriptionem Arabicorum*, I (Egypt: Mém, mis, arch. franç. au Caire) 19 (1894–1903), 254–65; J. Berkey, "Education and Society: Higher Religious Learning in Late Medieval Cairo (Egypt)," Ph.D. Dissertation (Princeton, 1989); Berkey, *The Transmission of Knowledge*; D. Brandenberg, *Die Madrasa: Ursprung, Entwicklung, Ausbreitung und kunsterliche Gestaltung der islamischen Mosche-Hochschule* (Graz, 1978); Y. Eche, *Les Bibliothèques arabes publiques et semi-publiques en Mésopotamie, en Syrie, et en Egypte au moyen âge* (Damascus, PIFD, 1967); I. Goldziher, "Education – Muslim," *Encyclopedia of Religion and Ethics*, vol. V, 198–207; Goldziher, *Muslim Studies*, S.M. Stern and C.R. Barber trans. (London, 1971); H. Halm, "Die Anfänge der Madrasa," *ZDMG*, suppl. III, 1, XIX (1977), 438–48; R. Hillenbrand, "Madrasa," *EI* (2); Leiser, "The Endowment of the al-Ẓāhiriyya"; Leiser, "The Restoration of Sunnism in Egypt: Madrasas and Mudarrisūn, 495–647/1101–1249," Ph.D. Dissertation (University of Pennsylvania, 1976); Leiser, "The Madrasa and the Islamization of the Middle East: the Case of Egypt," *JARCE* 22 (1985). See especially G. Makdisi's many articles and books in the bibliography. J. Pedersen, "Masdjid," *EI* (1); Pederson, "Some Aspects of the History of the Madrasa," *IC* 3 (1929), 525–37; H. Shumaysi, *Madāris Dimashq fī al-ʿaṣr al-ayyūbī* (Beirut, 1983); A. Shalabi, *History of Muslim Education* (Beirut, 1954); D. Sourdel, "Les professeurs de madrasa à Alep aux XIIe–XIIIe siècles d'après Ibn Shaddad," *BEO* 13 (1949–51), 85–115; Sourdel, "Réflexions"; J. Sourdel-Thomine, "Locaux d'enseignements et madrasas dans l'islam médiéval," *REI* 44 (1976), 185–98; A. Talas, *La Madrasa Niẓamiyya et son histoire* (Paris, 1939); A.L. Tibawi, "Origin and Character of the Madrasa," *BSOAS* 25 (1962), 225–38; G.L. Wiet, "La Madrasa Khaidariiya, à Damas," *Mélanges Gaudefroy-Demombynes* (Cairo, 1935–45); F. Wüstenfeld, *Die Academien der Araber und ihre Lehrer* (Göttingen, 1837).

As noted above, an earlier generation of scholars saw madrasas as institutions intended to develop the ideological cadres necessary for the "Sunnī Revival." George Makdisi, who performed such a signal service in demolishing these views, is himself a strong proponent of viewing madrasas as a form of "institutionalized education."[2] Having argued successfully against earlier interpretations, Makdisi continues to see madrasas as having an organized and differentiated student body, a specialized curriculum, a professoriate certified to teach, and an institutional educational goal – the certification of teachers and jurists. Where Makdisi recognizes that much learning was private, he still sees the madrasa as the major institution of higher education. In this view, students followed "the basic undergraduate law course," which led to "the license to teach."[3] Makdisi has been criticized for his use of anachronistic language, but at least it has the virtue of rendering the texts into familiar terms of reference. However, his interpretation of the structure of madrasas and the role they played in the specialization of education has remained dominant if not entirely unchallenged.

Other scholars have generally agreed with Makdisi that madrasas were a turning point in medieval cultural history. The outstanding political and social historians of the period have been interested in madrasas, both for the evidence they convey on other practices and for their roles in creating a unified cultural elite.[4] With respect to Damascus, the foundation of large numbers of religious institutions has been interpreted as a turning point in the social and cultural history of the city. Some of the finest historians of the city have seen madrasas as specialized institutions intended by their founders to recruit, train, and support jurists and bureaucrats, under the supervision of rulers of the city.[5]

Although scholars have largely agreed that madrasas were specialized institutions of higher education, some have questioned the extent to which madrasas dominated or monopolized education. D. B. MacDonald was perhaps the first scholar to stress the "personal" nature of medieval Islamic education, and A.L. Tibawi made the first explicit defense of an idea that has been repeated regularly since. To Tibawi the basic institution of education was the teacher-student relationship, which he held did not change with the advent of the madrasas.[6] Since then, Roy Mottahedeh has pointed out that many people who considered themselves learned in the Saljūk period were "outside the madrasa system," and Lapidus has underlined the centrality of the study-

[2] Makdisi, *The Rise of Colleges*, 281. [3] *Ibid.*, 96, 281, 181.

[4] See Bulliet, *Patricians of Nishapūr*; Cahen, *Pre-Ottoman Turkey*; Lapidus, *Muslim Cities*; Petry, *The Civilian Elite*.

[5] See Gilbert's suggestion that madrasas "professionalized" and "institutionalized" the scholarly elite: Gilbert, "The ʿUlamaʾ," 58–60; and Humphreys' conclusion that "madrasas . . . would ensure a solid education in Shāfiʿī or Ḥanafī fiqh, under the supervision of the prince and his close associates, for all potential ʿulamaʾ or bureaucrats": Humphreys, "Politics and Architectural Patronage," 166.

[6] A.L. Tibawi, "Origin and Character of the Madrasa"; Makdisi, *The Rise of Colleges*, 282ff.

circle in the culture of the learned elite in the Mamlūk period.[7] Most recently, Jonathan Berkey has affirmed the "informal" character of Mamlūk education and questioned the extent to which madrasas crowded out other forms of education.[8]

Yet these reservations have been largely a question of degree. Berkey's study is perhaps the most detailed description of the informal character of education in high and late medieval Cairo, an observation that he illustrates with important new material. Berkey also shows how the formal characteristics of the various types of institutions supported by waqfs tended to blur into one another, especially in the late medieval era. Yet in spite of the many merits of his study Berkey never entirely disengaged from the paradigm he sought to criticize. Rejecting some of Makdisi's views on the madrasa, Berkey still sought to analyze an "informal system of higher education," in which madrasas were "the primary forum for religious instruction throughout the Islamic Middle East," and "played a role of exceptional importance in the study and transmission of Islamic law and the religious sciences."[9] The examination of the madrasas also occupies the greater part of his book, because that was where his most original sources – the waqfiyyas – led him. Thus, while madrasas may not sustain all Goldziher's or Makdisi's interpretations, the idea that they were important institutions of higher learning that provided an advanced education to bureaucrats, jurists, teachers, and scholars has continued to inspire scholarship in the field. An even more dominant – and unexamined – idea is that a "system of education" is where elite strategies related to knowledge may be found.

This chapter will reexamine a number of these interpretations, at least insofar as they relate to high medieval Damascus. It will suggest that an examination of the uses of the madrasa within the social and political strategies of the aʿyān, rather than its institutional structures and routines, will produce a better understanding of its consequences. Furthermore, it will argue that studying the production of knowledge and the preparation of the young under the rubric of "higher education" is a fundamentally erroneous approach to relations between culture and society in the period.

These arguments address a single city, so one must ask whether what was true of madrasas in Damascus was also true elsewhere. Three considerations should be kept in mind. First, the material for Damascus has often been used as important sources on institutional histories of the madrasa. Second, none of the sources remarked that madrasas in Damascus had meanings, uses, and functions different from madrasas in other places in the high medieval period. Finally, the point of this study is to argue that cultural institutions and practices cannot be studied in isolation from their specific political and social contexts. Some of the uses of the madrasa discussed below will necessarily differ from their uses in other places and periods. Scholars who have studied

[7] Mottahedeh, *Loyalty and Leadership*, 140; Lapidus, *Muslim Cities*, 111.
[8] Berkey, *The Transmission of Knowledge*, 20–7, 43, 216–18. [9] *Ibid.*, 7–9, 16.

madrasas in eleventh-century Khurasān, late medieval Cairo, or eighteenth-century Istanbul or Central Asia will notice differences from their periods and places. That is to be expected and even desired. The object of this chapter is to understand the uses of the madrasa by the elites of a single city over a defined period. It is interested neither in origins nor in outcomes. Its aim is to urge that such institutions be studied within the context of specific struggles, rather than to force a reinterpretation of the ever-elusive "universal template" by which "Islamic institutions" can be understood.

Madrasas as institutions of higher education

To illustrate how the aʿyān of Damascus saw madrasas, it will be useful for comparative purposes to examine the educational institutions of the contemporary civilizations of the high medieval Latin West and Sung China. It is not difficult to define the extent to which the universities and academies of the Latin West and Sung China were specialized institutions of higher education.

While in early medieval Europe the young sought out individual masters and worked with them in their study-circles, by the thirteenth century universities thrived on both sides of the Alps. The Latin university existed where rulers allowed other social bodies partial autonomy and self-government. In Europe, universities were corporate bodies, with the same charter-based liberties as other groups. Before the term "university" acquired its final meaning of a body of scholars or students, it meant any organized group. For this reason, universities were not necessarily tied to specific places, as these groups were free to move from one city to another, and some in fact did so.[10] Universities as corporate bodies administered their wealth, their membership, and the granting of degrees. Together with other corporate groups, they were jealous of their autonomy, and struggled as institutions (or groups of individual corporations) against bishops and burghers, and occasionally against papal and royal authorities.[11] Universities also granted certificates of competence and membership and often had distinctive ceremonies of entrance and departure, curriculums, and organizational forms. Where it is just possible to conceive of the medieval Latin university without the state, it is impossible to conceive of it without its corporate organization and leadership.

By contrast, in Sung China imperial state structures, a learned officialdom, and a land-owning gentry survived the horse-warrior revolution that disrupted agrarian empires elsewhere. In the early Sung period the dynasty sought to reduce the control of the military over the administration by supplanting them with scholar-officials, and to reconcile new areas subjected

[10] F. Herr, *The Medieval World. Europe from 1100 to 1350* (London, 1963), 196. This comparison of madrasas to universities is in part taken from, and in part in agreement with, G. Makdisi, "Madrasa and University in the Middle Ages," *Islamica* 32 (1970), 255–64.

[11] Bourin-Derruau, *Temps d'équilibres*, 206–7; Herr, *The Medieval World*, 196–200.

to the dynasty's control.[12] In the Sung period government schools and the examination system bridged the gentry, the scholar-officials, the military, the imperial household, and disgruntled groups the dynasty tried to cultivate.[13]

Sung scholar-officials by definition were holders of a qualification granted by state agencies and produced by passing an examination. The examination system produced a status group of scholar-officials largely from among the military, gentry, and scholar-official families of the empire, though other elite groups – especially merchants – tried to turn their sons into officials through educational institutions. Although attempts to make school attendance mandatory for sitting the examinations ultimately failed, academies and universities as social institutions had an acculturating importance in Sung society second only to the family.[14] The gentry and others competed to insert their sons into the civil service by enrolling them in imperial and private universities and academies. The imperial household controlled the curriculum by selecting and disseminating the classics that formed the subject matter of the examinations. The bureaucracy itself staffed the imperial university, administered the examination system, and took some of the winners. The Chinese university or academy is conceivable without the gentry who made their sons its students – indeed the inevitably dubious claim of the system was that it was open to all. These institutions are hardly conceivable however without the civil service that staffed and administered them, gave the examinations, and inducted successful candidates.[15]

In both cases educational institutions were at once the objects and instruments of the social and political strategies of powerful groups. In the Latin West, resistance to the patrimonial claims of ruling groups permitted corporate forms of organization such as universities to become powerful entities in their own right. The relationship of authorities of various kinds to universities was often fractious and conflict ridden as a result, and universities themselves had strong collective identities and structures. Universities also served other groups, through the provision of educated individuals to the church, state, and

[12] Lo, *Civil Service*, 58, 93; Chafee, *The Thorny Gates of Learning*, 58.

[13] Chafee, "Education and Examinations in Sung Society," 92–100, 208–12; Lee, "Sung Education," 108–20; Lee, "Life in the Schools of Sung China," *Journal of Asian Studies* 37, no. 1 (November, 1977), 52–60; Lo, *Civil Service*, 79–86, 90–111, 218; B. McKnight, "Mandarins as Legal Experts: Professional Learning in Sung China," in Bary and Chafee, *Neo-Confucian Education*, 493–516; E. Balazs, *Chinese Civilization and Bureaucracy*; T. Wei-Ming "The Sung Confucian Idea of Education: a Background Understanding," in Bary and Chafee, *Neo-Confucian Education*, 139–50.

[14] Chafee, "Education and Examinations in Sung Society,"1, 208–12. It should be pointed out that even as educational institutions trained students in the classics that formed the subject matter of the examinations, there were nonetheless inevitable tensions between the Confucian imperative of moral cultivation – felt strongly by many in the schools – and the agonism of the examination system: Chafee, *The Thorny Gates of Learning*, 184–6.

[15] See Rodzinski, *A History of China*, vol. I, 119 for the contradiction between the apparent openness of the examinations to peasants and the practical limitation of entry to the sons of the rentier class.

religious orders and by giving a career path to the cadets of aristocratic families.[16] In Sung China, cooperation among the dynasty, the civil service, and the gentry made intermediate institutions among them viable. In both China and the Latin West, the existence of strong organizations – corporations or state agencies – made formal education a useful or necessary preparation for induction into the administrative, corporate, or religious body in which the young man would spend his productive life.[17] These educational institutions either controlled admission into social and political bodies or constituted social bodies themselves. It should be said that the universities of the Latin West and Sung China had no monopoly on the transmission of knowledge or culture, and in both places the acquisition of correct manners, correct deportment, and patronage were of great importance.[18] However, both had administrations, curriculums, and certificates that correspond reasonably well to the modern usage of these terms.

At first glance, the madrasas of high medieval Damascus seem at least roughly comparable to the educational institutions of these other societies. They gave personal and political benefits to ruling elites, they usually supported a lecturer, many housed and fed seekers after knowledge, and they usually but by no means always occupied a specific building. Thus Makdisi's reference to them as "colleges" in the medieval European sense seems only logical. They also resembled colleges in the Latin West (in one or two cases) in that they provided for the recitation (or singing as the case may be) of sacred texts for their founders at specified times.[19] Madrasas also resembled universities and academies in that they apparently imparted the legal knowledge and skills necessary to judges, officials, and scholars.

Yet in spite of these apparent similarities, were madrasas in high medieval Damascus part of a "system of higher education," however informal? Did Damascene madrasas have a curriculum, a privileged form of knowledge which they attempted to inculcate into students? Did they have any collective identity or organization? Did attendance at madrasas have anything to do with the transmission of elite status?

[16] See W.J. Courtenay, *Schools and Scholars in Fourteenth-Century England* (Princeton, 1987), 14–15, 118–46 for how relationships among educational capital, competence, birth, and patronage shaped career trajectories in fourteenth-century England.

[17] This was also true of the Ottoman empire, where medreses and the scholars they trained were integrated into the bureaucracy: A. Ugur, *The Ottoman ʿUlemā in the mid-17th Century*, xxxvii–lxxiv; M. C. Zilfi, *The Politics of Piety: the Ottoman Ulema in the Post Classical Age (1600–1800)* (Minneapolis, Bibliotheca Islamica, 1988).

[18] See Chafee, "Education and Examinations," 78–9, on the transmission of Confucian learning in Buddhist temples in the early Sung period, and 90 on specialized institutions in the Northern Sung; Lo, *Civil Service*, 82, on the importance in the oral examination of manners and deportment acquired within the household; Lee, "The Schools of Sung China," 59, on the acquisition of general culture and connections in Sung universities; Courtenay, *Schools and Scholars*, 88–91 on apprenticeship, religious orders, and cathedral schools as institutions that bypassed the university, and 118–46 on the importance of patronage in addition to education to a student's prospects.

[19] I owe this observation to a most enlightening conversation with William Courtenay.

Scholars have long noted that young people in the medieval Middle East sought out individual teachers rather than formal degree programs.[20] Scholars since Tibawi have remarked that the sources rarely mentioned study in madrasas in their biographies of their subjects.[21] The biographical notices of Damascenes mentioned their subjects' residence at only one madrasa – the Niẓāmiyya of Baghdād – because of the institution's great prestige as a gathering place for the foremost scholars of the period, and for the study-circles held there.[22] When discussing education, the sources cited their subjects' masters or shaykhs, not their madrasas; as Berkey justly puts it in the case of Cairo, "an education was judged not on *loci* but on *personae*."[23]

When the sources for Damascus mentioned madrasas in relation to a young person (and such a citation was rare), it was not as an institution in which he enrolled, but rather as a manṣab, consisting of a stipend (maᶜlūm, jāmikiyya) and a lodging.[24] We may see the provision of student manṣabs as a socially valuable and thus historically unproblematic educational project. The sources for Damascus, however, described the relationship of a student to a madrasa not in terms of "membership," but rather as the exploitation of a source of revenue that supported an individual. Because madrasas represented manṣabs above all, students had few of the corporate student identities characteristic of the educational institutions of the Latin West.[25]

A case in point is the early career of the great traditionist al-Nawawī (d. 676/1277). Having proved his ineptitude at commerce in his home village by "devoting himself to Qurʾan recitation instead of profits," he made his way to Damascus at the age of nineteen to seek knowledge. Once in the city Nawawī asked Ibn ᶜAbd al-Kāfī for advice, informed him of his purpose (aᶜrafahu maqṣidahu), and was taken by him to al-Fazārī, one of the great shaykhs of the period. Nawawī studied with Fazārī and became his disciple (yulāzimahu). However, Nawawī had no lodging, and Fazārī could be no help to him in this respect, because he had at that time only the Ṣārimiyya madrasa, which had no rooms for students. Fazārī was obliged to send him on to Kamāl al-Dīn Isḥāq,

20 Cf. *Encyclopaedia Britannica*, 11th edn., "Mahommedan Institutions," 413–14. After praising the "university" as the "glory of Muslim education," MacDonald cautioned that "the individual teacher, with his certificate, remained the object of the student; there was nothing corresponding to our general degrees."

21 See Tibawi, "Origins and Character of the Madrasa," 230–1; Berkey, *The Transmission of Knowledge*," 23; A.S. Tritton, *Materials on Muslim Education in the Middle Ages* (London, 1959).

22 For examples see Abū Shama, *Dhayl*, 35–6; Yūnīnī, 4/73; Ṣafadī, *al-Wāfī*, 21/293. The Taqawiyya was called the Niẓāmiyya al-Shām, not because of the education provided, but because of the illustrious shaykhs who gathered there: Nuᶜaymī, 1/84, 226; Abū Shāma, *Dhayl*, 136–7; Yunīnī, 4/143.

23 Berkey, *The Transmission of Knowledge*, 23.

24 An example of a rare citation of praise for a madrasa was Abū Shāma's description of the ᶜĀdiliyya: "It is a refuge and a place of lodging (wa-hyaʾl-māʾwī wa-bihāʾl-mathwī)": Abū Shāma, *al-Rawḍatayn*, 1/214. The house of one of the Banū Qudāma was also known as "a refuge for the people (māʾwī lʾin-nās)": Ibn Rajab, 2/95.

25 A rule-proving exception might seem to be the Bādharāʾiyya, which as a condition of its waqf stipulated that students there not be students elsewhere, and that they be devoted to seeking ᶜilm. The stipulation was condemned as the "cause of many evils": Ibn Kathīr, 13/196.

who had the manṣab of the lecturer (tadrīs) of the Rawāḥiyya, "in order that he might find lodging and take one of its stipends" (li-yaḥṣul lahu bihā bayt wa-yartafiq bi-maᶜlūmihā). Nawawī then lodged there "because it had been built by a wealthy merchant," and became Kamāl al-Dīn's student.[26] There is some evidence that Nawawī felt uneasy at accepting a stipend.[27] In his own biographical notice Nawawī listed at length the shaykhs with whom he had studied (giving no special attention to Kamāl al-Dīn Isḥāq), but made no mention of a madrasa.[28] Sibṭ Ibn al-Jawzī left an account of his own arrival in Damascus from Baghdād as a young man. He listed in some detail the shaykhs with whom he studied and the tombs he visited, but had not a word to say about madrasas.[29] Others were praised for refusing as much of the jāmikiyya of a madrasa as they could.[30]

Moreover, there is no evidence that the sons of the city's aᶜyān resided in madrasas rather than their households. On the contrary, religious scruples and social dignity inhibited some from settling in madrasas.The 128-page biography of Taqī al-Dīn al-Subkī (d. 744/1343–4) lists his every claim to intellectual distinction without specifying whether he ever resided when young in a madrasa at all.[31] Taqī al-Dīn forbade his own sons to settle in madrasas until they were old enough to assume the manṣab of the lecturer in one.[32] There is no evidence in the sources for medieval Damascus that students sought out specific madrasas, or, if they resided in one for a time, that they felt any special attachment to it. To students madrasas were stipends and residences – which they referred to as manṣabs – before they were anything else. And whether the children of aᶜyān households in Damascus ever resided in madrasas is a subject on which the sources maintain a relative if not utterly convincing silence – one broken only by the occasional hint that in fact they did not.

The words referring to students and teachers do not necessarily refer to holding a manṣab in a madrasa. There was no stable and specific term for a student engaged in full-time study. A *tilmīdh* was the disciple of a shaykh, not a student in a madrasa.[33] A *ṭālib* (pl. *ṭalaba*) was a seeker after knowledge, and usually though not always referred to one who sought out ḥadīth. The ṭalaba are occasionally referred to as a group, but there is no evidence that this group represented madrasa residents rather than young seekers after knowledge collectively. There were many other terms for students, including *mustafīdūn* (those who seek benefit), *mushtaghilūn bʾil-ᶜilm* (those who work on, or are

[26] Ibn Shākir 21/163; Ibn Shākir, *Fawāt*, 2/264; Yūnīnī, 3/284–5; Nuᶜaymī, 1/108, 268; Ibn ᶜAbd al-Hādī, *Ṭabaqāt*, 4/254; Pouzet, *Damas*, 167.

[27] One of the stories related of Nawawī was that when he resided in a madrasa he ate only bread brought to him from his family outside Damascus: Ibn Shākir, 21/160.

[28] Nawawī, *Tahdhīb al-asmāʾ*, 18, 19. [29] Sibṭ Ibn al-Jawzī, *Mirʾāt*, 8/517.

[30] Ibn Shākir, 21/160; Subkī, *Ṭabaqāt*, 6/242.

[31] See Subkī, Staatsbibliothek MS, esp. 6–7 but also throughout the text.

[32] Subkī, *Ṭabaqāt*, 6/253.

[33] For examples see Sibṭ Ibn al-Jawzī, *Mirʾāt*, 8/212, 213; Ibn Ḥajar, 1/81; Ṣafadī, *Aᶜyān*, 63a.

preoccupied by, knowledge) *mutaᶜallimūn* (those who would become learned), and *faqīh* (one learned in law). None of these terms referred necessarily to full-time study in madrasas, and all of these terms occasionally referred to people who were not young residents in madrasas. Of these terms, "faqīh" and "*mutafaqqih*" referred more specifically to students in madrasas, especially in waqfiyyas and fatwās. But faqīh was also used in many other contexts, and often referred to the learned in general, while the verb *tafaqqaha*, from which the term mutafaqqih was taken, was regularly used of very young people who learned law at home.[34]

Teachers also had few stable titles or honorifics. As the lists in biographical notices of shaykhs who taught individuals show, a large proportion of those who taught young people had no manṣabs. Learned men were called shaykh or ᶜālim and learned women *shaykha* or *ᶜālima*; but none of these terms refers to an appointment in a madrasa. Moreover, the biographical dictionaries did not describe shaykhs with manṣabs in strikingly different terms from shaykhs without them. When one of the great shaykhs of the city wrote an account of his career, he did not mention any of his manṣabs in madrasas, although he had held some of the major ones in the city, but rather celebrated taking over a study-circle in the Umayyad Mosque that had been in existence through five famous shaykhs before him.[35] While the title mudarris or lecturer is often cited in biographies of shaykhs, and biographies often list the positions that shaykhs held, these citations are usually in a longer list of the manṣabs that shaykhs held in their lifetimes. As was the case with students, the madrasa was a manṣab and occasionally a residence for a shaykh; but the mudarris was not a distinctive occupational type comparable to the professor or the mandarin. Only on rare occasions did the sources refer to the lecturers of the city collectively as a group.[36]

There is little evidence that holding a manṣab in a madrasa was critical to a shaykh's prestige. On the contrary, it appears that they expended some of their their hard-won prestige to gain manṣabs. There is abundant evidence that shaykhs who refused manṣabs were all the more highly regarded, and that benefiting from the waqfs of madrasas was seen as possibly polluting or corrupting.[37] Nawawī, for one example, refused out of piety to support himself on his stipend (jāmikiyya) at the Ashrafiyya; instead he ate food grown

[34] For example see the faqīh kabīr who was imām at the Rawāḥiyya: Ibn Ḥajar, 1/34; also the contrast of the fuqahāᵓ to the quḍāᵓ that named several famous shaykhs among the former in Ibn Kathīr, 14/45; for tafaqqaha see Subkī, *Ṭabaqāt*, 6/149: "tafaqqaha fī ṣigharihi ᶜalā wālidihi"; also Subkī, Staadtsbibliothek MS, 7.

[35] Subkī, *Ṭabaqāt*, 6/166; also Subkī, Staatsbibliothek MS, 37 for a study-circle founded in the Umayyad Mosque by Ibn ᶜAsākir.

[36] For one example see Ibn Khallikān, 2/464 in which it was said that someone's books were mentioned by the lecturers in their lectures: "wa-qad dhakarahā al-mudarrisūn fī durūsihim."

[37] See Ibn Kathīr, 14/109; Subkī, *Ṭabaqāt*, 6/6; Ibn al-Ḥājj, 1/14. See also Ṣafadī, *al-Wāfī*, 21/85 for a lecturer who resigned his manṣab at the Rukniyya "out of piety" because he was unable to abide by one of the stipulations of the waqf: "tarakahā tawarruᶜan."

on his family's land.[38] Similarly, the chief qāḍī Najm al-Dīn Ibn Ṣaṣrā (d. 723/1323) was said to have regretted having held the "worldly manṣabs" of the major madrasas.[39] Conversely, as students sought out teachers outside madrasas, so might they have held the lecturer of a madrasa in disdain. Teachers in madrasas faced criticism for their absences and inferior teaching. A great teacher might just as well work with students in jail, as did Ibn Taymiyya from the tower in Alexandria.[40] Another rode his animal accompanied by two or three students who recited his texts in turn.[41] It was a shaykh's prestige that got him a manṣab, and not a manṣab that put shaykhs in an occupational category.

Moreover, the lecturer was often not the only learned adult to reside in a madrasa. Founders of waqfs may have restricted residence in madrasas to young seekers after knowledge, but numerous adults also lived in them or benefited from waqf income in one way or another.[42] Shaykhs who gave lessons in study-circles (ḥalqa) and who were known as authorities in one field or another resided in madrasas even when they did not have manṣabs.[43] A distinguished scholar could also reside in a madrasa and receive a stipend there until a manṣab opened up elsewhere.[44] Finally, secretaries, amīrs, and holders of other religious offices also lived in madrasas, even though there was no provision in waqfiyyas for their residence.[45] As madrasas had no corporate administrative body, and ruling groups did not interfere in their administration consistently, there was little to prevent mature adults from settling in them. Ibn al-Ṣalāḥ al-Shahrazūrī wrote in a fatwā that the prevailing customs (*ᶜurf*) of madrasas can be taken as conditions (*sharṭ*) of the founder of the waqf, with respect to issues such as the permissibility of outsiders' entering the cells of the madrasa, attending open audiences (*majālis*, sg. *majlis*), and otherwise consuming resources and waqf income of the madrasa.[46]

Words for "studying" or "learning," as for "teacher" and "student," were various, and had little to do specifically with madrasas. There was no term for entering a madrasa, or matriculating, or taking up studies in one, or

[38] He was said never to have touched the jāmikiyya of a waqf out of the same ascetic resolve that had him season his food with no more than one condiment at a time: Yūnīnī, 3/288; Ibn Shākir, 21/160. See also Taqī al-Dīn al-Subkī who refused to consume any of the income of his manṣab at the Rukniyya because he did not make his five daily prayers there: Nuᶜaymī, 1/254.

[39] Ibn Kathīr, 14/106–7. [40] See Ibn Kathīr, 14/49.

[41] Ibn Khallikān, 3/27. See also Berkey, *The Transmission of Knowledge*, 43, for a shaykh who taught students while walking up and down the main street of Cairo with them.

[42] See for example Sibṭ Ibn al-Jawzī, *Mirʾāt*, 8/672. A shaykh who was learned in a variety of fields including medicine resided in the ᶜAzīziyya where he gave lessons in different fields of knowledge to large numbers of people: Ibn Abī Uṣaybiᶜa, 689. Occasionally an old scholar would finish out his years by taking up residence in a madrasa: Ṣafadī, *Aᶜyān*, 638b.

[43] Even a mature man known as a heretic (*zindīq*) and philosopher took up residence at the Nūriyya al-Kubrā: Abū Shāma, *Dhayl*, 200, 201. [44] Jazari, BN MS, 495–6.

[45] In 727/1326–7 for example the governor required bureaucrats and others who had put locks on their rooms in the ᶜAzīziyya to pay rent: Jazarī, Köp. MS, 128. For two amīrs who resided in the Ashrafiyya see Jazarī, BN MS, 348.

[46] Ibn al-Ṣalāḥ al-Shahrazūrī, *Fatāwā wa-masāʾil Ibn al-Ṣalāḥ*, ᶜAbd al-Muṭī Amīn Qalᶜajī ed. (Beirut, 1986), 1/369–70.

graduating from one.[47] The use of the term *darasa* to mean studying was rare.[48] Words loosely corresponding to "education" included *ṭalab al-ᶜilm* (to seek knowledge, a term that often but not exclusively referred to ḥadīth scholarship), *tashayyakha* (to take on a shaykh), *tafaqqaha* (to learn, especially law [*fiqh*] – which usually happened very early in a young person's career, before leaving home) – *intafaᶜa* or *istifāda* (to benefit or seek benefit), and *ishtaghala* (to work on something or with someone).[49] None of these referred specifically to study in a madrasa. There was no term for following a prescribed course of study, or for studying in a madrasa or dār al-ḥadīth.

Madrasas themselves as institutional types were fluid.[50] When waqf income was no longer sufficient to keep up the terms of the waqfiyya, or when it was usurped by warriors, madrasas changed their forms easily. For example, in 697/1297–8 the Muᶜaẓẓamiyya, one of the major madrasas on Mount Qāsyūn, became a mosque, the lecturer becoming its preacher (*khaṭīb*), because the waqf income was no longer enough to support a madrasa.[51] Moreover, a madrasa did not have to have anything at all to do with the transmission of knowledge to the young. Some madrasas had no stipends or places of

47 Makdisi, *The Rise of Colleges*, 171–80 contends that madrasas had a structured student body with classes of students, including beginning, intermediate, and advanced students, leading to "termination" after which graded ranks of graduate students began. His evidence is largely taken from legal literature, including Subkī's fatwās and his son's treatise entitled *Muᶜīd al-niᶜam wa-mubīd al-niqam*. Makdisi does not discuss the problematic nature of using these sources. The jurists usually mandated ideals before they described realities, and they tended to generalize the interests of their fraction of the aᶜyān into immutable prescriptions. Taking such sources at face value one can easily formalize legal ideals and normative categories into institutional structures. In both Subkī's fatwās and his son's treatise the intent was not to describe student life, but rather to define categories of beneficiaries of waqf income. To that end, the younger Subkī related the obligations of recipients of waqf income to their attainments, the more advanced being obliged to contribute more than the new students. Makdisi summarizes these arguments, but does not deal with the possibility that these gradations did not refer to formal status or classes, but rather to general levels of attainment and categories of stipends. The muntahī, for example, taken by Makdisi to be a member of the "terminal class," was described by Subkī in full: "The muntahī: he has a greater responsibility to discuss and debate than the others. If he should keep silent and take the muntahī's stipend because he believes he is more learned than the others present (*al-ḥādirīn*), he would not have been properly thankful for God's favor," Subkī, *Muᶜīd al-niᶜam*, 155. All the evidence adduced by Makdisi for the existence of distinct classes among the residents of a madrasa can just as easily be interpreted as categories of stipends. Another question is the degree to which these categories were in fact applied to madrasas at all. As was the case with so many other legal treatises, Subkī may have been describing a situation that was more ideal than real. See also Subkī, *Ṭabaqāt*, 6/253, 254, for confirmation in an anecdote that three categories existed among the residents of a madrasa. Association with the highest group (ṭabaqa al-ᶜalyāʾ) was "merited" (yastiḥiq), the term used to describe suitability for manṣabs generally. Here again what might appear to be distinct classes are just as likely to be categories of recipients of waqf income.

48 Two of the few examples I have found are Ṣafadī, *Aᶜyān*, 12b; Ṣafadī, *al-Wāfī*, 10/269.

49 For an example of ṭalaba referring to other forms of education see Ibn Abī Uṣaybiᶜa, 99, quoting Aristotle on his education, which he referred to as ṭalabī lʾil-ᶜilm. Most ways of expressing "to be a student" were transitive and referred to working with a teacher: "yatalamadhu lahu (he became his student)," "jālasa ash-shuyūkh (he sat in the company of shaykhs)": Ibn Shākir, 21/119; Ibn Rajab, 2/46; Ibn Jamāᶜa, 89.

50 Berkey, *The Transmission of Knowledge*, 45–60, illustrates this point nicely for Cairo, as does Pouzet, *Damas*, 167 for Damascus.

51 Jazarī, BN MS, 477, 485.

residence for students. One shaykh, Ismāʿīl Ibn Muḥammad al-Ḥarrānī, founded a madrasa in his own large house, became its shaykh, and invited older scholars to reside in it.[52]

Restricting higher education to the lecture (*dars*; pl. *durūs*) in a madrasa or a dār al-ḥadīth misses how most young people acquired knowledge – by working on texts with teachers and by attending lectures throughout the city. Words meaning "teaching" were *ishtighāl aṭ-ṭalaba* (working with students) *nashr al-ʿilm* (disseminating ʿilm), and especially *ifāda* (benefiting).[53] Because young people acquired ʿilm by working on texts with shaykhs, lectures inside madrasas or outside them were not necessarily the principal vehicle of learning. Some shaykhs gave lectures in madrasas. Others did not. One of the greatest shaykhs in the city, Ibn Qāḍī Shuhba, known as *shaykh aṭ-ṭalaba* and *mufīd aṭ-ṭalaba*, never gave a lecture.[54] Work with shaykhs and with one another on texts was the critical means by which the young acquired their learning, rather than a supplement to the lecture, which itself was often the public exposition of a preexisting text. In contrast to the near-total silence of the sources regarding attendance of lectures in madrasas, virtually all biographical notices of learned men and women recounted the shaykhs with whom they studied or whose circles they attended.

When young people resided in madrasas, they did not follow a specified course of instruction, and they did not necessarily study with the lecturer. Although I have found no exception in the case of Damascus to Makdisi's observation that madrasas usually had a single lecturer, the lecturer was not necessarily the sole source of knowledge in the madrasa. Shaykhs who represented various fields were present. *Muʿīd*s (a lesser manṣab for a scholar or assistant to the lecturer), the teacher of Qurʾān recitation (*shaykh al-iqrāʾ*), the lecturer of grammar, residents, and outsiders also gave lectures or worked with students inside madrasas.[55] Although some young people maintained close relationships with lecturers, death notices often provide long lists of shaykhs without manṣabs with whom young people studied, and whose

52 Ṣafadī, *Aʿyān*, 84b.

53 See the example of the shaykh who resigned from the lectureship of a number of madrasas and lived quietly as the imām of the ʿĀdiliyya al-Kubrā, still studying and "exercising" the students and "benefiting" them (ishtighāl aṭ-ṭalaba wa ifādatihim): Yūnīnī 3/282.

54 Ibn Kathīr, 14/126, 127.

55 See Ibn Shākir 21/162 and Yūnīnī, 3/284–5, for an account of Nawawī's becoming the muʿīd for his muʿīd's lectures. The minor employees in a madrasa or dār al-ḥadīth such as the Qurʾān readers could also be scholars in a variety of fields, and not necessarily specialists in the field for which they received a stipend: Ibn ʿAbd al-Hādī, *Ṭabaqāt*, 4/247. One shaykh of Qurʾān recitation gave lectures in his madrasa: Nuʿaymī, 1/323. See for another example the khaṭīb who taught in a madrasa: Ibn Kathīr, 13/173. Another example was the shaykh who upon retiring from a diwān resided in a dār al-ḥadīth, and was sought out by the ṭalaba: Yūnīnī 4/165. For another example of a resident in a madrasa in Cairo who delivered lectures see Ṣafadī, *al-Wāfī*, 13/24. The functions of the muʿīd may differ between Damascus and other places. Makdisi sees the muʿīd as an "advanced graduate student" whose function was akin to (if not a model for) that of the *repetitor* in the universities: Makdisi, *The Rise of Colleges*, 193–5. In Damascus, the muʿīd could be a mature man, and there is no record of a muʿīd acting in the manner Makdisi suggested. Mature visitors were given stipends and lodging in madrasas and dār al-ḥadīths as muʿīds: Ibn Shākir, 21/119, 162; Yūnīnī, 3/284, 285; Ibn Ḥajar, 2/61.

disciples they often became. The task for a young person was to select a shaykh and maintain a close relationship with him, and to study with as many distinguished shaykhs as possible. A young person's shaykh might or might not have been the lecturer of the madrasa in which he resided. When young people wanted to become shaykhs, they sought out the study-circle and intimacy with a shaykh.[56]

In addition to intimacy with individual shaykhs, what emerges from virtually every page of the biographies of major figures is the large number of their shaykhs. A young person's shaykhs were not necessarily of his legal school (*madhhab*) nor did they necessarily have manṣabs in madrasas.[57] The culture of the study-circle was the major form of high culture for the city's aᶜyān, and people of all madhhabs – and occasionally of different religious communities – joined them throughout their lifetimes.[58] Many shaykhs both with and without manṣabs in madrasas had study-circles in which they delivered lectures in the Umayyad Mosque.[59] Other study-circles, including those in which women delivered lectures to other women, were in private houses.[60] Moreover, a manṣab in lecturing could be established by waqf outside of a madrasa.[61] The Umayyad Mosque itself had various manṣabs for lecturers, including several customarily held by the chief qāḍī of various madhhabs.[62] Finally, residents in madrasas could also encounter various shaykhs as employees, residents, hangers-on, and deputies. Two of the most important madrasas in the city – the ᶜĀdiliyya and the Taqawiyya – had as their prayer leaders (*imāms*) eminent ṣūfīs.[63] As older men lived in madrasas, they could teach students in the fields they had mastered, as was the case of the

56 See Lapidus, *Muslim Cities*, 111, for the study-circle as the basis of ᶜulamāᵓ society; also Berkey, *The Transmission of Knowledge*, 86, for an example of the ḥalqas in the Mosque of ᶜAmr in Fusṭāṭ.

57 See for one example among many Dhahabī's biography of the Shāfiᶜī al-Nawawī in which he called the Ḥanbalī Ibn Qudāma Nawawī's "greatest shaykh": Ibn Rajab, 2/305. For another example of how study-circles cut across madhhab lines see Ibn ᶜAbd al-Hādī, *Ṭabaqāt*, 4/284.

58 See for example Zarnūji's comment: "The time for learning (extends) from the cradle to the grave," Zarnūjī, *Kitāb taᶜlīm al-mutaᶜallam ṭarīq al-taᶜallum* (Beirut, 1981), 58. An older shaykh could "cleave to" the majlis of a younger one, or a study-circle could be composed of equals: see Sibṭ Ibn al-Jawzī, *Mirᵓāt*, 8/675, 676, 701. For a study-circle in munāẓara at the Umayyad Mosque that brought in the elite of all the madhhabs ("al-akābir min kulli madhhab") see Ṣafadī, *al-Wāfī*, 21/341. For an example of a dars that brought in people from the four madhhabs and other learned adults see Ṣafadī, *al-Wāfī*, 13/23. See also Gilbert, "The ᶜUlamaᵓ," 118.

59 Ibn Shākir 21/119, 162; Ibn Shākir, *Fawāt*, 1/57; Yūnīnī 3/207; Ibn Kathīr, 14/141 for an example of a shaykh who taught in his own madrasa and in the Umayyad Mosque. For an example of a lecturer with a ḥalqa al-ishtighāl in the Umayyad Mosque see Ibn Kathīr, 14/103. Another example is the dars given in the Ḥanbalī study-circle (ḥalqa al-ḥanābila) which was endowed with a waqf: Sibṭ Ibn al-Jawzī, *Mirᵓāt*, 8/479. A Ḥanbalī lecturer gave lectures both in his madrasa and in the Umayyad Mosque: Ibn Rajab, 2/150; another Ḥanbalī had his own ḥalqa (ḥalqa lahu) in which he delivered lectures in fiqh: Ibn Rajab, 2/288. The ḥalqa was often a long-term regular session, which students could inherit from their teachers over generations: Nuᶜaymī, 1/248; Ibn Kathīr, 13/172–3.

60 See Ibn Rajab, 2/6; Dhahabī, *Tāᵓrīkh al-Islām*, Köp. MS, 16; Abū Shāma, *Dhayl*, 148.

61 For example the manṣab of the lecturer at the Zāwiya al-Gharbiyya in the Umayyad Mosque: Abū Shāma, *Dhayl*, 125.

62 Qalqashandī, 12/357.

63 Jazarī, BN MS, 366; Yūnīnī, 3/161.

philosopher who resided in madrasas and "corrupted" the beliefs of the young.[64]

There is little evidence in the sources that students considered themselves or were considered by others as a group with collective interests. It is difficult to specify what a student was. Moreover, many Damascenes who were not residents in madrasas or devoted to full-time study attended lectures and other occasions in which knowledge was transmitted. In Damascus there were no degrees, no enrollment into a student body, and no competition among certified or degreed graduates over induction into state, corporate, or religious bodies. What did occasionally animate collective student action was the defense of their manṣabs. In 698/1298–9 the Iranian students in the Ḥanafī madrasas rioted over the refusal of the lecturer to permit one of their countrymen to reside in the Qalījiyya.[65] When students took collective action on other occasions it was to ensure that waqf income be distributed according to the terms of the waqf – in other words again to defend their hold on manṣabs.[66] The conditions that gave students elsewhere common interests and identities were largely absent in Damascus.[67]

Curriculum

Did the madrasas of Damascus have an established course of study that produced general cultural competence or certified expertise? Having abandoned the notion that madrasas produced theologians as the ideological cadres of the "Sunnī Revival," recent scholars have seen the madrasa as an institution intended to train jurists and sometimes bureaucrats. Albert Hourani summed up this dominant interpretation concisely: "The judges who administered the sharīʿa were trained in special schools, the madrasas."[68] The case that madrasas taught the sciences of the law (*sharīʿa*) in order to produce a group of certified experts in law seems strong on its face. Some madrasa waqfiyyas in Syria and Egypt stipulated that the lecturer teach a certain subject within the broader range of the sciences of the sharīʿa.[69] Moreover, according to jurists such as Subkī, the lecturer should give the lecture in the field for which the madrasa was established; if not, he was a "thief" of the waqf.[70] Finally, jurists regularly held that the lecturer was to be knowledgeable in fiqh, and most lecturers were in fact learned in the various fields of the law.[71] This has understandably led scholars to concentrate on the legal "curriculum" of the madrasas.[72]

The case, however, stands on the interpretation of two problematic categories of evidence. First, although foundation deeds are good evidence on the intentions of founders, they are less reliable on the actual administration of

[64] Ibn Kathīr, 13/218; see also Pouzet, *Damas*, 167 for the residence of mature adults in madrasas.
[65] Jazarī, BN MS, 553–4. [66] Jazarī, Köp. MS, 61.
[67] See for comparison Lee, "Schools of Sung China," 54–7.
[68] A. Hourani, *A History of the Arab Peoples* (Cambridge, MA, 1991), 113–14.
[69] Subkī, *Muʿīd al-niʿam*, 152–4. [70] *Ibid.*, 153.
[71] Dhahabī, *Tāʾrīkh al-Islām*, BL MS, 18, for the censure of a young lecturer deficient in fiqh.
[72] Makdisi, *The Rise of Colleges*, 113; Berkey, *The Transmission of Knowledge*, 7.

waqfs. Even if the inaugural lecture was given in one of the sciences of the sharīʿa, and there were lectures on the sharīʿa in madrasas, there is little unambiguous evidence that madrasas in Damascus provided an advanced legal education that differed from the lectures and study-circles held elsewhere in the city. For all the attention that madrasas have received as providers of advanced legal education to their students, young people acquired advanced legal knowledge from their shaykhs long before the appearance of madrasas in the Middle East, as Muslims young and old do today in small study-circles all over the world. Second, jurists such as Subkī and Ibn Jamāʿa were not necessarily interested in describing actualities, but in condemning, for their own reasons, departures from the legal norms they defended. When Subkī wrote that the dars was to be given in the field stipulated by the founder, it is dangerous to assume that he intended to describe actual practices. He may just as well have been arguing on behalf of rules that were regularly ignored. In any case, Subkī's assertions cannot be used as evidence without further confirmation – of which in the case of Damascus at least there is surprisingly little.

Moreover, although there is no doubt that teachers gave lectures in madrasas, there are some indications that the provision in waqfiyyas that the lecturer teach law was at the least a matter of debate. Ibn al-Ṣalāḥ wrote a fatwā in response to the question whether recipients of waqf income in madrasas had to study fiqh. His solution allowed the *fuqahāʾ* – those who had acquired some learning – to study other fields; only beginners – *al-mutafaqqiha* – were obliged to study law. Nor was attendance at lectures necessarily mandatory for young holders of manṣabs in madrasas. Ibn al-Ṣalāḥ wrote that recipients of waqf income in madrasas were obligated to attend lectures only if it were the prevailing custom (*ʿurf ghālib*) of the madrasa.[73]

What the lecturer taught, if he taught anything at all, depended on the terms of the waqf, on his own interests, and occasionally on the efforts of rulers to mandate or proscribe subjects. Lecturers taught and wrote in fields other than fiqh.[74] While the lecturer was often expected to lecture in one of the sciences of the sharīʿa, many different forms of knowledge were taught, both in madrasas and in study-circles throughout the city.[75] Shaykhs taught the Hellenistic

[73] Ibn al-Ṣalāḥ, *Fatāwā*, 1/373–4.

[74] Prestige was attached to writing the basic texts for beginners (*qāʿida*, pl. *qawāʿid*) in several fields. Shams al-Dīn al-Isfahānī wrote qāʿidas in four fields, including the ʿuṣūlayn, and logic: Ibn Kathīr, 13/315. See also *ibid.*, 14/75 for a lecturer who composed books in kalām and uṣūl. Ibn Abī Uṣaybiʿa, 646–7, cited two lecturers who were learned in medicine and the natural sciences, and who taught students in those fields in grand madrasas such as the ʿĀdiliyya (where they were appointed in succession) and the Adhrāwiyya. For an example of the dars on various texts, in various fields, including logic and uṣūl al-dīn, see Ibn ʿAbd al-Hādī, *Ṭabaqāt*, 4/256; see also the student who read both law and the poetry of al-Ḥarīrī with Ibn ʿAsākir: Yūnīnī 4/165. Ibn Jamāʿa learned the same text from Ṣafadī: Ṣafadī, *al-Wāfī*, 18/557. See also the shaykh who learned adab from Tāj al-Dīn al-Kindī: Ibn Abī Uṣaybiʿa, 663.

[75] A philosopher said to have been a student of Fakhr al-Dīn al-Rāzī lived in madrasas and was accused of corrupting the beliefs of the students: Abū Shāma, *Dhayl*, 202; for a similar example see Ibn Kathīr, 13/218. Several lecturers were also physicians, and taught medicine to study-circles: see Ibn Abī Uṣaybiʿa, 647. One lecturer was best known for his ability to interpret dreams: Ṣafadī, *Aʿyān*, fol. 38a.

"rational" sciences in madrasas as elsewhere, in spite of attempts by the Ayyūbid rulers al-Muʿaẓẓam and al-Ashraf to forbid them.[76] There were also lecturers who were known as philosophers or ṣūfīs, and there is no reason to suspect that they did not teach philosophy or ṣūfism in their madrasas or wherever they held their study-circles.[77] It is therefore probable that one reason jurists demanded that lecturers teach according to the stipulations of the waqf was that lecturers were doing just the opposite.

The third and most critical point is that attending lectures in law in madrasas was not how young people became learned shaykhs. Young people typically studied a variety of fields, in a variety of places, often with a different shaykh in each.[78] A shaykh could also teach a variety of fields in a single ḥalqa.[79] Shaykhs learned in various fields taught them also in study-circles throughout the city.[80] Shaykhs in the Umayyad Mosque and in other places held study-circles in various fields that thrived long after the appearance of madrasas in the city.[81] If shaykhs taught law, poetry, medicine, philosophy, and other subjects in madrasas, they also taught these subjects elsewhere.

[76] Al-Ashraf, when he took power in 616, announced through the heralds that none of the fuqahāʾ should study any of the sciences but tafsīr, ḥadīth, and fiqh: Ibn Kathīr, 13/148. He and his successor al-Muʿaẓẓam threatened to expel anyone who taught any of the rational sciences, and in fact did so in the case of Sayf al-Dīn al-Amidī, who lost his manṣab at the Azīziyya: Sibṭ Ibn al-Jawzī, *Mirʾāt*, 8/681; Ibn Shākir, Vat. Ar. MS, 19; Ibn Kathīr, 13/148. However, this should not be taken as evidence that madrasas had a mandated curriculum in the sciences of the sharīʿa. Al-Ashraf and al-Muʿaẓẓam's policies were not universal even among Ayyūbid sulṭāns. The rational sciences in the city flourished under al-Muʿaẓẓam ʿĪsā, and al-Malik al-Nāṣir himself studied kalām with a student of Fakhr al-Dīn al-Rāzī, and was known to have studied the ʿulūm al-awāʾil as well: Ibn Kathīr, 13/124, 140–1,198; Ibn al-ʿImād, *Shadharāt*, 5/144. Lecturers learned in the rational sciences are attested throughout the period. Ṣafī al-Dīn al-Hindī, for example, who had a very successful career in the madrasas, was also a partisan of the rational sciences: Ibn Kathīr, 14/75. One of the most distinguished Ḥanafī lecturers in the city was also known as a muʿtazalī: Ibn Kathīr, 13/53. Another Ḥanafī taught logic and scholastic dialectic (jadal) in the Fārūkhshāhiyya madrasa and in the Umayyad Mosque: Ṣafadī, *al-Wāfī*, 21/88. Nūr al-Dīn al-Ardibīlī (d. 749/1348–9), a shaykh who held manṣabs at such major madrasas as the Jūrūkhiyya and the Shāmiyya al-barrāniyya, was known as an uṣūlī and a student of the rational sciences: Nuʿaymī, 1/230.

[77] For examples of lecturers known as philosophers, see Ibn al-Suqāʿī, 102 of the Arabic text; Dhahabī, *Tadhkirat al-ḥuffāẓ* (Hyderabad, 1955–8), 4/60. See Ibn Shākir, *Fawāt*, 1/55–6, for a ṣūfī lecturer who had "aṣḥāb wa-murīdūn."

[78] For one example see Ibn ʿAbd al-Hādī, *Ṭabaqāt*, 4/255.

[79] See for one example Jazarī, BN MS, 320.

[80] There was a follower of Ibn al-Rawandī in the early seventh century: Ibn Shākir, Vat. Ar. MS, 37. Also see the study-circle held in the house of a shaykh learned in grammar and the rational sciences, attended by Muslims, Jews, Christians, heretics, and Samaritans: Yūnīnī, 2/165. See also the blind shaykh ʿIzz al-Dīn al-Ḥasan al-Irbilī (d. 660/1262), who read philosophy and rational sciences with Muslims, ahl al-kitāb, and philosophers: Ibn Shākir, *Fawāt*, 1/362; Ṣafadī, *al-Wāfī*, 12/247; also the ḥalqa in the Umayyad mosque in which a shaykh taught the *Maqāmāt* of al-Ḥarīrī and other works of adab: Ibn Shākir, *Fawāt*, 2/346.

[81] This conclusion runs counter to Gilbert's thesis that "by degrees, specialized buildings replaced common teaching sites such as mosques, private homes, shops, libraries, and gardens": Gilbert, "The ʿUlamaʾ," 59. For one example of a shaykh who arrived in the city to give lessons in the Umayyad Mosque see Ibn Abī Uṣaybiʿa, 688; for a ḥalqa al-ishtighāl in the Umayyad Mosque, see Ṣafadī, *Aʿyān*, fol. 47a; for a ḥalqa al-taṣdīr in the Umayyad Mosque established by a qāḍī, with a stipend of 100 dirhams, see Jazarī, BN MS, 476.

Some had stipends for teaching fields such as belles lettres.[82] A shaykh known for his ḥurma held a study-circle in which Samaritans, Muslims, Jews, and Christians cultivated the Hellenistic sciences (*ʿulūm al-awāʾil*) together.[83] Another shaykh was known for holding study-circles in the many fields of knowledge he had mastered, including one for Christians in the New Testament and one for Jews in the Torah.[84] Medical learning was acquired in much the same way as other fields, through working on individual texts with single shaykhs, and was described in similar language.[85] Madrasas in Damascus were useful spaces for the interactions of the learned, as well as manṣabs for their residents and shaykhs. There is no doubt that they were important religious institutions, in that the learned often resided in them, prayed in them, interacted with one another in them, and taught students in them. But there is remarkably little evidence that they were specialized institutions of learning, as the knowledge that was transmitted in them was little different from that transmitted elsewhere. Most of what the young learned – in medicine, law, the Hellenistic or scholastic sciences, and other fields – was in fact transmitted as it had been previously, in relations between a single shaykh and a young person or small group of people. The production of knowledge – in readings, study-circles, recitations, and open audiences – was the main form of elite cultural life in the city, and people of all ages and varied intentions participated.[86] We can have no idea what it would be like to explain to a high medieval Damascene what "higher education" means, but we would fail if we used terms and concepts derived from modern experience. Our approaches have yet to explain how a young person became a learned shaykha or shaykh, why she or he would want to do so, and why others saw shaykhliness as such a valuable object of labor on the part of themselves and their children.

Finally, what emerges from the biographical notices of shaykhs is not only competence in law, but the wide range of their learning. The aʿyān of Damascus aimed for mastery (*riyāsa*, *imāma*, *siyāda*) in one or more subjects, which could be any one of those cultivated in the city, and knowledge of many fields. Entries in biographical dictionaries praised mastery of the fields of the law, but they also praised mastery in other subjects, including medicine, theology, mathematics, natural science, belles lettres, the Hellenistic sciences, and literature. The aʿyān valued poetry highly, as can be seen by the vast quantities of it quoted in the chronicles and biographical dictionaries, and many shaykhs tried to attain some distinction in it. Thus, even though many shaykhs were learned in law, and lecturers were expected to know something of it, the assertion that the madrasas were a form of higher education intended

[82] One example was the shaykh who was given a monthly stipend of 100 dirhams for teaching al-Ḥarīrī's *Maqamāt* and other works of adab in the Umayyad Mosque, a sum equal to what many lecturers received: Ṣafadī, *al-Wāfi*, 18/23, 24.

[83] Yūnīnī, 2/165. [84] Ibn Khallikān, 4/397.

[85] See Ibn Abī Uṣaybiʿa, 603–768, for many examples of the training of physicians that *mutatis mutandis* could apply to other fields of knowledge cultivated in the city.

[86] For one example see Ṣafadī, *Aʿyān*, 79a.

to produce specialists in law is both overstated and in some cases directly contradicted by the evidence. After all, there were qāḍīs all over the Islamic world long before the appearance of the madrasa, and in many cases they learned from the same books that the young read in Damascus, both inside madrasas and elsewhere.

In the education of the aᶜyān, exposure to many fields and many shaykhs was the ideal, rather than specialized training in single subjects. When biographers praised learned men, it was breadth of knowledge that they most lauded. A scholar learned in many fields was a "*kāmil*" (pl. *kamala*), a "complete" man.[87] Ibn Khallikān "acquired a good measure of learning in all fields"; while a writer praised another shaykh: "We never saw anyone who united more fields."[88] One shaykh was lauded for writing a single book that embraced twenty separate fields of knowledge.[89] Tāj al-Dīn al-Subkī praised his father as a polymath, "one who united every field of knowledge" (jāmiᶜ kull ᶜilm). At a time when he was also the disciple of a ṣūfī shaykh, the elder Subkī acquired *fiqh* (law), *ḥadīth* (accounts of the words and deeds of the Prophet taken as precedents in law and many other areas), *tafsīr* (the interpretation of the Qurᵓān), *qirāᵓa* (Qurᵓānic recitation), *kalām* (didactic theology), *uṣūl al-dīn* (speculative theology), *naḥw* (grammar and syntax), *lugha* (lexicography), *adab* (belles lettres or moral conduct), medicine, scholastic dialectic, *khilāf* (points of difference among the law schools), logic, poetry, *firaq* (heresiography), arithmetic, jurisprudence, and astronomy.[90] Other young people studied law and ḥadīth with noted jurists; and this did not prevent them from studying philosophy and Shīᶜism with other shaykhs.[91] The fields of knowledge were not specialized in the sense that mastering one field precluded studying others. Ibn Abī Uṣaybiᶜa's dictionary of physicians demonstrates that many physicians were also learned in belles lettres and the sciences of the law, and that many jurists in turn were learned in medicine.[92] And in no case did a death notice in a biographical dictionary assert that its subject studied law in a madrasa and other subjects outside it.

87 See for example the "kāmil" who knew law, astronomy and the use of astronomical instruments, history, the methods of government of the Mongols, Turks, and Indians, biographies of scholars, composition, diplomatic correspondence, and geometry: Ibn Shākir, *Fawāt*, 1/159. Another example was a member of the Banū Fāriqī who died in 689: Jazarī, BN MS, 2.

88 "Ḥasala min kulli fannin ṭarafan jayyadan": Yūnīnī, 4/150. "Mā rāᵓaynā ajmaᶜ li-funūn al-ᶜilmi minhu": Nuᶜaymī, 1/227. 89 Ibn Kathīr, 13/337.

90 Subkī, *Ṭabaqāt*, 6/146–7, 150, 168–9; Subkī, Staatsbibliothek MS, 3; also 41–4 for knowledge of the standard works of other madhhabs; Ṣafadī, 21/253–7; Ibn Kathīr, 14/252; Ibn Ḥajar, 3/134; Nuᶜaymī, 1/134–5.

91 Ṣafadī, *Aᶜyān*, fol. 47a. After his studies in philosophy and shīᶜism, one student went on to deliver lectures and fatwās.

92 For five consecutive examples, including chief qāḍīs who were also physicians, see Ibn Abī ᶜUṣaybiᶜa, 646–51; also, Jazarī, BN MS, 320–1; Nuᶜaymī, 1/229; Ṣafadī, *al-Wāfī*, 13/396. See Ibn Shākir, *Fawāt*, 1/48–9 for a physician who was known for learning the *Maqāmāt*, and who studied belles lettres, adab, and grammar, along with medicine and the rational sciences. He also copied out Avicenna's *Qānūn* three times. See *ibid.*, 2/316 for a physician learned in a variety of fields including architecture and astronomy.

There is little evidence that the madrasas marginalized fields other than law or that madrasas had a "curriculum" in law. Young people sought out shaykhs and studied with them in convenient locations – one hesitates to call it "private" or "informal" education because the categories of public/private and formal/informal are so problematically derived from Western experience. When young people set out to become learned shaykhs there is no evidence that they sought out an established curriculum. It is difficult to prove a negative, but scholars have been so committed to the notion that madrasas had a curriculum in law that reviewing the sources for high medieval Damascus can at the very least demonstrate a major exception. Moreover, in high medieval Arabic there is no word for "curriculum," "list of books," or "program of study." In the large literature for high medieval Damascus there is no evidence that students sought out prescribed programs of study, or enrolled in madrasas to master a specific body of knowledge. Rather, they chose their subjects for themselves, and sought out shaykhs who could "benefit" them.[93]

Writers of advice to young people stressed the voluntaristic nature of the subject matter of education. The young were told to seek advice constantly, because they made their own decisions.[94] "When undertaking the study of knowledge," Zarnūjī advised, "it is necessary to choose among all the branches of learning the one most beneficial to oneself."[95] Similar advice was given with respect to teachers: "regarding the choice of a teacher, it is important to select the most learned, the most pious, and the most advanced in years."[96] As the case of Nawawī illustrates, young people did not come to the city to enroll in specific madrasas for specific purposes, but rather sought advice concerning the teachers with whom they should study.[97] The case of Subkī is even more suggestive: it is difficult to imagine a mandarin refusing to allow his son to attend an academy until he had obtained mandarin status. In all the literature for high medieval Damascus there is not a single citation that this writer has found that any young person – much less one from an aᶜyān household – enrolled in a madrasa to acquire certified mastery of law. The notion that there was a curriculum in the madrasas has thus formalized the intentions of waqf and juristic prescriptions into an institutional "system." There is little evidence that in Damascus madrasas expelled non-sharīᶜa sciences from the city, and still less that they imposed their own advanced legal curriculum. The best available evidence suggests that the young acquired their learning – among which was their legal learning – and their distinction from individual shaykhs before and after the appearance of madrasas in the city.

Certification and qualification

Did madrasas produce a qualification or certificate of competence that had a social value? The uses and value of the qualification granted by the universities

93 For a fuller discussion of benefit see chapter 3 below. 94 Zarnūjī, 29. 95 *Ibid.*, 28.
96 *Ibid.* 97 Ibn Shākir, 21/163; Yūnīnī, 3/284–5.

and academies of the Latin West and Sung China are unmistakable. In both places a number of full-time students struggled to attain the degree. Makdisi holds that madrasas in Damascus were intended to produce a certified competence at least roughly comparable to that produced by the degree or the examination. He writes that the object of education was the *ijāza lʾil-iftāʾ* and the *ijāza lʾit-tadrīs,* certificates which granted the recipient the authority to issue fatwās and to teach: "The madrasa and the university in the Middle Ages had this in common: that they both had titular professors who had acceded to the professorship after having been duly licensed to teach."[98] Where the two differ, he holds, is in that the ijāza was granted by an individual, whereas the *licentia* was granted by the university as a corporation. This difference was only a matter of the identity of the authorizing body, as the granting of the ijāza was a formal process, completed only after "an oral examination satisfying the examining scholar as to the competence of the candidate," a competence which was demonstrated through mastery of disputation.[99]

However, in spite of the instructive contrasts he has drawn between the ijāza and the *licentia docendi*, Makdisi has not successfully demonstrated that the granting of the authority to write fatwās or to teach had anything to do with madrasas. There is no unambiguous evidence that lecturers gave ijāzas to students through such an examination in Damascus, or in fact that any type of the ijāza had any association with madrasas at all. As scholars have long recognized, the lecture was not restricted to madrasas. Moreover, the biographical dictionaries rarely if ever described lecturers as holders of an ijāza liʾt-tadrīs. There were, however, shaykhs without manṣabs who gave ijāzas. There were even fathers who got ijāzas for their sons by requesting them from many different shaykhs, a process they called *istijāza*, "seeking ijāzas."[100]

The forms ijāzas took, and how they were described and granted, make it difficult to credit the idea that the ijāza was a formal certificate or "system" for transmitting authority.[101] There were several different types of ijāza.[102] In Damascus the sources cited the ijāza liʾt-tadrīs less frequently than the ijāza lʾil-iftāʾ and the *ijāza liʾt-takallum*. The latter referred to the ability to discourse on behalf of the shaykh, and may occasionally have referred especially if not uniquely to matters of doctrine. Like the other ijāzas it was granted by a single shaykh.[103] These forms of authorization were not necessarily attested by a certificate, but were often expressed as much by the verbal form *yujūzu* as

98 Makdisi, *The Rise of Colleges*, 270; also 147–52, 270–2. 99 *Ibid.*, 271.

100 Ṣafadī, *al-Wāfī*, 7/247: "His father sought out ijāzas for him, from the shaykhs of his time, from Egypt and Syria (istajāza lahu wāliduhu mashayakha ʿaṣrihi minaʾd-diyār al-miṣriyya wʾash-shām)."

101 Berkey like Makdisi stresses that the ijāza was granted by a single shaykh to a single disciple, but unlike him makes no association of the ijāza with the madrasa. Still he tends to formalize the granting of ijāzas, writing of an "ijāza system" which was subject to "abuses": Berkey, *The Transmission of Knowledge*, 31.

102 For a detailed treatment of the ijāza as it applied to ḥadīth scholarship see Ibn al-Ṣalāḥ, *Muqaddima*, 262–77.

103 For examples, Ibn Kathīr, 14/115; Jazarī, Köp. MS, 495; Sibṭ Ibn al-Jawzī, *Mirʾāt*, 8/710.

through the verbal noun ijāza, and also by other verbs such as *adhana* or *aḥsana*.[104] These forms of the ijāza were granted when shaykhs deemed disciples ready to represent a body of knowledge and to exemplify its other carriers.[105] The ijāza did not necessarily refer to a single text, as shaykhs gave ijāzas for their knowledge as a whole or for a body of texts that they had learned.[106] In Damascus this may have included some kind of examination, but I have found no record of any ever having been given.

The ijāza as a form of "qualification" seems to have had little to do with madrasas. An extreme though revealing example of how Damascenes imagined the transmission of authority can be seen in how a blind holy man was persuaded to give an unpromising disciple permission to discourse (*adhana fīʾl-kalām*). The disciple, whom the shaykh had previously forbidden to discourse, had a vision of an interlocked chain in the sky. When he recounted the dream to his shaykh, the shaykh interpreted the meaning of the chain to be the *sunna* (normative pattern of conduct and belief derived from accounts of the Prophet's words and deeds) of the Prophet. After the vision the shaykh for the first time permitted the disciple to discourse in public.[107]

That the ijāza was not given as a result of study in madrasas is attested by the fact that even amīrs could acquire one, as was true of one governor of Egypt.[108] As a sign of the transmission of authority from shaykh to disciple, the ijāza was not a passport of entry into a category of persons, nor was it an institutional degree. It differed from the examination in China, the passing of which established a group of mandarins defined by their possession of a formal qualification. The ijāza was rather the sign of an authority that was transmitted within temporary social networks bound together through loyalties of love and service.[109] This authority was acquired through an ijāza from another shaykh, who himself had acquired it through personal contact. The ability to grant an ijāza was not restricted to holders of manṣabs, but was held by other bearers of ʿilm as well. What was granted was as much an emblem of a bond to a shaykh as a certificate with a fixed value in social relations. In this respect the ijāza resembled inclusion in the "register of auditors" kept in the mosque of Mount Qasyūn and other pieces of writing (markings in books, lists of auditors at open audiences, etc.) attesting to learning.

104 For the qualification of an ijāza as a written one (*ijāza bʾil-khaṭṭ*) see Ṣafadī, *Aʿyān*, fol. 122b.

105 One shaykh for example acquired permission to deliver fatwās from a shaykh while the two were traveling to Egypt: Ṣafadī, *Aʿyān*, 14b.

106 See Ibn al-Ṣalāḥ, *Muqaddima*, 265–7 for examples of ijāzas granted for "all my texts," or "all the accounts I have audited"; also Ibn Khallikān, 6/83.

107 Yūnīnī, 1/396; Ṣafadī, *al-Wāfī*, 10/245 adds that the shaykh told the disciple, "now divine benefit (an-niʿma) has descended upon you, my son." Another story that demonstrated the shaykh's paranormal knowledge is conveyed in Yūnīnī, 1/403. One day the shaykh approached someone and told him, "You have eaten ḥarām food. I see smoke coming out of your mouth." The man returned to where he had taken his last meal and discovered that what the shaykh said was true.

108 Ibn Kathīr, 14/155. See Berkey, *The Transmission of Knowledge*, 155–60 for ḥadīth transmission among the mamlūks of Cairo.

109 On loyalties of love (*ḥubb*) and service (*khidma*) see below, chapter 4.

Where scholars have examined the ijāza as a marker of capacity, the sources rarely relate ijāzas to the exploitation of waqf income at all. In fatwās, biographical dictionaries, and chronicles the possession or absence of ijāzas is rarely a matter of debate. Ijāzas seem to have been a small stake in social competition compared to the degree or the examination in the Latin West or China. This is not to say, however, that the sources were uninterested in what we would call "qualification" or "capacity" when it came to competition over manṣabs. Regularly, with respect to students, lecturers, qāḍīs, and others – in other words with respect to anyone who held a manṣab – sources debated the question of "suitability" (istiḥqāq), in the same manner as amīrs and soldiers were inspected for their istiḥqāq for iqṭāᶜs and soldiers' pay (jāmikiyya).[110] With regard to knowledge and distinction, the ijāza was just one part of a larger category of documents that attested to their learning; with regard to anything resembling temporary entitlement or capacity we must look elsewhere.

Madrasas in Damascus did not provide the aᶜyān of the city with cultural distinction, specialized knowledge, or formal qualifications, and they had many uses that had nothing to do with education. Following the establishment of large numbers of madrasas in the city, knowledge continued to be transmitted as it had been before – within lineages and groups of scholars tied together by bonds of love and service. Madrasas were foundations established in the interests of their founders, who were for the most part neither students nor teachers. As charitable foundations, they were a means by which elite households associated the prestige of ᶜilm and the protection of waqf with their own strategies. Madrasas were instruments by which the ruling elite controlled property. They were also useful to the ruling elite in providing a means of supporting the civilian elites upon whom they depended as a channel of influence into the city, as agents of social control and legitimation, and as religious specialists. Madrasas also provided useful platforms for their public activities and instruments of their political strategies. But in Damascus there is little evidence that they became specialized institutions of higher education in any useful sense of the term.

However, this is not to say that madrasas were without consequences for the aᶜyān. If madrasas did not in fact represent an institutionalized form of higher education, what effect did the establishment of madrasas have on the social and cultural struggles of the civilian elite? The next chapter examines how the proliferation of relatively large numbers of manṣabs transformed at once the arena and the prizes of their struggles for survival and success.

110 On istiḥqāq see chapter 1, notes 142–5.

CHAPTER 3

Manṣabs and the logic of fitna

A previous chapter has discussed how warriors ruled the city by making political and social use out of the foundation of "private" and "charitable" institutions such as waqfs. This chapter will examine the consequences for the aʿyān of the implantation of large numbers of household foundations in the city. The issue that this chapter will address is how the foundation of madrasas transformed aʿyān social strategies. It will suggest that the principal consequence of madrasas was to provide a package of prizes that changed the nature of aʿyān social competition.

To the aʿyān, madrasas were important religious and social institutions, with many purposes that had nothing to do with education. The learned elite not only often resided in madrasas, they used these institutions as stages for some of their important ceremonies, including the investiture of the chief qāḍī, Friday prayer, weddings, and ceremonies of mourning.[1] The aʿyān also resided, housed visitors, and imprisoned one another in madrasas under their control.[2]

[1] In the Mamlūk period, when a new chief qāḍī was appointed, he was given the appropriate robe of honor, whereupon he went to either the palace (dār al-suʿāda) or the Umayyad Mosque, where the appointment was read out in public, then returned to his madrasa, where the appointment was read out again in the main iwān. He then judged cases brought to him: Ibn Kathīr, 14/129, 153, 166; Jazarī, Köp. MS, 60, 255. For Friday prayer in the Shāmiyya al-Barrāniyya see Nuʿaymī, 1/294, Jazarī, Köp. MS, 258; in the ʿĀdiliyya: Jazarī, Köp. MS, 9; wedding: Ibn Kathīr, 13/330; mourning: Jazarī, Köp. MS, 536; Jazarī, BN MS, 580–1.

[2] For imprisonment in madrasas see Jazarī, BN MS, 237, 239; Ibn Kathīr, 13/302, 14/38, 70; Abū Shāma, *Dhayl*, 173; Nuʿaymī, 1/269. For madrasas as residences see Ibn Kathīr, 14/111, 148; Yūnīnī, 2/53, 350; Abū Shāma, *Dhayl*, 85, 110, 137, 239; Jazarī, Köp. MS, 225; Jazarī, BN MS, 347; Nuʿaymī 1/268. A wealthy Ḥanbalī founded a ribāṭ as a place of refuge for the ʿulamāʾ of Jerusalem during the crusades: Ibn Kathīr, 13/ 64. Visitors housed in madrasas: Jazarī, Köp. MS, 453, 589; Ibn Kathīr, 14/98; Nuʿaymī, 1/196. See Ibn al-Dawādārī, 9/27 for the residence of the shaykh al-shuyūkh in the ʿĀdiliyya; also Yūnīnī 1/453 for the stay of the ʿAbbāsid caliph in the Nāṣiriyya. Other religious buildings in the city were also used as residences. Three hundred people were living in the storerooms of the Umayyad Mosque when Baybars ordered them to decamp in 665/1266–7: Ibn Kathīr, 13/248. People also lived in the minarets of the Umayyad Mosque: Abū Shāma, *Dhayl*, 198, 217. It is also possible that madrasas were used to house visiting merchants, though the evidence for this is ambiguous and inconclusive: see for example Jazarī, BN MS, 553–4. See also G. Leiser, "Notes on the Madrasa in Medieval Islamic Society," *MW* 76 (1986), 19–20 for uses of madrasas as hostels. For the economic impact of madrasas in neighborhoods in Mamlūk Cairo see Berkey, *The Transmission of Knowledge*, 188–201; Leiser, "Notes," 20–3.

Perhaps the major consequence of the foundation of madrasas in Damascus was the competition for manṣabs that resulted, and the transformation of elite social life that the proliferation of monetized honors inaugurated. It is difficult to deduce how many lecturers there were from the number of manṣabs available. Manṣabs were rarely held for a lifetime, many lecturers held more than one manṣab, manṣabs were held like iqṭāᶜs and other property in "shares" (*mushāraka*) and many people were supported as "deputies" (*nāʾib*) of an absent lecturer. Moreover, the sources rarely cite the dates of an appointment, so it is impossible to determine how many manṣab-holders there were at a given moment. There were also scholars who were supported through the madrasa endowments as holders of lesser manṣabs or as residents.[3] However, even though it is impossible to establish the number of competitors for manṣabs at any one time, it is clear that the proliferation of manṣabs established the arena of competition within which most aᶜyān families struggled.

Fitna over manṣabs

Competition over manṣabs established by waqf strongly resembled amīrs' competition over iqṭāᶜs. As mentioned above, scholars often see the divide between civilians and the military as something of a social absolute. But the relationship of the two groups to property, their strategies of social survival, and their view and realization of social competition were similar. Even the categories of "social" civilian and "political" military competition introduce a misleading and anachronistic distinction.

The organization of elite social competition around monetized honors characterized both amīrs and aᶜyān, and both groups used similar language to represent their environments and their struggles within them. Amīrs and aᶜyān alike sought a *rutba* or rank, which meant both appointment and reputation.[4] Aᶜyān and amīrs competed for an appointment that brought with it a revenue source or stipend, and often a robe of honor. Appointments to manṣabs and imras could be divided into shares, which were often held in numerical fractions (half: *niṣf* or quarter: *rubᶜ*), or temporarily by deputies (nāʾib).[5] Secretaries, amīrs, shaykhs, and other beneficiaries of waqfs all "took in hand" (*bāshara*) their revenue sources, and could be "stripped" (*khuliᶜa*) of

[3] See for one example the very distinguished shaykh Sayf al-Dīn al-Āmidī, who supported himself in Cairo as the muᶜīd of the madrasa at Shāfiᶜī's tomb: Ṣafadī, *al-Wāfī*, 21/346.

[4] Both groups also used the term "rataba lahu" to indicate appointment: Yūnīnī, 2/223. For rutba as reputation or prestige see Ṣafadī, *al-Wāfī*, 11/200: "wa-lam tazil rutbatuhu ᶜindaʾl-mulūk taᶜlū wa tazdād ilā ākhiriʾl-waqt"; also Subkī, *Ṭabaqāt*, 6/217, 253, for rutbas with respect to fields of knowledge.

[5] For a "share" (mushāraka) in a revenue source for both aᶜyān and amīrs see Ibn Shākir, 21/37; Yūnīnī, 2/223. See Nuᶜaymī, 1/235 for a half-share (niṣf) of a revenue source; Nuᶜaymī, 1/287 for a father who left his manṣabs in niṣfs to his two sons. Nāʾib as a temporary military command: Ṣafadī, *al-Wāfī*, 11/36; nāʾib as a waẓīfa see Nuᶜaymī, 1/235, 239, 251, 254. See also Yūnīnī, 2/223; Ibn Shākir, 21/37.

them or "dismissed" (*ᶜazala*) from them. These groups could receive another imra or manṣab as "recompense" (*ᶜiwaḍ*) for one they lost.[6] They "resigned" (*nazala*) in favor of their intimates and protégés while they had the power to do so.[7] Shaykhs "competed" (*zāhama*) with one another over manṣabs, as amīrs "competed" over iqṭāᶜs. Scholars "seized" (*intazaᶜa*, or *intazaᶜa min yad*) the manṣabs of others, as rulers "seized" cities and fortresses and amīrs nabbed each others' iqṭāᶜs.[8] Amīrs and shaykhs both feared open competition as "factional disorder" (*ᶜaṣabiyya* or fitna), or enmity (*ᶜadāwa*).[9] In the case of amīrs and scholars alike, the "rules" they occasionally pointed to neither established nor described the terms of the competition. What we have interpreted in the sources as descriptions of rules was often part of the ordinance directed by one side against another in competitive struggle.

The hold of a civilian on a manṣab was similar in many respects to the hold of an amīr on an iqṭāᶜ. Neither had a legally enforceable title to office or revenue. Stipulations in waqfiyyas were in theory sacrosanct, but in practice were often suppressed. The case of Ibn Rawāḥa, founder of the Rawāḥiyya, is especially revealing in this respect. His desire to be buried in his madrasa was thwarted by the first lecturer; his stipulation that no Jew, Christian, or Ḥashawī (by which he meant Ḥanbalī) be permitted to enter was abrogated by a qāḍī; and the administrator he appointed lost his post to two shaykhs living in the neighborhood who swore that Ibn Rawāḥa had promised to give it to them.[10] Strictly speaking, the manṣabs were not fee benefices. They were not alienable or inheritable, and a claim to a manṣab could not generally be enforced through a qāḍī. The one possible exception to this was when an endowment deed specified that the manṣab go to the lecturer and his progeny. Since such a stipulation was usually hedged in by a restriction such as "those of his line who are qualified to hold the position," it should not be taken as evidence of a prescriptive right. An example was when the amīr al-Qaymarī appointed ᶜAlī Ibn Muḥammad al-Shahrazūrī to the lectureship of his madrasa, to be followed by those of his progeny who were qualified. The son of

6 For bāshara as receipt of waqf income, see Ṣafadī, *Aᶜyān*, 203b; Ibn Kathīr, 14/30; for dismissal of an amīr see Ṣafadī, *Aᶜyān*, 89b. For the ᶜiwaḍ of an amīr, who received iqṭāᶜs in return for others stripped from him, see Jazarī, BN MS, 122. For an Ayyūbid prince who received one province as ᶜiwaḍ for another see Ibn Khallikān, 4/173, 176. ᶜIwaḍ also referred to taking a post in the place of someone – as was the case of the sulṭān who sat on the throne in the place of his father – "jalasa fī takht al-mulk ᶜiwaḍ wālidihi": Jazarī, BN MS, 247. Finally, an amīr or ruler could receive another city as ᶜiwaḍ for one he had lost: Ibn al-ᶜAdīm, *Zubda*, 145.

7 For the nuzūl or the passing on of a post from one person to another, especially from fathers to sons or other members of their lineages, see Ṣafadī, *al-Wāfī*, 12/364; for the passing on of an imra as nuzūl. Also see below, notes 15–23.

8 For examples of warrior and learned intizāᶜ see Ibn Wāṣil, 4/231; Ibn Kathīr, 13/320, 336; Yūnīnī, 2/213; Nuᶜaymī, 1/220, 303, 304, 316; Ibn Khallikān, 4/174.

9 On competition over manṣabs as ᶜaṣabiyya or fitna see Yūnīnī 3/192–3; Sibṭ Ibn al-Jawzī, *Mirʾāt*, 8/771; Subkī, *Ṭabaqāt*, 6/252, 253; Ibn Rajab, *Dhayl*, 2/19. For factional enmities as ᶜadāwa see Ibn Shākir, *Fawāt*, 1/236; Ibn Kathīr, 14/48, 49.

10 Dhahabī, *Mukhtaṣar al-Jazarī*, Köp. MS, 26; Ibn Shaddād, 2/241; Nuᶜaymī, 1/265, 274; Abū Shāma, *Dhayl*, 136–7, 149, 187, 189; Ibn Kathīr, 13/116, 168, 304.

the first lecturer took over his father's post without a hitch. But in the third generation a dispute over the manṣab caused ʿaṣabiyya. The grandson of the first lecturer was not old enough to take the post when his father died, and had to wait until his suitability (istiḥqāq) was established. When the young man matured, his character and general fitness (*rushd wa-ahliyya*) were considered good enough, even though his knowledge of law was meager. The "temporary" holder of the post tried to make it permanent, and the case ended up in front of a qāḍī, who held in favor of the grandson. When he took the post, he began to study law, and eventually did become capable, and was even beloved by the students. He was the last of the Shahrazūrī lineage to control the manṣab.[11] As this example underlines, even if a stipulation in a waqfiyya was occasionally enforceable through a qāḍī, after a few generations the absence of a suitable candidate or usurpation often took the manṣab away from the control of the lineage.[12] Otherwise shaykhs won manṣabs by struggling for them.

As manṣabs were not inherited or attained through examination, and there was no concept of a "right" to them, acquiring and holding onto a manṣab was usually a reward for political dexterity. Relatively few lecturers lingered in a single post for a lifetime. Most engaged in a continuous play of seizing, resigning, increasing, trading or passing on, and defending their manṣabs. Some acquired whole galaxies of offices.[13] The waqf of the founder could forbid holding more than one post, but such a condition was rare, and in any case was regularly ignored.[14] Designation of a lineage in a waqf document was also relatively unusual.

More common was the temporary control an individual or lineage had over the manṣab of a madrasa.[15] This temporary control was often expressed as *nuzūl* – the "descent" or passing on of a post from its holder to some other.[16] Lecturers often chose their successors, and resigned in favor of sons, intimates, or men who paid them to move on.[17] Shaykhs also passed on appointments to their students.[18] Moreover, families negotiated with one another over man-

[11] Ibn Kathīr, 13/272–3, 301; Yūnīnī, 3/192–3; Nuʿaymī, 1/455–6.

[12] An example was the ʿAṣrūniyya. The grandson of the first lecturer was thought incapable of the post because of his lack of knowledge of fiqh: Dhahabī, *Taʾrīkh al-Islām*, BL MS, 18.

[13] For an extreme example see one of the Banū Qalānisī who according to Ibn Kathīr held more posts than anyone ever had: Ibn Kathīr, 14/154; Nuʿaymī, 198–9. For other examples see Ibn Kathīr, 13/322; Jazarī, BN MS, 57.

[14] See for example the Shāmiyya al-Barrāniyya, Nuʿaymī, 1/279.

[15] For examples of posts passed on to at least three people within a lineage see Nuʿaymī, 1/ 54, 55; 115–19, 158–66, 178–82, 193–200, 216–25, 236–40, 253–65, 277–300, 326–7, 373–82, 382–98, 398–406, 431–4, 455–6, 508–18, 572–6, 594–9; 2/30–41, 64–79, 79–86, 86–8.

[16] For a definition of the nuzūl see Qalqashandī, 12/353; for examples of it see Nuʿaymī, 1/224, 229. The term also applied to passing on military commands (imra) from father to son: Ṣafadī, *al-Wāfī*, 12/364; Ibn al-Ṣuqāʿī, 100–1.

[17] They also appointed deputies to their positions until their sons were capable of assuming them, much like the institution of the *atabek*: Yūnīnī, 2/143.

[18] Ṣafadī, *al-Wāfī*, 4/227; 22/300; Ibn Kathīr, 13/101.

ṣabs. The Banū Subkī, one of the important scholarly lineages in the city, and Ibn al-Khaṭīb arranged a swap of manṣabs that both parties found convenient. One of the Banū Subkī took Ibn al-Khaṭīb's manṣabs in Cairo, and Ibn al-Khaṭīb in turn took a manṣab vacated by another of the Banū Subkī in Damascus.[19] Lecturers could pass on their posts to others most easily at the height of their prestige, which was one reason why shaykhs passed on their posts to their sons while their sons were still of a young age.[20]

The nuzūl was not recognized in law, but depended on the prestige of the lecturer, on the expectation more generally that sons should inherit their fathers' positions, and on the lecturer's ability to enlist powerful supporters, such as the caliph or the sulṭān.[21] It also depended on external factors, such as the status of the candidate, the intensity of competition over manṣabs at the time, and the interest of the sulṭān. Because it depended on all of these other factors, attempts by manṣab-holders to "pass on" their manṣabs often failed.[22] Most manṣab-holders conceded that the nuzūl was more of a social hope than a right. Taqī al-Dīn al-Subkī could do no more than wish for "just three things: that my son here take up my posts, that I see my [dead] son Aḥmad in a dream, and that I die in Cairo."[23]

Powerful men rewarded their clients and scourged their detractors with manṣabs. The sulṭān, governors, wazīrs, and amīrs deposed shaykhs from their manṣabs and appointed others, and made appointments to vacant manṣabs.[24] At least one amīr intervened on behalf of the scholarly descendant of another amīr, though it was rare in Damascus for descendants of amirs to become lecturers.[25] Members of ruling households – including sulṭāns – recognized few impediments to making appointments themselves, though they never had the legal or administrative capacity that authors such as Qalqashandī argued for.

Throughout the Ayyūbid and Mamlūk periods, sulṭāns increasingly made

[19] Nuʿaymī, 1/240.

[20] See Ibn Kathīr, 14/184 for an example of a seventeen-year-old chief qāḍī who also delivered a lecture at a madrasa. Among many other examples of the passing on of posts are Ibn Kathīr, 13/327, 14/128; Nuʿaymī, 1/238.

[21] Nuʿaymī, 1/380; Ṣafadī, *al-Wāfī*, 18/522.

[22] See Subkī, *Ṭabaqāt*, 6/174 for the example of Dhahabī's attempt to "pass on" the dār al-ḥadīth al-Ẓāhiriyya to Tāj al-Dīn al-Subkī. After it failed ("lam yamḍīʾn-nuzūl"), Subkī's father told him: "I know that you are best suited (mustaḥiq), but there are others older than you who are more appropriate (awlā) to it." Later, Dhahabī on his deathbed again swore to pass on the manṣab to Subkī, but again Subkī's youth prevented him from taking it. See also Berkey, *The Transmission of Knowledge*, 123–6, for how a "deviation from the rule might engender a dispute."

[23] Later he went to the tomb of Shaykh Ḥamād outside the Bāb al-Ṣaghīr and sought the shaykh's intercession – "I have three sons, one of whom has gone to God, another is in the Ḥijāz and I know nothing of him, and the third is here. I want him to take my posts": Subkī, *Ṭabaqāt*, 6/175. For another shaykh who sought in dreams confirmation that his son would take his manṣabs see Jazarī, BN MS, 8a.

[24] For an appointment made by a wazīr see Ibn Kathīr, 13/114; for appointments by the governor Tankiz see Ṣafadī, *Aʿyān*, 144b.

[25] For one rare example see Ibn Kathīr, 13/325, 326.

appointments and by the eighth century made many appointments at a time.[26] Sulṭāns also dismissed lecturers for a variety of reasons. Lecturers lost their manṣabs for criticizing powerful men, for teaching sciences out of favor, for finding themselves on the wrong side in factional disputes, and to make way for favorites. The rational sciences (*al-ᶜulūm al-ᶜaqliyya*) flourished in the reign of al-Muᶜaẓẓam ᶜĪsa, and were banned by al-Malik al-Ashraf. Each hired and fired shaykhs who followed one or the other.[27] Al-Muᶜaẓẓam dismissed one lecturer who criticized his wine-drinking, and another for refusing to issue a fatwā deeming the practice legal.[28] Shaykhs did not have to be formally deposed by rulers to abandon their posts. Sulamī prudently left the city and his manṣabs after the sulṭān became angry at his attempt to remove innovations from the sermon.[29]

Holders of manṣabs also rose and fell with the leaders of their factions. When fitna broke out (*burūq al-fitna*), or the leader of a faction was deposed, one consequence was a reshuffle of manṣabs. When the Sulṭān Baybars al-Jāshnikīr's shaykh al-Manbijī was at the height of his power he dismissed at least one associate of his enemy Ibn Taymiyya from a manṣab.[30] Following the death of Baybars al-Jāshnikīr there was much rivalry (ᶜaṣabiyya) over manṣabs in Damascus. The supporters of Manbijī lost many of their manṣabs in Cairo and Damascus, while shaykhs who either opposed Baybars al-Jāshnikīr or supported Qalāwūn against him were rewarded with manṣabs of their own.[31] This year was remembered as "the year of the reapportionment of the waẓīfas" (sanna qisma al-waẓāʾif), of which there was another in 669/1270–1.[32]

Although it appears that rulers used manṣabs as a way of gaining control of the city, the aᶜyān often enlisted powerful men in their rivalries against one another. Throughout the period scholarly factions and lineages enlisted ruling groups in their struggles over manṣabs. Scholars arrived from Cairo with appointments to manṣabs from the sulṭān in hand.[33] In Damascus they

[26] See Jazarī, Köp. MS, 453, 590; Jazarī, BN MS, 304; Ibn Kathīr, 13/339 for examples. By Qalqashandī's time, if the ever-problematic *Subḥ al-aᶜshā* is to be credited, most major appointments were made by decree of the sulṭān, while the lesser manṣabs were granted by the governor, but throughout most of the period in question at least appointments were not entirely in the gift of the sulṭān: Qalqashandī, 12/6, 357; Gaudefroy-Demombynes, *La Syrie*, 166.

[27] Makdisi, *The Rise of Colleges*, 137; Nuᶜaymī, 1/393; 2/292; Ibn al-ᶜImād, *Shadharāt*, 5/144; Ibn Kathīr, 13/124,140–1,148; Ibn Shākir, Vat. Ar. MS, 119; Sibṭ Ibn al-Jawzī, *Mirʾāt*, 8/691.

[28] Ibn Kathīr, 13/101, 136; Ibn Shākir, Vat. Ar. MS, 103, 104.

[29] Subkī, *Ṭabaqāt*, 5/80–1.

[30] Ibn Kathīr, 14/50.

[31] Ibn Kathīr, 14/49, 57–9, 61, 65. For other examples of lecturers losing manṣabs due to their alignments in factional competition see Ibn Kathīr, 13/330; 14/56, 180.

[32] Nuᶜaymī, 1/190; see also the reshuffle of manṣabs after the fitna of 693/1293–4 recounted by Jazarī, BN MS, 235–6, and the reshuffle of 696/1296–7 in Jazarī, BN MS, 339–408.

[33] When Ibn al-Zamlakānī was appointed qāḍī of Aleppo, his successor arrived in Damascus with an appointment in hand: Jazarī, Köp. MS, 501. Ibn Jamāᶜa lost two madrasas in Damascus because he was resident in Egypt, but he got a decree from the sulṭān through Manbijī's intercession, and regained them for a time: Ibn Kathīr, 14/58. A scholar won a manṣab after securing an audience with the sulṭān in Cairo: Nuᶜaymī, 1/200.

ambushed the sulṭān with requests for manṣabs when he visited the city, hoping that "the glance of the sulṭān might fall upon them."[34] Civilians enlisted sulṭāns, caliphs, wazīrs, and amīrs to depose holders of manṣabs in favor of others, or to defend a client's hold on one, in a variety of ways. Payoffs and gifts were a common means of acquiring a manṣab.[35] Another tactic was to accuse a manṣab-holder of vice, immorality, impiety, or unbelief.[36] The most common strategy for gaining a manṣab was to seek the intercession (*shifāʿa*) of a powerful person, in the same manner that warriors rose through the intercession of other powerful people.[37] Amīrs, sulṭāns, governors, other civilians, and rulers from elsewhere found themselves enlisted to intervene on behalf of competitors for manṣabs.[38] As power was held by men at the top of temporary networks, competitors for manṣabs sought to muster as many powerful supporters as they could. Because the networks these people headed overlapped, cooperated, and competed with one another in different fields, a conflict over a manṣab could bring in several powerful people who worked out their relationships to one another gingerly.

This accounts in part for the impression of disorder in competition over manṣabs. Even the sulṭān's candidates could lose out. In 702/1302–3 a struggle erupted over the manṣabs of the recently deceased Zayn al-Dīn al-Fāriqī. The governor made a number of appointments to his posts, one on the advice of Ibn Taymiyya. Soon thereafter Ṣadr al-Dīn Ibn al-Wakīl arrived in the city on the post (*barīd*) from Cairo, bearing appointments to those manṣabs from the sulṭān, posts which he added to others he already held in the city. This set off a struggle over the manṣabs that the sulṭān's candidate eventually lost.[39] Similarly, Ḥusām al-Dīn al-Qaramī turned up in the city in 725/1325 bearing appointments from the sulṭān to two large madrasas. Both appointments were abrogated after the chief qāḍī of his madhhab held an audience concerning the

[34] Jazarī, BN MS, 351, 393. An example was the scholar who waited until al-ʿĀdil Kitbugha made a visitation to the Prophet's relics at a shrine outside the city to approach him, and obtained a manṣab for his deftness: Nuʿaymī, 1/281.

[35] See Nuʿaymī, 1/377 for an amīr discovered accepting payoffs from both sides in a competition over a manṣab. Periodic attempts were made to forbid the sale of manṣabs, such as Qalāwūn's order (made at the instigation of Ibn Taymiyya) that no one be appointed to office by virtue of a payoff, but there is no evidence that they succeeded: Ibn Kathīr, 14/66. See also Nuʿaymī, 1/255 for another example. See Ṣafadī, *al-Wāfī*, 18/137 for the story of a lecturer appointed to the Niẓāmiyya in Baghdad who "paid enough to build another Niẓāmiyya." Tankiz was praised for never accepting a payoff for any of the offices he controlled: Ṣafadī, *Aʿyān*, 144b.

[36] See Nuʿaymī, 1/193, 304; Ibn Kathīr, 14/59 for accusations of immorality and vice in a dispute over a post; see Ṣafadī, *al-Wāfī*, 21/346; Ibn Shākir, Vat. Ar. MS, 119; see Dhahabī, *Tadhkirat al-ḥuffāẓ* (Hyderabad, 1955–8), 4/60–1 and Ibn Khallikān, 2/455–6 for accusations against Sayf al-Dīn al-Āmidī of unbelief in fitnas over manṣabs that twice lost him manṣabs and once almost resulted in his execution.

[37] For examples of shifāʿa with respect to amīrs see Ibn al-Ṣuqāʿī, 25; Ibn al-ʿAdīm, *Zubda*, 160–1.

[38] Among the many examples that could be cited are the shifāʿa of the governor of Aleppo on behalf of a lecturer in Damascus: Nuʿaymī, 1/238, 282, 304; of amīrs: Nuʿaymī, 1/192–5, 304, 377; Ibn Kathīr, 13/325, 326; the shifāʿa of wazīrs and bureaucrats: Nuʿaymī, 1/186; of governors of the city: Nuʿaymī, 1/377.

[39] Ibn Kathīr, 14/28; Nuʿaymī, 1/304–5.

manṣab.[40] Even when the aᶜyān did not challenge a sulṭān's appointments directly, they had indirect ways of showing opposition. In 696/1296–7 Jamāl al-Dīn Ibn al-Sharīshī arrived in Damascus with appointments from the sulṭān in hand. The qāḍīs of the city, fearful of the manṣab-holder Jamāl al-Dīn deposed, steered clear of the inaugural lecture.[41] Finally, even when a manṣab in a madrasa supported a particular office, appointment to the office did not mean that the holder of the manṣab was automatically dismissed, even though this was often enough the case. When a new chief qāḍī was appointed, dismissing the holders of manṣabs associated with the qāḍīship could prove difficult, so new qāḍīs could wait for the deaths of their current holders.[42] As these examples illustrate, manṣabs were one element among several in the everlasting conflicts and negotiations of the major households and networks of the city. Attempts by jurists or proponents of the sulṭān's power to establish the legal capacity of one party or another to make appointments obscure how manṣabs were prizes of political and social struggles. They brought into play money, influence, factional alliance, and the power to intimidate, in addition to such formal legal capacity or administrative procedure as may have existed.[43]

We can observe how local households brought rulers into their struggles with one another, and how outside conquerors exploited local rivalries, in the Mongol seizure of Damascus in 658/1260. Several of the leading ᶜulamāᵓ of the city solicited the major manṣabs of Syria from the Mongol ruler Hulegu. Two who benefited were the chief qāḍīs Ibn al-Zakī and ᶜUmar al-Tiflīsī.[44] They obtained many of the major manṣabs in Syria, including a large number of madrasas, which they distributed among their families and protégés. The Mongol governor stepped easily into the ceremonial role of the Ayyūbid sulṭān, and a number of the aᶜyān were more than happy to cast him in it. At the investiture ceremony at the Qubba al-Naṣr in the Umayyad Mosque, the Mongol governor appeared with his wife for the reading of the appointments. Ibn al-Zakī himself appeared in great state for the ceremony. The sources treated the dealings of shaykhs with Mongols as expected events. When the Mongols decamped, Ibn al-Zakī and ᶜUmar al-Tiflīsī were not treated as traitors or collaborators; on the contrary, both judged their chances of survival optimistically enough to make large payoffs to retain their manṣabs. In time, however, they lost them, and Ibn al-Zakī withdrew to Cairo.

Najm al-Dīn Ibn Sanī al-Dawla also benefited from the Mongol invasion,

[40] Nuᶜaymī, 1/119; for an example from 694/1294–5 of appointments from Cairo that were abrogated see Jazarī, BN MS, 305.

[41] Ibn Taymiyya went to his house and heard his lecture there, "seeking its baraka": Jazarī, BN MS, 408.

[42] See Subkī, Staatsbibliothek MS, 23.

[43] For an example of how such evidence contradicts Qalqashandī's definitions of the formal capacities of the sulṭān and the governor to make appointments see Qalqashandī, 12/6–7.

[44] Yūnīnī, 1/357–8, 460; 2/13, 14, 124; Abū Shāma, *Dhayl*, 204–6, 214; Nuᶜaymī, 1/190; Subkī, *Ṭabaqāt*, 5/130–1.

and we can profit from his struggles over the next twenty years to learn something about the nature of aᶜyān competition.[45] His father, the chief qāḍī Ṣadr al-Dīn Ibn Sanī al-Dawla, had approached Hulegu with Ibn al-Zakī, but failed to obtain anything from him, and died soon afterwards. Najm al-Dīn took many of his father's manṣabs, and acquired the Amīniyya by his own efforts. Like the others after the Mongol defeat, he tried to hold on to his manṣabs by making large payoffs. However, Shams al-Dīn Ibn Khallikān arrived from Egypt with an appointment from the sulṭān to Najm al-Dīn's manṣabs as well as those his father had held. Ibn Sanī al-Dawla had to give them up. The spectacle gave rise to a poem much recited and long remembered:

The sun's light struck the star and incinerated him,[46]
and he sunk into the nether-regions and drowned.
The nights mourned him who was their sun; and fate, long-lived, revealed to him what had been obscure.
Lying hope promised that after adversity he would not know loss,
So he was prodigal with his money that his dominance (riyāsa) might endure.
He tore the tissue of law and piety, as if he needed neither,
And an arrow from the West [i.e. Ibn Khallikān, arriving from Egypt]
struck him; may its sender [i.e. the sulṭān] be exalted![47]

This was the opening bout of a rivalry that continued until their deaths in 680–1/1281–2. Ibn Khallikān went on to a brilliant career, becoming in time chief qāḍī, and achieving fame as a historian, judge, and administrator. Ibn Sanī al-Dawla also did well, regaining in time the Amīniyya and also becoming a chief qāḍī. In 679/1280–1 the conflict between Sulṭān Qalāwūn and Sungur al-Ashqar, a governor of the city who declared himself an independent sulṭān, caught the two rivals on opposite sides. While Sungur was at the height of his power, he gave Ibn Khallikān Ibn Sanī al-Dawla's manṣab at the Amīniyya as well as his position as chief qāḍī. As for Ibn Sanī al-Dawla, he was borne off to the muṣādara in Cairo. Some time later, Qalāwūn having subdued Sungur, Ibn Sanī al-Dawla quashed Ibn Khallikān, regained the chief qāḍīship, and repossessed his manṣab at the Amīniyya. Ibn Khallikān went off to imprisonment at the khanqāh al-Najībiyya; released, he was ordered to move his things out of the ᶜĀdiliyya to make way for Ibn Sanī al-Dawla. At the last moment a communication from the sulṭān arrived reprieving him, re-appointing him qāḍī (meaning that he could continue to reside in the ᶜĀdiliyya) and giving him a robe of honor, which he wore during the Friday prayer.[48] The unexpected

[45] For his rivalry with Ibn Khallikān see Abū Shāma, *Dhayl*, 214–15; Yūnīnī, 1/460; Ibn Kathīr, 13/290.

[46] These are puns on their honorifics, Shams al-Dīn, "the sun of religion" and Najm al-Dīn, "the star of religion." [47] Abū Shāma, *Dhayl*, 125, 275.

[48] For the events of 679/1280–1 see Ibn Kathīr, 13/291; Yūnīnī 4/37–9, 42, 43; Ibn Shākir, 21/242–6; Ibn al-Ṣuqāᶜī, 5, 6.

reversal gave birth to another poem: "The star has faded after its return, and morning has dawned; and the sun has risen after it set."[49] This was a long-standing but still typical example of a conflict over manṣabs that brought in rulers, other powerful men, and factions.

Where madrasas and dār al-ḥadīths were founded as a means of attaching the prestige of ᶜilm and the protection of waqf to the personal and political strategies of powerful households, their effect was to transform the nature of competition among the aᶜyān. What appears to be a system corrupted by money, office-mongering, and factional politics was in fact no "system" at all, much less a corrupted one. It was rather an arena of fitna in which various elites deployed the same competitive practices by which other social and political prizes were contested. Issues such as whether manṣabs were inheritable, whether and under what circumstances the sulṭān or qāḍī or nāẓir might make appointments, how the "process" was corrupted by power or money, what the "mechanisms" for making appointments were, all mistake the nature of social competition in the city. Struggles over manṣabs were much like struggles for all the monetized honors of the city. This is why such struggles were so often referred to as fitna. Amīrs and scholars imagined their rivalries in the same language and images, and advanced themselves by many of the same social and political tactics. Even the jurists were never able to elaborate a concept of the "right" to a manṣab, or the "capacity" to appoint others to one; all they could do was uphold suitability (istiḥqāq), and even here they often failed.

The uses of knowledge: conflicts external and internal

When Damascenes invested their painfully acquired knowledge to succeed in the world they experienced conflicts both internal and external. Many experienced a contradiction when they expended social capital acquired through learning and ascetic piety to purchase an elite status and style of life. Some among the civilian elite adopted a style not very different from that of wealthy and powerful amīrs. They wore luxurious clothing, rode about on caparisoned donkeys, kept slaves, and traveled about in state accompanied by large retinues.[50] Men at the top of scholarly and military networks had similar styles of self-glorification. The chief qāḍī had slaves (*ghilmān*) as one of the perquisites of office, traveled in state, and rode riding animals in the city like a high-ranking amīr.[51] When Ibn Jamāᶜa became qāḍī al-quḍā, he entered

[49] Yūnīnī, 4/143.

[50] See for example the scholar who became wealthy in the service of Saladin and was said to keep twenty concubines, each worth a thousand dinars, and kept a table that rivaled those of princes: Abū Shāma, *Dhayl*, 34–5; Sibṭ Ibn al-Jawzī, *Mirʾāt*, 8/515. See also Ṣafadī, *al-Wāfī*, 5/28; Yūnīnī, 1/356.

[51] Jazarī, BN MS, 240–1, for a chief qāḍī who entered the city in state like a prince ("dakhala fī mawkab hāʾil ka-dukhūl al-mulūk"); Sibṭ Ibn al-Jawzī, *Mirʾāt*, 8/590; Ṣafadī, *al-Wāfī*, 18/453.

Damascus "in great state, like the entrance of princes." Following his procession to the ʿĀdiliyya madrasa, he sat in the iwān and listened to panegyric poems written about him recited by the city's poets.[52]

Only a small number of the aʿyān, those most closely integrated into ruling groups, asserted themselves in this manner. A more significant consequence of the proliferation of manṣabs was the support of a larger group of aʿyān who competed for these, and whose use of knowledge for worldly purposes was often ambiguous. Men who struggled for manṣabs took much of their prestige from others who shunned them. Some shaykhs refused manṣabs, and the sources praised them for living quietly and benefiting students in their study-circles.[53] As others benefited from the waqfs of madrasas, they also admitted that they were polluted by them.

One of the paradoxes of the exercise of power in the city was that ruling elites tried to make use of the prestige of men who would have nothing to do with them. Shaykhs who resided in relatively "clean" madrasas shunned appointments to the major manṣabs (*manāṣib al-kibār*), such as the great madrasas and judgeships. Some writers praised the manliness (*murūʾa*) or the ascetic resolve of men who refused manṣabs.[54] Ibn ʿAsākir, to take one example, refused an appointment from the Ayyūbid sulṭān al-ʿĀdil and was obliged to flee town to escape his anger. Al-ʿĀdil afterwards was urged to forget what might have been an insult coming from someone else: "You should rather thank God that there is someone in your domain pious enough to refuse your appointments."[55] Others refused any appointments whatsoever. Those fastidious about accepting manṣabs saw them as a kind of pollution. A pious shaykh who made his living copying and gilding books "was not polluted by any appointment to office, nor by any appointment to any of the madrasas or notary-ships."[56]

These conflicts and tensions came out in poetry. A line of verse quoted by Subkī illustrates the cliché that the "true" manṣab of the learned man had nothing to do with the manṣabs of the madrasas and other foundations: "The perfection of the young man is in ʿilm not in manṣabs; and the rank of the learned is the most splendid of all ranks."[57] A larger poem, this one attributed

52 Jazarī, BN MS, 240–1. 53 For one example see Nuʿaymī, 1/239.

54 For a refusal to accept a post as qāḍī seen as murūʾa see Ibn Kathīr, 14/111; another refusal of appointment to the manāṣib al-kibār see Ibn Kathīr, 14/146. For refusal of manṣabs as ascetic renunciation see Ṣafadī, *al-Wāfī*, 13/182: "wa-zahida fiʾl-manāṣib wa-aʿraḍa ʿanhā iʿrāḍan kulliyyān." Also Subkī, Staatsbibliothek MS, 22; Ibn al-Ṣalāḥ, *Muqaddima*, 368.

55 Ibn Shākir, Vat. Ar. MS, 62; Ṣafadī, *al-Wāfī*, 18/235; Abū Shāma, *Dhayl*, 138.

56 Ibn Kathīr, 14/43, 109: "Lam yatadannas bi-shay' minaʾl-wilāyāt, wa-lā tadannasa bi-shayʾ min waẓāʾifiʾl-madāris wa-lāʾsh-shahādāt."

57 "Kamāluʾl-fatiyi bʾil-ʿilmi lā bʾil-manāṣibi wa-rutbatu ahliʾl-ʿilmi asnāʾl-marātib": Subkī, *Ṭabaqāt*, 6/161, 163; Subkī, Staatsbibliothek MS, 33, 34, and 35, where the line appears in another poem. See *ibid.*, 14 for reaching the "dharwa manṣabihi," the "acme of his manṣab," for reforming the chief qāḍīship of the city.

to Ibn Daqīq al-ᶜĪd, condemned the exploitation of ᶜilm in the struggle for manṣabs:

The manṣab-holders (*ahl al-manāṣib*) belong to this world and its high positions; while the people of virtue (*ahl al-faḍāʾil*) are abased among them.
They humiliate us because we are not of their breed (*jins*); they reckon us beasts, to be ignored.
What [little] they have of charity, it pains us to see; and what they have of ambition, gives us anxiety.
They have their happiness from ignorance and sumptuous wealth; while we have our exhaustion from ᶜilm and privation.

This poem inspired a ribald response that inverted its language to defend the association of learning with prestige and power:

What are manṣabs, or the things of the world, or high positions, to one who has acquired the ᶜilm that you possess not?
No doubt we have superior ability – that is what they saw – yet we reckon them inadequate; they are nothing to us.
They are but beasts, and we humans; our intelligence leads them where we wish, while they are but livestock.
They have nothing but their vapidity to distinguish themselves from us – because their opinions are a nullity.
Ours is the happiness of ᶜilm and privation; and theirs is the stigma of ignorance and shame.[58]

Similar conflicts came out in clothing. A fairly small number of the aᶜyān adopted the clothing styles of amīrs, as amīrs occasionally donned scholarly garb. A larger number flaunted styles that exaggerated the marks of learned status, especially large turbans and wide sleeves, which became larger and wider throughout the period.[59] The turban was the mark of the learned Muslim male, and the learned as a group called themselves "wearers of the turban" (*mutaᶜammamīn*) and "people of the turban" (*ahl al-ᶜimāma*). The *ṭaylasān* or *ṭarḥa* (a covering over the turban which ran down the back slightly) was awarded to distinguished visitors, as well as to holders of the manṣabs such as qāḍīs, the keeper of the treasury (*wakīl bayt al-māl*), the supervisor of waqfs (*nāẓir al-awqāf*), and market inspectors (muḥtasibs), for whom it functioned as a marker of authority.[60] It was also worn by some of the learned

[58] Subkī, *Ṭabaqāt*, 6/6. One irony of this exchange was the execution in Egypt in 701/1301–2 of the author of the second poem for unbelief: Ibn Shākir, *Fawāt*, 1/152–3; Ṣafadī, *Aᶜyān*, 55a-56b.

[59] Ibn Baṭṭūṭa, *Riḥla*, 1/383; Ibn Abī Uṣaybiᶜa, 643; Berkey, *The Transmission of Knowledge*, 182–3.

[60] The ṭaylasān was either similar to or identical with the ṭarḥa: see Lane, s.v. TRH; R. Dozy, *Dictionnaire des vetêments arabes* (Leiden, 1881), 254, 262. Qalqashandī, 4/42 had it that the ṭarḥa was worn by the qāḍī al-quḍā of the Ḥanafīs and the Shāfiᶜīs. See Nuᶜaymī, 1/270, Jazarī, BN MS, 473 for the use of the ṭaylasān/ṭarḥa to mark holders of the waẓīfas. For the ṭaylasān/ṭarḥa as a mark of authority, see for example the anecdote that had a lamp-carrier falsely identify someone as a qāḍī because of the ṭaylasān the latter was wearing. Also, see the new

as a marker of status, and a lecturer could wear it or be awarded it.[61] When the holder of a manṣab was humiliated, the ṭaylasān was publicly "thrown" from his head.[62]

As was the case with the manṣabs, where the "true" manṣab of the learned man was compared to worldly manṣabs, writers claimed that the "true" robe of honor of the learned was humble dress. Yūnīnī recorded a panegyric to a shaykh who criticized these styles: "O learned one, who stands as a guardian of religion, and to whom our wearing of the ṭaylasān is a heretical innovation (*bidʿa*)."[63] Even the intimates of learned men criticized them when they flaunted ostentatious dress. The daughter of Abū ʿUmar Ibn Qudāma, famous for her learning and piety, criticized her brother Shams al-Dīn for his "worldly" fabrics.[64] Men who refused manṣabs did so by refusing the robe of honor whose delivery announced the appointment.[65] Ibn al-Ḥājj sided himself with those who condemned the learned fashions of the age. He contrasted his age's obsession with fashion with the simplicity of the Prophet's companions: "God made pious fear (*khashya*) the robe of honor of the learned, but some have made the width, quality, and smoothness of their sleeves and robes their robes of honor."[66] Ibn al-Ḥājj also scorned the confusion of style with substance:

> Students should wear the correct clothes for audiences in which knowledge is transmitted (*majlis al-ʿilm*). These days students wear distinctive clothing as though it were a requirement, and as though one may not attend a lecture without such clothing. If a student attends a lecture wearing such clothing he is [considered] ignominious, insulting to a place of knowledge . . . All this comes from self-love. Dressing to distinguish oneself from one's contemporaries and colleagues is contrary to the sunna. One who dresses in such a manner is said to be a jurist (faqīh), so [people] distinguish [themselves] from the common people in that manner. [They] could not attain such a rank otherwise except after a long period of time, when [they] would attain a level of distinction (*faḍīla*) that would distinguish [them] from the common people. Only by [their] dress do [they] rise above them and associate [themselves] with the ʿulamāʾ. Thus is learning (fiqh) acquired by fashion and not by study (dars).[67]

Ibn al-Ḥājj not only objected to pretentiousness in dress, he also worried that the clothing of the learned would be taken as a marker of competence:

> Wearing the correct style can be misleading to the masses, because someone who is ignorant or nearly so can be sought out for legal advice by the common people . . . what

market inspector (muḥtasib), who was paraded around the city in his ṭaylasān and robe of honor: Ibn Kathīr, 14/43. For al-Malik al-Kāmil's giving the ṭaylasān as an honor to the visiting shaykh ash-shuyūkh from Baghdād, see Ibn Shākir, Vat. Ar. MS, 28.

[61] See Nuʿaymī, 1/558 for the qāḍī who wore the ṭarḥa when he gave the dars at the ʿIzziyya al-Ḥanafiyya madrasa. See also the ṭaylasān and the green robe of honor given to Ibn al-Qalānisī when he was appointed to the tadrīs of the Amīniyya: Jazarī, Köp. MS, 250.

[62] Ibn Kathīr, 13/37; Abū Shāma, *Dhayl*, 57.

[63] "Ayyuhāʾl-ʿālimuʾlladhī qāma liʾd-dīni ḥārisan/wʾalladhī mubdaʿātuhuʾlbisatunāʾṭ-ṭaylasān": Yūnīnī, 2/394.

[64] Ṣafadī, *al-Wāfī*, 11/304.

[65] Ibn Kathīr, 14/47.

[66] Ibn al-Ḥājj, 1/140.

[67] Ibn al-Ḥājj, 1/136–7.

he wears prevents him from admitting that he does not know because he would be associating himself with ignorance. He might deliver a fatwā based on his personal opinion (*rāʾī*) or on the principle of equity (*maṣlaḥa*).[68] He makes analogies with similar cases imagining that they are similar – and correct legal judgment (*al-ḥukm*) is not reached in this manner. He will lead others into error. This corruption occurs because of contradicting the sunna with respect to clothing.[69]

However, other members of the elite defended their characteristic clothing styles. When he was appointed chief qāḍī, for example, Ibn Jamāᶜa ordered that the other qāḍīs continue to wear the ṭarḥa.[70] Another shaykh found sanction for wearing luxurious clothing in a dream. Meeting a dead shaykh who was wearing luxurious clothing, he asked what God had done with him, and was told that he was forgiven.[71]

Status collided with gender in clothing. When elite women took to wearing the large turban, the governor of the city in 690/1291 forbade them to wear it.[72] Similarly, when men wore the ṭaylasān and wide and long sleeves they skirted dangerously close to gender boundaries. Ibn al-Ḥājj used any argument he could to criticize the width of sleeves and the wearing of the ṭaylasān, including the allegation that wearers of ṭaylasāns were occasionally hanged by them.[73] Critical in general of all emblems of superiority, he made use of gender boundaries to make a point about status. Condemning the ṭaylasān as a heretical innovation (*bidᶜa*), he wrote that those who wore it "can be taken from the side for women who fear to show their faces to men. Some of them even put a needle in their ṭaylasāns, pinning them to their turbans so that the wind does not carry them away, just as a woman does with her veil to keep her face from being exposed to those outside her family. Men should not resemble women."[74] Ibn al-Ḥājj also condemned the wearing of long hems and sleeves. He could find little in his own time to compare to the rough austerity of the Caliph ᶜUmar, who upon discovering that the sleeves of his robe were too long, cut them between two rocks and left the threads dangling.[75] Women, he wrote, could wear their hems long because of the demands of modesty, but there was no need for it in the case of men.[76]

Situated between those who sprinted to the Mongols at the first whiff of a manṣab, and those who lived eremitically, between those who flaunted their status and those who rejected all emblems of it, most of the aᶜyān occupied a middle ground. The sources often described the moral world of the scholar in absolutes, and assigned people to one category or another easily. But in fact the evidence suggests that many people were torn inwardly. Ibn al-Ḥājj captured nicely the urbane self-loathing that some experienced when they cashed in their distinction for manṣabs: "We deprecate the things of this world

[68] Mālikīs such as Ibn al-Ḥājj accepted neither rāʾī nor maṣlaḥa as jurisprudential principles.
[69] Ibn al-Ḥājj, 1/136–7. [70] Ibn Kathīr, 13/322. [71] Ibn Rajab, 2/108.
[72] Jazarī, BN MS, 59–60; Ibn Kathīr, 13/322. Ibn Taymiyya, *Mukhtaṣar al-fatāwā al-miṣriyya*, 318–23 wrote a fatwā condemning this practice.
[73] Ibn al-Ḥājj, 1/139. [74] *Ibid.*, 1/139. [75] *Ibid.*, 1/133. [76] *Ibid.*, 1/130.

with our tongues and pull them to us with our hands and feet."[77] Ibn Jamāᶜa, a jurist who advised students against seeking knowledge for worldly ends, such as gaining large numbers of students, fame, manṣabs, or money, was himself one of the most worldly of the learned, and held many major manṣabs in both Egypt and Syria.[78] Even men with the greatest success in the world learned to speak of it – or to be heard speaking of it – with disdain. Taqī al-Dīn al-Subkī, a man with great success in the struggle for manṣabs, and whose efforts on behalf of his sons are uniquely well documented, "saw the world as nothing but dispersed dust (habban manshūran), and he knew not how to gain a [single] dirham."[79]

Ibn al-Ḥājj, though a Cairene, expressed resentments towards the appropriation of learning for worldly ends that were common in Damascus. He was a Mālikī, and as Mālikīs rejected waqf as practiced by the other schools, part of his criticism at what he encountered in Egypt and Syria can be understood as the position of his legal school on foundations. But as he furnished the most detailed expression of this attitude his opinions are worth some consideration. Expressing his disdain for the acquisition of knowledge as a social investment, he called up a germane ḥadīth: "You have learned ᶜilm in order to be called ᶜālim." He regretted the perversion of knowledge into manṣab-seeking: "People learn ᶜilm, then investigate it, then want manṣabs and leadership (*riyāsāt*); [they] delight in ostentatious display (*maḥabba aẓ-ẓuhūr w'ar-rafᶜa*), and [are] avid for high standing with rulers, amīrs, the ᶜulamāᵓ, and the common people (*ᶜawāmm*); frequenting their doors is an incurable disease." As in the poem quoted above, he contrasted the struggle for manṣabs with the "true" manṣab of the learned man: "By frequenting those in power, they deprecate their great manṣab with respect to the sharīᶜa (al-manṣab ash-sharᶜīᵓl-ᶜazīm)."

According to Ibn al-Ḥājj, competition for manṣabs caused the learned to ignore their true pastoral function: "The occupation of the ᶜulamāᵓ is riᶜāyya (pastoral guidance) and the occupation of the stupid is riwāya (narration). He whose heart God has enlightened has reached a high rank (*rutba ᶜuliyāᵓ*), and those whose hearts God has not enlightened are either devils or thieves."

The idea that the manṣabs interfered with rather than facilitated the acquisition of ᶜilm did not divide the aᶜyān into those who sought out manṣabs and those who did not; rather it created an interior divide within many people that was never bridged. A typology of learned people might be constructed that would place the lone ascetic copyist or ḥadīth scholar on one end and on the other a chief qāḍī with the manṣabs of many household waqfs, a retinue including mamlūks and caparisoned donkeys, and a household noted for the number of its slave girls. As with all such charts, however, many aᶜyān would have been able to imagine themselves at most points. The author of the poem

77 This and the following section are taken from Ibn al-Ḥājj, 1/14–20.
78 See for example his advice in *Tadhkira al-sāmiᶜ*, 12–13, 19.
79 Subkī, Staatsbibliothek MS, 3.

lamenting the abasement of the "people of virtue" at the hands of the "people of manṣabs" himself had manṣabs in a number of madrasas. Fathers also found it difficult to explain to their sons the compromises needed to survive in the world. One of the Banū Subkī hoped to spare his son a youth's disdain of hypocrisy by explaining how he lobbied on his behalf for the chief qāḍīship of the city. "Never, never," he warned, "seek the qāḍīship with your heart in addition to your acts."[80] A paradox often remarked was that social power came to those who refused it most. ᶜIlm had a high exchange value in social relations, one which could be cashed in easily. The resentments and interior conflicts that this set off ran through the social life of the period.

Conclusion

Scholars have studied madrasas primarily as institutions of education, yet the complex interrelations among household waqfs, the cultivation of knowledge, and the social strategies of elites has been an unresolved problem. Madrasas together with other waqfs were both objects and arenas of fitna. They had no autonomous leadership or administration, nor were they permanent and impersonal instruments of outside groups. Rather, power held by others – the sulṭān, governor, households of amīrs, qāḍīs, lecturers, scholarly factions, and lineages – intersected at madrasas, as these groups struggled to control revenue sources and the uses to which they could be put. Juristic literature mandated that appointments to madrasas were to follow the prescriptions of waqf. Administrative literature gave the sulṭān or the governor the authority to make appointments and oversee the affairs of the madrasas more generally. But these sources have to be understood in terms of the social and political strategies they were intended to advance. As the chronicles and biographical dictionaries make abundantly clear, the formal legal or administrative "capacity" of qāḍīs, jurists, and even the sulṭān was just one element in wider struggles to control waqfs.

The effect of the foundation of large numbers of madrasas in the city was less to change the nature of education than to redirect the nature of social competition. Manṣabs became prizes of social competition among the aᶜyān much as iqṭāᶜs were objects of competitive struggle among amīrs. Terms such as "eligibility," "ineligibility," "appointment," "stipend," "dismissal," and "seizure of a post," among many others, were not restricted to "education," but referred to a more universal set of competitive practices, both "educational" and "military," "social" and "political."

When young Damascenes wanted to become learned shaykhs they imitated their exemplars. If we can speak of an object of "education" at all it was a quality of exemplarity that was desired, rather than any formal qualification or affiliation. In Damascus social honor was not enshrined in titles of nobility

80 Subkī, *Ṭabaqāt*, 6/175.

or certificates of educational competence. The object of education was not a credential with a fixed or expected value. What appear as credentials were tokens not only of an individual's acquisition of the texts carried by his shaykh, but of the whole complex of manners, moral conduct, deportment, and scripted forms of self-presentation that in sum made up the notion of adab. How the aʿyān acquired this symbolic capital, and the uses they made of it, are the subjects of the next two chapters.

CHAPTER 4

Social and cultural capital

Nothing takes longer to acquire than the surface polish which is called good manners. Tocqueville, *L'Ancien Régime et la Révolution* (Paris, 1856)

They are more proud of the title Cartesian and of the capacity to defend his principles than of their noble birth and blood.
Giovanni Marana, *Letters Writ by a Turkish Spy* (Paris, 1684)

This chapter examines how the aᶜyān, through cultivation of ᶜilm, inculcated in their young a talent or knack for acquiring social and cultural capital. It will argue that the aᶜyān acquired their critical loyalties and social distinction by making social use of cultural practices associated with ᶜilm. It will argue further that where in other societies many of these practices are specialized in formal domains such as "higher education" and "book production," in medieval Damascus they are better studied as a single group of ritual, mimetic, and performative practices.

Young people and their shaykhs

As with much else in the cultural history of Islamic societies, the association of learning with loyalty was summed up in a quotation attributed to ᶜAlī Ibn Abī Ṭālib: "I am the slave of whoever who teaches me one letter of the alphabet. If he wishes he may sell me; if he so desires he may set me free; and if he cares to he may make use of me as a slave."[1] In quoting this sentiment, Zarnūjī was typical of his contemporaries. The aᶜyān of Damascus constructed their most intimate and socially critical social bonds through the cultivation of ᶜilm. Bonds of dependence and loyalty between shaykhs and their disciples, and among shaykhs themselves, were the basis of the aᶜyān's social networks.

The ties that bound teachers to students had much in common with those that bound ṣūfīs to their disciples. Learned shaykhs claimed the prestige of

[1] Zarnūjī, 32. Ibn Jamāᶜa also wrote that the student should be like a slave to his teacher: Ibn Jamāᶜa, 90.

ṣūfism and the intimacy of its human relationships for themselves. Writers of advice to the young did not hesitate to refer to a teacher as a spiritual guide or *murshid.*[2] One wrote that it was the ᶜulamāᵓ who were meant by the term *ahl al-dhikr* (a term usually referring to ṣūfīs) in the Qurᵓān.[3] When the biographical dictionaries described the relationship of students to their shaykhs, it is clear that they saw the teacher as more than an expert in a body of knowledge. Yūnīnī's biographical notice of one learned man, an entry typical of hundreds of others, shows how the learned represented relations between shaykhs and young people as moral and mimetic as well as intellectual: "He became his student, and was known by his companionship (*ṣuḥba*) of the shaykh, and he devoted himself to the shaykh's ṣuḥba. The light of the shaykh and his baraka reflected upon him, and he modeled himself after the shaykh in his morals and manners."[4] The loyalties between young people and their shaykhs were sanctified, and long outlasted the relatively short period of their "companionship." Dead shaykhs haunted their students in their dreams.[5] Some were "known by" their shaykhs.[6] Others adopted distinctive clothing on the model of their shaykhs.[7] Men also requested burial with their shaykhs after their deaths, even when they had their own family tombs.[8] Shaykhs were also models for opinions on the questions of the time. When the Shāfiᶜī chief qāḍī ᶜMuḥī al-Dīn Ibn al-Zakī (d. 658/1260) became the disciple of Ibn ᶜArabī, he began to set ("yadhhab ilā tafḍīl") ᶜAlī over ᶜUthmān, on the model of his shaykh. This difficult transgression of the usual beliefs of his group worked its way into his dreams, which confirmed for him ᶜAlī's superiority.[9]

When young Damascenes set out to become learned shaykhs, they did not conceive of their training as impersonal, restricted to a specific time of life, in a specialized location, to a limited end. The family was the model for intimate relationships, and the aᶜyān used language taken from the family to represent the ties they acquired with their shaykhs. Shaykhs occasionally compared knowledge explicitly to blood: "If one is ignorant of knowledge," wrote one writer, "it is as though he is ignorant of his father. Knowledge for one who seeks it is a father, only better."[10] A poet made this association even more

2 Ibn Jamāᶜa, 88. 3 Ibn al-Ḥājj, 1/91.

4 "Talammadha lahu wa-ᶜurifa bi-ṣuḥbatihi waᵓkhtaṣṣa bi-khidmatihi wa ᶜāda anwāruᵓsh-shaykh wa-barakatuhu ᶜalayhi wa-takhallaqa bᵓikhlāqih": Yūnīnī, 2/57.

5 "Ẓahara lahu baᶜda mawtih": Ṣafadī, *al-Wāfī*, 22/431, 4/79, 12/258; Ibn Kathīr, 13/52; Subkī, *Ṭabaqāt*, 6/217.

6 "Wa-ᶜurifa bihi": Subkī, *Ṭabaqāt*, 6/250. For one of the muwallahīn whose niṣba included his shaykh's name see Jazarī, BN MS, 577.

7 See for example Yūnīnī, who wore his *qabᶜa* – a small felt cap – with the wool on the exterior, on the model of his shaykh: Ibn Kathīr, 13/229.

8 Jazarī, BN MS, 26–7, 372; Ibn Shākir, *ᶜUyūn al-tawārīkh*, 21/75; Ibn Shākir, *Fawāt*, 1/180; Abū Shāma, *Dhayl*, 66, 187; Ibn Kathīr, 13/318; Nuᶜaymī, 1/86; Yūnīnī, 3/229. See also an anecdote concerning al-Khaṭīb al-Baghdādī related approvingly by Ibn Jamāᶜa. The Khaṭīb, getting his customary three wishes after sipping the holy waters of zamzam, asked first to be permitted to write the *Tāᵓrīkh Baghdād*; second that the book fill the Manṣūr Mosque; and third that he be buried next to Bishr al-Ḥāfī: Ibn Jamāᶜa, 139. 9 Ibn Kathīr, 13/258

10 Ibn al-Ṣalāḥ al-Shahrazūrī, *Ṭabaqāt al-Fuqahaᵓ*, Hamidiye MS 537, fol. 2.

explicit: "The blood-tie of ᶜilm," he wrote or recited, "is superior to the blood-tie of kinship."[11] Writers often compared family loyalties to loyalties among scholars. Shaykhs were "like fathers" to their disciples, and referred to them as their "sons."[12] The prestige that attached itself to lineages in other societies adhered to scholarly pedigrees in Damascus, as cultivation of ᶜilm gave civilians their entry into the "nobility of learning."[13] "Knowledge," wrote Ibn Qutayba, "is the highest nobility, just as love is the highest of ties."[14] An example of this association was a poem in praise of himself that Abū Shāma quoted with sincere approval: "Concerning the names in his lines of transmission, and their contents, he knows them as if they were part of his clan."[15]

When the aᶜyān inserted themselves into lines of transmission of ᶜilm they gained a pedigree that was in some respects more useful to them than that provided by their blood-line. Writers advised cutting off family ties in order to obtain ᶜilm, both to facilitate the arduous business of studying and to enter the "nobility of ᶜilm and the ᶜulamāʾ."[16] Ibn Jamāᶜa quoted al-Baghdādī on the displacement of blood by ᶜilm: "No one will attain knowledge who does not close his shop or let his garden rot, and leave his brothers, and die far from his family with an unwitnessed funeral."[17] Whoever wanted ᶜilm should cut family ties to obtain it: "He who marries is sailing on a sea, and when he has a child he is sunk."[18] Although families provided the language and images for intimate relationships, they could not directly bestow the social status of their members. It was their cultural capital that constituted their true patrimony.

Making social bonds

How did elites imagine their place in the world and construct the social bonds necessary to their survival? The previous chapter discussed in passing several similarities between the struggles of the aᶜyān and amīrs for monetized honors. It might seem logical to think of these two groups of elites as so dissimilar that they do not really bear comparison, much less study as a single group. Yet, in spite of the obvious differences between them, aᶜyān and amīrs faced many of the same constraints and possibilities in forming households and groups and reproducing their status in time. Thus it should not be surprising that both

11 "Luḥmatuʾl-ᶜilmi taᶜlū luḥmataʾn-nasab": Ṣafadī, *al-Wāfī*, 21/342.

12 For three examples see Abū Shāma, *Dhayl*, 136; Yūnīnī, 3/205; and especially Jazarī, BN MS, 437 for a shaykh who "was in the position of a father" to an amīr. Zarnūjī wrote, "He who teaches you one letter of those you need for your religious instruction is your father in religion": Zarnūjī, 32.

13 For examples of sharaf al-ᶜilm, see Yūnīnī, 2/52; Ṣafadī, 21/94.

14 Quoted in F. Rosenthal, *Knowledge Triumphant: the Concept of Knowledge in Mediaeval Islam* (Leiden, 1970), 257.

15 Abū Shāma, *Dhayl*, 40.

16 For sharaf al-ᶜilm see Ibn Jamāᶜa, 70; for a book entitled in part "sharaf al-ᶜilm wʾal-ᶜulamāʾ" see Ṣafadī, *al-Wāfī*, 21/266. For a similar sentiment from Buyīd Iran, see Mottahedeh's quote of al-Rāmhurmuzī: "It is sufficient nobility for the transmitter that his name be joined with the name of the Prophet and be mentioned along with mention of Him and His family and His companions": *Loyalty and Leadership*, 141.

17 Ibn Jamāᶜa, 70.

18 Ibn Jamāᶜa, 72.

groups represented the social universe, conceived of the nature of loyalties, and forged their social bonds in similar ways.

Both amīrs and aʿyān imagined their positions and their trajectories in the social universe in terms of "benefit." In the absence of any "natural" social order (or theodicies of privilege such as superior breeding, lineage charisma, divine selection, or natural superiority that often underpin one) most members of the elite represented their status as compensation for the altruistic "benefit" they provided others.[19] Most exchanges among surplus-consuming groups, whether economic, political, cultural, or social, were represented as the bequeathing of benefit from one person to another. The cure of the physician, the exploit of the soldier, the service of the clerk or secretary, the favor of the powerful, the intercession of the influential, the friendship of the scholar, the waqf of the benefactor, the edicts and appointments of the ruler, and the productions of the ʿulamāʾ were all represented as "benefits."[20] This experience of the world in terms of benefit extended to the cosmos: the sun when it rises also spreads benefit.[21] In the biographical dictionaries, the various words for benefit (nafʿ, fāʾida, maṣlaḥa, and their derivatives) often appear many times in a single entry.

The aʿyān represented their honorifics, honors, cultural productions, initiations into texts, and social bonds as benefits. A common honorific for a shaykh was *mufīd* (one who provides benefit), and the reputation of a scholar among the common people was partly due to the "benefit" they received from him or her.[22] The learned elite also represented their cultural productions – lectures,

[19] For the social and political uses of "benefit" among ruling groups in Buyīd Iraq, from which my reading of Damascus has benefited greatly, cf. Mottahedeh, *Loyalty and Leadership*, 73–9, 82–4.

[20] The terms nafʿ and ifāda appear so frequently and in so many contexts in the sources that it would be impossible to attempt to cite them all. The following are a number of examples of a way of imagining social life that is inscribed in virtually every page of the chronicles and biographical dictionaries: ʿilm a nafʿ: Ibn Kathīr, 13/325; a marginal commentary a benefit: Ibn Khallikān, 1/91; relating ḥadīth a benefit: Ibn al-Ṣalāḥ, *Muqaddima*, 359; Jazarī, BN MS, 68; lessons a benefit to students: Ibn Jamāʿa, 216; building mosques, lavatories, and baths a benefit: Ibn Kathīr, 13/337–8; 14/103, 116; Abū Shāma, *Dhayl*, 82; medicine provides or fails to provide nafʿ: Sibṭ Ibn al-Jawzī, *Mirʾāt*, 8/550; Ṣafadī, *al-Wāfī*, 13/388; the cure of the physician provides nafʿ: Ibn Shākir, *Fawāt*, 2/317; Ibn al-Ḥājj, 1/88; friendship as nafʿ: Ibn ʿAbd al-Hādī, *Ṭabaqāt*, 4/274; prayer a nafʿ: Ibn Rajab, 2/101; the duty of the sulṭān to employ people who will provide benefit: Subkī, *Muʿīd al-niʿam*, 28; patronage of the learned a nafʿ: Ṣafadī, *al-Wāfī*, 11/200; nafʿ as political favor: Ibn Abī Uṣaybiʿa, 729, 730; Ibn Kathīr, 14/56; Nuʿaymī, 1/235–6; Jazarī, BN MS, 223; making clocks and astrolobes a nafʿ: Ibn Kathīr, 14/168; waqf as nafʿ: Subkī, *Muʿīd al-niʿam*, 145; donating a library to "benefit the Muslims": Yūnīnī, 4/185; giving advice about a blunder in adab an ifāda: Ibn Jamāʿa, 93; political mediation a benefit: Ṣafadī, *al-Wāfī*, 10/260; Ibn Taymiyya's meeting with the Mongol Ghazān in 699/1299–1300 a nafʿ: Ibn Kathīr, 14/7.

[21] Qalqashandī, 12/19.

[22] See for example the love of amīrs, soldiers, merchants, notables, ʿulamāʾ, and common people for Ibn Taymiyya, because "he was devoted to their benefit, night and day, with tongue and pen": Ibn Nāṣir al-Dīn, BL MS, 3; Ibn ʿAbd al-Hādī, quoting Dhahabī, *Taʾrīkh al-Islām*, Köp. MS, 47. Among the many honorifics other than the very common use of mufīd by itself are:

debates, public readings and other open audiences, fatwās, and books – as benefits.[23] Writers, copyists, public readers, and commentators gave as the reason for their efforts the provision of benefit.[24] Of Ibn al-Qalānisī the historian, to cite one example among many, it was said, "no one approached him, or became his companion, without gaining benefit from him."[25] When shaykhs came together it was to benefit one another, and they regretted the deaths of their companions because it meant the end of the benefits to be obtained from them.[26] Shaykhs also saw their manṣabs as recompense for the "benefits" they conferred.[27] In a world in which social honor and position were won rather than inherited, gaining and giving benefit was seen as the point of life.

The initiation of the young was seen as a process in which young people

"muḥaddith Baghdād wa-mufīduhā": Ibn Rajab, 2/353; "mufīd Baghdād": Ṣafadī, *Aᶜyān*, fol. 44a; "mufīd al-umma": Ibn Nāṣir al-Dīn, BL MS, 5, 7; "mufīd al-muʾadhdhinīn": Ibn Nāṣir al-Dīn, BL MS, 7; "kanz al-mustafidīn": Ibn Nāṣir al-Dīn, BL MS, 11; "shaykh aṭ-ṭalaba wa-mufīduhum": Ibn Kathīr, 14/126; "mufīd al-warā": Ṣafadī, 21/86. For a later example of how a suggested format for an ijāza at-tadrīs referred to teaching as "ifāda," see Qalqashandī, 14/325. Misreadings of the term ifāda and its derivatives are characteristic of how scholars have formalized juristic literature. Discussing the muᶜīd and the mufīd, Makdisi, *The Rise of Colleges*, 176 writes: "These two posts may be compared to those of the modern 'teaching fellows' or 'assistants,' held by graduate students working towards their doctoral degrees." Berkey, *Transmission of Knowledge*, 40–2, largely follows Makdisi's sources and conclusions on the muᶜīd and mufīd as "teaching assistants," adding that the latter functioned "informally." Neither Makdisi nor Berkey reads their main source – Subkī's *Muᶜīd al-niᶜam* – critically on this issue. Berkey, 40, sees the source as a tract written by an "experienced educator" intended to define "the proper behavior of those employed in a variety of academic, religious, bureaucratic, and economic tasks." Neither Makdisi nor Berkey deals with the possibility that by abstracting from legal discussions of suitability for receiving waqf income, we risk formalizing legal distinctions into differentiated institutional structures and functions. There is no evidence that in Damascus mufīds were thought of as advanced students or even that they had any "functions" or "duties." What neither Makdisi nor Berkey mentions is that perhaps the most common term for teaching of all kinds was ifāda – the provision of fāʾida or benefit. One of the most common honorifics for teachers and shaykhs in the biographical dictionaries for Damascus was mufīd. Taking everything into consideration, a fair guess might be that the mufīds mentioned in the juristic literature were mature men who resided in madrasas, some of whom consumed enough endowment income to warrant the occasional fatwā concerning their legal status.

23 Lessons and lectures were "beneficial" ("mufīda yantafiᶜū bihā an-nās"): Ibn Kathīr, 14/179; a ḥadīth session loses its benefit if it goes on too long: Ibn al-Ṣalāḥ, *Muqaddima*, 369; a debate produced "benefit": Yūnīnī, 2/142; a lecturer demonstrated his benefits after his appointment to a madrasa: Ṣafadī, *Aᶜyān*, fol. 45b; a Qurʾān reader benefited whoever read with him: Ṣafadī, *al-Wāfī*, 10/267; a book was beneficial ("nāfiᶜ mufīd"): Subkī, *Ṭabaqāt*, 6/245; a writer was referred to as the "benefactor of the Muslims" because of his writings: Birzālī, *Muᶜjam al-shuyūkh*, Ẓāhiriyya MS, 21a.

24 The adjective most often employed to praise a book was mufīd, repeated thousands of times in the sources. Books written for fāʾida: Ṣafadī, *Aᶜyān*, 3b; Jazarī, Köp. MS, 311. Marginal comments to a text were fāʾidas, as in "wa-zāda ᶜalā aṣl fawāʾida jalīla": Yūnīnī, 3/75; copying a text a fāʾida: Ibn al-Ḥājj, 4/84

25 Ibn Shākir, 21/32; Yūnīnī, 3/37, 38. For another example of ṣuḥba conceived as benefit see Ibn Khallikān, 2/230.

26 For death as the end of a shaykh's benefits to others see Abū Shāma, *Dhayl*, 131.

27 See Ibn Shākir, *Fawāt*, 2/264.

sought, and shaykhs provided, benefit.[28] The point of seeking out a shaykh was to find benefit, and the point of taking on a disciple was to provide it.[29] Students and other seekers after knowledge were often called mustafīdīn, those who seek fāʾida, as teaching and reciting ḥadīth were called ifāda, providing benefit.[30] When a traveling scholar arrived in the city, he sought a place to "set himself up to benefit."[31] One grammarian fished for students by standing in front of the ʿĀdiliyya al-Kubrā and shouting to passers-by: "Is there anyone who would benefit, is there anyone who would become learned?"[32] When women taught other women, they "benefited" them.[33] In the biographical dictionaries, ifāda was probably the most common term for education itself. Fields of knowledge were rated for the benefit they provided their scholars. The study of ḥadīth, for example, was lauded by one of its partisans as "the most beneficial of all of the beneficial sciences (anfaʿ al-funūn an-nāfiʿa)."[34]

The elites of Damascus as elsewhere divided the social universe into insiders and outsiders. Here the principle of social division was not between the pure and the impure, or between the naturalness of the well bred and the affectation of the social climber, but rather between the beneficial and the useless. "The worst of people," quoted Ibn al-Ḥājj from a ḥadīth, "is a learned man who does not benefit others by his learning."[35] Moralists advised young people not to associate with anyone who would not bring them benefit and whom they would not benefit themselves. "It is important for the student to abandon socializing – this is the most critical thing a student may do, especially those without family (jins). The defect of socializing is that it is a waste of time without benefit (fāʾida)."[36]

Loyalties

Even more than in Sung China or the Latin West, where political relationships were also experienced as ties of affection, the political and social history of the medieval Middle East cannot be addressed without consideration of the

[28] For several examples among many of the description of teaching as benefit, see Ibn Nāṣir al-Dīn, BL MS, 13: "istafāda wʾafāda"; Ṣafadī, *Aʿyān*, 122b for a shaykh who sat on the steps of the Umayyad Mosque, "benefiting listeners (yanfaʿ aṭ-ṭālibīn)." A commonplace in a death-notice was "he sought out benefit and benefited [others]": see Ibn Khallikān, 2/366 for one example.

[29] See two admonitions by Ibn Jamāʿa: "If the person whose baraka you seek is obscure, then the nafʿ is all the greater, and what one gains from him is all the more complete"; "To get the nafʿ of the teacher, you should regard him as the very eye of perfection": Ibn Jamāʿa, 86–8.

[30] Ṣafadī, *al-Wāfī*, 13/457: "samiʿa bi-ifāda khālihi"; see also Ibn al-Ṣalāḥ, *Muqaddima*, 359.

[31] Ṣafadī, *al-Wāfī*, 4/76: "thumma qadima Dimashqa wʾantaṣaba lʾil-ifāda."

[32] "Hal min mustafīd hal min mutaʿallim": Shumaysī, *Madāris dimashq*, 134. See also Ibn Kathīr, 14/50 for an example of shaykhs seeking benefit from Ibn Taymiyya ("yataradid ilayhi al-akābir wʾal-aʿyān wʾal-fuqahā . . . yastafīdūna minhu").

[33] Ibn Kathīr, 14/189.

[34] Ibn al-Ṣalāḥ, *Muqaddima*, 75.

[35] Ibn al-Ḥājj, 1/65.

[36] Ibn Jamāʿa, 83.

history of sentiment.[37] In a monetized society in which warrior households continuously redistributed property and status, aᶜyān and amīrs could not inherit their socially or politically useful affiliations through legal mechanisms. Instead, both groups experienced their critical bonds as ties of intimacy. They especially valued practices rooted in patriarchal households that gave them useful intimacy with powerful men.[38]

The military had few or no hereditary affinities; neither did they have any legal or contractual ties to ruling groups. Rather, as mentioned above, soldiers acquired their critical relationships within households and commands. These ties were expressed in the language of household intimacy, a language that is surprisingly similar to that of the Latin West, but one which was all the more powerful for the absence of any form of *stabilitas loci*. We can see this especially in examining how socially and politically useful ties were conceived in terms of "love." There were several more or less interchangeable terms for love, including *ḥubb*, *maḥabba*, *mawadda*, and *tawaddud*. The significance of all these terms differs from sentimental love in the modern sense, and includes associations of "friendly feeling," and "esteem." It was closely allied to "friendship" (*ṣadāqa*), and had uses and meanings that were similar to *amicitia* in the Latin West. Powerful men displayed their love for others publicly through gifts, manṣabs, and honors. The formula for the favor of a powerful man for a client, one which appears again and again in the sources, was "he loved him and honored him" (aḥabbahu wᵓakramahu). Sovereigns expressed their relations to one another as bonds of love.[39] They also experienced their ties to their subjects as ties of love, as their subjects (in theory) loved them in return.[40] Within ruling groups, love was also the basis of political loyalty. Sulṭāns, governors, and amīrs did not command secretaries, amīrs, and shaykhs; rather, they "loved" them, as they loved members of their households.[41] In return, they pretended not to expect automatic obedience to their sovereign wills so much as voluntary service (khidma), itself represented as animated by love.[42] Given the constant formation and reformation of warrior factions around the households of amīrs and sulṭāns, "love" was as much an instrument of politics as it was an emotion.

As crucial as love was in establishing new ties, it was also disruptive. The

[37] The pioneering study in this regard is Mottahedeh, *Loyalty and Leadership*.

[38] Cf. Mottahedeh, *Loyalty and Leadership*.

[39] See for example the mawadda Berke Khan had for Baybars: Yūnīnī, 2/365. For some examples among many of the love of rulers or governors for their amīrs see Yūnīnī, 3/68; Ṣafadī, *Aᶜyān*, 25a; Ṣafadī, *al-Wāfī*, 11/196. For the love of an amīr for a bureaucrat: Ṣafadī, *al-Wāfī*, 5/14.

[40] For example see Jazarī, BN MS, 247.

[41] See Nuᶜaymī, 1/217 for the "love" Saladin had for his nephew (ibn ᶜamm) al-Malik al-Muẓaffar, leading him to grant him Ḥamā and eventually many other cities.

[42] For a few examples of hundreds that might be cited of rulers and amīrs who "loved" the ᶜulamāᵓ and other civilians, see Sibṭ Ibn al-Jawzī, *Mirᵓāt*, 8/647, 696, 702; Ṣafadī, *al-Wāfī*, 12/36; Ṣafadī, *Aᶜyān*, 84a; Yūnīnī, 2/354, 398, 4/67; Nuᶜaymī, 2/10. See the governor Tankiz's reception of a secretary returning from Cairo: "Greetings to one whom we love and who loves us (marḥaban bi-man nuḥibbuhu wa-yuḥibbunā)": Ṣafadī, *al-Wāfī*, 10/260.

"excessive" love the sulṭān conceived for a new client or mamlūk threatened his longer-serving supporters.[43] Ḥubb was also dangerous when political relations turned sexual, or vice versa. When Sulṭān Muḥammad Ibn Qalāwūn conceived a sexual passion for the son of one of his amīrs, and gave him the command of a thousand horse, this "excessive love" (*maḥabba ghāliyya*) was much resented.[44] From the perspective of established elites, love could cut across established loyalties dangerously. The learned elite feared the loyalties of the common people to holy men as *ḥubb ghālī*, excessive love, one that could lead to "disruptive" conflict (*taʿaṣṣub*).[45] When the followers of a ruler became the spiritual disciples of a shaykh, the love they bore the shaykh could be politically dangerous. The ruler of Mosul complained of a shaykh who attracted his entourage (*khawāṣṣ*), "they love him more than they love me."[46] Because of its utility and its danger, elites tried both to mobilize love for their own purposes and to control its effects when it was used by others.

Acquired relations of intimacy were also critical to aʿyān strategies of social survival. The aʿyān experienced their useful loyalties as love, and expressed them in similar language taken from the patriarchal household. As was true of warriors, shaykhs created their crucial loyalties from scratch through love. Shaykhs served amīrs and rulers because of their love for them, as amīrs and sulṭāns "loved" ʿilm and the ʿulamāʾ.[47] Shaykhs constructed their relations with one another, with their disciples, and between themselves and the rest of the population through bonds of love. Love could bring one shaykh into the intimate circle (*khūṣūṣiyya*) of another.[48] The love between two shaykhs could be so strong they would move from one city to another to be with one another.[49] Shaykhs would also "cleave to" the audiences of others out of love.[50] Young people in turn approached shaykhs, and gained benefit from them, through strategies of love. This is one reason why the disciples or admirers of a shaykh were represented as his *muḥibbūn* – those who loved him.[51] Shaykhs also "loved" dead shaykhs, as was the case of the physician

[43] See Ṣafadī, *al-Wāfī*, 10/299; Ibn al-ʿAdīm, *Zubda*, 151. [44] Ṣafadī, *Aʿyān*, 25a.
[45] Ṣafadī, *al-Wāfī*, 18/396. For excessive love of the common people for a holy man who reveled in dirt see Ibn Kathīr, 13/298. For a shaykh who experienced excessive love for another see Jazarī, BN MS, 4. [46] Ibn Shākir, 21/299: "wa-hum yuḥibūnahu akthar minī."
[47] Dhahabī, *Taʾrīkh al-Islām*, BL MS, 28; Jazarī, BN MS, 415.
[48] Subkī, Staatsbibliothek MS, 20; Subkī, *Ṭabaqāt*, 6/253 for love as a bond between shaykhs.
[49] Yūnīnī, 3/95. [50] Sibṭ Ibn al-Jawzī, *Mirʾāt*, 8/675–6.
[51] For two examples of the relationship between young people and their shaykhs as a tie of love, see Ṣafadī, *Aʿyān*, 14b, 17a. For two examples of muḥibbūn referring to followers or admirers see Dhahabī, *Taʾrīkh al-Islām*, BL MS, 56: "lahu aṣḥāb wa-muḥibbūn"; and Ibn Nāṣir al-Dīn, BL MS, 3: "lahu muḥibbūn minaʾl-ʿulamāʾ." Examples of the love of the population for the learned are frequent in the sources. Of Birzālī, for example, it was said that people of all groups (ṭawāʾif) loved him: Ibn Kathīr, 14/185. When Ibn Qudāma resided in Isfahan, so great was the love of the city for him that if he had wanted to rule it he could have: Ibn Rajab, 2/14. Another Damascene, Ibn al-Zamlakānī, was said to have excited love in the hearts of everyone who saw him: Ṣafadī, *al-Wāfī*, 4/215. The love that large numbers of people bore a shaykh was considered a kind of divine gift; of one shaykh it was said, "God made the love of him descend into the hearts of the people (wa-qad awqaʿa Allah maḥabbatahu fī qulūbiʾl-khalq)": Dhahabī, *Taʾrīkh al-Islām*, BL MS, 14.

who "became enamored" of Auicenna through loving his discourse.[52] Finally, shaykhs "loved" knowledge, and applied to it the language of affection that they applied to one another.[53] Amīrs and aᶜyān conceived of love in a similar manner, and made use of it to form their ever-shifting social networks.

Ties of service and attendance: khidma, mulāzama, taraddud, ṣuḥba

Both military and civilian elites understood their ties of loyalty, dependence, and reciprocal obligation as voluntary service or khidma. Unlike such forms of service in the Latin West as vassalage or the contract of the stipendiarii, the duties of khidma were not defined in a legal or contractual sense, nor were there formal ceremonies of homage associated with it, though the language by which it was expressed had a number of similarities.[54] Khidma referred in the first place to household ties, especially to the personal service of children and servants to their elders and masters, and to the obligations of hospitality.[55] Khidma also referred to service at courts, which were themselves structured as households, and in foundations, diwāns, and the retinues of powerful men.[56] With khidma as with ḥubb, elites made use of practices rooted in the patriarchal household to forge useful ties of intimacy.

Most ties of subordination or dependence were understood as khidma. The dependant or supporter, civilian or military, of a powerful man was known as his "servant" (*khādim*).[57] The court of the ruler was known as the khidma. Amīrs, mamlūks, and people who received stipends from a ruler were said to be in his service.[58] When one ruler supported another, his political support

[52] "Wa-kāna yuḥibbu kalāmaʾsh-shaykh Ibn Sīnā fiʾṭ-ṭibbi mughramān lah": Ṣafadī, *al-Wāfī*, 14/129.

[53] See for example the love for ḥadīth that mature men bore in Ibn al-Ṣalāḥ, *Muqaddima*, 75.

[54] On the contractual relationship of the stipendiarii to a ruling household see M. Chibnall, "Mercenaries and the *Familia Regis* under Henry I," *History* 62 (1977); Contamine, *War in the Middle Ages*, 90–1; J.O. Prestwich, "The Military Household of the Norman Kings," *English Historical Review* 96 (1981), 1–35.

[55] For a son who "served" his mother see Yūnīnī, 1/395. See the proverb: "There are four things which the superior man cannot disdain, even if he be an amīr: standing when meeting his father, service to a learned man one learns something from, asking questions about subjects one knows nothing about, and service to a guest": Ibn Jamāᶜa, 110.

[56] For the labor of a physician in a hospital (*bimāristān*) as khidma, see Ibn Abī Uṣaybiᶜa, 659; for the retinue of the sulṭān as his khidma see Ibn Shākir, *Fawāt*, 1/183.

[57] Nuᶜaymī, 1/532; Ibn Kathīr, 14/154. For a soldier (*jundī*) who entered the service of an amīr see Ṣafadī, *al-Wāfī*, 1/232; for a physician in the service of an envoy on a diplomatic mission see Ibn al-Ṣuqāᶜī, 78; for learned men, lecturers, poets, and literati in the service of sulṭāns or amīrs see Sibṭ Ibn al-Jawzī, *Mirʾāt*, 8/693–4, 743; Yūnīnī, 2/142; Jazarī, BN MS, 330; for an example of the relationship of an amīr to the sulṭān as khidma see Yūnīnī, 2/8; for an amīr in the service of a powerful civilian see Ṣafadī, *al-Wāfī*, 4/87; for the khidma, ordered by the sulṭān, of the qāḍī of Nablus to the emperor during his visit to Jerusalem see Ibn Wāṣil, 4/244; a physician in the bimāristān or a secretary in a diwān were thought of as being in khidma: Ṣafadī, *al-Wāfī*, 6/48, 18/515; Dhahabī, *Tāʾrīkh al-Islām*, BL MS, 86; Ibn Ḥajar, 1/76.

[58] For example, see the learned men, poets, and literati in the khidma of al-Malik al-Nāṣir, who received high stipends from him: Yūnīnī, 2/142. For amīrs and mamlūks in the khidma of the sulṭān see *Tāʾrīkh al-salāṭīn wa al-mulūk*, 74r.

was represented as service.[59] To support a contender in fitna, or to come to the aid of one's khushdāsh was to "enter his service."[60] An army's organization was not in formal regiments, but was conceived rather as the service of its various amīrs to its most powerful amīr.[61] Although it carried no contractual obligations, service was bound by reciprocal obligations: an amīr was never to forget his obligations to a mamlūk in his khidma.[62] Rulers and amīrs, themselves beneficiaries of the service of others, liked to represent their relationship to the learned as being one of service to them. Al-Malik al-Nāṣir Yūsuf said of his relationship to a shaykh he had appointed to the Ribāṭ al-Nāṣirī: "We did not make him the shaykh of this place so that he could serve us, but rather that we might serve him."[63] In a similar manner, the deputy sulṭān in Egypt put himself in the service of the ṣūfī shaykh al-Khaḍir al-Mehrānī, who had a following among the ruling amīrs of Egypt.[64] It was by such small symbolic reversals that the military maintained both the fiction of the sovereignty of religion and the reality of their ideological dependence on civilians.

The aᶜyān also conceived of their bonds to one another as ties of service. The aᶜyān served men to whom they were not related, and in turn expected service from those who owed them deference due to their learning.[65] Many of the aᶜyān of the city spent some time in the service of a great shaykh, and considered themselves to have life-long obligations to him.[66] The aᶜyān represented their service in the domain of knowledge as analogous to service to individuals or the courts of the powerful: shaykhs were in the khidma of knowledge.[67] Service among shaykhs was not restricted to education; nor

[59] One Ayyūbid ruler who supported another "served him excellently (khadamahu khidmatan ᶜaẓīma)": Sibṭ Ibn al-Jawzī, *Mirʾāt*, 8/618. The relationship of the bedouin leader ᶜĪsā Ibn al-Muhannā to Sunqur al-Ashqar was expressed as his service to him: Ibn Shākir, 21/243–4.

[60] "Jāʾa fī khidmatihi," said of one amīr during a fitna: Ibn Kathīr, 13/305; for the relationship of khidma to khushdāshiyya during a fitna ("huwa khushdāshī wa-anā fī khidmatih") see Jazarī, BN MS, 397.

[61] Jazarī, BN MS, 497, for amīrs' entry into the khidma of the commander of an army. For one example of how the organization of an army was conceived as the retinues of individuals rather than regiments, see Jazarī, BN MS, 559, for the arrival of the Egyptian army in Damascus in 698/1298–9. The people of Damascus described it by the names of the amīrs in it.

[62] Ibn Shākir, 21/38. See also Ibn Wāṣil, 4/255 for an account of the sulṭān's frequenting someone in gratitude for service to his uncle.

[63] "Mā jaᶜalnāhu shaykhan fī hādhāʾl-makān illā li-nakhdimahu lā li-yakhdimanā": Yūnīnī, 4/300. [64] Yūnīnī, 3/265.

[65] Makdisi sees the khādim as a servant to wealthy students or to lecturers: *The Rise of Colleges*, 222–3; Makdisi, "La corporation à l'époque classique de l'Islam," 204.

[66] See for example Ibn Jamāᶜa's detailed prescriptions for the service of shaykhs: the student must support the shaykh during the shaykh's lifetime, and look after his loved ones and family after his death, and undertake to visit his tomb and to pray for him: Ibn Jamāᶜa, 87–90. Some students served their shaykhs by living in their houses: Yūnīnī, 4/184. For Shaᶜrānī's later discussion of the role of khidma in ṣūfism – "he who draws near to his shaykh through acts of service draws near to God (man taqarraba ilā shaykhihi bʾil-khidam taqarrabaʾl-ḥaqqa taᶜālā)": Shaᶜrānī, *al-Anwār al-Qudsiyya fī maᶜrifa al-qawāᶜid al-ṣūfiyya*, Taha ᶜAbd al-Bāqī Sarūr and al-Sayyid Muhammad ᶜId al-Shāfiᶜī eds. (Beirut, n.d.), 2/16.

[67] Ṣafadī, *Aᶜyān*, 13a.

should we confuse it with servitude. It was a relationship that they entered upon willingly without expectation of material reward.[68] Even though service appears in the sources most frequently in the context of the relationship of young people to their shaykhs, it was also one dimension of a bond between shaykhs.[69] Service produced ties of deference and obligation between people for their lifetimes, but these ties did not extend beyond the tomb or attach themselves to lineages. After his death the followers of an important lecturer attended a lecture of his son, "as a service to him (khidmatan lahu)," but the son did not inherit the father's loyalties.[70]

Service was accompanied by a number of other forms of personal attendance, among them *mulāzama*, *ziyāra*, *taraddud*, and *ṣuḥba*. Scholars have studied these practices as aspects of higher education or everyday piety.[71] However, their social uses were more varied, and aʿyān and amīrs alike made use of them. Lāzama, which meant "he kept, confined himself, clave, clung, or held fast, to him," referred to the continuous physical propinquity of a follower to a powerful man. In the case of amīrs this produced advancement; in the case of shaykhs lāzama was a initiatic relationship that produced baraka.[72] Mulāzama was often associated with service, as in the case of the amīr who was ordered to the mulāzama and the service of Baybars.[73] It also expressed the tie between shaykhs and favored young people. Ibn Taymiyya, for example, impressed by a boy's performance in a session of Qurʾān interpretation, promised him: "If you cleave to me (lāzamanī) for a year, you will benefit."[74] Taraddud meant to "frequent" someone, often expressed in visits.[75] Where mulāzama implied constant propinquity, taraddud meant

68 For examples see the amīr who served one of the aʿyān: Ṣafadī, *al-Wāfī*, 4/87, and the group of young men who, upon hearing that an Andalusian ṣūfī was making the ḥajj, "went out to serve him (takharraja fī khidma)": Ṣafadī, *al-Wāfī*, 18/62. Ṣūfī shaykhs also received khidma from their followers: Ibn Kathīr, 14/151.

69 A shaykh attended a majlis given by a visitor to his town and served him: Sibṭ Ibn al-Jawzī, *Mirʾāt*, 8/768. One of the followers (aṣḥāb) of a shaykh accompanied him from Egypt, dwelt in the shaykh's madrasa, and served him for forty years: Abū Shāma, *Dhayl*, 207–11; another shaykh was known for his service to people in prayer: Ibn Rajab, 2/49.

70 Ibn Kathīr, 14/153. Zarnūjī advised students to treat their shaykhs' families with respect, and quoted with approval the example of a student who rose to his feet whenever the sons of his lecturer passed by: Zarnūjī, 33.

71 See for examples Berkey, *The Transmission of Knowledge*, 34–5; Makdisi, "Ṣuḥba et riyasa dans l'enseignement médiéval," in *Recherches d'Islamologie. Recueil d'articles offerts à Georges C. Anawati et Louis Gardet par leurs collègues et leurs amis* (Louvain, 1978).

72 Lane, *suppl.*, s.v. LZM. For examples see Yūnīnī, 3/46; for Sulṭān Baybar's mulāzama of his shaykh Khaḍir see Ṣafadī, *al-Wāfī*, 13/334; for the baraka gained by mulāzama or ṣuḥba see Jazarī, BN MS, 72.

73 Ibn Shākir, 21/37. Mulāzama also meant something like "take care of" as with the keeper of the clock at the Umayyad Mosque, whose labors were described as mulāzama: Ṣafadī, *al-Wāfī*, 14/128.

74 The boy did so, and reported later: "There fell upon me during his discourse benefits (fawāʾid) which I never heard from anyone else, nor encountered in a book": Ṣafadī, *al-Wāfī*, 7/22.

75 For two examples of the many that could be cited of taraddud, see Abū Shāma, *Dhayl*, 141, 179. See also the valorization of taraddud aṣ-ṣulaḥāʾ – frequenting the virtuous to seek baraka from them: Ṣafadī, *al-Wāfī*, 4/226.

regular contact. To "frequent" someone's doors was usually how those who had little power or prestige approached those who had. The civilians of the city who wanted to acquire some of the baraka and prestige of learning would "frequent" the ʿulamāʾ; and people who were in the ṣuḥba of one shaykh would "frequent" others.[76] As was the case with ṣuḥba, when powerful men "frequented" shaykhs, they showed to the world at large their dependence on them.[77]

Another way of acquiring socially useful ties was the visitation or ziyāra. Visitation was a nearly universal practice in the pre-modern Middle East, and Christians as well as Muslims practiced it.[78] Scholars have generally restricted their examination of ziyāra to the visitation of tombs in ṣūfism or popular religion. However, ziyāra included a much wider variety of practices of visiting people, living or dead, and sacred places, for the baraka to be gained from them. Almost all sections of the population, including rulers, sought baraka through visitation.[79]

Learned shaykhs were both practitioners of ziyāra and objects of it. Among the young and their shaykhs alike the ziyāra or the single visit to a scholar was at one end of a continuum of practices that ended on the other with the constant companionship of ṣuḥba and mulāzama.[80] Learned men with baraka and their tombs or birthplaces were objects of popular visitation, much as ṣūfīs were.[81] Fathers also took their sons to shaykhs for

[76] For one example of someone who frequented the ʿulamāʾ see Abū Shāma, *Dhayl*, 179.

[77] A sulṭān frequented an amīr who had served his uncle al-Malik al-Nāṣir: Ibn Wāṣil, 4/255; al-Malik al-Muʿaẓẓam frequented a scholar to read al-Zamakhsharī's grammar with him: Ibn Kathīr, 13/72.

[78] For Christian ziyāra as viewed by Muslim writers, see Yūnīnī, 3/111 for a priest who was sought out for his baraka; and Ibn Wāṣil, 4/244 for the pilgrimage of the emperor to the holy places during the truce of 626/1228–9 understood as ziyāra. The military incorporated ziyāra into their own relations. The tomb of Kutuz became an object of ziyāra after his death until Baybars made it inaccessible: Ibn Kathīr, 13/225–6. On ziyāra to holy places around Damascus see ʿAlī b. Abū Bakr al-Ḥarawī, *Kitāb al-ishārāt fī maʿrifat al-ziyārāt*, J. Sourdel-Thomine ed. (Damascus, 1953), trans. by J. Sourdel-Thomine as "Guide des lieux de pèlerinage" (Damascus, 1957). On ziyāra in Mamlūk Egypt see C. Taylor, "The Cult of the Saints in Late Medieval Egypt," Ph.D. Dissertation (Princeton University, 1989).

[79] For examples of rulers who made a visitation to learned shaykhs see Sibṭ Ibn al-Jawzī, *Mirʾāt*, 8/548, 616, 688; Yūnīnī, 2/142; Ṣafadī, *al-Wāfī*, 18/133; Ibn Kathīr 13/299.

[80] For evidence that these practices were imagined as a continuum, see Ibn Shākir, 21/299, for the holy man who grew food for "those who were of his ṣuḥba, those who frequented him, and those who visited him." See also Jazari, BN MS, 72 for a distinction made between ṣuḥba and mulāzama – "ṣāḥabahu aw lāzamahu."

[81] For an example of a ziyāra to a living scholar for his baraka see Ibn Kathīr, 14/4–5. Tombs of scholars visited included those of Ibn ʿArabī, Ibn Taymiyya, and Ibn ʿAsākir: Sibṭ Ibn al-Jawzī, *Mirʾāt*, 8/641; Ibn ʿAbd al-Hādī, Köp. MS, 134. For ziyāra to a shaykh's birthplace see Ibn Khallikān, 2/417. Abū ʿUmar Ibn Qudāma's tomb illustrates how a scholar and holy man's tomb became an object of veneration. He was buried by the roadside outside the city, and the place of his burial soon became an object of ziyāra. Al-Shāfiʿī was enlisted to approve the visitation of the tomb by his appearance in a dream declaring that he too visited Abū ʿUmar. Eventually a saying emerged that "he who visits the tomb of Abū ʿUmar on a Friday night, it is as though he has visited the kaʿba; take off your shoes before praying there": Abū Shāma, *Dhayl*, 74–5. See Ibn Ṭūlūn, *al-Qalāʾid al-jawhariyya*, for the posthumous fates of some of

baraka.[82] Young people who could not "cleave to" shaykhs or enter their service visited them to acquire their personal baraka or the baraka of their learning.

Shaykhs also made use of visitation to sanctify their bonds amongst themselves.[83] The ziyāra overlapped with traveling in search of ḥadīth, as scholars moved from place to place "visiting" other scholars.[84] The learned also represented their socializing with one another as a form of ziyāra.[85] Ziyāras of this nature could have (and one suspects often did) political uses, as in the visitation of Ibn al-Ṣalāḥ to Sibṭ Ibn al-Jawzī, the point of which was to seek his intercession with the ruler.[86] Becoming an object of visitation was also a sign of distinction. To the learned elite, having visitors arrive from the four quarters (*al-afāq*) was one of the highest marks of scholarly prestige.[87] Such people in turn were constrained by the obligations of hospitality. One shaykh, known for treating the amīrs, poor people, the rich, and the powerless equally, greeted them all with a single formula: "Your khidma has brought us joy – how blessed is this hour."[88] Like mulāzama, khidma, and taraddud, ziyāra was a practice that transmuted propinquity into useful intimacy.

Another practice by which military and civilian elites constructed social bonds was ṣuḥba.[89] Together with mulāzama and service, references to ṣuḥba in the sources are so frequent that it is easy to become blinded by their

these twelfth- and thirteenth-century scholars in the early sixteenth century, when their tombs were visited and venerated in a manner similar to the ziyāra to tombs of ṣūfīs. Living scholars were also objects of popular veneration. This was the fate of the Ḥanbalī scholar Muwaffaq al-Dīn Ibn Qudāma, brother of the above. Expelled from Damascus for his uncompromising advocacy of Ḥanbalī theology, while living "in obscurity" in Cairo he nonetheless found it difficult to walk to the mosque for the number of people who awaited him in the streets to seek his baraka: Ibn Rajab, 2/14. The same was true of Ibn Taymiyya, who after his release from prison became an object of ziyāra: Ibn Kathīr, 14/47. See also the shaykh in Ḥimṣ who held two majālis, one for the ṭalaba al-ʿilm, and the other for the groups (*wufūd*) who came to visit: al-Ṣafadī, *al-Wāfī*, 6/79. For the ziyāra to the shaykh Ibn Qawām see Ṣafadī, *al-Wāfī*, 10/245; Ibn Shākir, *Fawāt*, 1/224. Funerals of the major scholars of the city were often major events, attended by much of the population: see L. Frescobaldi, *Viaggi in Terra Santa di Lionardo Frescobaldi e d'altri del secolo XIV* (Florence, 1862), 28, on funerals he witnessed in Damascus in 1384–5: "Hanno di costume quando e'muore uno cittadino da bene de farlo seppellire a'loro cimiteri, che sono fuori della terra in un campo . . . ed acompagnarlo gran numero di cittadini, secondo la condizione dell'uomo." [82] See for example Yunīnī, 3/191.

[83] For people among the learned who made ziyāras, see Sibṭ Ibn al-Jawzī, *Mirʾāt*, 8/457, 614. For an expedition to a holy man, see the ziyāra made by a group of eighteen who visited a holy man and stayed with him for a month: Yūnīnī, 1/405.

[84] See Ibn Khallikān, 3/294: "No one visited Irbil without hastening to visit shaykh (bādara ilā ziyāra) . . . Ibn al-Mubārak, and they approached his heart from all directions." The shaykh was learned in ḥadīth and its ancillary sciences, and a large number of other fields.

[85] Sibṭ Ibn al-Jawzī, *Mirʾat*, 8/747; Yūnīnī, 2/54, 330; Ibn Shākir, *Fawāt*, 1/73 of the Cairo 1951 edition. [86] Sibṭ Ibn al-Jawzī, *Mirʾāt*, 8/758.

[87] See for example Ṣafadī, *al-Wāfī*, 22/299. [88] Jazarī, BN MS, 369.

[89] On ṣuḥba see Makdisi, *The Rise of Colleges*, 128–33; Makdisi, "Ṣuḥba et riyasa," 207–11. Makdisi was the first scholar to raise the importance of ṣuḥba to Islamic education, but has restricted his interest so far largely to the teacher-student relationship. Berkey, *The Transmission of Knowledge*, 34–5, has largely followed Makdisi on the issue. However, looking at ṣuḥba solely in the context of education or as a form of "discipleship" misses many of its wider meanings and uses.

ubiquity. Ṣuḥba is usually translated as "companionship" or "fellowship," and can often be translated verbally, such as "he began accompanying someone," or "he joined someone." Its meanings and uses, however, were wider than that which is implied by companionship or fellowship, and ranged from affiliation to a group to subordination to a powerful individual. Among aᶜyān and amīrs alike ṣuḥba was the basis of the temporary groups that constituted the main social networks of the city.[90] The political elite represented its social bonds as the pairing of ṣuḥba to khidma. When the bedouin leader ᶜĪsā Ibn al-Muhannā allied himself to Baybars, the sources wrote that he entered his ṣuḥba and his khidma.[91] Factional affiliation was thought of as a tie of ṣuḥba, and ṣuḥba was itself one of the most common words for faction.

Ṣuḥba, like service, was considered a duty that carried with it the considerable obligations of hospitality. An anecdote quoted for its moral value recounted the dilemma of a Muslim holy man taken prisoner by Crusader bandits (*ḥarāmiyya*). In the middle of the night, tied up while his captors were sleeping, he heard some Muslim bandits approaching. Although he could have saved himself by raising the alarm, he woke his captors and went into hiding with them. When they asked him why he saved them when he could have been freed, he replied, "It was because I was your companion (ṣaḥibtukum) and ate your bread. Truly ṣuḥba is a mighty thing (innaʾṣ-ṣuḥba ᶜazīza)."[92]

Ṣuḥba referred to a variety of loyalties among the civilian elite, including ties between a civilian and an amīr, ties among the civilian elite, and ties between older and younger men. Even though it can be translated "friendship, discipleship, companionship, affiliation," it implied the attendance of one person on the person of another. As ṣuḥba and khidma referred to the critical political bonds among the military, they were also paired among civilians, as in the case of the shaykh whose companions (*aṣḥāb*) served him.[93] Ṣuḥba was one of the fundamental means by which people acquired their useful loyalties. Ṣuḥba was also the basis of the temporary scholarly factions that were the critical groups of the learned.[94]

Young people became shaykhs through the ṣuḥba of a single shaykh and his disciples, just as a mamlūk entered the ṣuḥba of his ustādh.[95] The follower of a

[90] For an example of one civilian who entered the ṣuḥba of al-Malik al-Muᶜaẓẓam ᶜIsā, see Ibn Abī Uṣaybiᶜa, 646. For a shaykh in the ṣuḥba of an amīr: Ibn Shākir, 21/63–4; Yūnīnī, 3/106. For an amīr in the ṣuḥba of shaykhs see Ṣafadī, *Aᶜyān*, 121a. A shaykh could be both ṣāḥib and ṣadīq or friend to another: Sibṭ Ibn al-Jawzī, *Mirʾāt*, 8/718; Yūnīnī, 3/136. Ṣuḥba as a bond between shaykhs: one shaykh reported that "I went to him again and again because of the ṣuḥba that was between us": Subkī, *Ṭabaqāt*, 6/228.

[91] Ibn Shākir, 21/243–4. [92] Sibṭ Ibn al-Jawzī, *Mirʾāt*, 8/689. [93] Yūnīnī, 4/151.

[94] For ṣuḥba as a scholarly faction defined by its loyalty to a single individual see the fate of Manbijī's ṣuḥba after the death of Baybars in Ibn Kathīr, 14/57, and of ᶜAbd al-Ghanī Ibn Qudāma's ṣuḥba, who suffered during the fitna surrounding his trial: Ibn Rajab, 2/19. For a scholar who attained a high position (rutba ᶜāliyya) by virtue of his ṣuḥba of a shaykh see Subkī, *Ṭabaqāt*, 6/44.

[95] For an example of how people became learned through the initiatory power of ṣuḥba, see Yūnīnī, 3/203: "ṣaḥiba jamāᶜa minaʾl-ᶜulamāʾ wʾal-mashāyakh." According to Ibn Jamāᶜa, the point of residing in a mudrasa was muṣāḥaba al-fuḍalāʾ: Ibn Jamāᶜa, 220. Medical education was also conceived of as ṣuḥba: see Ibn Abī Uṣaybiᶜa, 637.

shaykh was his ṣāḥib, and group loyalties were understood as ṣuḥba.[96] To Damascenes, ṣuḥba created loyalties more intimate and useful than the formal group affiliations they may have had. The ṣuḥbas of famous shaykhs, for example, cut across madhhab lines.[97] When the sons of the aᶜyān encountered scholars brought in from outside the city, they forged and sanctified their ties through ṣuḥba.[98] Some considered ṣuḥba to be exclusive, as was the case of the shaykh who forbade his disciples (*murīds*) to enter the ṣuḥba of anyone else, for fear that they might be endangered.[99]

What unites these various practices is that they engendered loyalties among elites who otherwise had few useful ties to one another. Aᶜyān and amīrs alike both faced the problem of constructing alliances in a society that was considerably more monetized than the Latin West, one in which wealth, power, and status were constantly reshuffled. The elites of Damascus made social and political use of such household ties. These ties had their origins in the patriarchal household, but they were also strategies by which a resourceful elite formed its critical groups. Thus within the domain of knowledge civilians acquired loyalties similar to those the military realized in the domains of war and fitna.

Imitation

ᶜIlm, the sources repeat again and again, was a form of baraka, and as with other sources of baraka, Damascenes of all types labored to acquire it. Some among the learned were objects of popular practices for the incorporation of baraka. Damascenes seeking "benefit" and baraka drank the water in which Ibn Taymiyya did his ablutions; and after his death some vied to drink the water with which his corpse was washed.[100] Another example was the wealthy Damascene who acquired ᶜAbd al-Ghanī Ibn Qudāma's robe, intending to use it as his own burial shroud. People who fell ill or suffered headaches wore the robe and were cured by its baraka.[101] Use of such objects for their baraka was little different from other widely practiced ways of seeking useful grace.

Young people became disciples of their shaykhs for the baraka to be gained from them and to imitate them to gain exemplarity. The jurists who wrote our

96 For example, see the lecturer who dropped his manṣabs and entered the ṣuḥba of the antinomian ḥarāfīsh: Ibn Kathīr 13/314.

97 Ibn Rajab, 2/95. For Ḥanbalīs, Ḥanafīs, and Mālikīs joining the other followers of an esteemed Shāfiᶜī shaykh, see Ṣafadī, *al-Wāfī*, 21/341.

98 This was true of Ibn ᶜAsākir's relationship to Ibn al-Ṣalāḥ al-Shahrazūrī, and of ᶜIzz al-Dīn Ibn al-Qalānisī's relationship to Tāj al-Dīn al-Kindī, both of which were relationships of ṣuḥba between sons of established families and scholars brought in by rulers. ᶜIzz al-Dīn's relationship to al-Kindī was described thus: "ṣaḥiba shaykhanā Tāj al-Dīn wa-kāna mulāziman lahu wʾantafaᶜa bih": Sibṭ Ibn al-Jawzī, *Mirʾāt*, 8/631.

99 He cautioned his followers: "The patient consults a single physician, who prescribes medicine for him, and if another physician were also to participate in caring for him it might lead to the death of the patient": Yūnīnī, 4/79.

100 Ibn ᶜAbd al-Hādī, Köp. MS, 133; Ibn Shākir, *Fawāt*, 1/76 of the Cairo 1951 edition.

101 Ibn Rajab, 2/27.

sources advised young people to submit themselves to their shaykhs and to model themselves consciously after them. Learned people advised the young to model themselves not just on the moral and intellectual example of their shaykhs, but also on the shaykhs' "ḥarakāt wa-sukna," or "movements and stillnesses," words which in this instance as in others echoed the vowelizing of texts ("ḥarakāt wa-sukūn").[102] To Aḥmad Ibn Ibrāhīm al-Wāsiṭī, "the student must love guidance, as the teacher must love to guide. This condition is legally binding on them."[103] Ibn Jamāᶜa wrote that in relation to their shaykhs, students should be "as the sick man is to the expert physician."[104] He wrote his book of advice to the young partly to affirm the mimetic character of their ties to their shaykhs, quoting with approval one of the companions of the Prophet: "O my son, cleave to the ᶜulamāʾ and the fuqahāʾ, and learn from them and acquire their adab; for that is preferable to me than your learning many ḥadīth."[105] One reason that writers reassured the young that they should not be too troubled by errors their shaykhs committed was to put the importance of the imitation of shaykhs over and above the knowledge their shaykhs conveyed. Wherever the shaykh points the student, there the student should follow, and set aside his own opinion, "for the error of the guide (murshid) is more beneficial than being correct himself – as was the case with Moses and Khiḍr. In spite of Moses' great rank he kept silent."[106] The shaykh was as much a model of bodily norms as he was a carrier of truths. Training of the self and shaping its presentation was an important part of the capital of young people: adab was "the inheritance of the prophets," by which they "attained the first rank."[107]

When dealing with pre-modern agrarian societies, historians are apt to give tradition a large role in explaining cultural practices. And there is no doubt that in Damascus the imitation of cultural exemplars was one of the critical social practices of the city's elites. Yet despite their frequent invocation of the past, what is striking about the greatest shaykhs is the frequency with which writers praised their inventiveness and individual virtuosity. Exemplary shaykhs were carefully scrutinized, and their slightest deviation from established practice was noted and queried. When Ibrāhīm Ibn ᶜAbd al-Wāḥid went to the mosque, his concern for ritual purity was as inventive as it was scrupulous: "Whenever he pulled a hair from his beard, or whatever he picked from his nose, he put it in his turban; whenever he sharpened a reed-pen, he was careful that the shavings did not fall." When he discovered a spot of dust

102 "The student must support his teacher during his life, and look after his relatives and loved ones after his death, and undertake the visiting of his tomb . . . and follow his path (yaslik maslakahu), and preserve his way in ᶜilm and dīn, and be guided by his movements and his stillnesses (ḥarakāt wa-sukna) in his customs and manner of worship, and adopt his adab, and never abandon being guided by it": Ibn Jamāᶜa, 90.

103 Quoted in Ibn ᶜAbd al-Hādī, Köp. MS, 113.

104 Ibn Jamāᶜa, 87. For another example of the fairly common association of the shaykh with the physician, see Ibn al-Ḥājj, 1/117. For another reading of these passages by Ibn Jamāᶜa, see Berkey, *The Transmission of Knowledge*, 36–9.

105 Ibn Jamāᶜa, 2. 106 Ibn Jamāᶜa, 88. 107 Ibn Jamāᶜa, 2.

on his robe in the mosque, he would depart to clean it off. In prayer, Ibrāhīm raised his voice during the takbīr, contrary to the local practice. When an onlooker pointed out to him that the local practice followed the example of the Prophet and gave a ḥadīth as evidence for his view, Ibrāhīm countered with a ḥadīth of his own which seemed to support his way of doing things.[108]

Ibrāhīm's transgression cast him paradoxically as an arbiter of the practices by which the aʿyān gained their distinction. This standing outside the rules appears again and again in the biographies of the learned men of the city. Through such epigrammatic gestures the aʿyān gained distinction not by imitating cultural forms but by gently transgressing them, thereby casting themselves as arbiters of the ordinary rules of interaction. Shaykhs did not duplicate an unchanging body of cultural forms. Rather, they struggled to acquire a sense of deportment that allowed them to manipulate these apparently fixed cultural forms gracefully and naturally, much as athletes or musicians repeat single movements in ever-changing situations. Also like athletes and musicians, they lauded unexpected virtuosity in the use of an apparently invariable "tradition."[109]

Mastery of the text so that it could be produced instantly and faultlessly from memory, and the constant companionship and service of the shaykh, had a similar object. The goal was virtuosity and what we would call "naturalness" in public performances, as much as trained competence in specific fields of knowledge. This may be why praise of deftness in difficult and unexpected situations was such a constant refrain, and why error-free ease in public performances was so highly valued.[110] Memory and imitation had, and were put to, similar uses.

The advantage in this kind of initiation went to those exposed to great

[108] Ibn Rajab, 2/98.

[109] For other examples of such virtuousity, see Nawawī's apparently eccentric refusal to eat fruit or enter a bath, which he justified in a similar manner: Ibn ʿAbd al-Hādī, *Ṭabaqāt*, 4/256–7; also the shaykh who fasted only on the sixth of Shawwāl and who wore the clothing and cap he slept in to prayers at the mosque, "astonishing the common people." He transgressed his own norms by wearing the ṭaylasān during the procession of the sulṭān through the city, "astonishing" his son and justifying it by similar unassailable counter-intuitive logic: Subkī, *Ṭabaqāt*, 6/173–4. Other examples: Abū Shāma lauded Ibn ʿAsākir for "his own characteristic manner" of reading fatwās: Abū Shāma, *Dhayl*, 37. A noted shaykh never changed his cotton robe or turban: Ibn Shākir, *Fawāt*, 2/82. A pious and famous shaykh, when standing in the miḥrāb of a masjid, thrice demanded that those in attendance depart and perform their ablutions: Jazarī, BN MS, 369–70. A shaykh refused to eat or to speak to anyone until after the evening prayer: Jazarī, BN MS, 505–6. A shaykh would spend the night at the head of John the Baptist in the Umayyad Mosque, and at dawn went home with his clogs in his hand: Jazarī, BN MS, 195. See also Subkī, Staatsbibliothek MS, 46 on an eccentric style of writing.

[110] For examples of the praise of virtuosity displayed through writing, lecturing, or memorizing effortlessly and quickly, or speaking and quoting without preparation, see Ibn al-Ṣalāḥ, *Muqaddima*, 208; Abū Shāma, *Dhayl*, 131; Yūnīnī, 2/55–6; Nuʿaymī, 1/250; Subkī, *Ṭabaqāt*, 5/14, 6/170, 200, 201; Ibn Kathīr, 14/46; Ibn Rajab, 2/91; Ibn ʿAbd al-Hādī, Köp. MS, 3. The effect of such displays of memory on their audiences can be seen in a typical reaction of an onlooker to one: "I couldn't control my astonishment at what I saw": Ibn Shākir, *Fawāt*, 1/159.

shaykhs at young ages. It was also why lineages able to pass on ʿilm to their offspring had such an advantage in imparting to them the whole package of signs and emblems associated with knowledge. The ideal was something like the early life of the Ibn Taymiyya, who was "raised in the best way, in the rooms of the ʿulamāʾ, drinking from the cups of understanding, cavorting in the fields of learning (tafaqquh) and in the trees of books."[111] Fathers also reinforced what their offspring learned from shaykhs. Subkī described how his father encouraged his discipleship of Mizzī, with whom the father had long associated. "Whenever I came home from a meeting with Mizzī, my father would say, 'you have arrived home from the shaykh.' He would explain the shaykh's expressions in a loud voice, and I am certain that he did so because he wanted to fix [Mizzī's] greatness in my heart and encourage me in [my] discipleship."[112]

The ritualization of knowledge

As with the ritual practices of many other societies, the cultivation of knowledge joined together fundamental oppositions and correspondences in a sanctified space and time.[113] The biographical dictionaries convey numerous examples of the majlis al-ʿilm uniting the inner and the outer, the individual and the collective, the origin and the outcome, the ritually pure and the true.

Damascenes together with many other medieval Middle Eastern peoples imagined the world as polarized between purity and pollution. Purity was associated with the sunna, truth, moral conduct, good government, the boundaries of the community of Muslims, the absence of fitna (itself conceived as pollution), and the social honor of elites.[114] Shaykhs tested all vehicles of baraka for ritual purity, and guarded them against pollution. Shaykhs ordered nursing women not to eat ḥarām foods, lest children lose the "baraka of the milk."[115] As the literate elite looked to ʿilm as their prime source of baraka, they cared for it as they cared for other sacred substances, and protected the purity of its vehicles of transmission.

The conflation of ʿilm and purity caused shaykhs to describe transactions of knowledge in the same terms as other ritual transactions that demanded

[111] Ibn ʿAbd al-Hādī, Köp. MS, 3. [112] Subkī, *Ṭabaqāt*, 6/253.

[113] For a review of social science literature on ritual see C. Bell, *Ritual Theory, Ritual Practice* (Oxford, 1992).

[114] Examples of how the world was imagined in terms of purity and pollution include the association of scholarly fitna with pollution: Subkī, Staatsbibliothek MS, 9; the conflation of the sunna with purity: Ibn al-Ḥājj; 2/87, Ibn al-Ṣalāḥ, *Fatāwā*, 1/401–2; the prayer (*duʿā*) to "purify our tongues from lies": Ibn Rajab, 2/100; God "purified" all of Syria: Qalqashandī, 12/22, as Damascus under a good ruler was "pure"; Sibṭ Ibn al-Jawzī, *Mirʾāt*, 8/740, and a good ruler "purified" his realm: Sibṭ Ibn al-Jawzī, *Mirʾāt*, 8/595; Nuʿaymī, 1/610. Muslims were "the partisans of God (*al-ḥaqq*) who . . . are purified": Qalqashandī, 12/353, as Franks were polluting: Ibn al-Ṣuqāʿī, 12–13. On the association of purity with social honor see Yūnīnī, 2/56. Appointments from the sulṭān were seen as pollutions: Ibn Kathīr, 14/43, 109.

[115] Ibn al-Ḥājj, 4/295.

purity: "Just as prayer – which is the [form of] worship of the external body (ʿibāda al-jawāriḥ al-ẓāhira) – is not valid until after the purification of the exterior from pollution . . . If the heart is made ready for ʿilm, then its baraka will appear and it will increase as the plowed earth will produce and thrive; if it be corrupted, then the body will be corrupted in its entirety."[116] At Ibn Taymiyya's Friday morning session in Qurʾān interpretation, those in attendance benefited from the "baraka of his prayer (duʿā) and the purity of his person (ṭahāra anfāsihi) . . . the purity of his exterior and interior (wa ṣafā ẓāhirihi wa-bāṭinihi), and the agreement of his words and deeds."[117] Similarly, in the transmission of ḥadīth, the ḥadīth-transmitter was told both to be in a state of ritual purity and to "purify his heart from worldly ambitions and their pollutions (aghrāḍ ad-dunyāwiyya wʾadnāsuhā)."[118] A particularly pious shaykh could be known as a *muṭahhur* – one who purifies by his very presence.[119]

Objects used in the transmission of ʿilm excited some of the ritual fastidiousness that ritual objects inspired. As the shaykh giving the dars should attain a state of ritual purity, so books, ink, and paper transmitting ʿilm were to be made of pure materials. Writers advised booksellers to inquire into the probity of people they purchased books from, to protect the "purity" (*ṭahāra*) of the buyers. They were not to sell or buy books to or from anyone who contradicted the sharīʿa.[120] These writers also advised copyists to perform ablutions before copying.[121] Inks were to be made from ritually pure materials.[122] Shaykhs also worried about the purity of paper. They promised that copyists fastidious about obtaining unpolluted writing materials would gain a reward in the afterlife (*thawāb*) and baraka.[123] One mid-seventh-century fatwā addressed the question whether paper-makers could use the ashes of polluted substances to dry paper in the manufacturing process.[124] Another writer advised copyists to ensure that their paper was not made in enterprises in which workers "uncovered their private parts," as workers often wore a kind of loincloth which "failed the demands of modesty."[125] Moreover, writers advised copyists to be careful not to purchase recycled paper that had once contained sacred texts or the names of prophets, angels, the companions of the prophets, or the ʿulamāʾ. Paper that had sacred things written on it was not to be pulped again, because it would either end up underfoot while being pulped or be overwritten.

As the learned considered themselves vessels of ʿilm, they admonished one

116 Ibn Jamāʿa, 67. 117 Ibn ʿAbd al-Hādī, *Ṭabaqāt*, 4/286.

118 Ibn al-Ṣalāḥ, *Muqaddima*, 359, 363.

119 Birzālī, *Muʿjam al-shuyūkh*, Ẓāhiriyya MS, 21a. 120 Ibn al-Ḥājj, 4/80.

121 Ibn al-Ḥājj, 4/85. For a similar sentiment, see Ibn Jamāʿa, 173: "If one copies a portion of a book in fiqh, then one must be in a state of purity as if ready for prayer (mustaqbal al-qibla), pure of body and of robe, with pure ink (bi-ḥibr ṭāhir)." Of course, that jurists associated the transmission of ʿilm with ritual purity did not mean that they succeeded. See al-Nāsikh al-Fārisī, whose passion for the grape – "he did not depart from it for even an hour" – did not interfere with his reputation as a copyist: Sibṭ Ibn al-Jawzī, *Mirʾāt*, 8/759.

122 Ibn al-Ḥājj, 4/89; Ibn Jamāʿa, 173. 123 Ibn al-Ḥājj, 4/82.

124 Ibn al-Ṣalāḥ, *Fatāwā*, 1/222–3. 125 Ibn al-Ḥājj, 4/81–2.

another to be alert to the dangers of pollution. Even though the ʿulamāʾ were not a closed caste of Brahmins, some occupations degraded them through something like pollution: "The learned man should keep away from the basest professions, because they are despicable according to both revelation and custom, such as the art of cupping (*hijāma*), dyeing, money changing, and gold-smithing."[126] Writers advised young people and their shaykhs to attain a state of ritual purity before transmitting ʿilm: "The student should enter into the shaykh's presence in a state of ritual perfection (kāmil al-hayʾa) pure of body and of dress (muṭahhar al-badan wʾath-thiyāb) . . . especially when a student goes into a majlis al-ʿilm."[127] So too the shaykh: "When a learned man decides to hold a lecture, he should purify himself from pollution (al-ḥadath wʾal-ḥabath) . . . by way of exalting ʿilm and the sharīʿa."[128]

When writers associated ʿilm with purity, this was just one way they conceived of the cultivation of ʿilm as a ritual practice. As the learned compared ʿilm to prayer, so they associated the transmission of knowledge with other collective liminal experiences.[129] Ibn Jamāʿa quoted a ḥadīth that made one such explicit link: "He who would wish to know the character of the audiences of the prophets, let him look to the audiences of the learned."[130] The first lecture was said to be the teaching of the Qurʾān, either *talqīnan* (one-to-one "inculcation," a term associated with the transmission of knowledge [maʿrifa] among ṣūfīs and with memorization more broadly) or on a paper or board.[131] The lecture itself was a partly ritual occasion, one that "provided baraka" to its audience.[132] Ibn al-Ḥājj provides the most detailed description of the lecture from the period. His descriptions were prescriptive in ways we find difficult to fathom; at the very least, he intended to criticize the practices of other legal schools and what he saw as the corruptions of his time. But from him we can at least learn how these practices were valorized as socially useful cultural ideals, if not how the actual practices were in all cases played out. Ibn al-Ḥājj's description of the dars is worth quoting at some length, not only because it is the most detailed description of the dars available, but also because he demonstrates how some among the learned elite sought to associate one of their critical rituals with the sacred power of other rituals:

When the Qurʾān-reciter finishes, [the lecturer] is to recite the fātiḥa [the first verse in the Qurʾān], taking refuge thereby from Satan, protecting the audience from his evil in the audience. Then God should be named, because Satan abandons everything that begins

126 Ibn Jamāʿa, 19; see also R. Brunschwig, "Métiers vils dans l'Islam," *SI* 16 (1967), 41–60.

127 Ibn Jamāʿa, 95.

128 Ibn Jamāʿa, 30. See Jazarī, BN MS, 375, for a majlis known for its purity; also Ṣafadī, *al-Wāfī*, 13/63 for a sixth-century shaykh in Marwarūdh renowned for never giving a dars except in a state of purity: "kāna lā yulqīʾd-dars ilā ʿalāʾṭ-ṭahāra."

129 For one association of ʿilm to prayer see Ibn Jamāʿa, 64: the faḍīla of ʿilm is superior (*afḍal*) to prayer in a Friday mosque; by it the *sharaf* (nobility or eminence) of the world and the hereafter is acquired. 130 Ibn Jamāʿa, 11. 131 Ibn al-Ḥājj, 1/94.

132 See for one example Ibn Khallikān, 2/374. A very typical account of a visit to a study-circle mentioned the baraka obtained in it: "I happened to attend a study-circle he presided over, and experienced his baraka as something amazing (jalastu ʿindahu fī ḥalqa marāran fa-wajadtu min barakatihi shayʾ ʿaẓīm)": Ṣafadī, *al-Wāfī*, 5/11.

with the naming of God, and his presence is banned. Then [he should] pray for the Prophet because it will bring baraka to his audience. Then he should express his satisfaction with the companions [of the Prophet], because they are the foundation upon which all is built. Then he should say lā ḥawl wa-lā quwwa illā lʾillah three times, or seven if possible, as the correct among the ʿulamāʾ do. Then he should consign his affairs to God and put his trust in his guidance (yatawakkul). He should . . . clear his mind of all [the fruits of] his knowledge, understanding, studying, and conversations – so that now [it is as though] he knows nothing. If God were to reveal some knowledge to him, it is from God, and not from his own past reading, studying, and thinking. He should ask the aid of God in avoiding slips of the tongue, the insinuations of Satan, and mistakes and corruptions. Then he should discourse on whatever knowledge he has acquired concerning the issue that the Qurʾān-reciter has read. He should cover what the ʿulamāʾ have said on the matter. He should survey their doctrines, and then he should go over the foundations in the Qurʾān and the sunna upon which they constructed their judgments. When he discusses the ʿulamāʾ, he should be gentle and express satisfaction with them. He should also discourse on the ʿulamāʾ according to their rank, virtue, and precedence. As Abū Ḥanīfa said, "relating stories about the learned and sitting in attendance upon them (mujālasatihim) is preferable to me than much learning (fiqh), because they represent the adab of the people and their morals too." Then he should advance the position of his school and support it, on condition that he refrain from partisanship [by imputing] error to authorities not of his school. For example, if you are a Mālikī do not permit the defects of al-Shāfiʿī or other authorities to register with you. They are the physicians of your religion. Whenever something in religion gets crooked, they fix it. When you fall into error they have the medicine to cure you. Physicians have various courses of treatment. When you go to a physician and get from him a course of treatment, this does not mean that you despise other physicians.[133]

The learned associated themselves with other forms of ritual power by linking their ʿilm to ṣūfism. One way they did this was by casting themselves as "true" ṣūfīs or *ahl al-dhikr*.[134] The learned elite were often ṣūfīs themselves, and identified with ṣūfism in a number of ways, but they still competed with ṣūfīs for the capacity to represent ʿilm.[135] When Taqī al-Dīn al-Subkī

[133] Ibn al-Ḥājj, 1/115–17. For similar advice concerning sessions of ḥadīth transmission see Ibn al-Ṣalāḥ, *Muqaddima*, 363–7.

[134] Ibn al-Ḥājj, 1/89: "It is the ʿulamāʾ who are meant by the term ahl al-dhikr by the Qurʾānic verse, 'if you do not know something, ask the ahl al-dhikr'". He also quoted a ḥadīth: "Sitting in attendance upon learned men is preferable to God than a thousand years of worship (ʿibāda)."

[135] This competition went both ways, as ṣūfīs appropriated the authority of ʿilm and the learned tried to appropriate the immediacy and significance of ṣūfī maʿrifa. Ṣūfīs themselves had a long tradition of associating maʿrifa with ʿilm. Qushayrī for example said that every ʿilm was a maʿrifa and every maʿrifa an ʿilm, and every ʿārif (i.e. ṣūfī) was an ʿālim: Rosenthal, *Knowledge Triumphant*, 166. Al-Sarāj called ṣūfism the "ʿilm al-bāṭin" (Rosenthal, 181), and ʿilm itself was experienced as a kind of ʿishq, a physical love felt for the divine (Rosenthal, 241, quoting Ibn Qayyim al-Jawziyya's *Rawḍa al-Muḥibbīn*). Rosenthal, 177, wrote that ṣūfīs "tried very strenuously to appear as a 'science' as well as keep in step with the various scientific views of the meaning of knowledge." Ibn al-Ḥājj tried to associate the dars with the liminality of ṣūfī dhikr and the majālis of the Prophet, while keeping the subject matter devoted to fiqh: "The majlis of ʿilm should be a majlis of the permitted and forbidden (ḥalāl and the ḥarām, i.e., its

enumerated in a poem the various fields of knowledge, he related to his readers that the object of learning was "to seek by your ʿilm the face of God."[136] Some argued that the cultivation of ʿilm was a collective invocation of God (dhikr) similar to worship (*ʿibāda*), or to other occasions in which baraka was to be gained.[137] This association of ʿilm with worship and baraka was partly to compete with ṣūfism, by demonstrating that the ʿilm of the ʿulamāʾ was "true" knowledge, and that the ritual cultivation of ʿilm rivaled the liminality of ṣūfī dhikr. The learned advised young people to imagine the lecture as a ritual occasion similar to the dhikr: "The student must empty his heart of all corruption, impurity (*danas*), envy, and false belief in order to receive knowledge, remember it, and be able to meditate on its meanings and the depths of its truth. Knowledge – as someone has said – is the prayer of the innermost self (ṣalā as-sirr), and the worship of the heart (ʿibāda al-qalb), and the vehicle of the inner truth (qurba al-bāṭin)."[138]

An anecdote related by Ibn al-Ḥājj illustrates the association of patrimony, knowledge, and the ritual character of the majlis al-ʿilm. After the Prophet's death, Abū Hurayra went to the market and "announced to the people that the estate of the prophet was to be divided in the mosque, so the people left the market and went to the mosque. Inside they discovered people learning the Qurʾān and ḥadīth, and the ḥalāl and the ḥarām [the permitted and the forbidden, i.e., law]. So they said to Abū Hurayra: 'Where is what you mentioned?' He replied: 'This is the estate of the prophets; they leave behind them not a dirham nor a dinar, rather they leave behind ʿilm.' Religion is the rememberance (dhikr) of God through one's knowledge of the ḥalāl and the ḥarām; this is preferable to the dhikr of the tongue."[139]

It was not only formal occasions such as the dars or the majlis al-ʿilm that were experienced as liminal moments. Many banal interactions between students and shaykhs were ritualized and scripted: "When the student enters into the company of the shaykh, or sits with him, he should have his mind free from preoccupations (*shawāghul*) and his mind should be pure, untroubled by anxieties, drowsiness, anger or strong hunger or thirst, in order that his breast may be open to what is said, and that he may heed what he hears."[140] Advice to young people prescribed the proper attitude of the student in the presence of the shaykh, hedging in the majlis al-ʿilm with numerous restrictions:

> Do not look at anything but the teacher, and do not turn around to investigate any sound, especially during discussion. Do not shake your sleeve. The student should not uncover his arms, nor should he fiddle with his hands or feet or any part of his body

subject matter should be law); determining what is permitted and forbidden, recommended or despised, in such areas as prayer, sex, ablutions, and commerce, through close textual study, including parsing the text correctly. This is the way things were in Madina": Ibn al-Ḥājj, 1/87.

136 Subkī, Staatsbibliothek MS, 31.

137 Ibn Jamāʿa, 95. Transmission of ḥadīth was conceived as an occasion in which collective baraka was to be gained: "[One aspect of the] baraka of ḥadīth is that [its transmitters] benefit one another (min baraka al-ḥadīth ifādatu baʿḍihim baʿḍ)": Ibn al-Ṣalāḥ, *Muqaddima*, 370.

138 Ibn Jamāʿa, 67. 139 Ibn al-Ḥājj, 1/87. 140 Ibn Jamāʿa, 96.

parts, nor should he place his hand on his beard or his mouth, or pick his nose or play with it, or open his mouth, or gnash his teeth. He should not lean against a wall, or a cushion, or put his hand against [them] in the presence of his shaykh; nor should he turn his back or his flank to his shaykh, nor should he sit on his hands, nor should he speak too much without need, nor should he try to say anything funny or offensive; and he should not laugh except out of surprise. If something overcomes him he should smile without giving voice. He should not clear his throat unnecessarily, nor should he spit if he can help it, nor should he drool, but should wipe his expectorate on his sleeve or in a scarf. If he sneezes he should try to do it quietly and cover his face with a handkerchief, and if he should yawn he should cover his mouth after first trying to fight it off. It is a sign of respect to the shaykh not to sit between him and the direction of prayer, nor to his side, nor on a cushion.[141]

Similarly, in ḥadīth audiences, seekers after ḥadīth should not speak to the ḥadīth-transmitter; nor should the session be allowed to last long, otherwise the "benefit" of the session was lost.[142] These prescriptions went beyond school-rules or proper etiquette; they were also a means of making young people conscious of themselves as they entered the partly sacred space around the shaykh. Within this space, students were encouraged to think of themselves as ritually polluting: "The student should not let his hand or foot or any part of his body or his clothing touch the clothing of the shaykh or his cushion or his prayer rug . . . the student should not sit in the presence of the shaykh on [his] prayer rug (*sajāda*) nor pray on it if the place is pure (*ṭāhir*)."[143] These are just a few examples of the admonitions, restrictions, and prohibitions that governed the relationship of the young person to the shaykh. One effect of these admonitions was to ritualize the space around the shaykh and his followers, and to bring their interactions outside ordinary time.

Reversal and transgression

One way of understanding the ritualized character of the transmission of knowledge is by examining how the ʿilm and adab of the learned were adopted by others. Although the aʿyān often punished severely transgressions of their control over ʿilm and the adab associated with it, a group of marginal holy men known as the *muwallahīn* lampooned their dominance with impunity. They achieved fame, and avoided repression, even when they subverted the rituals, performances, and idioms of purity of the learned.

One of the most famous of the muwallahīn was Yūsuf al-Qamīnī (d. 657/1259). Yūsuf had a particularly ribald version of the ʿilm and adab of the learned elite. As the learned were noted for their attention to purity, Yūsuf lived on or in the refuse heap of Nūr al-Dīn's hospital, wore clothes stained with dirt, urinated in his robes, and used little water. Where the learned marked their status by large turbans and wide sleeves of fine cloth, Yūsuf went

[141] Ibn Jamāʿa, 98–100. [142] Ibn al-Ṣalāḥ, *Muqaddima*, 369. [143] Ibn Jamāʿa, 108–9.

bare-headed and let his sleeves drop, "giving a bizarre effect." Where the learned were known for discoursing endlessly, Yūsuf was famous for his long silences. Where learned men exerted themselves to adopt a moderate gait, of Yūsuf it was said that "one of the world's great oddities is that he would stagger in his gait, without running into anyone, and not care."[144]

Nonetheless, the common people (ʿawāmm) and others described as his "followers" esteemed him, not just as a typical holy man, but because "he made things clear to them."[145] "The people (*an-nās*)," recounted Jazarī, "believed that he was righteous (*ṣalāḥ*), and spoke of his marvels and wonders (ʿajāʾib wa-gharāʾib), and [believed that] his mind was sound (ʿaqlahu thābit)."[146] He also healed the sick whom physicians had failed.[147] Abū Shāma, who lived near the hospital and probably would have encountered him frequently, said he "benefited us."[148] Yūsuf's transgressions were often as striking as those of others who suffered terrible punishments. However, he was paradoxically an object of much esteem from the common people, and even from the aʿyān.

Others were described as holding counter-performances of the rituals of the elite on dunghills and garbage heaps and wearing polluted clothing. Ibrāhīm Ibn Saʿīd al-Shāghūrī (d. 680/1281–2) either sat or held majālis in polluted substances, and wore clothing from which polluted substances (najasāt) had been brushed off but not washed, meaning that according to Islamic law it remained polluted. He supposedly never prayed or purified himself from pollution. He had a large following among "the ʿawāmm and those who do not reason."[149] The sources accused him of "mental confusion" without citing any examples of what he said, so we do not know what was simultaneously so compelling as to attract crowds and so innocuous as to spare him from persecution. But it is clear that many did not see him as a marginal individual or madman.[150] On a more modest level, ʿIzz al-Dīn al-Irbilī, a philosopher on the sidelines of the struggle for manṣabs, was known for criticizing the aʿyān and flaunting polluting substances.[151]

Marginal or insane people became famous for reversing the normal order of things. Ḥasan al-Kurdī (d. 724/1324), known for wearing polluted substances and walking barefoot, spoke what one sceptical source described as "mindless drivel" (*hadhayānāt*), but which he acknowledged resembled a form of esoteric

[144] The most detailed study of the muwallahīn in the context of the religious history of the city is L. Pouzet, *Damas*, 222–32. On Yūsuf al-Qamīnī (possibly Iqmīnī in Damascene dialect; his niṣba means "of the stokehold" after the stokehold of the baths at the Nūriyya bimāristān) see Abū Shāma, *Dhayl*, 202–3; Yūnīnī, 1/348; Ibn Kathīr, 13/216–17, 298; C.E. Bosworth, *The Medieval Islamic Underworld. The Banū Sasān in Arabic Society and Literature* (Leiden, 1976), vol. 1, 121–2.

[145] Yūnīnī, 1/348. Ibn Kathīr accepted that Yūsuf had knowledge of the unseen, but criticized the willingness of people to follow him, as such knowledge "has its source in possession by jinn," Ibn Kathīr, 13/216–17.

[146] Jazarī, Gotha Ducale MS 1559, year 657.

[147] *Ibid.*

[148] Abū Shāma, *Dhayl*, 203.

[149] Ibn Kathīr, 13/298.

[150] Ibn Kathīr, 13/217, 298; Ibn Shākir, 21/297–8; Yūnīnī, 4/100.

[151] Ibn Shākir, *Fawāt*, 1/362–3.

knowledge (*ᶜilm al-mughayyabāt*) that gained him some disciples.[152] Similarly, Aḥmad Ibn Ibrāhīm al-Maqdisī (d. 710/1310–11), one of the Banū Qudāma, had a conventional religious education, then after "a defect entered his mind," he stood in the road, "reciting useful things, and relating things new and old," and mixing "the serious with the frivolous."[153] Ibn Ḥajar and Ṣafadī related that he had disciples (talāmidha) while he was in this state.[154] Another of the Banū Qudāma, Aḥmad Ibn ᶜAbd al-Raḥmān, interpreted visions and dreams, and produced miracles.[155] Ibn Taymiyya was quoted as saying that a jinn followed Aḥmad around ("lahu ṭābiᶜ minaʾl-jinn") and prompted him with esoteric knowledge. In spite of the unorthodox character of his ᶜilm, which exposed him to suspicion, he successfully cast himself as a learned shaykh. He was known as a man with ḥurma and lectured in the Jawziyya madrasa without recorded interference. In contrast to other carriers of esoteric knowledge, he wrote a book about his ᶜilm.

Some of the common people saw the knowledge and manners of these marginal people as a meaningful usurpation of the ᶜilm and adab of the learned elite. The common people treated the muwallahīn as powerful patrons treated great shaykhs. The common people "loved and honored" Ibrāhīm Ibn Saᶜīd (aḥabbahu wʾakramahu), the usual formula for the favor of a man with power for a shaykh or amīr. The common people also gave him the kind of well-attended funeral that was usually accorded great scholars and amīrs. They had a carved headstone made for him and built over it a small mausoleum decorated with some of the architectural details of the major madrasas and dār al-ḥadīths, including a miḥrāb and muqarnas.[156] They also gave Yūsuf al-Qamīnī a decorated tomb with a carved headstone, and a group of them remained by the tomb reciting the Qurʾān, thereby casting him in death in the role of the founders of the great tomb-foundations.[157] This tomb, in which others of the muwallahīn were buried, became known as *Sayyidīʾsh-shaykh Yūsuf al-Iqmīnī*, or the *turba al-muwallahīn*.

What these figures had in common was not just their prestige, but their apparent immunity from persecution. Some writers associated their ᶜilm with insanity, consumption of ḥashīsh, or possession by jinn, but the learned elite never silenced them.[158] There is little evidence that they tried. Ibn Kathīr was one of the few writers who was generally scornful of these figures. Of

152 Ibn Kathīr, 14/116.

153 "Kāna yaqifu fīʾṭ-ṭuruq wa-yunshidu ashyāʾa mufīda, wa-yaḥkī ashyāʾa qadīma wa-jadīda": Ṣafadī, *Aᶜyān*, 22b.

154 "Wa-lahu talāmidha fī tilkaʾl-ḥāl": Ibn Ḥajar, 1/81; Ṣafadī, *Aᶜyān*, 22b.

155 Ibn Shākir, 1/86–88; Ṣafadī, *al-Wāfī*, 7/84; Ibn Rajab, 2/336.

156 Ibn Kathīr, 13/298.

157 Ibn Kathīr, 13/217, 298. Sahar von Schlegell has told me that the tomb was maintained by the Nabulusī family until the mid-twentieth century, when its guardian built an apartment building on it.

158 See the case of Ḥasan al-Kurdī, who supposedly had a jinn who followed him around and spoke through him: Sibṭ Ibn al-Jawzī, *Mirʾāt*, 8/638. Another marginal type named ᶜAlī al-Kurdī (d. 631) was also said by some to have been used by jinn and by others to have knowledge of the unseen: Ibn Shākir, Vat. Ar. MS, 117. Ibn Kathīr also attributed Yūsuf al-Qamīnī's ᶜilm to the insinuations of jinn: Ibn Kathīr, 13/216. For accusations of insanity see the accusation that Aḥmad Ibn Ibrāhīm al-Maqdisī had a "defect" (inḥirāf in Ibn Ḥajar,

Sulaymān al-Turkmānī (d. 714/1314–15), he said that "one of the riff-raff (*al-hamaj*) had a teaching (*ᶜaqīda*) about him, suitable for the low-lifes who follow everyone who caws like a bird. They believed that he revealed the unseen (*yukāshifu*) and was a decent man."[159] However, Ibn Kathīr's hostility was largely absent in more contemporary sources.

What accounts for the absence of any recorded attempt to suppress or silence these marginal people? Several possibilities suggest themselves. First, even though they claimed to possess a form of ᶜilm, they neither challenged the learned elite's control over the production of knowledge nor struggled for their honors or status. By virtue of their pollution, they were ineligible for manṣabs, and their clownishness could then be tolerated even by very grave men. Second, the ribaldries of these marginal individuals had much in common with the rituals of reversal and transgression seen in many other pre-industrial societies. Such reversals, by inverting the normal order, paradoxically often serve to affirm it. The ribald performers seen on the margins of many pre-modern societies often enjoyed a kind of immunity as a result.[160] Finally, the learned elite lauded these marginal people in language they usually reserved for ṣūfīs and holy men, describing their careers as ascetic athleticism, "holding to a path (*ṭarīqa*) hard on the self."[161]

Even if some among the elite regarded these people as possessed, there were few practices by which elite groups could diagnose, segregate, and silence the insane. There were also fewer reasons to do so than we have today. It is likely that to many of their audiences these men worked new meanings out of cultural practices usually controlled by the aᶜyān. These were people who transformed the performances, truths, and texts of the learned into productions that were equally significant but that had different meanings and audiences. By bringing meaning and the social order into temporary congruity – however ribald that correspondence was – they affirmed the relationship of ᶜilm to the social order, masked the aᶜyān's control over the production of knowledge, and gained their acceptance if not their gratitude for it.

Rituals of reading, rituals of writing

Another way of understanding the local and disputed uses of knowledge is by looking at the oral and written transmission of texts. By deciphering an apparently universal cultural practice – the production and reproduction of books – we can examine in a new light three of the principal problems this

inkhirāṭ in Ṣafadī) in his mind, caused by eating too much ḥashīsh, and that he would fall in and out of states of derangement: Ibn Ḥajar, 1/81; Ṣafadī, *Aᶜyān*, 22b. See also the shaykh who dropped out of the group of the learned and began to eat ḥashīsh, calling it the "morsel of invocation of God and thought (luqaymatuʾdh-dhikr wʾal-fikr)": Dhahabī, *Tāʾrīkh al-Islām*, BL MS, 75.

159 Ibn Kathīr, 14/72. For similar language used to scorn Yūsuf al-Qamīnī and Ibrāhīm Ibn Saᶜīd al-Shāghūrī see Ibn Kathīr, 13/216–17, 298.

160 See Crone, *Pre-Industrial Societies*, 117–22; P. Stallybrass and A. White, *The Politics and Poetics of Transgression* (Cornel, 1986), 125–48 and bibliography.

161 "Mulāzamatuhu li-hādhihiʾṭ-ṭarīqatiʾsh-shāqa ᶜalāʾn-nafs": Abū Shāma, *Dhayl*, 202–3.

study has addressed. First, we can understand how cultural productions such as books had specific social uses. Second, we can question the extent to which formal domains such as education and book production are constructions of our own making. And third, we can compare Damascus to other societies in an area that has usually been seen as a universal cultural practice and largely without local meanings.

Interpreting the social uses of familiar cultural objects in such a distant society poses its own difficulties. Perhaps the most formidable is their very familiarity. Books are such universal cultural artifacts that scholars often take them for "blank" objects that differ little from society to society. A number of scholars have recently tried to examine more specific social and cultural meanings and uses of the production of texts. Inspired by anthropological pioneers such as Jack Goody and adopted by historians, this approach has studied the production and reproduction of texts not only as a subject interesting in itself, but also as a means of addressing wider issues.

Partly because it was social scientists who first treated the production and reproduction of texts as cultural phenomena, the modeling of societies based on their various modes of transmission of texts has influenced the approach since its inception. Scholars have been especially interested in trying to understand differences among oral, manuscript, and print cultures.[162] This strategy, having benefited scholars by treating the production of texts as a cultural and social practice that can open up other issues, nonetheless has several drawbacks. At the least, it assumes that pre-modern peoples wrote, read, and reproduced books for many of the same reasons they did in later periods. It also tends to lump together different societies at similar stages of technological development.

The most serious problem with this approach, from the perspective of a historian, is that universal types such as "oral," "scribal," or "print" cultures, however useful they may be in the broadest sense, tend to obscure the particular social uses texts had in societies that possessed similar technologies. Goody's study was one of the first and remains one of the most influential studies of the social and cultural consequences of technological changes in book reproduction. However, his wide comparative framework misses some of the different uses of books in the pre-modern world. He also tends to reify culture as a static entity transmitted from one generation to the next, ascribing differences among oral, manuscript, and mechanical reproduction of texts to their efficiency in transmitting information more than anything else.[163] He sees the production and reproduction of texts largely as a problem of "memory storage," which was improved first with alphabetic writing and then finally

[162] See W. J. Ong, *Orality and Literacy: the Technologizing of the Word* (London, 1982) and Brian Street, *The Theory and Practice of Literacy* (Cambridge, 1984); E. A. Havelock, *The Muse Learns to Write. Reflections on Orality and Literacy from Antiquity to the Present* (New Haven, 1986).

[163] J. Goody, *The Interface between the Written and the Oral* (Cambridge, 1987), esp. 37,165; J. Goody, ed., *Literacy in Traditional Societies* (Cambridge, 1968); R.W. Neitzen, "Hot Literacy in Cold Societies," *CSSH* 33, no. 2 (Apr. 1991).

resolved with the advent of mechanical printing. Other scholars have followed Goody in being mainly interested in the pre-modern uses of books largely as they conduced to modern book production. These approaches have seen the production of books in the pre-modern world as a kind of imperfect precursor to a modern book production which "freed" writing from the problem of "memory storage." By privileging those uses of books in the past that conduced to modern book production, these scholars have often assumed the existence of a kind of technological determinism. The strategy imposes a teleological progression to the reproduction of texts, and carries often unexamined assumptions of technological "progress," if not European cultural triumphalism.

When we read backwards from outcomes in this way, one effect has been to obscure the various social uses of books in different pre-modern societies. When the text itself is treated as an inert vessel of information, and the mechanism of reproduction becomes the object of study, then the issue might justifiably become one of "efficiency." However, if we ask what the relationship between producing and using books was, and how each imposed its logic on the other, then we better understand the varied uses and meanings of texts in various societies at similar levels of technological development.

Once we concentrate on such differences in the uses of books, it is striking how the social uses of book production in medieval Damascus diverged from other societies that have been better studied. Book production and reproduction resembled neither the commodified nor the bureaucratic cultural production of the modern world.[164] It little resembled the organized production of manuscripts for patrons, for the market, or in the scriptoria of the high

164 Though books were certainly commodities, even if authors were typically not paid for composing them. There was a sūq al-kutub in Damascus, but it is not mentioned in the sources as often as the one in Cairo: Ṣafadī, *al-Wāfī*, 5/309; Nuᶜaymī, 1/95; Abū Shāma, *Dhayl*, 234. There was also an international trade in books, as one book merchant, who was also a copyist and librarian, traveled around ᶜIrāq, the Jazīra, and Syria in the trade: Ṣafadī, *al-Wāfī*, 12/218. In Damascus, booksellers gathered together every Friday: Ṣafadī, *al-Wāfī*, 4/89. There was also a market in Arabic manuscripts to provide pulp for Genoese paper manufacturers: L. Febvre, *The Coming of the Book* (New York, 1934), 30. Books left as waqfs were often stolen or seized and sold: Abū Shāma, *Dhayl*, 98; Ibn Kathīr, 14/8. There were collectors of books, who created a market for books as luxury products: see for examples of such luxury production and consumption Ibn Kathīr, 13/24; Abū Shāma, *Dhayl*, 183–4, 196; Nuᶜaymī, 1/64; Jazarī, Köp. MS, 204; Ibn Shākir, Vat. Ar. MS, 162; Ṣafadī, *al-Wāfī*, 12/6, 258; Ṣafadī, *Aᶜyān*, 66b. Ibn Abī Uṣaybiᶜa, 676 ff., 655 for a physician who had in his employ three full-time copyists. On book collecting among Mamlūks see Haarmann, "Arabic in Speech, Turkish in Lineage," 93–4. It was copyists and booksellers who made money from the book trade. Copyists could be well paid for producing books as luxury items, as was the case with Nuwayrī, who wrote out al-Bukhārī's *Saḥīḥ* eight times, selling each volume as soon as he could have it bound, for 700 dirhams; he also sold a chronicle for 2,000 dirhams: Ṣafadī, *Aᶜyān*, 42a. However, the majority of the thousands of books composed in Damascus in this period were not written for sale or for patrons, but were produced in a few copies for their "benefit" (nafᶜ) and baraka. For a noted shaykh who copied 2,000 texts in his lifetime "for money and for his own use" see Ibn Shākir, *Fawāt*, 1/81. The physician-collector cited above himself copied many books. Paper production was also an industry in the city, until from 1354 Italian production began first to equal then surpass it: A. Blum, *Les Origines du papier, de l'imprimerie et de la gravure* (Paris, 1935). For one paper-making enterprise, see Abū Shāma, *Dhayl*, 86.

medieval Latin West.[165] Finally, book production was utterly unlike the printed literature of Sung China, either the state printing and distribution of classics for bureaucrats and examination candidates or the popular literature produced for commercial purposes.[166]

The aᶜyān of Damascus were conscious of an ambiguity in their uses of books. On the one hand, much of the culture of the city was centered on texts. The public reading was one of the major forms of cultural production in the city, and some of the great shaykhs were known for their readings. Some shaykhs had stipends for reciting certain texts in public.[167] Moreover, political protests occasionally took the form of a public reading of certain texts. In protest against the first audience held to investigate Ibn Taymiyya, Ibn al-Mizzī read a portion of *al-Radd ᶜala al-jahmiyya* in the Umayyad Mosque, inciting the chief qāḍī Ibn Ṣaṣrā to imprison him.[168]

Books were also emblems of prestige for the elite.[169] Rulers tried to write books and to memorize them, with varying degrees of success, and they rewarded others for memorizing texts.[170] Shaykhs also gained prestige by

165 See E. Eisenstein, *The Printing Press as an Agent for Change* (Cambridge, 1979), 9–42 for bibliography on manuscript production in the high and late medieval Latin West. For the organization of manuscript production in thirteenth-century France, see Bourin-Derruau, *Temps d'équilibres*, 31–7.

166 On book production in Sung China see Gernet, *Chinese Civilization*, 331–8; T.H.C. Lee, "Sung Education," 107–8; H.K. Chan, *Control of Publishing in China, Past and Present* (Canberra, 1983); T.F. Carter, *The Invention of Printing in China and its Spread Westward*, ed. and revised by L.C. Goodrich (New York, 1955) and esp. Ming-Sun Poon, "Books and Printing in Sung China, 960–1279," Ph.D. Dissertation (University of Chicago, 1979), 28–66, 73–4, 84–7, and 100–12 on the impact of the examination system on the printing of books; 113–44 on printing by the Sung state; 22–4, 167–81 on commercial printing in private hands.

167 Abū Shāma, 113; Ibn Abī Uṣaybiᶜa, 655; Jazarī, Köp. MS, 164. Subkī, *Muᶜīd al-niᶜam*, 162–3, distinguished between the qāriᶜ al-kursī, who read moralistic literature, ḥadīth, and tafsīr in mosques, madrasas, and khanqāhs and the qāṣṣ, who recited memorized texts in the street.

168 Ibn Kathīr, 14/38.

169 For example, it was said of al-Firkāḥ, one of the most famous shaykhs of the city, that "his books are proof of his standing (*makān*) with respect to ᶜilm": Nuᶜaymī, 1/109. See also a book that "demonstrated [a shaykh's] great learning (yadullu ᶜalā ᶜilm ᶜaẓīm)": Subkī, *Ṭabaqāt*, 6/29; and another shaykh whose compositions "confirm his standing with respect to ᶜilm (yadullu ᶜalā maḥallihi minaʾl-ᶜilm)": Ibn Shākir, *Fawāt*, 2/263.

170 Ayyūbid princes found memorization of books desirable if occasionally unreachable. Al-Ashraf was quoted as saying, "If I could memorize the Qurʾān, even though doing so would cost me my power, I would still memorize the Qurʾān": Abū Shāma, *Dhayl*, 31. For another example see the ten-volume compendium of Ḥanafī fiqh that al-Malik al-Muᶜaẓẓam ordered written for him. He was seen reading it constantly, and at the end of each volume wrote: "ᶜĪsā . . . b. Abī Bakr b. Ayyūb has completed this book by committing it to memory (anhāhu ḥifzan)." Sibṭ Ibn al-Jawzī pointed out to the sulṭān that this claim might expose him to criticism, as "the greatest lecturer of Syria was able to memorize al-Qudūrī only because of his freedom from responsibilities, while the sulṭān was preoccupied with ruling the kingdom." Al-Muᶜaẓẓam replied that what he meant by memorizing was the meaning, not the articulation (*lafẓ*) itself: Sibṭ Ibn al-Jawzī, *Mirʾāt*, 8/647. Al-Muᶜaẓẓam gave prizes for memorizing books. Having studied Zamakhsharī's *Mufaṣṣal* by "frequenting" a shaykh, he considered himself its champion, and offered a prize of thirty dirhams to anyone who memorized it. He also offered prizes of 100 dirhams to anyone who memorized the more daunting *Jāmiᶜ al-kabīr* by Kirmānī or the *Idāḥ* by Abū ᶜAli: Ibn Kathīr, 13/72; Nuᶜaymī, 1/580; Sibṭ Ibn al-Jawzī, *Mirʾāt*, 8/577; Ibn Khallikān, 3/162 reported that the prize for

learning, reciting, copying or composing books, to the extent that a shaykh's nickname could refer to a book he had memorized.[171] Many of those with a claim to learning wrote at least one book, and some wrote hundreds.[172] The scale of book production was very large relative to the number of learned people in the city, and though it is impossible to count the number of texts composed in the period, it was surely in the thousands. Furthermore, the possession of a book in memory and the ability to teach it were the stock-in-trade of the learned elite. Books were at the core of the initiation of the young, and much of a student's training was devoted to memorizing them and working on them with shaykhs. In studying texts with shaykhs young people could learn an astonishing number of texts from a single individual.[173]

Finally, books had talismanic power as carriers of baraka.[174] They were objects of the ritual fastidiousness that other sacred things excited, and were protected for their purity. A measure of the effect books had on imaginations in Syria in a later period is conveyed in ʿAbd al-Ghanī al-Nabulusī's book of dream interpretation: "A book in a dream means power. He who sees a book in his hand in a dream will acquire power (*quwwa*)."[175]

However, even though Damascenes valued books for all these reasons, they

memorizing the *Mufaṣṣal* was one hundred dinārs and a robe of honor. See Nuʿaymī, 1/579 for a book "written" by al-Malik al-Muʿaẓẓam, with the aid of a scholar. The Ayyūbid ruler of Ḥamā, al-Malik al-Manṣūr (d. 617/1220–1), wrote a ten-volume chronicle: Abū Shāma, *Dhayl*, 124.

171 Ṣafadī, *Aʿyān*, 60b, for the shaykh known as "al-Taʿjīzī" because he had memorized the *Taʿjīz*.

172 See for example the 300-volume *Kitāb al-shāmil*, Dhahabī, *Tāʾrīkh al-islām*, Köp. MS, 21. Ibn Taymiyya was said to have filled 4,000 fascicules: Ibn ʿAbd al-Hādī, Köp. MS, 11.

173 Ṣafadī, *Aʿyān*, 65a, for an informant of Ṣafadī's who supposedly mastered 120 volumes from a single shaykh of the Banū ʿAsākir.

174 See for an example the story of the family that inherited the books of Nawawī, who kept two of them "for baraka (lʾit-tabarruk)": Yūnīnī, 4/185. The Qurʾān of ʿUthmān (Muṣḥaf ʿUthmān), kept in the Umayyad Mosque, was one of the most sacred objects in the city, and like other sacred objects it was veiled. Rulers, the aʿyān, and other groups associated themselves with it. In 735/1334–5 a new white silk veil costing 4,000 dinars and taking a year and a half to make was completed: Jazarī, Köp. MS, 415. When Ibn Qudāma died, someone said, "I saw in a dream the Muṣḥaf ʿUthmān fly into the sky from the Umayyad Mosque": Abū Shāma, *Dhayl*, 141; Sibṭ Ibn al-Jawzī, *Mirʾāt*, 8/629. In 711/1311–12 a demonstration took the Muṣḥaf ʿUthmān along with caliphal standards and relics of the Prophet and marched in protest against new exactions: Ibn Kathīr, 14/62. Another example of the brandishing of the Qurʾān was its use by one of the aʿyān of the quarter of the date-merchants, Zayn al-Dīn Ibn Bakrān, during the reign of al-Malik al-Ādil. He hung spears and other weapons at the entrance to the quarter, and whenever the sulṭān's troops or a messenger from Baghdād appeared, he would meet them on a riding-animal with a copy of the Qurʾān in a pouch, the people of the quarter watching from rooftops above: Abū Shāma, *Dhayl*, 230. Reading sacred texts also had magical or talismanic uses: the Sūra al-Nūḥ was also recited 3,336 times because of a vision during the plague: Ibn Kathīr, 14/226. In the famine brought about by the drought of 695/1295–6 the chief qāḍī requested that a certain shaykh read Bukhārī's *Saḥīḥ* in the Umayyad Mosque for its baraka: Jazarī, BN MS, 338. See also Subkī, *Ṭabaqāt*, 6/4; Ibn Kathīr, 14/225. For comparative material on the talismanic uses of books in the pre-modern world more generally see W.A. Graham, *Beyond the Written Word: Oral Aspects of Scripture in the History of Religion* (Cambridge, 1987), 58–66.

175 Nabulusī, ʿAbd al-Ghanī, *Taʿṭīr al-anām fī taʿbīr al-aḥlām* (Beirut, 1384 A.H.), 2/178.

held books in suspicion, and occasionally derided them.[176] Throughout the period, young people were chided for reading books without the personal supervision of shaykhs. Although Ibn Jamāᶜa advised students to purchase or borrow the books they needed, as these were their "tools of knowledge," he also warned that ultimately "knowledge is not gained from books, which are some of the most damaging of all corruptions."[177] He also cautioned against trying to become learned without a shaykh: "One of the greatest calamities is taking texts as shaykhs."[178] Writers told young people to avoid thinking too highly of themselves and doing without a shaykh: "This is the mark of ignorance and lack of discernment. What escapes him is greater than what he learns."[179] Young people "should guard against relying on books, but should instead rely on whomever is best in that field."[180] Nor could scholarly careers be advanced by the pen alone. Shams al-Dīn al-Sarkhadī, "the greatest polymath of his age," had nonetheless a sharper pen than a tongue, "and had little good fortune in the world, never obtaining a manṣab."[181]

Moreover, there were ways of acquiring ᶜilm that bypassed the mediation of written texts. Most people experienced the Qurʾān and ḥadīth as oral performances rather than texts, and indeed the memorization of the Qurʾān has long been central to the education of children.[182] Oral transmission also was the preferred, in some respects the sole, acceptable means of learning ḥadīth. Ḥadīth scholars not only insisted that ḥadīth should be learned orally from someone in a direct line of transmission to the Prophet, some also claimed that ḥadīth should not be put in writing at all. One debated issue was whether a scholar could claim a place in an *isnād* (the chain of transmission of a ḥadīth) if he copied down ḥadīth in a ḥadīth-session, even as he memorized it

[176] For the latter, see for example the poem written by Abd Allah Ibn ᶜAsākir; a ṣūfī described as one of the aᶜyān al-mashāyikh, who responded to criticism of ṣūfī practices: "Poverty is [the ṣūfīs'] glory, and truth (*al-ḥaqq*) their excellence, and grace (*luṭf*) their distinction . . . this is their virtue (*faḍl*) not reading in books (ad-dars fʾil-kutub); this is their glory, not money or lineage": Ibn Shākir, 21/41–2; Sibṭ Ibn al-Jawzī, *Mirʾāt*, 8/53–4.

[177] Aḍurr al-mafāsid: Ibn Jamāᶜa, 123, 163. Makdisi, *The Rise of Colleges*, 89, has quoted a similar sentiment from Ibn Abī Uṣaybiᶜa, 691: "I commend you not to learn your sciences from books, even though you may trust your ability to understand. Resort to professors for each science you seek to acquire; and should your professor be limited in his knowledge take all that he can offer, until you find another more accomplished than he."

[178] "Min aᶜẓam al-baliyya tashayyakhaʾṣ-ṣaḥīfa": Ibn Jamāᶜa, 87. Also Berkey, *The Transmission of Knowledge*, 26.

[179] *Ibid.*, 134. For a similar sentiment, see the poem quoted by Subkī: "If you want knowledge without a shaykh, then you have departed from the path of the mustaqīm; and things will become so obscure for you that you will become more errant than Thomas the Ḥakīm": Subkī, *Ṭabaqāt*, 6/35.

[180] Ibn Jamāᶜa, 113–15.

[181] Nuᶜaymī, 1/223.

[182] Recent studies of the uses of oral transmission and the public performance of sacred texts in the Islamic world include F. Denny, "Qurʾān Recitation: a Tradition of Oral Performance and Transmission," *Oral Tradition* 4 (1989); D. Eickelman, *Knowledge and Power in Morocco* (Princeton, 1985); and Graham, *Beyond the Written Word*, esp. 99–115. See also Weber, *Economy and Society*, vol. II, 790, for a comparison of the importance of oral transmission of sacred texts in Islamic and Hindu law. See Pouzet, *Damas*, 177–99 for instruction in the Qurʾān and ḥadīth in the city; Pouzet, "Prises de position autour du samaʾ en Orient musulman au VIIe/Xiiie siècle," *SI* 57 (1983), 119–34.

from a recognized authority. Some authorities held that when scholars transcribed ḥadīth they were prevented from understanding them.[183] Great ḥadīth scholars were lauded for dispensing with written texts entirely. A famous ḥadīth scholar, al-Dhahabī, holder of the manṣab at the dār al-ḥadīth al-Ashrafiyya, related ḥadīth without error and "never glanced at a book [of ḥadīth] or of *rijāl* [a genre that listed transmitters of ḥadīth]."[184] An illustration of the importance Damascenes placed on oral transmission of ḥadīth was the mode of transmission of Bayhaqī's *Sunan* into Damascus. A shaykh heard two volumes of the work from Ibn al-Ṣalāḥ al-Shahrazūrī (himself an immigrant), and related it on Ibn al-Ṣalāḥ's authority to anyone who wanted to hear it.[185] People were said to have come from as far as Aleppo to audit a text that existed in numerous copies throughout the region.

This incorporation of lines of transmission continued throughout life. Shaykhs traveled to learn ḥadīth throughout the period, as they had since the early Islamic era: "There are four [categories of people] from whom one should not accept guidance: the guard of a neighborhood (ḥāris al-darb); the crier of the qāḍī (munādī al-qāḍī); the son of a ḥadīth scholar; and a man who writes [down ḥadīth] in his own city and does not travel in search of ḥadīth."[186] With sacred texts such as the Qurʾān and ḥadīth, oral transmission had a triple purpose: it connected auditors to revelation and the Prophet directly; it linked them to all who had transmitted the text in the past; and the moment of transmission was itself a ritual moment.

The sense that transmission established a tangible link between the auditor and the Prophet is why elderly transmitters were valued so highly. An example of this, an unlikely one to Damascenes, was the rich man Ibn al-Shihna (d. 730/1329–30). He was well over a hundred years old when his name was discovered in the "book of auditors" in Qasyūn as having audited ḥadīth in 630/1232–3. He had lived most of his life "without telling ḥadīth scholars anything," and once discovered he began to relate ḥadīth and give ijāzas in the Umayyad Mosque.[187] Adults took young children (and also themselves) to old shaykhs, in order to shorten the links of transmission between them and the Prophet.[188] Some criticized this practice because children were less likely to understand what they memorized. Critics also worried that the practice reduced confidence in the chain of transmission, out of fear that "one's shaykhs and their shaykhs were too young to understand the content of what they transmit-

[183] Ibn al-Ṣalāḥ, *Muqaddima*, 206–7: "He may say, 'I attended,' and not [so and so] related to us, or [so and so] informed us (yaqūl 'ḥadartu' wa-lā yaqūl 'ḥadathanā' wa-lā 'akhbaranā')." See *ibid.*, 296 ff. for debate over whether ḥadīth and "al-ʿilm" should be written down at all.

[184] Subkī, Staatsbibliothek MS, 48.

[185] Ṣafadī, *Aʿyān*, 45a.

[186] Ibn al-Ṣalāḥ, *Muqaddima*, 369.

[187] Ṣafadī, *Aʿyān*, 64a.

[188] See for one example the shaykh who "connected the young with the aged (alḥaqaʾṣ-ṣighar b'il-kibar)": Abū Shāma, *Dhayl*, 62; also Tāj al-Dīn al-Kindī, famous at the end of his career for being the longest living link in an isnād on earth ("aʿlā ahl al-arḍ isnādan") in Qurʾān recitation, as he lived eighty-three years after first learning it: Ṣafadī, *al-Wāfī*, 15/51.

[189] Ṣafadī, *al-Wāfī*, 5/67.

ted."[189] But it demonstrates that some of the aᶜyān at least believed that the incorporation of the line of transmission was as important as the content of what was transmitted.

The insertion of young people into lines of transmission of texts was a central part of their initiation into the culture of the aᶜyān. We know almost nothing about early education in this period, because the sources were largely uninterested in childhood. Beyond the occasional mention of a Qurʾān school (*maktab*) what we know of the education of children comes largely from the biographical notices, necessarily written after their deaths, of the children of the authors of our sources.[190] As few and as touching as they are, these texts give us a rare glimpse into how fathers raised their children. When the historian Abū Shāma's son died at the age of eight, his father wrote in his biographical notice that he had taken him to hear ḥadīth and other texts from over 170 shaykhs. Abū Shāma himself read books to another son, including works of famous Damascenes such as Ibn ᶜAsākir and Ibn Abī ᶜAṣrūn which he had learned from their authors.[191] Other shaykhs read texts to their daughters.[192]

Yet it was not only sacred texts that were transmitted without the necessary mediation of books. Many other texts were learned and transmitted orally. The lecture was often the oral production of a pre-existing text. Other forms of knowledge were acquired without any exposure to a text, oral or written, at all. Some shaykhs, such as the famous blind shaykh Ibn Qawām (d. 658/1260), a member of a famous aᶜyān household, acquired and transmitted other forms of ᶜilm paranormally. Once, while giving an exegesis of the Qurʾān, someone asked the shaykh how he came up with an original interpretation, "yet you neither read nor write? Where did you get this from (min ayna laka hādhā)?" The shaykh responded: "Just as I hear the questions, so I hear the response."[193] Another example of paranormal transmission of ᶜilm was one of the most noted and most dubious holy men in the city, al-Bājirīqī (d. 724/1323–4). The head of the physicians of the city was sitting with Bājirīqī in a garden when a peasant who worked there came upon them. Bājirīqī ordered the peasant to sit before him. Once the peasant was settled, Bājirīqī began to stare at him, then ordered the peasant to speak to the raʾīs "until he woke up." The raʾīs related what happened next: "The peasant began to discourse with me in all fields of medicine – the general principles of medicine and its specific applications (fī kulliyyātiʾṭ-ṭibb wa-juzᶜiyyātihi) – concerning the various modes of treatment, using the most specialized technical terms which only a

[190] For two maktabs in Damascus see Ibn Kathīr, 13/335; Nuᶜaymī, 1/225.

[191] Abū Shāma, *Dhayl*, 84 176; Ibn Kathīr, 13/274. In another citation of childhood education, of one of the Banū Subkī it was said that his father got him ijāzas from the "shaykhs of his time" in Egypt and Syria: "istajāza lahu wāliduhu mashayikh ᶜaṣrihi minaʾd-diyār al-miṣriyya wʾash-shām"; the father then brought son to ḥadīth-sessions where he heard ḥadīth from the shaykhs of his city ("mashayikh bilādihi"): Ṣafadī, *al-Wāfī*, 7/247. For another shaykh who read texts to his son see Ṣafadī, *Aᶜyān*, 86a. For shaykhs who took their sons to other shaykhs to read texts see Ṣafadī, *Aᶜyān*, 59a; Jazarī, BN MS, 492.

[192] Ṣafadī, *al-Wāfī*, 15/117.

[193] Yūnīnī, 1/399; Ṣafadī, *al-Wāfī*, 9/245; Ibn Shākir, *Fawāt*, 1/225.

small number of skilled [physicians] know." After an hour the peasant regained his normal consciousness and reported that he was not aware of what he was saying, but that the words fell from his tongue (jarā ᶜalā lisānī).[194] As this anecdote and others like it show, ᶜilm did not require texts to contain it, but existed independently of the books we consider its necessary vessels and vehicles. The shaykhs who carried ᶜilm acquired it without the necessary mediation of texts.

What accounts for this paradoxical suspicion of written texts within a culture that so highly valued them? The reason is partly to be found in a relationship between the production and reproduction of texts that was different from that in many other societies. The idea that books are singular products of individual wills, belonging to their authors as unmistakably as their personalities, is a modern one that would not have been understood in Damascus. Authors of books generally did not see themselves as creators of unique commodities, although there were some exceptions. Nor did those engaged in the production and reproduction of books always see themselves as instrumental carriers of information.

Damascenes rarely wrote, copied, acquired, or read books purely for the information they contained. On the contrary, books had other uses and meanings. Authors of books, copyists, booksellers, owners, and readers experienced their ties to one another in part as personal altruistic bonds. Booksellers were not in business just for profit (*matjar*), but to benefit others (intifāᶜ).[195] Authors often composed books in single copies for specific individuals, much as they composed fatwās. When others copied such works, it was often to make a personal copy of a useful text.[196] Readers as individuals who perused texts in private for the information they contained were condemned throughout the period. While there were exceptions, especially with respect to the basic manuals (qawāʾid) or bluffer's guides (the "man lā yaḥduruhu" literature) in various fields, private reading was a subject of debate. Damascenes were advised to read books not silently and in private but aloud with a shaykh or a group.[197]

194 Ibn Ḥajar, 4/13. 195 For an example see Yūnīnī, 2/355.

196 See for example Ibn Taymiyya's explanation of how the *ᶜAqīda al-Wāsiṭiyya* came to be written and distributed: "A qāḍī came from Wāsiṭ, and complained of the practices of the people of that city [who suffered] under a regime of usurption, ignorance, and lack of instruction (durūs) in ᶜilm or religion. He asked me to write a creedal statement (ᶜaqīda) that would be a support to him. I declined, saying that others had [already] recorded the doctrines (ᶜaqā'id) of the imāms of the sunna. He said 'no, I want you to write one,' so I wrote it and many copies were made of it, and it spread through Egypt and Irāq and other places": Ibn ᶜAbd al-Hādī, Köp. MS, 84. Ibn Jamāᶜa, 165–7, advised students that they should not occupy themselves with prolonged copying, unless they lacked the purchase price or rental fee of a book.

197 See for example how a son of Abū Shāma read even his father's books with a shaykh: Abū Shāma, *Dhayl*, 176. For another example see the relationship between Ṣafadī and his student Tāj al-Dīn al-Subkī. Subkī learned Ṣafadī's books with him, and Ṣafadī in turn both copied and recited one of Subkī's books in a ḥalqa: Subkī, *Ṭabaqāt*, 6/94. Ibn Jamāᶜa suggested that the dars begin with praise for the author of a text and end with prayers for his sake: Ibn Jamāᶜa, 162. See also Berkey, *The Transmission of Knowledge*, 24–8.

This is why the sources claimed that the selection of a book involved consideration of the shaykh who would teach it, and why Damascenes believed that the selection of a book had social and moral consequences. Some writers quoted older arguments to the effect that learning from books was superior to learning from teachers, but these were exceptions rare enough to merit mention.[198] The advice literature cautioned young people not to rely on books when they wanted to master a field, but to seek out whomever was "best" in it, according to criteria that included piety, probity, and compassion.[199] Moreover, reading a book with a shaykh was not just a means of ensuring accuracy, as some western scholars have occasionally believed.[200] When Damascenes learned a book with a shaykh, they entered a line of transmission that stretched back to the author, and they appropriated some of the authority of the others in the chain. Damascenes gained a reputation for learning a book with its author or with someone who learned it from the author.[201] When Damascenes read books, they often recognized the handwriting of their intellectual ancestors as a physical link to them, and having completed the book with a shaykh they often inscribed their own names in it.[202] Mastery of a book was in part a means of acquiring the authority of older or more powerful men.

This forging of a personal connection to powerful men is one reason why some people collected large numbers of ijāzas, certificates from a shaykh that a book they taught they had acquired from another shaykh. This was especially true in the case of prestigious ijāzas that reached back many generations.[203] Many ijāzas did not refer to single books, but rather to all that one shaykh could relate.[204]

Even when people had books but no shaykhs with whom to study them, they sought a kind of intimacy with authors of texts. A shaykh who studied the works of Ibn ʿArabī made visitations repeatedly to his tomb ("yulāzim ziyāra qabrihi") and read his books there, "cleaving to" (lāzama) the texts of Ibn

198 See for example Ṣafadī, *al-Wāfī*, 21/106–7 and Ibn Abī Uṣaybiʿa, 2/99–106 for the views of Ibn Riḍwān (d. 460), the famous Egyptian physician: "wa-lahu muṣannaf fī 'annaʾt-taʿallum minaʾl-kutub awfaq minaʾl-muʿallimīn." His views were refuted by another famous physician, Ibn Buṭlān, quoted in part in Ibn Abī Uṣaybiʿa, 2/99–106.

199 Ibn Jamāʿa, 113–15.

200 See for example J. Pedersen, *The Arabic Book*, G. French trans. (Princeton, 1984), 27–36.

201 See for example Ibn Ḥajar, 2/59.

202 For one example see Ibn Khallikān, 2/461.

203 Ijāzas have received much scholarly attention, though their social uses remain largely unstudied: see Berkey, *The Transmission of Knowledge*, 31–3; Pedersen, *The Arabic Book*, 31–6; Makdisi, *The Rise of Colleges*, 140–52; Goldziher, *Muslim Studies*, I, 175–80; G. Vajda, *Les certificats de lecture et de la transmission dans les manuscrits arabes de la Bibliothèque Nationale de Paris* (Paris: Publications de l'Institut de recherches et de l'histoire des textes, VI, 1957). Ibn Jamāʿa had over 700 ijāzas, Birzālī over 3,000, and Dhahabī heard ḥadīth and learned texts from 1,200 shaykhs: Jazarī, Köp. MS, 311; Nuʿaymī, 1/79, 112, 113. Ijāzas could extend over many generations of scholars: one recorded by Jazarī had thirteen names written on it: Jazarī, Köp. MS, a note glued on to page 158 in Jazarī's hand. Rulers also tried to acquire ijāzas, and some even granted them for texts they had learned: Yūnīnī, 1/429.

204 For one example of the ijāza in "what [the shaykh] related (mā yarwīhi)" see Abū Shāma, *Dhayl*, 163.

ʿArabī, just as one would "cleave to" a shaykh.[205] In a dream another shaykh associated the body of a shaykh with the words of a text. Sayf al-Dīn al-Āmidī dreamt that he heard a voice calling to him: "This is the house of the Imām Ghazālī." In the dream he entered the house, and finding Ghazālī's tomb inside he opened it (kashaftuhu); then finding Ghazālī's corpse within wrapped in cotton he unveiled his face (kashaftu ʿan wajhih) and kissed it. When he awoke, "I told myself that I should memorize [some of] Ghazālī's discourse (kalām al-Ghazālī). I picked up his book, *al-Muṣṭasfā fī ʿuṣūl al-fiqh*, and memorized it in a short time."[206] The "reading" of a book was thus for Sayf al-Dīn in part a means of conjuring up the intimate presence of its author.

Damasceues brandished texts such as ijāzas and *mashyakhas* (lists of shaykhs with whom scholars audited texts) as emblems of prestige when they attested to their positions in chains of transmission. While ijāzas and mashyakhas have long attracted scholarly attention, other written testiments to the oral reception of texts existed. At a banquet held by the amīr Fakhr al-Dīn Lūʾlūʾ, forty ḥadīth were recited, and one of those attending the banquet recorded the names of all those present.[207] One of the highest emblems of scholarly honor was a large mashyakha, especially the *arbaʿīn buldāniyya*, "the forty by city," usually an enormous book that listed forty ḥadīth audited from forty shaykhs in each of forty cities to which a scholar had traveled.[208] Other records of learning texts were preserved. In the Jabal Qasyūn, there was a "booklet of auditors" (kurrāsa's-sāmiʿīn) that recorded the names of all who heard Bukhārī's *Saḥīḥ* there.[209] On a more modest level, after having memorized some ḥadīth and the sciences associated with it, one shaykh "had some writings of shaykhs (khuṭūṭ al-ashyākh) confirming his knowledge."[210]

Whereas ḥadīth transmitters were scrupulous about reproducing narratives exactly, written texts were mutable. The classical literature from the ʿAbbāsid period was often copied as integral single texts, especially for the luxury market. But with respect to their own book production, Damascenes did not necessarily reproduce texts as exact copies of single products. This was a common characteristic of much pre-modern manuscript production: before commodified production gave publishers an incentive to produce unique products, exact reproduction was generally guaranteed only to sacred texts or classics. Nor was there any cult of individual genius that would call for the exact reproduction of books.

Books in Damascus were not of necessity produced as single acts of a creative autonomous will. Texts were rather enacted fortuitously in time, and could be incorporated in other texts in different ways. Texts were often

[205] Dhahabī, *Taʾrīkh al-Islām*, Köp. MS, 40; BL MS, 86; Ibn Shākir, *Fawāt*, 1/180.
[206] Ṣafadī, *al-Wāfī*, 21/341–2. [207] Ibn ʿAbd al-Hādī, Köp. MS, 118.
[208] Birzālī wrote one in twenty volumes: Nuʿaymī, 1/122–3; Ibn ʿAsākir also wrote one: Nuʿaymī, 1/101. For a large mashyakha in ten volumes covering one hundred shaykhs see Jazarī, BN MS, 72. [209] Ṣafadī, *Aʿyān*, 64a. [210] Ṣafadī, *Aʿyān*, 60b.

shortened, lengthened, amended, and interpreted in their margins. Even titles were not unique. Subkī took the title of one of his father's books as the title of one of his own, "by way of gaining the baraka of his father's work (ṣanīᶜ al-wālid)."[211] The relationship between authorship and copying, between the production and reproduction of books, was not, as might be expected, a question of seniority and intellectual prestige. Scholars with the highest intellectual prestige copied or abridged texts out of what they described as the desire for benefit, baraka, or out of "love" (ḥubb or maḥabba) for the author.[212] Where poetry and other forms of literature were often copied as integral texts, living poets made liberal use of the verses of others, and certain lines appear repeatedly in different poems and contexts.

Some also believed that copying had a talismanic power that would give them spiritual benefit. Ibn al-Jawzī requested that after his death the pens he used to copy ḥadīth be collected and heated in the water with which his corpse was washed; this was done, and benefit was obtained from the liquid.[213] Others copied as a means of bringing themselves into the presence of the author of the text, living or dead. This was the case of the shaykh who became an ascetic, living off his meager savings, and "cleaved to" the books of Ibn ᶜArabī, copying a number of them while constantly visiting Ibn ᶜArabī's tomb.[214] Another shaykh who experienced such "love" for Ibn ᶜArabī that he was buried in his tomb, copied two pages of his work a day, as he copied two pages of ḥadīth.[215] Copying was also hedged in by ritual restrictions. The copyist was to use ritually pure inks and paper, and was not to orphan the word "ᶜabd" in a name such as ᶜAbd Allah," at the end of a line.[216] Copying also had ritualistic promise. One writer related the ḥadīth "he who writes some ᶜilm from me, and writes his prayer for me with it, will never cease to receive reward as long as that book is read."[217]

The boundaries between written and oral reproduction of texts were not

211 Subkī, *Ṭabaqāt*, 6/213–14.

212 For abridging a text out of love for its author, see Ṣafadī, *al-Wāfī*, 21/343, for a shaykh who copied Sayf al-Dīn al-Āmidī's *al-Iḥkām fī 'uṣūl al-aḥkām* "out of his love for him (min maḥabbatihi lahu)." Some examples of copying for benefit or baraka: one of Saladin's secretaries had a passion for copying books: Nuᶜaymī, 1/91. A shaykh who was a qāḍī and shaykh of a dār al-ḥadīth copied out 500 volumes: Ibn Kathīr, 14/158. An amīr who had been governor of Egypt (d. 731) was known for having audited al-Bukhārī and for copying the entire text in his own hand: Ibn Kathīr, 14/155. Ibn Asākir made two fair copies of the *Tarikh Madinat Dimashq* in his own hand: Ibn Shākir, Vat. Ar. MS, 5. Abū ᶜUmar Muhammad Ibn Qudāma made copies of many books for his family and friends without payment: Ibn Rajab, 2/ 52; Sibṭ Ibn al-Jawzī, *Mirʾāt*, 8/547; Abū Shāma, *Dhayl*, 69–71; Ibn Kathīr, 13/59. Birzālī's daughter wrote out al-Bukhārī in thirteen volumes, and Birzālī recited it in the Umayyad Mosque under the Qubba al-Nasr. This copy became the definitive text ("aṣl muᶜtamad") from which the people would copy: Ibn Kathīr: 14/185. One possible reason that copying was generally such an informal practice, taking place outside the guilds and religious bodies that controlled reproduction of texts in the Latin West, was the easy availability of cheap paper long before its diffusion in Europe after 1350.

213 Ibn Khallikān, 2/321.

214 Ibn Shākir, *Fawāt*, 1/180.

215 Ibn Kathīr, 13/318.

216 Ibn al-Ṣalāḥ, *Muqaddima*, 306.

217 Balqīnī, *Maḥāsin al-Iṣṭilāḥ*, in the marginal commentary to Ibn al-Ṣalāḥ, *Muqaddima*, 307. Several similar ḥadīth are quoted by the same author.

fixed. Shaykhs reproduced texts from memory in public performances. They also copied texts and composed books of ḥadīth as a means of inscribing them in the memory.[218] The true possession of a book, the authors of the period repeated again and again, was internal, as the "two wings" of ᶜilm were memory and oral discussion.[219] A commonplace in the biographical dictionaries was the preservation of texts in the memory after their destruction by fire. Ibn Khallikān related the story of a fifth-century Khurasānī scholar who boasted that if all of al-Shāfiᶜī's books were burned he could write them out himself from memory.[220] A similar story was told of the fourth-century Baghdādī who was able to quote from the entirety of his library after it burned down.[221] In Damascus shaykhs rated one another based on the speed with which they memorized texts and the quantity and difficulty of what they memorized.[222] Phrases such as "he never heard anything without memorizing it, and never memorized anything and then forgot it" appear frequently in the biographical dictionaries.[223]

Writers warned against learning from anyone who read from a sacred text rather than memory: "Do not acquire ᶜilm from one who reads it from a written copy of the Qurʾān or off a piece of paper; in other words, do not recite the Qurʾān after one who reads it from a written text; or ḥadīth or other texts from one who takes it from a piece of paper."[224] Ibn Jamāᶜa suggested that young people not purchase books, because books should be an aid to memorization and not a substitute for memory. He made his point with a line of verse: "If you are incapable of memorizing, then accumulating books will do you no good."[225] Shaykhs who lacked confidence in their own memories forbade others from relating narratives on their authority. "Concerning oral narratives (*riwāya*)," warned one cautious shaykh, "I forbid anyone to relate my accounts of the texts I have audited. This is because of the difficulty of fulfilling the conditions set down by our authorities requiring the verification of the accuracy of memory from the moment a text is audited until it is related.

218 Ibn al-Ṣalāḥ, *Muqaddima*, 374–5.
219 Ṣafadī, *al-Wāfī*, 13/415. This word may refer to armies rather than birds, as the order of battle of many armies of the period had "two wings" and a center as their principal tactical units.
220 Ibn Khallikān, 2/370.
221 Abū al-Hilāl al-ᶜAskarī, *al-Ḥathth ᶜalā ṭalab al-ᶜilm*, Asir Effendi MS 433, 74.
222 For other heroic memories, see Subkī, Staadtsbibliothek MS, 48: "He never heard anything without memorizing it"; the shaykh who memorized the *Ṣaḥīḥ* of Muslim in four months, also able to memorize seventy ḥadīth in a single sitting: Yūnīnī, 2/59; the shaykh who memorized the *Mukhtaṣar* of Ibn al-Ḥājib in nineteen days, in spite of the difficulty of the language: Ṣafadī, *al-Wāfī*, 4/226–7; the shaykh able to memorize a fascicule in a single day: Ṣafadī, *al-Wāfī*, 3/227; the shaykh who memorized the *Maqāmāt* of al-Ḥarīrī in fifty nights: Abū Shāma, *Dhayl*, 130. For more typical praise of a shaykh as "speedy of memory (sarīᶜ al-ḥifz)" see Jazarī, BN MS, 8b. These are just several of the many examples that could be cited. See also Berkey, *The Transmission of Knowledge*, 28–31.
223 See for example Subkī, Staatsbibliothek MS, 48.
224 Ṣafadī, *al-Wāfī*, 21/109: "lā taʾkhudhuʾl-ᶜilma min ṣaḥaf wa-lā muṣḥaf yaᶜnī lā yaqrāʾuʾl-qurʾān ᶜalā man qarāʾa min muṣḥaf wa-lāʾl-ḥadīth wa-ghayrahu ᶜalā man qarāʾa dhālika min ṣuḥuf." Also see Graham, *Beyond the Written Word*, 103–7.
225 Ibn Jamāᶜa, 164.

The books I have audited are not fixed in my memory."[226] Finally, to have acquired texts merely by reading them could subject an individual to suspicion. One shaykh was said to have had "no studies and no knowledge except from reading."[227]

Authors were also fearful of the spiritual consequences of writing books. An anecdote Ibn Khallikān related to his contemporaries concerning al-Mawārdī (d. 450/1058) illustrated the spiritual dangers writers perceived in composing books: "None of his books appeared in his lifetime, but rather were put in a storage-place. When death approached him he said to someone he had confidence in, 'the books that are in a certain place owned by a certain person are all my compositions. I did not publish them because my motives towards God were not pure, so if death comes upon me, when I fall into my death-agonies take my hand in yours. If I grab your hand and squeeze it know that nothing has been accepted from me, and go and throw the books into the Tigris at night. If my hand remains open and does not grasp yours know that they have been accepted, and that I have triumphed with respect to [the purity of] my intentions.'" Mawārdī's friend related: "When death approached him I put my hand in his, and his remained open and did not grasp mine. I knew that this was the sign of acceptance, and I published his books afterwards."[228] The writing of books, like the reading of them, was an act that had its dangers.

Because Damascenes valued the acquisition of a book in memory so highly, they gave much thought to mnemonic techniques and the psychology and even psycho-pharmacology of memory.[229] Ibn Jamāʿa suggested that young people should avoid anything that interferes with memorization, including "reading inscriptions on tombs, walking between two camels haltered in a line, or flicking away lice." He also followed ancient dietary advice in advising young people to avoid foods that will render them "senseless and stupid" such as sour apples, baklava, vinegar, and anything that by increasing congestion "dulls the mind, such as too much milk or fish." God, he pointed out, has provided such mind-strengtheners as gum, rose water, honey, sugar, and eating twenty-one raisins daily, all of which "aid the memory and prevent illness by reducing congestion."[230] Our sources do not provide us with examples of the training of memory nearly as detailed as those found in

[226] "Wa-ʾammaʾr-riwāya faʾinnī lam asmaḥ li-aḥad bi-ʾan yarwaya ʿannī masmūʿātī li-ṣuʿūba mā sharaṭahu aṣḥābunā fi-ḍabṭi bʾil-ḥifẓi min ḥayn samiʿa ilā ḥayn rawā, wʾanna al-kutub allatī samiʿtuhā lam takun maḥfūẓa ʿindī": Ṣafadī, *al-Wāfī*, 21/89.

[227] "Kāna lā ishtighāl lahu wa lā ʿilma min ghayrʾil-muṭāliʿa": Ṣafadī, *Aʿyān*, 57b.

[228] Ibn Khallikān, 2/444.

[229] See for comparison on mnemonics and the social uses of memory, M. Carruthers, *The Book of Memory: a Study of Memory in Medieval Culture* (Cambridge, 1990), esp. 16–45, 80–188; J. Parry, "The Brahmanical Tradition and the Technology of the Intellect," in J. Overing ed., *Reason and Morality* (New York and London, 1985); F.A. Yates, *The Art of Memory* (Chicago, 1966); D. Eickelman, "The Art of Memory: Islamic Education and its Social Reproduction," *Comparative Studies in Society and History* 20 (1978), 485–516; Pedersen, *The Arabic Book*.

[230] Ibn Jamāʿa, 77. Also Berkey, *The Transmission of Knowledge*, 29. On medieval European ideas of the effect of diet on memory see Carruthers, *The Book of Memory*, 50.

medieval Europe. We do not encounter any examples of the architectural mnemonics so characteristic of the training of memories in Europe – though scholars may some day encounter evidence of them. Nonetheless, with respect to the care of the memory, there appear to be a number of similarities between the Middle East and Europe, due partly to the influence of Arabic literature on Europe, and partly to the common origins of the ideas of both in Galen.[231]

In the lecture, boundaries between the text studied, the script of the lesson, and the record of the lecture blurred. Not only was the lesson itself often a memorized text about a text, those in attendance took the lesson itself as a text which they then memorized, and later wrote down.[232] For mature scholars, the texts they had memorized as young people now became scripts for oral performances.[233] Lecturers shaped their lectures, as writers shaped their texts, to make memorization easier.[234] Ibn al-Zamlakānī was praised for lessons that "caused his listeners to memorize without having to practice."[235] Great shaykhs discoursed effortlessly, "as though reading from a book," and they lectured "as though delivering a sermon."[236] Even writing was a public performance, as biographers much lauded the ability to write fair copy without notes quickly, "from the tip of the pen" (min rāʾs al-qalam) – praising in one case a writer who composed on horseback.[237] When Damascenes

231 *Ibid.*

232 For an example of a dars as a performance from a memorized script see Dhahabī, *Tāʾrīkh al-Islām*, BL MS, 58, in which a shaykh was praised for his ability to assimilate three pages at a glance, and then to give the dars without error. Another shaykh praised for giving lectures straight from memory: Ibn Kathīr, 14/169. Ibn Ṣaṣrā was praised for memorizing four lectures a day: Ṣafadī, *al-Wāfī*, 8/16. Even the length of a lecture could be reckoned in terms of the size of the script: a dars of 600 lines (slightly larger than the single standard Syrian fascicule – qaṭᶜ baladī – of 500 lines) was praised for being well delivered: Nuᶜaymī, 1/59. Students were told to memorize the "benefits" (fawāʾid) of the majlis of a shaykh. When departing the majlis they were advised to concentrate on collective memorization (*mudhākara*) of the discourse of the shaykh, "because in collective memorization there is great benefit": Ibn Jamāᶜa, 143. See Ibn ᶜAsākir, *Majlis min majālis al-ḥāfiz Ibn ᶜAsākir fī masjid dimashq* (Damascus, 1979), esp. 18, for an example of how the disciple of a shaykh transcribed the proceedings of a majlis al-ᶜilm, and then read and corrected it with his master. This was also true in ḥadīth scholarship, where listeners copied ḥadīth they heard in ḥadīth-sessions, and reproduced them orally: Ibn al-Ṣalāḥ, *Muqaddima*, 206–8.

233 See for example Ṣafadī, *Aᶜyān*, 201a. For an Irbilī shaykh's lectures taken from a memorized section of Ghazālī's *Ihyāʾ* ("wa-kāna yulqī fī jumla durūsihi min kitāb al-iḥyā darsan ḥifzān"), see Ibn Khallikān, 1/90.

234 See for example the complaint made of a book: "Its complicated and difficult pronunciation leaves no trace on the mind as an aid to memory (faʾinna alfāẓ al-mukhtaṣar qaliqatun ᶜuqdatun mā yartasimu maᶜnāhā fī dhihn li-yusāᶜida ᶜalāʾl-ḥifz)": Nuᶜaymī, 1/248.

235 Ṣafadī, *al-Wāfī*, 4/214.

236 A shaykh was said to have held a dars in which he asked for someone to choose a Qurʾānic verse for discussion "and when they selected one, he discoursed on it with felicitous expressions and great learning, as though he were reading from a book (kaʾinnamā yaqrāʾ min kitāb)." This shaykh was also known for being able to recite a text from memory immediately after having read it but once: Subkī, *Ṭabaqāt*, 5/14. For praise of a shaykh who gave the lecture as though it were a khuṭba see Ṣafadī, *al-Wāfī*, 21/343.

237 Subkī's father for example was known for writing out ten pages of final copy extemporaneously ("min ẓahri qalbih") at a sitting, without making a draft copy: Subkī, *Ṭabaqāt*, 6/170. The author of the 300-volume *Kitāb al-shāmil* wrote extemporaneously without revision,

memorized books, it was not a "private" act. Young people relied on others to prompt them, and after memorizing a text they amended it and corrected it with a shaykh.[238] For this reason, writers warned, "reading with a shaykh is preferable and more advantageous than reading alone."[239] A fine illustration of the blurring of the dars, writing, and memory is an anecdote Ibn Khallikān related of al-Qushayrī (d. 465/1072). Qushayrī sat at the feet of a shaykh for several days, when the shaykh admonished him that the particular field of knowledge could not be acquired solely by auditing, but that it had to be written down as well ("hādhā'l-ᶜilm lā yuḥsal b'il-samāᶜ wa-lā budda mina'ḍ-ḍabṭi b'il-kitāba"). Qushayrī then "astonished" the teacher by repeating exactly everything he had heard in his days of attendance. The shaykh then honored him and told him, unusually: "You do not need the dars; it will be sufficient for you to read my books."[240]

This endless circular displacement between the oral and the written, between production and reproduction, identifies the production of texts as a ritual practice. When students read books with shaykhs it was not just to check them for accuracy, but also to inscribe them in the memory so that they could later be performed orally, and to gain the baraka of the line of transmission. Because of this ritual aspect of the reproduction of books, the writer and the reader were never entirely differentiated from the shaykh and the disciple. Books were never so much read as performed, and learning a book was in part an imitation of the shaykh's performance of the text, including his pronunciation, intonation, and gestures. It was partly for this reason that reading alone without a shaykh was discouraged.[241]

Thus, to answer our original question, what excited suspicion of books was not the texts themselves. The reason that books were objects of such simultaneous esteem and disdain was that the transmission of ᶜilm was not

ready for composition ("kāna yaktub min ṣadrihi min ghayr murājaᶜa kitāb ḥālatu't-taṣnīf"): Dhahabī, *Tā'rīkh al-Islām*, Köp. MS, 21. While in prison Ibn Taymiyya wrote from memory without other books as sources: Ibn ᶜAbd al-Hādī, Köp. MS, 12. Ibn Taymiyya wrote at a rate of a volume (*mujallad*) a day, and was capable of writing out forty pages in a single sitting: *ibid.*, 26; see also Ibn Kathīr, 14/164. See Ibn Abī Uṣaybiᶜa, 687, for a shaykh who wrote without making a draft copy. See Ṣafadī, *al-Wāfī*, 13/85 for Ibn al-Mutahhar al-Ḥillī, witnessed composing on horseback: "kāna yuṣannif wa-hwa rākib"; Ṣafadī, *al-Wāfī*, 13/341 for a bureaucrat who drafted decrees extemporaneously, "from the tip of his pen (min rā's qalamih)." See Subkī, Staatsbibliothek MS, 46 for a shaykh who wrote a commentary entirely from memory ("ᶜalā ẓahr qalbih"). With only pen, ink, paper, and a copy of the text, he quoted voluminously from other commentators, "astonishing" his onlookers.

238 For prompting, see the shaykh who "benefited" students by "facilitating" (ashala) their readings of texts of fiqh: Abū Shāma, *Dhayl*, 149. See Nawawī's account of memorizing books: after listing two books that he memorized, including the *Tanbīh*, the standard of Shāfiᶜi fiqh in the city, "I began to comment on and confirm" the reading of the texts with the aid of a shaykh: "jaᶜaltu ashraḥu wa-'uṣaḥḥiḥu ᶜalā'sh-shaykh": Yūnīnī, 3/285. See also Berkey, *The Transmission of Knowledge*, 30.

239 "Fa'l-qirā'a ᶜalā'l-ᶜulamā' afḍal w'ajdā min qirā'ati'l-insān li-nafsih": Ṣafadī, *al-Wāfī*, 21/109. See Graham, *Beyond the Written Word*, 32–3 for an acute discussion of solitary reading in the pre-modern world more generally.

240 Ibn Khallikān, 2/375.

241 Cf. Graham, *Beyond the Written Word*, 131–42, 160–1, 164–5.

entirely alienated from the ritual nature of its production. Books in medieval Damascus were not yet separated from the oral performances in relation to which they functioned both as records and as scripts. Reading had not yet entirely lost the character of oral forms of transmission. Readers often entered into the physical presence of one another, where their interactions were partly ritual and mimetic; and when readers read books in private they sometimes took them as fetishes standing in for absent shaykhs. Book production was thus only a partially commodified form of cultural production, perhaps closer in this respect to modern music than to modern publishing. In any case, the shaykhs of Damascus could no more expect to be "freed" by the printing press than modern musicians were liberated by the phonograph record. "Education" and "book production" thus reveal themselves as aspects of the same group of ritual and performative practices, rather than formal domains.

Were debates over the relationship of books to memory connected to the struggle for manṣabs? There is some evidence in the sources that the increasing social value of acquired texts made the instrumental use of books a subject for disagreement. Ibn al-Ḥājj argued: "If the stipend (maᶜlūm) of one of us is cut off he resents it and says, if he is a beginner, 'how can I be cut off when I have read the book of so and so and have memorized such and such?' We see students among us say, 'how could so and so receive such and such when I am of greater discernment and understanding, and have memorized more books and narratives (riwāya)?' And the older students compete with their contemporaries for manṣabs in lecturing; such positions come only from standing at the door of the powerful. So how can he gain enlightenment? We study because of stipends."[242] One possibility is that the sources condemned solitary reading so vehemently precisely because the struggle for manṣabs detached texts from the ritual nature of their transmission. It also threatened the monopoly of shaykhs over the transmission of knowledge. This was also partly true in Sung education, in which teachers had ritual roles, were concerned with moral cultivation, and saw the examination system as a threat to the neo-Confucian ideals they inculcated into the young.[243]

Given the importance they attached to the incorporation of paths of transmission of texts, it is not surprising that Damascenes devoted a substantial literature to their intellectual ancestors. The *mashyakha* or *muᶜjam* was a genre that listed the shaykhs with whom an individual had studied, or heard ḥadīth from, and many of the important shaykhs of the city either had one or were subjects of one.[244] Biographies (tarjama) and biographical dictionaries

[242] Ibn al-Ḥājj, 1/18–19. [243] Chafee, *The Thorny Gates of Learning*, 186.

[244] Often written on the occasion of the death of a shaykh, for example Ibn Kathīr, 14/185. See Ṣafadī, *al-Wāfī*, 13/80 for a seventeen-volume mashyakha written by Birzālī for one of the Banū Ṣaṣrā; Ibn Shākir, *Fawāt*, 2/263 for another written by Birzālī for Tāj al-Dīn al-Firkāḥ in ten small volumes. For a "thick" mashyakha as a positive attribute of a shaykh see Ibn Shākir, *Fawāt*, 2/159. For the terms mashyakha and muᶜjam used interchangeably see Ibn Kathīr, 13/337. On mashyakhas and majmūᶜas the fundamental work has been done by G. Vajda, but scholars have been largely uninterested in their social or cultural uses: see G.

(ṭabaqāt) were popular books, and many of the important shaykhs of the cities both wrote biographies and had biographies written of them.[245] Although only the major ṭabaqāt and a few smaller biographies of great shaykhs have survived, a fairly large number of the shaykhs in the city wrote tarjamas of their contemporaries. As large numbers of shaykhs from Iran and the Jazīra settled in the city in the Ayyūbid period, there was a demand for biographies of the shaykhs in lines of transmission emanating from those places.[246]

Such biographies in some respects represented the "real" history of the city as much as documents did in European cities. The aᶜyān of Damascus took few measures to ensure the survival of documents, save those which testified to their positions within a chain of transmission. However, they exerted themselves daily to preserve the memory of shaykhs through whom ᶜilm passed. They rarely flourished documents other than ijāzas as proof of status or honor, but moment by moment they brandished the names, gestures, anecdotes, and texts of their shaykhs. The aᶜyān did not see themselves as members of institutions or formal groups, but rather as exemplars of great shaykhs living and dead. It was exemplarity, a quality of shaykhliness, rather than formal affiliation, that they looked to to secure themselves a place in the world. As the aᶜyān acquired their critical intimacies and affiliations, they gained their social honor more from the incorporation of the adab and baraka of their shaykhs than their bloodlines.

The lecture, the transmission of ḥadīth and of books, and of everyday interactions among students and their teachers were in these respects less a form of higher education as we see it in other societies than a set of ritual and initiatory practices. The bond with the shaykh initiated the young person into the adab of the learned shaykh, a set of acquired dispositions that scripted virtually every aspect of daily life. The student–teacher relationship was thus also a master–disciple relationship.

When young people mastered a text with a shaykh, or attended a lecture, or "served" the shaykh as in his ṣuḥba, the subject matter of education – the texts they studied – was in some respects arbitrary. There were no canons of privileged texts, or the lists of books characteristic of European universities, for the same reason that there were no degrees or professional qualifications:

Vajda, "La liste d'autorités de Manṣūr Ibn Sālim Wajīh al-Dīn al-Hamdānī," *JA* 253 (1965), 341–406; G. Vajda, "Un magmuᶜ damascain du VIIe/XIIIe siècle," *JA* 245 (1957); G. Vajda, *Les certificats de lecture*; and his collected articles in Variorium reprint, N. Cottart ed., *La transmission du savoir en Islam (VIIIe–XVIIIe siècles)* (London, 1983); Berkey, *The Transmission of Knowledge*, 33–4; Ibn al-Ṣalāḥ, *Muqaddima*, 375–6.

245 For one example among many see the biography of Ibn Qudāma: Ṣafadī, *al-Wāfī*, 6/36. Books were also written as accounts of a shaykh's majālis, or of his words and deeds: Subkī, *Ṭabaqāt*, 5/11.

246 For example, Ibn al-Ṣalāḥ al-Shahrazūrī (d. 642/1244–5), a shaykh from the Jazīra who had studied in Khurasān, wrote a *Ṭabaqāt al-fuqahaʾ* in which he related the biographies of the great shaykhs of the Jazīra, Khurasān, and Iran more generally to his associates and students in Damascus. He wrote that his motive for composing it was "maᶜrifa al-insān biʾaḥwāl al-ᶜulamaʾ" – "informing the people about the lives of the learned," Ibn al-Ṣalāḥ al-Shahrazūrī, *Ṭabaqāt al-Fuqahaʾ*, Hamidiye MS, 537.

there were no state or corporate bodies to mandate them. When some books were read more often than others, it was because these were the books that their shaykhs carried, and that they themselves in turn passed on. More important for the long-term strategies of the aʿyān was the latent "curriculum," which permitted the young to incorporate the bodily norms, ritual competencies, and performative techniques of older and more powerful men.

The cult of the well-groomed personality was characteristic of elites throughout agrarian civilizations, and indeed has begun only recently to lose its importance (or change its form) in some areas of the modern world. But compared to the high medieval Middle East, in the other places we have considered correct manners and a sense of style were accompanied by formal mechanisms of social survival. What makes high medieval Damascus different was that exemplarity and the loyalties created by the same ritual and mimetic practices that produced it constituted the most reliable coin of the aʿyān's survival.

CHAPTER 5

Truth, error, and the struggle for social power

This chapter addresses how law or sharīʿa intersected with other social and cultural practices. Medieval Islamic societies are often thought to be unique in the extent to which elites took their social authority from sacred law, just as Islam is thought to be uniquely legalistic. On the surface, there is much to recommend this view. There is no doubt that the aʿyān learned the sciences of the sharīʿa partly to qualify themselves as exponents of sacred law. Moreover, the all-encompassing nature of the sharīʿa, which included matters of cult, ethics, and family relations in addition to criminal, commercial, and administrative law, meant that legal forms of authority and argumentation were applied to many areas of social life. Finally, the representative social type of the civilian elite is often thought to be the qāḍī or muftī, whose position and authority were derived largely from knowledge of the law. Secretaries too were advised to become learned in the law so they would not be dependent as the *muqallad* or follower of a legal scholar.[1] There would thus seem to be little reason to reject the widespread characterization of Islamic societies as "nomocracies."

However, there are at least two reasons to qualify this perception. First, the extent to which the aʿyān's cultivation of law distinguished Islamic societies from others is at least debatable. As Weber pointed out, in a number of agrarian societies in which elites competed for prebends they cast themselves as carriers and interpreters of sacred law.[2] Second, even when the aʿyān's social struggles were cast in legal terms, their struggles for authority and prestige among themselves, and vis-à-vis others, often had little to do with the sharīʿa in the strictest sense. The legal aspect of their social power is perhaps both less unique and less comprehensive than scholars have generally recognized. In concentrating on the legal capacity of the learned elite, we may have overlooked or downplayed other uses of their knowledge.

Rather than contribute to the already large body of literature on the legal roles and functions of the aʿyān, this chapter suggests that we might interpret

[1] See Ibn al-Firkāḥ, *Kitāb Sharḥ wa-iqrār Imām al-Ḥaramayn*, BN MS 1226 Arabe, 178a-179b.
[2] Weber, "The Chinese Literati," 126; Weber, *Economy and Society*, vol. II, 784–808.

the practices by which the learned elite made use of their knowledge in social struggles among themselves and against others. It covers two related issues. It first examines how the aᶜyān imagined the social world and the nature of social competition. It then interprets how the aᶜyān made use of their control over law and knowledge in social competition.

ᶜIlm and making social hierarchies

To amīrs and aᶜyān both, status, power, and wealth were prizes won through competitive struggle. The sources described the marks of distinction of both groups in similar language. Amīrs and civilian elites alike were shuyūkh, khawāṣṣ, aᶜyān, and akābir (elders, elites, notables, and grandees).[3] As the military were "lords of the sword" (*arbāb as-sayf*), the civilian elite were also "lords," either of the pen or of the stipendiary posts (arbāb al-qalam or arbāb al-manāṣib).[4] Shaykhs represented leadership with language taken from warriors, such as the waqf established for the "amīr of the Ḥanbalīs" (amīr al-ḥanābila), and the shaykh described as the "sulṭān of the learned" (sulṭān al-ᶜulamāʾ).[5]

The aᶜyān also portrayed distinction and social competition in the language of military heroism. Scholars were the "swords of God in Syria" (suyūf Allah fiʾsh-shām), and shaykhs were the "standard-bearers" of their fields, madhhabs, or groups.[6] The scholars of a field of knowledge were its "horsemen" (*fāris*) or "armies" (*juyūsh*), and their words were "the swords of books."[7] Ḥadīth scholars described themselves as "a little troop, few in number, low on supplies."[8] Learned heroes were dubbed the "swords of the theologians" (sayf al-mutakallimīn), the "swords of debaters" (sayf al-munāẓirīn), and the "horsemen of the Ḥanbalīs."[9] Damascenes also associated great scholars with legendary heroes such as ᶜAntar and Marwān Ibn al-Ḥakam.[10] They imagined

[3] For amīrs as shaykhs see Ṣafadī, *Aᶜyān*, 102a; for the aᶜyān al-umarāʾ see *ibid*., 89a; Yūnīnī, 3/46, 238.

[4] For examples of the arbāb as-sayf contrasted to the arbāb al-manāṣib or arbāb al-qalam, see Ibn Wāṣil, 4/228; Ṣafadī, *al-Wāfī*, 13/190. Such martial metaphors also described scholarly competition in the Latin West; see for example the honorific of Abelard as the "chevalier de la dialectique": Makdisi, *The Rise of Colleges*, 130.

[5] For the amīr al-ḥanābila see Nuᶜaymī, 2/99. For the honorific sulṭān al-ᶜulamāʾ, applied to Ibn ᶜAbd al-Salām, see Subkī, *Muᶜīd al-niᶜam*, 70. Leadership of other groups was expressed through the term sulṭān: for the term sulṭān al-ᶜārifīn (sulṭān of the ṣūfīs), see Ṣafadī, *al-Wāfī*, 4/219; for the sulṭān al-harāfīsh see W. M. Brinner, "The Significance of the Ḥarafīsh and their Sulṭān," *JESHO* 6 (1963), 190–215.

[6] For the "swords of God" see Jazarī, BN MS, 240; for standard-bearers of fields or groups see Ibn Kathīr, 14/40, 137; Ibn ᶜAbd al-Hādī, Köp. MS, 5, 11; Ibn Shākir, *Fawāt*, 1/72 of the Cairo edition; Subkī, *Ṭabaqāt*, 6/251–2.

[7] Subkī, *Ṭabaqāt*, 6/217, 227, 251. See also Ibn Shākir, *Fawāt*, 1/158, for the "furūsiyya" or horsemanship of a scholar in his field.

[8] "Hum shirdhima qalīlatuʾl-ᶜadad ḍaᶜīfatuʾl-ᶜudad": Ibn al-Ṣalāḥ, *Muqaddima*, 76.

[9] Ṣafadī, *al-Wāfī*, 1/243, 21/253; Ṣafadī, *Aᶜyān*, 30b; Ibn Ḥajar, 1/160.

[10] Ṣafadī, *Aᶜyān*, 199a; Ṣafadī, *al-Wāfī*, 4/214.

competition for status and position through metaphors taken from the hippodrome.[11] A debate was a duel in the lists, an argument a sword or a knife. The debater triumphed with the "sword of eloquence," "slashing through obscurities men of the sword have never known," finally "killing the feeble-minded opponent."[12] A scholar "unsheathed the sword of the tongue of eloquence to make war on his opponent."[13] Through such symbolic equivalencies shaykhs and amīrs imagined dominance and distinction in similar terms.

Because Damascus had no "natural" or bureaucratic social hierarchies, and because there was no educational system to reproduce existing social divisions, the aʿyān continuously renegotiated status among themselves. One striking quality of the authors of the biographical dictionaries and their subjects (who were often enough intimates of the authors), was the effort they put into ranking the world and its inhabitants. Both the authors of the sources and their subjects as they describe them learned to imagine the world in hierarchies. The aʿyān sorted out hierarchies among themselves based on their learning in a wide variety of fields, and on their skill in practices such as lecturing, debate, and writing fatwās.[14]

At the top of a hierarchy of relations to ʿilm was leadership or dominance (riyāsa or imāma; or *rāʾasa*, *fāqa*, or *sāda* when expressed in verbal form).[15] Riyāsa of course was also a quality the military tried to acquire.[16] Being the dominant authority in a field could make a shaykh the *mushār ilayhi*, the "authority of reference."[17] Riyāsa often was an honorific and not a recognized position (physicians appear to be an exception), such as the "leadership of the learned" (riyāsa al-ʿulamāʾ)" said to have characterized Ibn Jamāʿa, or the "leadership of the universe" (imāmatuʾd-dunyā) attributed to the father of

[11] For example, Subkī, *al-Rasāʾil al-Subkiyya*, 94; Subkī, *Ṭabaqāt*, 6/160.

[12] Subkī, *Ṭabaqāt*, 6/61–2; Ṣafadī, *al-Wāfī*, 4/227; Nuʿaymī, 1/248. [13] Subkī, *Ṭabaqāt*, 6/61.

[14] Ibn Kathīr, 14/141. For riyāsa in medicine, see Dhahabī, *Tāʾrīkh al-Islām*, BL MS, 72; for uses of the verbal forms fāqa and sāda see Ibn Kathīr, 13/325 and Dhahabī, *Tāʾrīkh al-Islām*, Köp. MS, 11. For an example of riyāsa in calligraphy see Dhahabī, *Tāʾrīkh al-Islām*, BL MS, 20.

[15] Cf. riyāsa in the Buyīd Iran and ʿIrāq: Mottahedeh, *Loyalty and Leadership*, 129–50. See also Makdisi, *The Rise of Colleges*, 129–33. To Makdisi, riyāsa was a formal status: "The system whereby the fitness of a candidate to teach could be determined . . . is to be found in the institution of riyāsa": Makdisi, *The Rise of Colleges*, 130. According to Makdisi, riyāsa was attained through skill in disputation: "No one could claim riyāsa without mastering the new art." By restricting riyāsa to the madrasa, and by claiming that madrasas went only to those who mastered jadal, Makdisi intends to advance his argument that madrasas dominated intellectual life, and that lecturers were a social and occupational type. However well his formulation may work for other places, in Damascus there were many people who had riyāsa in one field or another without an appointment in a madrasa; and in madrasas there were many people who had appointments without riyāsa in anything being attributed to them. Disputation was rarely associated with riyāsa, though there were people who had riyāsa in disputation, as in other fields. See also Makdisi, "Ṣuḥba et riyāsa," 207–11. Riyāsa was the term for leadership in most fields and groups. Physicians had a raʾīs aṭ-ṭibb, who was appointed by the sulṭān: Qalqashandī, 12/6–7. Leadership of the Jewish community of Syria was also understood as riyāsa: *ibid.*

[16] See Nuʿaymī, 1/218 for an example of al-Malik al-Muẓaffar's riyāsa.

[17] Yūnīnī, 3/95; Nuʿaymī, 1/227.

Ibn Daqīq al-ᶜĪd.[18] Following riyāsa in status was having a leading position (*taqaddum*). Scholars could also have a "share" (mushāraka) in a field like the "share" in a manṣab or an iqṭāᶜ. Where civilian elites reckoned the "share" to be a mediocre distinction, or a compromise between rivals, to the military a share in a field of knowledge was a mark of high prestige.[19] At the bottom of this scheme of classification was having a taste (*dhawq*) for a field of knowledge.[20]

Perhaps the most desirable sign of status, and a fixed target of social struggle, was fame or renown (*shuhra, dhikr, samᶜa* – also *sumᶜa* – and *ṣīt*). Aᶜyān and amīrs alike regarded having a name that extended beyond the city or better still beyond Syria as one of the surest marks of social distinction.[21] The aᶜyān as a group were occasionally referred to as "the famous" (*al-mashāhīr*).[22] The sources were alert to the first signs of celebrity, and described gaining a reputation outside the city as a stage in a scholarly career.[23] A young man "flashed his merit like a bright star rising on the horizon."[24] Another saw his name "fly to the horizons, to fill the regions of the earth, and soar above the universe."[25]

This attention to fame was not merely the meaningless repetition of literary commonplaces. The biographical dictionaries enumerated in detail areas in which their subjects were famous.[26] When shaykhs composed their own biographies they paraded the first signs of their fame as an all-important mark of distinction. An anecdote Abū Shāma recounted of his own birth allows us to see how fame was seen by shaykhs themselves, and not just by their biographers, as a mark of social honor. When he was a boy, Abū Shāma informed his readers, he took unusual pleasure in his lessons. When acquaintances expressed surprise at the joy he took in learning, his mother had a ready answer: "Do not be surprised. When I was pregnant with him, I dreamt that I was at the top of a minaret delivering the call to prayer. When I mentioned this to an acquaintance, he said, 'you will give birth to a male child, whose fame will spread throughout the earth.'"[27] Fame rather than title was also the marker of

[18] Ibn Ḥajar, 1/39; Subkī, *Ṭabaqāt*, 6/19. See also the "riyāsatuʾd-dīn wʾad-dunyā" attributed to Fakhr al-Dīn Ibn ᶜAsākir: Ibn Shākir, Vat. Ar. MS, 61.

[19] For example, a learned governor of the city, founder of a madrasa, had a mushāraka in various fields of knowledge: Nuᶜaymī, 169–70; al-Malik al-Amjad had a share in the sciences he had studied: Ṣafadī, *al-Wāfī*, 12/6.

[20] Ṣafadī, *al-Wāfī*, 5/15.

[21] See for a few examples the soldier who had ṣīt among the Franks: Yunını, 4/56; the princes of the "people of unbelief" (ahl al-kufr) fear the sumᶜa of mamlūk amīrs: Qalqashandī, 12/15; for "famous" amīrs of Damascus, including one "famous for horsemanship," see Ṣafadī, *Aᶜyān*, 89a, 89b. For examples of scholarly fame see Yūnīnī, 3/14; Subkī, *Ṭabaqāt*, 6/31; Ṣafadī, *al-Wāfī*, 7/19; Jazarī, BN MS, 369.

[22] For one example see Ibn al-Dawādārī, 9/23.

[23] See Ṣafadī, *Aᶜyān*, 200a; Ibn ᶜAbd al-Hādī, *Ṭabaqāt*, 4/283; Subkī, *Ṭabaqāt*, 6/245; Subkī, Staatsbibliothek MS, 14.

[24] Ṣafadī, *Aᶜyān*, 125b.

[25] Subkī, *Ṭabaqāt*, 6/156; for a similar expression, "his name flew to fill the regions," see Subkī, Staatsbibliothek MS, 21.

[26] For one example, see Yūnīnī 4/101 for an enumeration of the fields in which a scholar had ṣīt.

[27] Abū Shāma, *Dhayl*, 38. For other dreams of fame on the part of parents see Ibn Khallikān, 2/331, 325.

social capacity. Someone in need of a fatwā or medical care, or who desired to learn a certain field of knowledge, sought out not a specific office but an individual "famous" in the field.[28] With fame, as with so many other aspects of the struggle for status, pedigreed, certified, or chartered capacity was of little use; rather, it was an acquired honorific that was the object of competitive struggle.

As is often the case in elite struggles for scarce markers of status, some stood on their dignity and represented themselves as above the fray. Most, however, had an ambiguous relationship to self-assertion. On the one hand, acquiring ʿilm for the sake of fame was denounced as a misappropriation of learning for worldly ends.[29] On the other, self-assertion was expected and often lauded as a virtue: of amīrs and ʿulamāʾ the highest praise was: "No one equaled him, and no one opposed him in anything he did."[30]

Ranking

Without formal distinctions of rank or birth, Damascenes were all the more alert to subtle gradations in prestige. The biographical dictionaries rated people against others, and reported on how people rated one another. As there were few formal distinctions of status, much less inherited ones, prestige was an elusive prize of competitive struggle. Examining their subjects for signs of superiority, the sources seized upon any indication of it, including everyday activities such as prayer.[31] In many entries, "surpassing [one's] contemporaries" was represented as the object of social labor.[32] As always, we can never know whether specific individuals in fact possessed the qualities attributed to them, but the abundant use of these terms in the sources demonstrates that the aʿyān understood their struggles in such language.

Such honorifics could have immediate practical uses, and appointments to manṣabs often mentioned them. The appointment of Ibn Khallikān to the tadrīs of the Amīniyya referred to him as "the unique one who has no peer (al-awḥad alladhī lā naẓīr lahu)."[33] In a competition over the tadrīs of the Khātūniyya, one party had the "imāms of Syria" write out a document on his behalf, which they loaded with his praises.[34] The praises that occupy so much space in the biographical dictionaries thus were not merely literary commonplaces, nor did they merely reflect social struggle: they were objects of it.[35]

[28] For an example of fame for knowing a particular text, see Yūnīnī, 3/75; see also Subkī, *Ṭabaqāt*, 6/31 for a famous marginal commentary. For seeking out qāḍīs and others "famous" for their fatwās, see Ṣafadī, *al-Wāfī*, 22/449. See Ibn Abī Uṣaybiʿa, 637, 672, for "famous" physicians. [29] Ibn Jamāʿa, 19.

[30] For amīrs see Yūnīnī, 3/46; also Ibn Khallikān, 1/165; see Ṣafadī, *Aʿyān*, 141b, for a secretary who had killed "any who opposed him"; for civilians see Subkī, *Ṭabaqāt*, 6/174.

[31] For example, "I never saw anyone pray as well as he": Dhahabī, *Tāʾrīkh al-Islām*, BL MS, 14.

[32] For fāqa ahl ʿaṣrihi, see Yūnīnī, 3/79; for an example of sāda ahla zamānihi see Ibn Kathīr, 13/12. [33] Yūnīnī, 4/143. [34] Ibn Ḥajar, 1/43.

[35] For a later example of how such praise figured in a suggested format for an ijāza see Qalqashandī, 14/322.

The biographical dictionaries ranked many of their subjects in hierarchies, including ascetics, soldiers, scholars of all types, and artists and musicians.[36] The terms ʿadīm al-naẓīr (without peer), waḥīd dahrihi (the unique of his age), aḥdhaq an-nās (the most intelligent of the people), awḥad (the unique), ashar ahl zamānihi (the most famous of the people of his time), afḍal aqrānihi (the best of his contemporaries), awḥad al-ʿaṣr (the unique of the age), farīd ad-dahr (the singular of the age), baraka al-waqt (the baraka of the age), baraka al-ʿilm (the baraka of ʿilm), aʿlam ʿaṣrihi ʿilman (the most learned of his time in ʿilm), shaykh al-waqt (the shaykh of the age), sayyid ahl al-islām fī zamānihi (the leader of the people of Islam in his time) appear so frequently in the biographical dictionaries that they became the points around which narratives were constructed.[37] Even in death shaykhs were rated against others, as their funerals were objects of competitive ranking.[38] Many who merited more than a cursory line or two in a death-notice were said to be the best, the unique, the singular, in one field or another. One reason for the existence of the genre was to provide a means by which carriers of ʿilm in the past as in the present could be rated.[39]

After listing several such honorifics, biographers often proceeded to a more expanded version of them. "He surpassed the people of his age in the East and the West (fāqa ahl zamānihi sharqan wa-gharban)."[40] "He carried the day against all of his contemporaries (ḥāza qasabaʾs-sabq)."[41] "He surpassed the minor and the major (fāqa al-asāghir wʾal-akābir) with respect to ʿilm."[42] One entry referred to "the unique of his time in the number of his fields (awḥad zamānihi fī taʿaddud al-faḍāʾil)."[43] In many death-notices, such rankings took up the greater part of an entry, and they occasionally fill long passages. Subkī for example wrote two-and-a-half dense pages comparing his father to dozens of other scholars.[44]

Such honorifics were not just "formulas," as scholars who have waded through the biographical dictionaries have occasionally dismissed them. It is true that we often do not know whether an honorific attributed to a single individual in the sources was in fact applied to him by his contemporaries –

[36] See Yūnīnī, 3/135 for an example of ranking of ascetics by their piety. For ranking of musicians see the punning praise of a fiddler: "lam yakun ka-man rāḥ wa-lā ka-man jā" (of those who came and went, there was no one like him), playing off kamanjā, the two-string fiddle: Ṣafadī, *Aʿyān*, 9a. For ranking of a calligrapher see Ṣafadī, *al-Wāfī*, 10/259. For a complex ranking of the ḥadīth scholars of the city see Subkī, *Ṭabaqāt*, 6/252.

[37] For these, which constitute a small number of the total, see Jazarī, BN MS, 69–71, 194; Abū Shāma, *Dhayl*, 131; Dhahabī, *Tāʾrīkh al-Islām*, BL MS, 5, 15; Ibn Nāṣir al-Dīn, BL MS, 6, 7; Ṣafadī, *al-Wāfī*, 4/144, 21/340, 349; Ibn Rajab, 2/307, 308; Nuʿaymī, 1/226. These were applied to different fields of knowledge, including medicine: see Ibn Abī Uṣaybiʿa, 636, 646, 661, 663 for physicians known as "the unique of his age (awḥad zamānihi)" in medicine and in other fields such as time-keeping and astronomy.

[38] See for example Subkī, *Ṭabaqāt*, 6/216.

[39] See for one example Ṣafadī, *al-Wāfī*, 11/420.

[40] Ibn Kathīr, 13/71.

[41] *Ibid.*, 13/325.

[42] Ibn Shākir, 21/261.

[43] Dhahabī, *Tāʾrīkh al-Islām*, BL MS, 16. See Kazimirski for "science" in the French sense as one of the meanings of the word faḍāʾil.

[44] Subkī, *Ṭabaqāt*, 6/179–82; in Subkī, Staatsbibliothek MS, 18–19, he quoted a long passage from Ṣafadī's *Aʿyān* comparing his father to others in rhyming prose.

though in the case of Damascus, because of its unusually detailed sources, often enough in fact we do. The possibility that an anecdote may be untrue is why scholars have been wary of these sources. That these honorifics were advantageous in social struggle, however, there should be no doubt – as can be seen in the effort the authors of our sources put into describing themselves with such language when given the opportunity. Both biographers and their subjects as they describe them struggled for such honorifics and often made use of them when they possessed them.

The very ubiquity of such honorifics in the sources shows that negotiating these terms was ingrained in the rhetorical forms by which the biographical dictionaries and their subjects represented the social universe. When biographers – and their subjects as they depicted them – described themselves and others, they were impatient with relations of equivalence. Again and again we see them struggling with orders of precedence. When a young person set out to learn ḥadīth, he should begin with the "best of his shaykhs with respect to their ᶜilm, their fame (shuhra), or their eminence (sharaf)."[45] An example of how this propensity to rank shaped the aᶜyān's experience of the world was the quandary one Damascene fell into and resolved in a dream. In his dream he encountered his brother, who had been dead for a year. When he learned that his brother resided in the garden of Eden, he could only think to ask him: "Which of the two is better, the Ḥāfiẓ ᶜAbd al-Ghanī or Abū ᶜUmar?" He was referring to two brothers of the Banū Qudāma, both known for their piety, learning, and asceticism, whom it would have been difficult to rank. The brother replied: "I do not know, but in the case of the Ḥāfiẓ, a chair is set up for him every Friday beneath the divine throne (*al-ᶜirsh*), and ḥadīth are read to him, and pearls and jewels are scattered upon him."[46] Some aᶜyān even ranked their children, and others their ancestors, as in the shaykh who wrote that his grandfather was "greater" than his father.[47]

Such rankings also compared the living to their dead exemplars. Subkī wrote of a shaykh, in punning Arabic whose full effect cannot be conveyed: "In tafsīr, he was the imprisonment of Ibn ᶜAtiyya, and the fall of al-Rāzī into disaster (*razīʾa*); in qirāʾāt he was the exile of al-Dānī, and the impoverishment of al-Sakhāwī . . . in ḥadīth – what a catastrophe for Ibn ᶜAsākir, and as for al-Khaṭīb (al-Baghdādī), better not to mention it; in uṣūl, how dull was Fakhr al-Dīn (al-Rāzī's) sword-edge, and how his excellence was tormented by injustice; in fiqh [he was] the perdition of al-Juwaynī . . . and he pulled al-Rafiᶜī to the depths; in logic he was the flight of Dabīrān; in khilāf he was the destruction of al-Naṣafī."[48] Damascenes also compared shaykhs to dead exemplars out of outrage at social failure. When al-Mizzī lost his manṣab at the dār al-ḥadīth al-Ashrafiyya during a fitna, the shaykh who dismissed him said: "My skin crawled and my mind reeled. I said to myself, 'this is the Imām of the muḥaddithūn! By God, if Dārulquṭnī were alive he would be ashamed to

[45] Ibn al-Ṣalāḥ, *Muqaddima*, 369. [46] Ibn Rajab, 2/31.
[47] Ibn Abī Uṣaybiᶜa, 691; Jazarī, BN MS, 330. [48] Subkī, *Ṭabaqāt*, 6/154.

give the lecture in his place!' "[49] This constant comparison of the living with the dead was one way the aʿyān made use of the past to make sense of the present and secure the future.

The biographical dictionaries' criteria of inclusion and ranking could become a subject of dispute. When Ibn Abī Uṣaybiʿa was composing his dictionary of physicians, one of his teachers came across a draft copy and complained that while Shihāb al-Dīn al-Suhrawardī was included, others of greater virtue, himself included, were not.[50] In a world in which status shifted constantly, elites weighed and evaluated one another unendingly. The loyalties they nurtured over lifetimes could fracture in a single invidious comparison. Similarly, the conflicting imperatives between the instinct to rank and the experience of social bonds as ties of intimacy produced inevitable inner conflicts. On his death-bed a shaykh named ʿAlī told Tāj al-Dīn al-Subkī that the absence of Tāj al-Dīn's brother Aḥmad was harder on him "than either his illness or his son's absence." Tāj al-Dīn continued: "And it reached him that my brother's lectures were superior to his, so he said, 'the lectures of Aḥmad are better than the lectures of ʿAlī, and that in ʿAlī's opinion is his highest hope.' "[51] The resolution of this socially produced inner tension was in playing off the names of the people involved, as the Prophet Muhammad was known as Aḥmad, and his son-in-law and cousin ʿAlī Ibn Abī Ṭālib could take second place in the normal course of things.

Social combat and the imagination of status in space

As there were few formal or "natural" criteria of social classification, the sources, and their subjects as they described them, were especially alert to the negotiation of status in the protocol of spatial arrangements. Shaykhs felt the need to work out hierarchies immediately, as one individual in each group had to have precedence in speaking, standing, sitting, and praying. Ibn Jamāʿa suggested how protocols of deference might be worked out in the lecture: "If the shaykh be [seated] in the middle . . . then the superior (faḍl) of the group deserve to be on his [immediate] right and left; and if the shaykh should sit on the edge of a bench, then the most venerable and respected should be against the wall, or facing him. It is customary in the lecture-session (majlis at-tadrīs) for the most distinguished (*mutamayyizīn*) to sit facing the lecturer, and it is important for those in attendance (*al-rufaqāʾ*) to sit to one side in order that the shaykh may look upon them as a group during the explication (*sharḥ*) and not to have to single out one over the others."[52]

When shaykhs gathered in groups, they worked out the ever-shifting hierarchies among themselves. In the dars, for example, the lecturer should begin by "honoring all those present, dignifying the most notable among them

[49] Subkī, *Ṭabaqāt*, 6/253. [50] *Ibid.*, 647. [51] Subkī, Staatsbibliothek MS, 36.
[52] Ibn Jamāʿa, 148–9.

(afāḍilahum) by knowledge, age, piety, honor (sharaf), according to their precedence. He should be kind to the others and honor them by the excellence of his greeting. He should not disdain to rise for the most important among the people of Islām (akābir ahl al-islām) in order to honor them, as concerning the honoring of the ʿulamāʾ and seekers after knowledge (ṭalaba) there are many precedents."[53] Without established protocols of deference, they made up their own as they struggled for precedence.[54]

Such codes never assigned unambiguous meaning to each action, but were rather subject to rearrangement to express a variety of meanings. For example, traversing apparent hierarchies expressed "genuine" intimacy or esteem. We might note for this purpose a story Yūnīnī related of an amīr in Cairo. The amīr entered the house of another amīr, who was holding a session of samāʿ. Observing his host's entourage (khawāṣṣ) and mamlūks seated in the iwān, and a group of ṣūfīs (*fuqarāʾ*) seated in the courtyard, he paused and did not enter. He said to the owner of the house and to the amīrs: "You have made a mistake. It is the ṣūfīs who should be seated above, and you below." The amīr would not enter until they exchanged places.[55] Another example of a paradoxical reversal of established protocols of deference was when the father of Yūnīnī, dining with Shaykh ʿUthmān, a noted holy man, commenced to eat without waiting for the shaykh. When someone expressed surprise, Yūnīnī replied: "The point here is to obtain the baraka of Shaykh ʿUthmān, so let us leave the decision of whether to eat to him."[56] Thus he simultaneously expressed his esteem for the shaykh and cast himself in an exemplary light as defender of a deeper norm than the one his interlocutor invoked. This surprising contradiction of the expected order appears as a recurring mark of distinction or humiliation. One of the highest marks of social power was the capacity to invert or reverse expected hierarchical relations.[57]

When chroniclers reported major events, they focused on the reflection of status in the relative positions of the participants. An account of an inaugural lecture given in the ʿĀdiliyya described the positions of the participants around the sulṭān according to their waẓīfas.[58] The author then ranked the lecture in

[53] Ibn Jamāʿa, 33. See also *ibid.*, 152–3: "The student must treat those in attendance upon the shaykh with adab, for his good manners are for [the sake of] the shaykh, and respect for his majlis, for they are his companions (rufaqāʾ) . . . he should honor his superiors (kubarāʾahu) by not sitting in the middle of the ḥalqa, nor in front of anyone, except in case of necessity . . . He should not separate two friends (rafīq), nor two companions (mutaṣaḥib) except with their permission, and [nor should he sit] above someone who is superior to him (man huwa awlā minhu). When someone arrives, it is incumbent on those present to welcome him and to make a space for him; people should not crowd him out, or turn their sides or backs to him."

[54] For one example see the Mālikī chief qāḍī who demanded to sit above the other qāḍīs because of his age and his priority, presumably in office ("the date of his hijra," also used to refer to the beginning of the service of warriors to their ustādhs or the sulṭān): Ṣafadī, *Aʿyān*, 12a.

[55] Yūnīnī, 2/351. A similar story is related in Jazari, BN MS, 496. [56] Yūnīnī, 2/47.

[57] Anecdotes attesting to the power of the sulṭān to invert expected hierarchies are not rare in the sources. One anecdote intended to illustrate al-Kāmil's sense of justice related that a squire complained of an injustice received at the hands of his ustādh. Al-Kāmil had them exchange cloaks and riding animals, and had the ustādh serve his squire for six months: Ibn Kathīr, 13/149; Ṣafadī, *al-Wāfī*, 1/194; Nuʿaymī, 2/279. [58] Ibn Shākir, Vat. Ar. MS, 54–5.

relation to other audiences, concluding that only an audience held in 623/1226 equaled it.[59] Virtually the entire narrative consisted of rankings in space, in time, and in prestige. Another example of how this rhetoric of ranking structured historical narratives was the description of an audience held by Qalāwūn. Accounts of the audience first described in detail the positions of the participants relative to one another, then showed how those positions were undermined. When Ibn Taymiyya, who enjoyed Qalāwūn's esteem, entered the room, Qalāwūn broke with established practice and walked across the room, took Ibn Taymiyya by the hand, and walked with him before praising him to the group.[60] Structuring narratives around the spatial arrangement of the participants, followed by the undermining or inversion of those arrangements, was one way elites charted ever-shifting status relationships and plotted their own movements within them.

Shaykhs organized not only themselves, but also things, through the same classificatory schemes. Throughout the sources, questions of priority appear again and again, addressed to a wide variety of objects. What city is the best, the most sacred, the most pious? Which field of knowledge is the most beneficial?[61] Who was superior, ʿAlī or Abū Bakr?[62] In giving a series of lectures, which subject should have precedence?[63] When shaykhs discussed texts, they sought to determine the most correct version, and rated them as they rated shaykhs.[64] The elaborate practices applied to ranking texts and arranging them in space mirrored identical practices of ranking and arranging people, the ordering principles in both cases being their fame (shuhra), their benefit (nafʿ), and their eminence (sharaf). As Ibn Jamāʿa described them, these practices were both precise and emphatic:

Books should be stored in the order of precedence of [first] the field of knowledge they belong to, [second] their eminence (sharaf), [third] their authors, and [fourth] their excellence. The most eminent should be placed above the rest, and then the others [follow] by order of precedence. If there is a Qurʾān among them, it should occupy the place of precedence . . . then books of ḥadīth, then interpretation of the Qurʾān, then interpretation of ḥadīth (tafsīr al-ḥadīth), then dogmatic theology (uṣūl al-dīn), then jurisprudence (uṣūl al-fiqh). If two books pertain to the same branch of knowledge, then the uppermost should be the one containing the most quotations from the Qurʾān and ḥadīth. If they are equivalent in that respect, then [the criterion is] the prestige (*jalāla*) of the writer. If they are equal in that respect, then [the criterion is] the most correct of them.[65]

[59] *Ibid.* [60] Ibn Kathīr, 14/52, 53; Ibn ʿAbd al-Hādī, Köp. MS, 98–9.

[61] Ibn al-Ṣalāḥ, *Muqaddima*, 75 for a claim that the ḥadīth scholarship was "the best of the excellent sciences (afḍal al-ʿulūm al-fāḍila); the most beneficial of the beneficial fields of knowledge."

[62] See Ibn Khallikān, 2/322, for a struggle in Baghdād between sunnīs and shīʿa over the question, eventually calmed by Ibn al-Jawzī, who cast the solution to the question in the form of a riddle that allowed both sides to believe their claims vindicated.

[63] One suggested order went as follows: first tafsīr, then ḥadīth, uṣūl al-dīn, uṣūl al-fiqh, khilāf, naḥw, and jadal: Ibn Jamāʿa, 35–6. [64] Sibṭ Ibn al-Jawzī, *Mirʾāt*, 8/671.

[65] Ibn Jamāʿa, 171. Al-Zarnūjī suggested a simpler form of ranking: tafsīr should be placed over all other books, and no book should be placed above the Qurʾān: Zarnūjī, 35.

These practices of classification were especially important in a society in which status was the prize of negotiation, assertion, and struggle. They did not only reflect the social world: learning to classify was a necessary skill of social combat. The talent of classification, the distinguishing of the higher from the lower, the inner from the outer, and the better from the worse, thus extended to many objects and practices within the scope of the aᶜyān's vision. As both an object and a tool of social labor, this way of seeing was also a skill of social action.

There was another consequence to the necessity of acquiring status on one's own. Distinction was seen as the reward of labor, not of any intrinsic quality. The learned elite had no cult of "natural" intelligence or genius. What they valued was a form of knowledge, and a form of deportment associated with it, that subjected the young to agony. As one shaykh advised: "He who knows not the pain of learning will never taste the pleasure of ᶜilm."[66] In the ancient world, where a notable's dignity depended on his reputation as a "man of leisure," the cultivation of knowledge was known by terms such as *otium*' derived from words meaning ease or leisure. Medieval Muslims by contrast stressed the laborious nature of learning. Students were known as *mushtaghilūn* – those who labor, as teaching was *ishghāl* or *ishtighāl*, making students work.[67] Writers cherished signs of exhaustion in their subjects. A poem Abū Shāma quoted in praise of himself went: "O envious ones! He (Abū Shāma) is one who exhausted himself, as a boy, a youth, and a man with the incessant labor of study."[68] Zarnūjī warned his readers that becoming a shaykh required labor: "Who desires advancement without fatigue wastes his life in quest of the absurd."[69] The sources fixed on signs of fatigue that left their marks on the bodies of the learned, such as the scholar's weak eyesight – a prize of "too much reading and weeping."[70] When Taqī al-Dīn al-Subkī arrived at the dār al-ḥadīth al-Ashrafiyya, he "was on the point of exhaustion," from "rousing the students from the couches of indolence."[71] The aᶜyān of Damascus had no cults of the "natural" distinction and taste of hereditary aristocracies or the "giftedness" of the modern upper middle classes. They acquired their distinction through labors that took the self and its presentation as their objects.

ᶜIlm, error, and fitna

The aᶜyān of Damascus were as alert to error as aristocrats elsewhere were to points of honor. Chroniclers and biographers described many edifying

[66] Ibn Abī Uṣaybiᶜa, 692.
[67] For one example of the common use of this term see Ṣafadī, *al-Wāfī*, 4/194.
[68] Abū Shāma, *Dhayl*, 41.
[69] Zarnūjī, 39. The remainder of the passage reads: "No gain of riches is possible without difficulties that you must take upon yourself. Hence, how is it possible for learning [to be acquired without difficulty]? . . . It is by much hard work that you will gain the highest distinction. Therefore, he who seeks learning stays awake at night."
[70] Ibn Kathīr, 13/39. [71] Subkī, Staatsbibliothek MS, 14–15.

struggles against error. One exemplar of vigilance against error was the shaykh who heard a mistake in the recitation of the Qurʾān at his own funeral, and revived long enough to correct it.[72] A similar story was told of the great ḥadīth scholar al-Mizzī, who would awaken instantly from a nap to correct any error, "as though someone had awakened him."[73] An especially revealing incident was the interrogation in 718/1318–19 of a shaykh concerning an error he made in a dream. In the aftermath he was forbidden to deliver fatwās or contract marriages.[74] Questions of truth and error have a social dimension in many societies; in Damascus, where the aᶜyān derived their power and social honor largely from their learning, there were few social antagonisms that were not also experienced as conflicts between the sound and the specious.

As the aᶜyān made frequent written and oral productions extemporaneously, in every performance there lurked the possibility of a public and humiliating error.[75] Error-free performances were difficult for several reasons. One was the challenge of reciting unpointed and grammatically difficult Arabic texts.[76] Another was that much of the learning of the ᶜulamāʾ consisted of memorized lists of relatively random words, especially genealogies and isnāds.[77] Blunders in spelling, pronunciation, or recitation of one of these motley lists brought humiliation.[78] One of the main objects of working on texts with shaykhs was to give elites the knack or practical know-how of making successful "spontaneous" performances out of such challenging material. The biographical dictionaries repeatedly praised scholars for reciting memorized texts without error.[79] This is also one reason why mastery of grammar was so important to them. Knowledge of grammar was a critical skill not just in understanding or composing texts, but also in these performances that tested the aᶜyān's social honor.[80]

Alertness to error, and the uses of error as the point of honor in elite social

[72] Yūnīnī, 4/183. [73] Subkī, *Ṭabaqāt*, 6/252. [74] Ibn Kathīr, 14/88.

[75] Errors in fatwās were taken with a seriousness that could be deadly, as in the case of the shaykh who was nearly executed for errors in his fatwās: Ibn Kathīr, 14/35.

[76] For an example of how a slip in Arabic grammar could be disastrous, see Ṣafadī, *al-Wāfī*, 7/20. The recitation of a long or difficult work without error was a somewhat heroic event, and if successful could figure in an individual's death-notice. See Ibn Kathīr, 14/149 for a series of nine majālis in which Muslim's *Saḥīḥ* was read without error. Delivering the khuṭba was also a dangerous performance. See for one example the khaṭīb praised for making his way through the khuṭba "without hesitating or stuttering": Ibn Shākir, *Fawāt*, 1/56.

[77] See for example the shaykh Abū Shāma ridiculed for getting his own genealogy wrong: Abū Shāma, *Dhayl*, 189. Yūnīnī, 2/428 also related an account of someone who got his ancestry wrong. For examples of how errors in ḥadīth transmission were perceived see Ibn Rajab, 2/7; Ṣafadī, *al-Wāfī*, 4/193; Nuᶜaymī, 2/14.

[78] See for example the chief qāḍī who pronounced the qāf as a hamza in a reading of the Qurʾān during Friday prayer, provoking al-Malik al-Muᶜaẓẓam to laugh out loud and end the prayer: Ibn Wāṣil, 4/172–3. See also the shaykh who misspelled two words in a text, provoking another shaykh to make two humiliating puns on his misspellings: Ṣafadī, *al-Wāfī*, 22/300.

[79] For one example see Ṣafadī, *Aᶜyān*, 201a: "wa-yunshidu mā yaḥfaẓuhu jayyidan min ghayri laḥn wa-lā taḥrīf."

[80] For an example of how studying Zamakhsharī's *Mufaṣṣal* was expected to confer a kind of performative mastery, see the case of Ṣadr al-Dīn Ibn al-Wakīl, who was said to have made many solecisms even though he had studied the text: Ibn Kathīr, 14/80. Also Ṣafadī, *al-Wāfī*, 7/20.

competition, cut across the liminal and ritual character of the occasions in which knowledge was transmitted. Although ḥadīth were recited ideally without reference to a text, the possibility of error in a purely oral performance gave pause even to a distinguished shaykh. When ʿAbd al-Ghanī Ibn Qudāma was asked why he read ḥadīth from a text, he replied: "Because I fear surprises."[81] This ambiguity between the liminality of ritual and the agonism of public performance came out especially in the case of formal debates. Debates (*jadal, munāẓara*) were suspect because they excited a rancor incompatible with the ritual character of the transmission of knowledge, and because of their association with Hellenistic learning.[82] An anecdote related of Dhahabī illustrates this point nicely. Tāj al-Dīn Subkī asked Dhahabī, his shaykh, to debate before his disciples. Dhahabī agreed only out of his "love" for his student and "for [Subkī's] instruction." In the event he allowed the students to select the subject of the debate (*masʾāla*), then told them to leave and study the problem. When they returned they found him reciting the Qurʾān with Jazarī, "the Ḥanbalī." The story illustrates three ways in which debate could be conceived as contrary to a shaykh's true purpose in life. Dhahabī engaged in it out of deference to the duties of the master–disciple relationship; instead of preparing for it he occupied himself with an act of piety; and when his students came upon him he was with a Ḥanbalī of the sort these students wanted to learn to refute.

However, in spite of the suspicion in which they were held, debates were also highly regarded because they were the most purely agonistic form of interaction among the learned elite.[83] Of all the cultural productions of the learned elite, formal debates best demonstrate this two-sided character of their interactions. When modern scholars have studied debate, they have concentrated on describing the rules that structured it and the relationship of debate to Hellenistic antecedents. However much formal debates were devoted to determining the true from the false, the sources were at least as interested in debates as contests of social honor between individuals. To Damascenes, the

[81] Ibn Rajab, 2/7.

[82] See Ibn Jamāʿa, 40: "It is not appropriate for the people of ʿilm to engage in competition or enmity, because these are the cause of aggression and anger. The goal of the meeting should be directed towards God, in order to bring benefit in this world and to obtain happiness in the hereafter." See also Ibn Abī Uṣaybiʿa, 693. For condemnations of jadal as Hellenistic, see Abū Shāma, *Dhayl*, 32, 217. When the Hellenistic sciences were suppressed, jadal was included with them. The chief qāḍī of the city once banned jadal along with logic, and tore up books about it in the presence of students: Makdisi, *The Rise of Colleges*, 137; Abū Shāma, *Dhayl*, 32. For another description of jadal as a Hellenistic distraction "that gives no benefit," see Ibn Kathīr, 13/237. Ibn Taymiyya wrote a tract entitled *The Book of Admonishing Intelligent Men from the Fabrication of Useless Jadal*. In it he admitted that the first Muslims (salaf) refuted heretics and innovators through debate, but he criticized jadal for its jargon, its elevation of suppositions into certainties, and its adducing as proofs everyday examples that do not constitute evidence: Ibn ʿAbd al-Hādī, Köp. MS, 14.

[83] A debate could arise out of any formal majlis, as in the case of the visit of the four chief qāḍīs to a lecture where they debated with one of the shaykhs present: Ibn Ḥajar, 2/59. Debates were also arranged for visiting scholars, and were one way for those arriving in the city to gain a good reputation there: Dhahabī, *Taʾrīkh al-Islām*, Köp. MS, 35.

debate was a kind of agonistic performance, similar to modern sports, in which points scored were at least as important to audience and participants as the rules by which the contest was regulated. As in the case of sport today, the disinterested outsider wants to know the rules of the game; but to participants and spectators what was important was the play on the field and the result.

Caustic replies to error were the basis of a cult of the deadly witticism (*ajwiba nādira* or *ajwiba laṭīfa*) much like the cult of the *bon mot* in early modern European court society.[84] In a debate in Baghdād in 605/1208–9, a shaykh quoted a ḥadīth containing a problematic preposition. Tāj al-Dīn al-Kindī interrupted and pronounced the preposition according to one school of thought. The shaykh turned to the wazīr and asked who his interlocutor was, and the wazīr responded: "He is one of the Kalb, so let him bark."[85] The pun was so esteemed that it was lauded in poetry composed to commemorate the event and reported in chronicles written long afterwards.[86] In a later debate in Damascus, Kindī won victor's laurels. A debate was arranged between him and a visiting shaykh from Cairo. After each party accused the other of error in the vocalization of a phrase, the debate degenerated. Kindī denied his opponent's claim to an illustrious ancestry, saying that the ancestor he claimed had no issue. His opponent then tried to make a fool out of Kindī, at one point claiming: "I possess books the equal to Baghdād in value." Kindī responded: "That is impossible. There are no books in the world to equal Baghdād. I, however, possess books the mere covers of which equal your neck!"[87] It was such anecdotes that were reported of debates, and that gave debaters the fame that was so much the object of social labor.[88] The formal structures of debate, which have occupied the greater part of scholarly attention, were perhaps less important to the audience or the participants than the contest they regulated.

Scholars described such competitions in the language of war. They glorified individuals skilled in debate with images of military heroism.[89] The debate was a battle, often glamorized as the "thick of debate" (*ḥawma al-baḥth*).[90]

[84] The devastating *bon mot* was much appreciated at court in Cairo too: see for example Jazarī, BN MS, 420.

[85] Kinda, from which Tāj al-Dīn took his niṣba, was one of the tribes of Kalb, "dog" in Arabic.

[86] Abū Shāma, *Dhayl*, 65. Ṣafadī, *al-Wāfī*, 15/53 carried a different version and described how the event set off a long rivalry. Other derisive puns were made by inverting the meaning of one part of an individual's name. Ibn al-Muṭahhar, as noted below, note 101, was insulted as Ibn al-Munajjas. Another was Ibn al-Mukhṭār, mukhṭār meaning "invested with the authority to judge or choose." Inclined to philosophy and logic, he was the object of a witty versification: "Ibn al-Mukhṭār is not capable of independent judgment; rather, his unbelief is the result of his acceptance of the authority of unbelievers (laysaʾbnu Mukhṭār fi kufrin bi-mukhṭār/ wʾinnamā kufruhu taqlīd al-kufār)": Ṣafadī, *al-Wāfī*, 5/15. For another example of praise for a caustic witticism see *ibid.*, 22/300.

[87] Yūnīnī, 2/428.

[88] For other examples see Sibṭ Ibn al-Jawzī, *Mirʾāt*, 8/515; Ibn Kathīr, 13/39

[89] An especially common term was fursān al-baḥth: see Ṣafadī, *Aʿyān*, 203b. For a study of the pairing of the pen and the sword in literary debates see G.J. van Gelder, "The Conceit of Pen and Sword: On an Arabic Literary Debate," *JSS* 32 (1987), 329–60.

[90] For two examples among many that could be cited, see Nuʿaymī, 1/248, and Ṣafadī, *al-Wāfī*, 4/227.

Formal debates were "contests in the hippodrome," the debater "galloping onto the field of eloquence," attacking like the legendary hero ᶜAntar, struggling against falsehood with ᶜAlī's legendary sword Dhūʾl-faqār.[91] Victory in debate was "striking the opponent with an arrow," "cutting [him] off," or "taking him to the impasse of surrender."[92] When a scholar set out to write a refutation (*radd*), he "unsheathed his sword."[93] Refutations often sported a military image in their titles. Al-Malik al-Muᶜaẓẓam's tract against al-Khaṭīb al-Baghdādī was called *al-Sahm al-muṣīb fī al-radd ᶜalā al-khaṭīb* ("The Bull's-eye in Refutation of the Khaṭīb [al-Baghdādī]").[94] Another radd was entitled *al-Sayf al-ṣaqīl fī al-radd ᶜalā Ibn Zafīl* ("The Burnished Sword in Refutation of Ibn Zafīl").[95]

Such martial metaphors structured whole narratives of scholarly competition. In a 6,000-verse panegyric, Ibn Taymiyya was described in warlike images: "And I strike all who would strip God of His attributes (kull muᶜaṭṭil) with the sword of inspiration (sayf al-waḥī), the blow of a holy warrior (mujāhid) . . . he who would enter the lists (mā dhā yubārizu), let him come forward! Or he who would contest me hand to hand in the hippodrome! . . . Fear not the tricks and snares of the enemy, for their manner of fighting is lies and slander. The soldiers of the followers of the Prophet are angels; and their soldiers are the troops of Satan."[96] Accounts of his debates described them in the language of war. Between Ibn Taymiyya and an opponent in debate there were "military campaigns, battles Syrian and Egyptian," which Ibn Taymiyya, the "brandished sword," won, "with a single bow-shot."[97] These martial images also entered decrees appointing shaykhs to manṣabs. When Muḥammad Ibn ᶜAlī al-Miṣrī was appointed as lecturer and administrator of the Duwlāᶜiyya, the decree referred to him as a man who in the "thick of debate" "cuts through obscurities with proofs [sharper] than a sword."[98] The appointment of Ṣalāḥ al-Dīn al-Alāʾī described the ink that flowed through his pen as the blood that flows from a martyr.[99] The aptness of this language to describe social competition among civilians, and to construct a heroic narrative for civilian careers, was not merely metaphoric license; it was also because shaykhs identified with warriors as engaged in mortal combat.

In addition to these martial invocations, civilian elites also associated the true and the false with the pure and the polluted. As their productions of ᶜilm were "pure," so did they conceive of error as ritual impurity. Scholars treated books that contained errors as pollutions, and washed – the term used was *ghasala*, a term often associated with ritual purity, as removing ritual

91 Ṣafadī, *al-Wāfī*, 12/373; 4/214; Subkī, Staatsbibliothek MS, 9.
92 Ṣafadī, *al-Wāfī*, 7/19; Ṣafadī, *Aᶜyān*, 55a–66b. 93 Subkī, *Ṭabaqāt*, 6/151.
94 Ibn Wāṣil, 4/212; see Subkī, *Ṭabaqāt*, 6/124 for the image of the "bull's-eye" in another title.
95 Subkī, *al-Rasāʾil al-Subkiyya*, 81. 96 *Ibid.*, 94.
97 Ibn ᶜAbd al-Hādī, Köp. MS, 4; Ibn Ḥajar, 1/159. For more military metaphors describing Ibn Taymiyya's skill in jadal see Ṣafadī, *al-Wāfī*, 7/19. 98 Nuᶜaymī, 1/248.
99 Ṣafadī, *al-Wāfī*, 13/415. For another use of this image in a decree appointing a shaykh to a manṣab see Qalqashandī, 12/15.

impurities required cold water – or burned them.[100] Debaters linked their opponents' errors or characters with ritual pollution.[101] The association of error with pollution entered the titles of books, such as the refutation of Ibn Taymiyya entitled *The Purification of Knowledge from the Pollution of Belief.*[102] Writers also represented struggles over the capacity to determine the true from the false as a form of purification. Ibn Taymiyya explained his debates and imprisonment in Egypt in a letter to Damascus: "[The relationship of a] believer to another believer is like one hand washing the other – the dirt is not carried away without a little roughness."[103] This conflation of purity and pollution with truth and error appears again and again in the sources.

As the occasions in which knowledge was transmitted were stages for ritual performances, they were also arenas. Makdisi compared the debater to the gunfighter in the wild west, and some Damascenes did see their competitions in such a light.[104] However, where scholars have viewed these contests as formal competitions by which candidates for appointments were selected, there is not much evidence that debates in Damascus produced candidates for manṣabs. The connection between the formal debate and the manṣab was more indirect. Debates were one way a competitive group of elites demonstrated and tested their social honor – which could then be translated into a manṣab. They were the open and visible manifestation of a form of competition over social honor that made truth and error the contested matter.

Heresy and fitna

Although the contest over correct belief was one of the premier forms of social combat in the city, it remains poorly understood. One reason is that in Damascus, as in many other pre-Ottoman Islamic societies, heresy and orthodoxy were problematic categories: there were no state or corporate bodies that promulgated correct doctrine. In Damascus there were partisans of several systems of belief, including shīʿīs, philosophers, ṣūfīs of various kinds, Ḥanbalīs, practitioners of kalām, and even at least one partisan of Ibn

[100] See for example the shaykh who was publicly censured, and four of his books washed, at the ʿĀdiliyya: Dhahabī, *Taʾrīkh al-Islām*, BL MS, 63. Books containing errors were burned in public in Baghdād: Abū Shāma, *Dhayl*, 56. When a Shīʿī opponent of Ibn Taymiyya died, a book was found in his effects that supported Jews and the "other corrupt religions (al-adyān al-fāsida)." Taqī al-Dīn al-Subkī washed it (ghasalahu): Ibn Kathīr, 14/101.

[101] In the case of those who debated Ibn al-Muṭahhar al-Ḥillī, his name especially invited puns (ṬHR = purity), as in a poem Ibn Taymiyya composed around the time he wrote his refutation *Minhāj al-sunna al-nabawiyya*: "wʾabnuʾl-muṭahhar lam taṭhur khalāʾiquh; dāʿin ilāʾr-rafḍi ghālin fiʾt-taʿaṣṣub (and then there is Ibn al-Muṭahhar, whose character is not pure; he is an agitator for Shiʿism and excessive in taʿaṣṣub)": Subkī, *Ṭabaqāt*, 6/170; Ṣafadī, *al-Wāfī*, 21/262; Subkī, Staatsbibliothek MS, 30, attributed the second half of the line of verse to someone else's long poem. Ibn Taymiyya was said to have referred to Ibn al-Muṭahhar as Ibn al-Munajjas (NJS = pollution): Safadī, *al-Wāfī*, 7/19; 13/85.

[102] *Taṭhīr al-fawāʾid min danas al-iʿtiqād*: Subkī, *al-Rasāʾil al-Subkiyya*, 75.

[103] Ibn ʿAbd al-Hādī, Köp. MS, 92.

[104] Makdisi, *The Rise of Colleges*, 133.

al-Rawandī.[105] Where accusations of false belief were implicit in their interactions, in general these groups lived peaceably if uncomfortably with one another, and they rarely coerced others to abandon their beliefs.

Another reason that the suppression of heresy is poorly understood is that scholars who have studied it have tended to stress the role of the state, of formal practices, and of specialized agencies in its suppression. E. Ashtor, the scholar who studied the suppression of heresy in the Mamlūk period in greatest detail, saw it as a form of "inquisition" carried out by state "tribunals." Ashtor attributed to the Mamlūks a conscious political strategy for the suppression of heresy: "One common trait in all these trials [of heretics] was the great role played by the government, which interfered incessantly in the affairs of the theologians . . . The court knew very well that in the East theological differences often ended in political or social movements, which could give fatal blows to governments."[106] Moreover, Ashtor gave military and civilian elites defined spheres of jurisdiction and a division of political labor in the suppression of heresy: "The Turkish military aristocracy, reserving jurisdiction in criminal matters to itself, gave local judges the freedom to prosecute their enemies, who were also their own." He saw the suppression of heresy carried out by "inquisition tribunals" which had a special "jurisdiction" because "ordinary judges did not have the right to judge crimes against the faith."[107]

Ashtor did an important service both in bringing these materials to light and in treating heresy as a social and political phenomenon. The most critical thing one might say of him is that he no more than others escaped the search for formal and permanent "public" institutions, especially those backed by the state and regulated by law, that have dominated European historiography on Europe and the world outside it. However, the inquisition tribunal, like the other formal domains of knowledge we have examined, is an object of our own creation. By formalizing the practices by which the capacity to define truth was contested, Ashtor like others mistook their social context and meaning.

Contrary to Ashtor's description, there is no evidence for the existence of state or corporate bodies with jurisdiction over heresy. There were no suppressions of heresy by public entities. Rather, struggle over the capacity to define correct belief was understood as fitna or ʿaṣabiyya, as were other forms of elite competition in the city.[108] Fitna in this case as in others was the environment in which the logic of elite social competition must be interpreted.

One difficulty in understanding fitnas over belief and unbelief is the nature of the evidence. From the sources it is clear that there were dozens of fitnas over belief. Unfortunately, concerning most of these fitnas, we know next to

105 Ibn Shākir, Vat. Ar. MS, 37.
106 E. Ashtor, "L'inquisition dans l'état mamlouk," *RSO* 25 (1950), 14, my translation.
107 *Ibid.*, 17, 24.
108 Jazarī, BN MS, 302–3; Abū Shāma, *Dhayl*, 168; Ibn Kathīr, 14/38, 75, 101; Ibn Rajab, 2/21; Nuʿaymī, 1/97–8.

nothing beyond that they occurred. Evidence on them is scarce both because there were no records kept by officially constituted bodies and because the losers in general left behind few surviving accounts of any kind. There is no alternative to observing these events from the perspective of the learned elites who wrote the literary sources.

Of the fitnas over belief cited by the sources, only in fitnas involving Ḥanbalīs do we have accounts from both sides. In spite of the fame of great Ḥanbalī scholars such as Ibn Taymiyya and Ibn Qudāma, the madhhab's situation in the city was insecure. In theory, each of the four madhhabs tolerated the doctrines of the others. In practice, however, Ḥanbalī positions on theological issues varied from those of others to the extent that conflict was latent in their relations. On the issues of the created character of the Qurʾān, the visitation of tombs, and the divine attributes, the Ḥanbalīs of Damascus espoused doctrines that were fundamentally incompatible with the beliefs of the Shāfiʿīs and often the other madhhabs as well. Examples of the suspect status of the Ḥanbalīs appear frequently in the sources. Some Damascenes rejected the claim of the Ḥanbalīs to be Muslims.[109] One waqf for a madrasa specified that "no Jew, Christian, Magian, or Ḥanbalī enter" it.[110] Shāfiʿīs who controlled madrasas in at least one instance tried to keep Ḥanbalīs from entering or benefiting from them.[111]

Yet in spite of strong doctrinal differences, Ḥanbalīs were by and large immune from persecution for their beliefs. When a fitna over theological issues broke out between Ḥanbalīs and others, the sources usually attributed a social dimension to it. One reason for the conflict between Ḥanbalīs and others was the recent arrival of many Ḥanbalīs in the city. Ḥanbalīs included immigrants who had fled Mongols and Crusaders in the Jazīra and Palestine, in addition to arrivals from the region around Damascus.[112] Some of the established aʿyān of the city resented the Ḥanbalīs as outsiders. Once in the city, Ḥanbalī immigrants clashed with Shāfiʿī elites, especially the Banū Zakī and the Banū ʿAsākir. The conflict between newcomers and established households provided the context and often the direct cause of the theological fitnas between Ḥanbalīs and others.

One arena of this conflict was the Umayyad Mosque, the use of which Ḥanbalīs disputed with the Shāfiʿī aʿyān. A fitna over the use of the Umayyad Mosque produced an accusation of unbelief against ʿAbd al-Ghanī Ibn Qudāma, one of the most prominent Ḥanbalīs in the city. The two protagonists were the Banū ʿAsākir, one of the most noted Shāfiʿī families in the city, and a group of Ḥanbalīs that included ʿAbd al-Ghanī, a member of a noted household that arrived in Damascus from Palestine fleeing crusaders. We have accounts from both parties. Abū Shāma, himself a Shāfiʿī who was an admirer of Fakhr al-Dīn Ibn ʿAsākir, wrote that the "ignorant" among the Ḥanbalīs hated the Banū ʿAsākir because they were the aʿyān of the Shāfiʿī ʿulamāʾ. This

[109] Ibn Shākir, Vat. Ar. MS, 69. [110] *Ibid.*, Dhahabī, *Mukhtaṣar ... al-Jazarī*, Köp. MS, 26.
[111] Yūnīnī, 2/337. [112] Pouzet, *Damas*, 80–105.

hatred was supposedly so intense that Fakhr al-Dīn Ibn ʿAsākir feared walking through the Mosque for fear that the Ḥanbalīs "would commit some sin."[113]

The Ḥanbalī Ibn Rajab interpreted the fitna differently. In his account, the cause of the conflict was the envy (*ḥasd*) of the Shāfiʿī aʿyān for ʿAbd al-Ghānī Ibn Qudāma. One of the Banū ʿAsākir supposedly insulted ʿAbd al-Ghānī, and was beaten up in revenge by a group of Ḥanbalīs. Ibn Rajab related that the victim proceeded to the governor and complained that the Ḥanbalīs "wanted fitna." An audience was then convened to discuss the issue, at which the governor, "understanding nothing," ordered that the pulpit (*minbar*) of Ibn Qudāma and the Ḥanbalī library in the Mosque be destroyed. According to Ibn Rajab, the Shāfiʿīs intended to expel all madhhabs but their own from the Umayyad Mosque, and it was only by protecting their area of the mosque with soldiers (jund) that the Ḥanafīs kept their chamber (*maqṣūra*) from being destroyed as well.[114]

All accounts agree that Ibn Qudāma himself was accused of anthropomorphism. A majlis was held for him, at which he responded with the standard Ḥanbalī theological positions. Finally he left the city before a fatwā authorizing his death was drafted, and died in Cairo before he could be repatriated.[115] This was one of the major fitnas in the period, and writers agreed that the reason for it was competition between new immigrants and older elites over the use of the mosque and the dominance of Shāfiʿī aʿyān in the city.

The sources also attributed the accusations of unbelief directed against Ibn Taymiyya to fitna. Of the six occasions on which he was jailed, five were caused by friction between him and factions of the aʿyān of Damascus and Cairo.[116] One resulted from an alliance between the sulṭān and his supporters in Cairo and a number of aʿyān families in Damascus. Ibn Taymiyya was known as an opponent of Sulṭān Baybars al-Jāshnikīr and of his powerful shaykh al-Manbijī. Ibn Taymiyya criticized both openly, saying at one point of al-Jāshnikīr that "his day has passed and his leadership has come to an end."[117] This incited Manbijī's enmity (ʿadāwa), and soon afterwards some of his supporters requested the governor in Damascus to persecute Ibn Taymiyya. This began Ibn Taymiyya's long series of tribulations. Describing one of the later persecutions, Ibn Kathīr attributed Ibn Taymiyya's imprisonment in Alexandria to a scheme by Manbijī to use his relatives there to murder him. When Qalāwūn prevailed over Baybars al-Jāshnikīr, he apparently expected that Ibn Taymiyya would want to take revenge against Manbijī's partisans. He

[113] Abū Shāma, *Dhayl*, 138; Ṣafadī, *al-Wāfī*, 18/235; Ibn Shākir, *Fawāt*, 2/290.

[114] Ibn Rajab, 2/20, 21. See also Ibn Shākir, Vat. Ar. MS, 4; Sibṭ Ibn al-Jawzī, *Mirʾāt*, 8/521, 522.

[115] On fitnas surrounding ʿAbd al-Ghanī Ibn Qudāma see Ibn Shākir, Vat. Ar. MS, 4; Sibṭ Ibn al-Jawzī, *Mirʾāt*, 8/521, 522; Ibn Kathīr, 13/20, 21, 39; Ibn Rajab, 2/20–5; Abū Shāma, *Dhayl*, 46–7.

[116] D. Little, "The Historical and Historiographical Significance of the Detention of Ibn Taymiyya," *IJMES* 4 (1973), 311–27. Little is less interested in the social than the historiographical issues raised by Ibn Taymiyya's jailings, and follows other scholars in seeing the fitnas surrounding him as inspired by the state: 312–13.

[117] Ibn Kathīr, 14/49: "zālat ayyāmuhu waʾntahat riyāsatuhu wa-qarubaʾ inqiḍāʾ ajlih."

asked Ibn Taymiyya for a fatwā authorizing their execution, but Ibn Taymiyya refused.[118] In spite of this refusal, the scholarly factions associated with Jāshnikīr continued to work against him. In the year after Qalāwūn's death these groups and others moved against Ibn Taymiyya again.

The aʿyān fought out many of their conflicts over belief without bringing in ruling groups. When Ibn al-Wakīl made a play for the manṣab at the Adhrāʾwiyya madrasa, his opponents made a case against him by accusing him of unbelief and immorality. He escaped execution at the hands of his own madhhab by seeking the aid of the Ḥanbalī chief qāḍī.[119] In the case of a follower of al-Bājirīqī, killed in 741/1340–1 for "major sins in speech (aẓāʾim minaʾl-qawl)," an audience was held in the hall of justice (dār al-ʿadl) in the palace (dār al-suʿāda). The audience was attended by the aʿyān and the qāḍīs of all the madhhabs but the Shāfiʿīs, but there is no record of the presence of amīrs. Accused of claiming divinity, deprecating the prophets, and associating with skeptics, the accused insulted the qāḍīs present, who condemned and then killed him forthwith. The trial and killing supposedly went against the wishes of both the governor and the Shāfiʿī qāḍī, neither of whom was present.[120] In this as in other cases, heresy was not suppressed by a legally constituted body with a defined sphere of jurisdiction; it rather shows how power was always the prize of a never-ending competition that brought in many groups.[121]

What these examples illustrate is that the suppression of heresy was not carried out by any sovereign or legally constituted state or corporate body, but was rather one dimension of the fitna that was the inescapable environment of elite social life. Ashtor believed that sulṭāns and governors often took the initiative in suppressing heresy. His evidence for this is inadequate and largely from the later Mamlūk period, which he did not distinguish from earlier times. Ruling groups in the high medieval period were generally reluctant to interfere in scholarly fitnas, in spite of the attempts of scholars to enlist them. Only a few rulers and governors ever tried to enforce a set of doctrines, and these attempts did not last.[122]

On the contrary, instead of enforcing orthodoxy, amīrs, governors, and sulṭāns generally suppressed fitnas over belief when they broke out. One such event occurred in 636/1238–9, when a fitna broke out between Ḥanbalīs and Ḥanafīs in the Umayyad Mosque, where each group had a separate area for prayer. Al-Malik al-Kāmil attributed the fitna to the fact that each group had its own khaṭīb, and ordered them thereafter to pray behind a single khaṭīb.[123] Another example was the fitna of 705/1305–6, which broke out at a time when

118 *Ibid.*, 14/54. 119 Nuʿaymī, 1/305. 120 Ibn Ḥajar, 2/441–2; Ibn Kathīr, 14/189–90.

121 See Ibn Kathīr, 14/53, 54, 56, 58, 65; Dhahabī, *Kitāb al-ʿibar*, 341–2; Ṣafadī, *al-Wāfī*, 7/18–22; also Ṣafadī, *Aʿyān*, 65b, 65a, for the Māliki chief qāḍī Aḥmad Ibn Yasīn al-Riyāḥī (d. 764) who beheaded a number of Damascenes for unbelief before being chased out of the city, and repeated what he had done there in both Cairo and Aleppo.

122 See attempts by al-Malik al-Muʿaẓẓam and al-Malik al-Ashraf to ban the rational sciences. Al-Azīz wanted to expel the Ḥanbalīs from Cairo but never carried it out: Ibn Kathīr, 13/18.

123 Abū Shāma, *Dhayl*, 166.

the governor was absent from the city. He quelled the fitna when he returned by ordering that none of the ᶜulamāᵓ discourse on questions of belief, on penalty of forfeit of life and property.[124] Still another theological fitna between Ḥanbalīs and Shāfiᶜīs in 716/1316–17 ended when the governor Tankiz summoned both parties and forced them to make peace.[125] For a final example, when a group of scholars (jamāᶜa minaᵓl-fuqahāᵓ) summoned Ibn Taymiyya to question him about his *ᶜAqīda al-Ḥamawiyya* an amīr beat some of them to quiet the situation.[126] In these cases rulers and governors sought to quell fitna rather than suppress "heresy."[127]

Rarely in fitnas over belief did ruling groups take action unbidden. Aᶜyān determined to silence others enlisted rulers, amīrs, and other powerful men in their struggles.[128] When the Mālikī qāḍī attacked Shihāb al-Dīn al-Baᶜlabakkī for his positions on a number of theological issues, he brought him before the sulṭān, then the governor, before he jailed and beat him himself.[129] When Ibn Taymiyya wished to punish a Christian accused of blaspheming the Prophet, he and another shaykh approached the governor and asked permission to proceed.[130] In another instance, Sibṭ Ibn al-Jawzī asked al-Muᶜaẓẓam why he revoked the authority of a shaykh to deliver fatwās, and was told that a group of scholars had written him requesting that he do so, because of the shaykh's bad character and the mistakes in his fatwās.[131] This was also true in the cases of the trials of Ibn Taymiyya and Ibn Qudāma, both of whom were attacked by groups of scholars who persuaded rulers to take action against them. The "state" thus had no specialized agencies capable of acting independently. The aᶜyān silenced one another through the same diffuse practices by which they contested other social and political prizes.

Shaykhs approached rulers especially to silence others through violence. While in some incidents shaykhs killed people without bringing in rulers, in others the aᶜyān hesitated to act on their own.[132] In 712/1312–13, Ibn Zahra al-Maghribī, who "discoursed" in al-Kallāsa (on what we do not know), incited the ire of a group of the learned. In a petition to the governor they accused Ibn Zahra of deprecating the Qurᵓān and the ᶜulamāᵓ, then brought Ibn Zahra to the dār al-ᶜadl where he capitulated and saved himself.[133] An

[124] Nuᶜaymī, 1/97–8; Ibn Kathīr, 14/37; Birzālī, *al-Muqtafā li-tāᵓrīkh al-shaykh Shihāb al-Dīn Abū Shāma*, 2 vols. Topkapisaray, Ahmad III MS 2951, year 705; Ṣafadī, *Aᶜyān*, 635b.

[125] Ibn Kathīr, 14/75–6. [126] Ibn Kathīr, 14/4.

[127] For another example of the "taskīn" or quelling of fitna over belief see Jazarī, BN MS, 237. See also chapter 1, note 32.

[128] For examples of scholars attacked by other scholars through ruling groups, and forbidden from delivering fatwās or silenced, see Ibn Rajab, 2/21; Ibn Shākir, Vat. Ar. MS, 91; Sibṭ Ibn al-Jawzī, *Mirᵓāt*, 8/696; Ibn Kathīr, 14/123; Ṣafadī, *al-Wāfī*, 7/22; Jazarī, Köp. MS, 103, 493; Ibn ᶜAbd al-Hādī, Köp. MS, 131. [129] Jazarī, Köp. MS, 495.

[130] Ibn Kathīr, 13/335–6. [131] Sibṭ Ibn al-Jawzī, *Mirᵓāt*, 8/710.

[132] See for example Aḥmad al-Rūsī, executed in 714/1314–15 by the Mālikī qāḍī for licentiousness, deprecating the Qurᵓān and ḥadīth, and laxity in his religious duties: Ibn Kathīr, 14/74. Another qāḍī, ᶜAlī al-Bakrī, was almost killed by the sulṭān for his readiness to execute people for irreligion, but was instead exiled and forbidden from discoursing or giving fatwās: Ibn Kathīr, 14/70. Some among the ᶜulamāᵓ planned to execute a shaykh for mistakes in his fatwās, but he was saved by the governor: Ibn Kathīr, 14/35. [133] Ibn Kathīr, 14/66.

episode in Cairo in 704/1304–5 illustrates the absence of formal agencies and procedures in that city too. A Christian who converted to Islam and then apostatized was taken before the sulṭān. When the Christian refused to reconvert, the learned parties involved debated what to do with him, and failed to come to a decision. One group then brought the man to a madrasa and decided there to kill him, whereupon they paraded his head about on a spear to show "what Islamic justice (al-ʿadl al-islāmī) ordered in his case."[134]

By including members of ruling groups in their struggles against one another, the aʿyān were also able to make use of their instruments of coercion and communication. When Ibn Zahra was punished, he was whipped, then seated backwards on a mule, with his head uncovered, and led about the city with the heralds calling out: "This is someone who discourses on ʿilm without true knowledge (maʿrifa)." When Ibn Taymiyya's opponents persecuted him for a creedal statement (ʿaqīda) he had written, they sent the criers around the city to proclaim its falsity.[135] These were not state bodies; they were rather groups of the aʿyān who made use of rulers' resources of coercion and communication. The same holds largely true for the places in which these debates and examinations were held: there was no stable and specific location in which they were held. Without reliable control over instruments of violence, when shaykhs or qāḍīs composed fatwās authorizing the killing of an unbeliever they lacked the capacity to enforce them, especially when they did not have the body of the accused under their control. One example was the shaykh known as al-Ḥarīrī (d. 645/1247–8), accused of inciting passions for singing, dancing, and pederasty among the sons of the elite (*kubarāʾ*) of the city. Several fatwās were issued calling for his death; however, Ḥarīrī proved to be untouchable, and these fatwās were not carried out.[136]

Powerful men were often interested in the outcome of these competitions, although they did not necessarily take part in them. Those condemned to death could escape it if a powerful individual interceded on their behalf. In 737/1336–7 a Shāfiʿī faqīh was summoned to an audience, accused of holding Qarmaṭī beliefs, and sentenced to death. Before he could be killed, a group of amīrs and aʿyān interceded, and he was spared.[137] But others without such influence suffered death before the very men who struggled to spare others. Such was the fate of Ibn al-Ḥaythamī, whose only claim to distinction was his residence in a madrasa and his memorization of a work in Shāfiʿī fiqh. Accused of heresy, he had no patron to intercede on his behalf, and his execution was witnessed by the aʿyān of the city.[138] In fitna over belief as in fitna over manṣabs, intercession was one of the critical practices; and in both cases shaykhs made use of rulers for their own purposes.

We have also misunderstood fitnas over belief by treating them as trials before legally constituted bodies such as tribunals of inquisition. Just as the

[134] *Kitāb tāʾrīkh al-salāṭīn wa al-ʿasākir*, BN MS, 58–9.
[135] Ṣafadī, *al-Wāfī*, 7/22. [136] Abū Shāma, *Dhayl*, 180.
[137] Ibn Kathīr, 14/177. See *ibid.*, 14/70, for another person whose life was spared by the intercession of amīrs with the sulṭān. [138] Ibn Kathīr, 14/122–3.

aᶜyān acquired social capacity informally from individual shaykhs, there were no formal procedures for withdrawing it.[139] The silencing or censuring of individuals followed the same political forms as competitions over the manṣabs, and brought in similar groups of learned elites, lineages, ruling groups, and scholarly and political factions. As there were no specialized agencies for determining truth from error, there were no specialized procedures such as trials or inquisitions. The form the identification and suppression of error took was usually the debate, in which a powerful amīr or a group of scholars invited the object of their suspicion to debate with a shaykh in an audience before the aᶜyān. This crossing of the procedures of the trial before a qāḍī with the debate among scholars raised inevitable ambiguities.[140] As the debate was the principal means by which heretics were tried, and the result of the debate could be the death of one party, the association of scholarly struggle with military violence was occasionally not just metaphor. Taqī al-Dīn al-Subkī's son took some pride that though his father "made war with his disputations (jadālihi), he never splattered with blood the sword-edge of his struggle."[141] As was the case in other forms of fitna, when participants in these contests made reference to an external set of rules, it was more often a weapon of social combat than a description of a formal procedure or mechanism.

The capacity to articulate truth and use violence in its defense was a reward of competitive struggle. It was acquired for a time, and was not held by virtue of a right, patent, or office. There was no sovereign or autonomous body capable of planning and carrying out long-term ideological strategies. Although many involved in such events were qāḍīs, the "suppression" of heresy did not take the form of an official trial but of fitna. When we encounter fatwās and debates dealing with the struggle to define truth, these were objects and instruments of political competition and not formal mechanisms or procedures. When the ruler or governor took part in these struggles, it was usually at the instigation of an outside group; and in any case his interest was usually in maintaining a balance between social peace and the satisfaction of the scholarly factions that supported him. In the case of "heresy," as in the case of "education," western scholars have formalized practices of social competition into social and institutional structures, but in fact there were no legally constituted or socially authorized agencies for determining the true from the false. The capacity to define and suppress heresy was a prize of fitna like other symbolic, social, and political prizes of the city.

[139] A shaykh could however revoke the authority of one of his disciples to discourse in public or to deliver fatwās. See for example the shaykh who, after criticizing Ibn Taymiyya, was banned from discoursing in public by his shaykhs: "anta lā taḥsan ᶜan tatakallam": Ibn Kathīr, 14/115.

[140] See for example one of Ibn Taymiyya's interrogations, in which he complained that his opponent in debate was also his judge: Ibn ᶜAbd al-Hādī, Köp. MS, 71. See also the debate of Shihāb al-Dīn al-Suhrawardī with the learned of Aleppo, after which his opponents wrote a document demanding his execution: Ibn Abī Uṣaybiᶜa, 642. See also Ibn Kathīr, 14/275 for the interrogation/debate in 762/1360–1 of a man who claimed that Pharoah converted to Islam. Also *Kitāb tāʾrīkh al-Salāṭīn wa al-ᶜasākir*, BN MS, 6r.

[141] Subkī, Staatsbibliothek MS, 9.

Conclusion

Law, institutions, even knowledge itself cannot be thought of as formal domains. They were rather simultaneously instruments and arenas of a never-ending struggle for social power and status. No contest over the right to represent truth was without a social dimension that gave it a point. By the same token, few competitions among the aʿyān and against others were imagined in terms of naked interest without bringing in the fundamental structuring values of truth/falsity, legality/illegality (ḥalāl/ḥarām), and purity/pollution. It is difficult to discern a purely political or social dimension within cultural conflicts, or a cultural dimension within political and social conflict, because truth and interest interpenetrated one another.

The competition over the capacity to determine the legal from the unlawful and the true from the false took the forms of other types of competition in the city. The learned elite struggled to keep the right to represent ʿilm within a single group. They also used their control over ʿilm to struggle against one another and against others. But they did not possess institutional means of limiting to a small number the socially recognized capacity to articulate truth through degrees, certification, or ordainment. Even the social power of qāḍīs was not that of an elite with state or corporate instruments of coercion behind them. Rather, "capacity" was the temporary reward of struggle by individuals and their groups against others. These struggles took many forms and were played out in many fields.

Summary

"In an era of upheaval," writes Charles Maier of a similarly resourceful elite, "it is continuity and stability that need explanation."[1] In this study I have tried to identify some of the practices by which the elite of a medieval Middle Eastern city acquired power, resources, and prestige, and reproduced their status in time. One of the principal aims of the study has been to question the often uncritical application to the medieval Middle East of the concepts and methods of European social history. The social history of structures, agencies, and formal processes and routines, constructed from original documents, appeared in Europe answering to particular European social imperatives. It was partly (though not entirely) through such mechanisms that individuals, lineages, and groups in Europe struggled for power, property, and prestige, and passed them on to their descendants. These historiographical practices have been well applied to societies such as Sung China where formal institutions and well-defined social bodies had roles that to Europeans were familiar or made sense. In the cases of Sung China and the Latin West, scholars have been able to identify (and identify with) a familiar principle of legitimate "order." The transposition of either principle to the medieval Middle East works only by positing the continuous "corruption" of the order we have sought to find.

High medieval Syria, however, together with much of the medieval Middle East, was not a society of specialized institutions, state agencies, or of well-defined corporate bodies. Power in all its aspects was relatively undifferentiated, because it was mainly the household and not the agency or public body that held power, and held it in most of its social, political, and economic aspects. As we have seen, because of the nature of political power in the period, elites could not make use of autonomous corporate bodies or state agencies in their strategies of social reproduction. The institutions, groups, and structures historians have studied were little more than aspects of a larger set of practices.

Western scholars may no longer see sulṭāns and amīrs as kings and barons; but still they often conjure up an image of Europe in the medieval Middle East.

[1] C.S. Maier, *Recasting Bourgeois Europe: Stabilization in France, Germany, and Italy in the Decade after World War I* (Princeton, 1975), 3.

It is only by assuming the existence of the structures they analyze that Western scholars have found "systems of education," "colleges," "inquisitions," "the government," and "schools." In each case, scholars have taken practices by which elites competed with one another as evidence for permanent structures and agencies. Scholars have often recognized that these institutions did not regulate social competition as might be expected. But in general this realization has not led them to question the existence of the "systems" they analyze. Rather, they have often seen departures from them as one of two things: an "informal" analogue or a "corruption" of the "system." This is why the period has seemed both "personal" and "disorderly." However, as we have seen, constant unregulated competition over status, power, and revenue sources was the aᶜyān's inescapable environment.

There was no "system" of education, patronage, appointment, or of government. Damascus did not have agencies, autonomous social bodies, or institutions with the power to organize such systems. Rather, Damascus and its revenue sources are better viewed as arenas for competitive practices of political and social struggle. These practices were somewhat restrained by commonly held values and expectations; but they were nonetheless carried out without sovereign or autonomous entities to regulate them. When we formalize practices used in social and political competition into entities such as schools, tribunals of inquisition, systems of education, and the state we may miss many of the critical practices of the city. As we have seen, even the distinctions between the realms of the "political" and the "social" or the "public" and the "private" reads modern relations between state and society into a medieval past that cannot sustain such a clear-cut division.

In the case of the implantation of madrasas in the city, what appear to be specialized institutions were in fact instruments and objects of two separate struggles. To the households of amīrs and a few wealthy civilians, madrasas represented one strategy for the long-term control of property. When members of elite households founded madrasas, they sought to benefit from them as household waqfs. To the aᶜyān madrasas constituted another arena, in which manṣabs became prizes of their own struggles. However, as we have seen, madrasas did not create or train an institutional elite, still less a bureaucratic one. They were not the means by which the state trained its cadres or by which civilian elites transmitted social and cultural capital to their descendants. Instead, to the civilian elite, madrasas represented manṣabs, residences, and spaces in which they interacted. There is no doubt that many who used madrasas experienced them as important religious institutions, but we will mistake the intersection between the transmission of knowledge and the foundation of household waqfs if we study them as the constitution of a new form of higher education.

In Damascus it is difficult to speak of specialized education at all, much less of a "system of education," formal or otherwise. There was no evidence of specialized training in schools, nor was there any form of specialized culture that could be acquired only through formal institutions. The transmission of knowledge did not belong exclusively either to schools or to the period of youth. The primary form of higher culture was one of knowledge production, of wide dissemination, into which the young were initiated; taking it as a whole, as a "system of education," mistakes how the aʿyān acquired knowledge and made use of it throughout their lifetimes. This is also (parenthetically) true of the transmission of knowledge in many Muslim groups today in the Middle East, Asia, Europe, and the Americas.

The aʿyān did not seek to reproduce their status through equipping their descendants with formal qualifications. Rather, in addition to learning law and other fields, they wanted their young to master ritual practices and an often innovative style of deportment and manners. The bonds created by interactions with their shaykhs and others in the ritualized environment of the production of knowledge forged this elite's useful intimacies. Their social and cultural capital – as they themselves expressed it – became the dominant currency in fitna, both in their struggles for manṣabs and in their rivalries for eminence more generally. It is by interpreting the strategies by which they acquired their distinction that historians might break free of paradigms they distrust but are reluctant to abandon.

Once we look for practices and strategies rather than institutions and rules, at the strategic rather than the taxonomic, we are in a much better position to exploit the records that medieval Damascenes composed and preserved. This study has suggested that it is the biographical dictionary rather than archive that constituted the main repository of their critical practices of social survival. The concepts of right, capacity, entitlement, or exemption, whether natural, legal, or divine, are conveyed by the title, charter, degree, or deed, and Damascenes had few of these. Instead, they contested their social prizes through competitive performance of a mass of emblems and signs associated with ʿilm, and on these topics the biographical dictionaries carry masses of information. As with elites of other societies they brandished the past to secure their futures, but what they invoked was neither deed nor title but their memories of their shaykhs. These humble, elusive, and "formulaic" sources not only preserved the memory of the individuals through whom cultural prestige passed. As the useful past, they were also archives of the practices by which households survived over time.

Bibliography

Primary sources

Abū Shāma, *Kitāb al-rawḍatayn fī akhbār al-dawlatayn* (Cairo, 1956)

Tarājim rijāl al-qarnayn al-sādis wa al-sābiʿ al-maʿrūf bi al-dhayl ʿalā al-rawḍatayn, M. al-Kawtharī ed. (Beirut, 1974 repr.)

ʿAskarī, Abū Hilāl, *al-Ḥathth ʿalā ṭalab al-ʿilm wa al-ijtihād fī jamʿih*, Süleymaniye Kütüphanesi, As. Effendi MS 433

Balqīnī, *Maḥāsin al-Iṣṭilāḥ*, in the marginal commentary to Ibn al-Salāḥ, *Muqaddima*

Birzālī, ʿAlam al-Dīn, *al-Muqtafā li-tāʾrīkh al-shaykh Shihāb al-Dīn Abū Shāma*, 2 vols. Topkapisaray, Ahmad III MS 2951

Muʿjam al-shuyūkh, Ẓāhiriyya MS, Majmūʿ 62

Dhahabī, *Kitāb al-ʿibar fī khabar man ʿabar*, Köprülü Kütüphanesi MS 1052

Kitāb al-ʿibar fī khabar man ʿabar, Ṣalāḥ al-Dīn al-Munajjid and F. Sayyid eds., 6 vols. (Kuwait, 1963–6)

Kitāb duwal al-Islām, 2 vols. (Hyderabad, 1356, 1364 S.H.); annotated translation of years 447/1055–6 to 656/1258 by A. Nègre (Damascus, 1979)

Mukhtaṣar min tāʾrikh al-shaykh Shams al-dīn . . . al-Jazarī, Köprülü Kütüphanesi MS 1147

Tadhkirat al-ḥuffāẓ, 4 vols. (Hyderabad, 1955–8)

Taʾrīkh al-Islām, British Library, Or. MS 1540; Köprülü Kütüphanesi MS 1048

Frescobaldi, L., *Viaggi in Terra Santa di Lionardo Frescobaldi e d'altri del secolo XIV* (Florence, 1862)

Ḥarawī, Ali b. Abu Bakr, *Kitāb al-ishārāt fī maʿrifat al-ziyārāt*, J. Sourdel-Thomine ed. (Damascus, 1953), trans. by J. Sourdel-Thomine as *Guide des lieux de pèlerinage* (Damascus, 1957)

Ibn ʿAbd al-Hādī, *Kitāb fī dhikr ḥāl shaykh al-Islām Taqi al-Dīn Abī al-ʿAbbās Aḥmad Ibn Taymiyya wa-dhikr baʿḍ manāqabihi wa muṣannafātih*, Köprülü Kütüphanesi MS 1142

Ṭabaqāt ʿulamāʾ al-ḥadīth, vol. IV, Ibrāhīm al-Zaybaq ed. (Beirut, 1409/1989)

Ibn ʿAsākir, *Majlis min majālis al-ḥāfiẓ Ibn ʿAsākir fī masjid dimashq* (Damascus, 1979)

Ibn Abī al-Wafāʾ, *al-Jawāhir al-muḍiyya fī ṭabaqāt al-ḥanafiyya*, 2 vols. (Hyderabad, 1914)

Ibn Abī Uṣaybiʿa, *ʿUyūn al-anbāʾ fī ṭabaqāt al-aṭṭibāʾ* (Beirut, 1965)

Ibn al-ʿAdīm, *Zubda al-ḥalab fī tāʾrīkh ḥalab*, Sami Dahān ed. (Damascus, 1968)

Ibn al-Athīr, *al-Kāmil fī al-tāʾrīkh*, vol. XII, C.J. Thornberg ed. (Beirut, 1965)
Ibn al-Dawādārī, *Die Chronik des Ibn al-Dawadarī*, 3 vols., U. Haarmann ed. (Wiesbaden, 1960–1)
Kanz al-durar wa jāmiʿ al-ghurar, Ṣalāḥ al-Dīn al-Munajjid et al. eds. (Cairo, Deutches Archäologisches Institut, 1960–72)
Ibn al-Firkāḥ, *Kitāb Sharḥ wa-iqrār Imām al-Ḥaramayn*, BN MS 1226 Arabe
Ibn al-Furāt, *Tāʾrīkh al-duwal wa al-mulūk*, 7 vols. Costi K. Zurayk and Najla Izzeddin eds. (Beirut: American University in Beirut Press, 1936–42). Partial translation by M.C. Lyons as *Ayyubids, Mamluks, Crusaders: Selections from the Tāʾrīkh al-Duwal wʾal-Mulūk* (Cambridge, 1971)
Ibn al-Ḥājj (al-ʿAbdarī), *Madkhal al-sharʿ al-sharīf*, 4 vols. in 2 (Cairo, 1929)
Ibn al-ʿImād, *Shadharāt al-dhahab*, 8 vols. (Cairo, 1931–2)
Ibn al-Qalānīsī, *Dhayl tāʾrīkh dimashq*, H.F. Amedroz ed. (Leiden, 1908)
Ibn al-Ṣalāḥ al-Shahrazūrī, *Ṭabaqāt al-fuqahaʾ*, Süleymaniye Kütüphanesi MS Hamidiye 537
Fatāwā wa-masāʾil Ibn al-Ṣalāḥ, ʿAbd al-Muṭī Amīn Qalʿajī ed. (Beirut, 1986)
Muqaddima Ibn al-Ṣalāḥ wa-maḥāsin al-iṣṭilāḥ, ʿĀʾisha ʿAbd al-Rahmān ed. (Cairo, 1974)
Ibn al-Shihna, *Les perles choisis*, J. Sauvaget trans. (Beirut, 1933)
Ibn al-Ṣuqāʿī, *Tāli kitāb wafayāt al-aʿyān*, J. Sublet ed. (Damascus, 1974)
Ibn Baṭṭūṭa, *Riḥla Ibn Baṭṭūṭa al-masammā tuḥfa al-nuẓẓār wa ʿajāʾib al-ʾasfār*, vol. I (Beirut, 1981)
Ibn Ḥabīb al-Dimashqi, *Tadhkirat al-nabīh fī ayyām al-manṣūr wa banīh*, M.M. Amin ed. (Cairo, 1976–86)
Durrat al-aslāk fi dawlat al-atrāk, Süleymaniye Kütüphanesi MS, Yeni Cami 849
Ibn Ḥajar al-ʿAsqalāni, *Al-durar al-kāmina fi aʿyān al-mīʾa al-thāmina*, 4 vols. (Beirut, n.d.)
Ibn Jamāʿa, *Tadhkira al-sāmiʿ wa al-mutakallim* (Beirut, 1974)
Ibn Jubayr, *Riḥla* (Beirut, 1964)
Ibn Kathīr, *al-Bidāya wa al-nihāya fī al-tāʾrīkh*, vols. XIII and XIV (Beirut, 1981 repr.)
Ibn Khallikān, *Wafayāt al-aʿyān wa anbā abnāʾ al-zamān*, 6 vols. M. ʿAbd al-Hamīd ed. (Cairo, 1948)
Ibn Nāṣir al-Dīn, *Tarājim Ibn Taymiya*, British Library Or. MS 7714
Ibn Qaḍī Shuhba, *Tāʾrikh* (Damascus, 1977)
Ibn Qayyim al-Jawziyya, *Rawḍa al-muḥibbīn*, A. ʿUbayd ed. (Cairo, 1375/1956)
Ibn Qudāma, *al-Ṣārim al-munkī fī al-radd ʿalā al-subkī* (Cairo, 1964)
Kitāb al-ṭawābīn, G. Makdisi ed. (Beirut, 1974)
Censure of Speculative Theology, G. Makdisi ed. and trans. (London, 1962)
Ibn Rajab, *Kitāb al-dhayl ʿalā ṭabaqāt al-ḥanābila* (Beirut, n.d.)
Ibn Ṣaṣrā, *al-Durra al-muḍīʿa fī al-dawla al-ẓāhiriyya*, W.M. Brinner ed. and trans., *A Chronicle of Damascus 1389–1397*, 2 vols. (Berkeley and Los Angeles, 1963)
Ibn Shaddād, *al-Aʿlāq al-Khaṭīra*, S. Dahān ed. *La Description de Damas d'Ibn Shaddād* (Damascus, 1956)
al-Nawādir al-sulṭāniyya wʾal-maḥāsin al-yūsufiyya (Cairo, 1903)
Ibn Shākir (al-Kutubī), *Fawāt al-wafayāt*, ed. Muhi al-Din ʿAbd al-Hamīd, 2 vols. (Cairo, 1951)
ʿUyūn al-tawārīkh, Köprülü Kütüphanesi MS 429
ʿUyūn al-tawārīkh, Biblioteca Apostolica Vaticana, Vaticano Arabo MS 736

ᶜ*Uyūn al-tawārīkh*, partial trans. by H. Sauvaire, in *JA* 9, series t. VI (1896), 369–421
ᶜ*Uyūn al-tawārīkh*, vol. XXI, Nabīla ᶜAbd al-Munᶜim Dāwūd and Fayṣal al-Sāmir eds. (Baghdād, 1984)
Ibn Taghrībirdī, *al-Manhal al-ṣāfī*, vol. I (Cairo, 1957)
al-Nujūm al-ẓāhira fī mulūk miṣr wʾal-Qāhira, vol. II, part 2, no. 1, W. Popper ed. (Berkeley and Los Angeles, 1909–23)
Ibn Taymiyya, *Mukhtaṣar al-fatāwā al-miṣriyya* (Lahore, 1368 A.H.)
Ibn Ṭūlūn, *al-Qalāʾid al-jawhariyya fī tāʾrīkh al-ṣāliḥiyya* (Damascus, 1980)
Ibn Wāṣil, Jamāl al-Dīn al-Ḥamawī, *Mufarrij al-kurūb fī akhbār banī ayyūb* (Cairo, 1953)
al-Jāhiz, *Kitāb al-tāj*, trans. by C. Pellat as *Livre de la couronne* (Paris, 1954)
Jazarī, *La Chronique de Damas d'al-Jazari (Années 686–698)*, J. Sauvaget ed. and trans. (Paris, 1949)
Tāʾrīkh, Köprülü Kütüphanesi MS 1037
Ḥawādith al-zamān, Bibliothèque Nationale, fonds arabes MS 6739
Ḥawādith al-zamān, Gotha Ducale MSS 1559, 1600, 1601
Kitāb tārīkh al-Salāṭīn wa al-ᶜasākir wa al-mulūk, Bibliothèque Nationale, fonds arabes MS 1705
Maqrīzī, *Ighātha al-umma bi-kashf al ghumma* (Cairo, 1940)
Kitāb al-sulūk li-maᶜrifa duwal al-mulūk, M. Ziyāda ed. (Cairo, 1934–9)
Nabulusī, ᶜAbd al-Ghanī, *Taᶜṭīr al-anām fī taᶜbīr al-aḥlām* (Beirut, 1384 A.H.)
Nawawī, *Bustān al-ᶜārifīn*, M. al-Ḥājjār ed. (Aleppo, n.d.)
Fatāwā al-Imām al-Nawawī (Aleppo, 1971)
Minhāj al-ṭālibīn wa ᶜumda al-muftīn, L.W.C. Van den Berg ed. (Batavia, 1882–4)
Tahdhīb al-asmāʾ, F. Wüstenfeld ed. (Göttingen, 1842–87)
Nuᶜaymī, *al-Dāris fī tāʾrīkh al-madāris* (Damascus, 1367–70/1948–51)
Dūr al-Qurʾān fī dimashq (Damascus, 1942)
Nuwayrī, *Nihāya al-arab fī funūn al-adab*, vol. VIII (Cairo, 1931)
Qalqashandī, *Subḥ al-aᶜshā*, vol. XII of the 18-vol. set (Cairo, 1914–28)
Qifṭi, ᶜAlī Ibn Yūsuf al-Shaybānī, *Rawḍa al-ᶜulamāʾ fī tāʾrīkh al-hukamāʾ*, otherwise known as *Ikhbār al-ᶜulamāʾ bi akhbār al-ᶜulāmaʾ*, Süleymaniye Kütüphanesi MS, Yeni Cami 854
Ṣafadī, Khalīl Ibn Aybak, *Aᶜyān al-ᶜAṣr*, Süleymaniye Kütüphanesi, Atif MS Effendi 1809
al-Wāfī bi al-wāfayāt, H. Ritter et al. eds., *Das Bibliographische Lexicon*, vols. I–XXII (Istanbul, 1931–)
Shaᶜrānī, ᶜAbd al-Wahhāb, *al-Anwār al-Qudsiyya fī maᶜrifa al-qawāᶜid al-ṣūfiyya*, Taha ᶜAbd al-Bāqī Sarūr and al-Sayyid Muhammad ᶜĪd al-Shāfiᶜī eds. (Beirut, n.d.)
Sibṭ Ibn al-ᶜAjamī, *Kunūz al-dhahab fī tāʾrīkh ḥalab*, J. Sauvaget ed. and trans., as *Les Trésors d'or* (Beirut, 1950)
Sibṭ Ibn al-Jawzī, Yusuf Ibn Quzlughu, *Kanz al-mulūk fī kayfiyyat al-sulūk*, G. Vitestam ed. (Lund, 1970)
Mirʾāt al-zamān fī tāʾrīkh al-aᶜyān, vol. VIII, part 2 (Hyderabad, 1370/1952)
Subkī, Tāj al-Dīn, *Fatāwā al-subkī* (Cairo, 1936–7)
Subkī, Taqī al-Dīn, *Muᶜīd al-niᶜam wa mubīd al-niqam*, D. Myhrman ed. (London, 1908)
al-Rasāʾil al-Subkiyya
Ṭabaqāt al-shāfiᶜiyya al-kubrā, vols. V and VI (Cairo, 1964–76)

Tarjama, Berlin, Staatsbibliothek preuss. Kulturbesitz Or. 8 MS no. 1440
Yūnīnī, *Dhayl mirʾāt al-zamān*, vols. I–IV (Hyderabad, 1374–80/1954–61)
Zarnūjī, Burhān al-Dīn, *Kitāb taʿlīm al-mutaʿallam ṭarīq al-taʿallum* (Beirut, 1981)

Secondary sources

Amīn, M.M., *al-Awqāf wa al-ḥayā al-ijtimāʿiyya fī miṣr* (Cairo, 1980)
Catalogue des documents d'archives du Caire de 239/853 à 922/1516 (Cairo, 1981)
Anderson, P., *Lineages of the Absolutist State* (London, 1980)
Ashtor, E., "L'inquisition dans l'état mamlouk," *RSO* 25 (1950), 11–26
"L'administration urbaine en Syrie médiévale," *RSO* 31 (1956), 73–128
"Town Administration under the Early Mamluks," in *Proceedings of the Twenty-second Congress of Orientalists*, vol. II (Leiden, 1957)
A Social and Economic History of the Near East in the Middle Ages (London, 1976)
The Medieval Near East: Social and Economic History (London, 1978)
Atiya, A.S.,"An Unpublished XIVth Century Fatwā on the Status of Foreigners in Mamluk Egypt and Syria," in *Paul Kahle Festschrift, Studien zur Geschichte und Kultur des Nahen und Fernen Ostens* (Leiden, 1953), 55–68
The Arabic Manuscripts of Mount Sinai (Baltimore, 1955)
Ayalon, D., "L'Esclavage du Mamlouk," *Oriental Notes and Studies* 1 (Jerusalem, 1951), 29–31
"The Wāfidiyya in the Mamlūk Kingdom," 25 (1951), 89–104
"Mamlūk," *EI* (2)
"Studies on the Structure of the Mamluk Army," *BSOAS* 15 (1953), 203–28, 448–76; 16 (1954), 57–90
"The System of Payment in Mamlūk Military Society," *JESHO* 1 (1957–8), 37–65, 257–96
"The Euro-Asiatic Steppe – a Major Reservoir of Power for the Islamic World," *Proceedings of the Twenty-fifth Congress of Orientalists* (Moscow, 1960)
"The Muslim City and the Mamluk Military Aristocracy," in *Proceedings of the Israel Academy of Sciences and the Arts*, vol. II, no. 14 (1967), 311–28
"Aspects of the Mamlūk Phenomenon: Ayyūbids, Kurds, and Turks," *Der Islam* 54 (1974), 1–32
"Preliminary Remarks on the Mamlūk Institution in Islām," in Perry and Yapp, *War, Technology, and Society*, 44–58
The Mamluk Military Society (London, 1979)
Baer, G., "The Evolution of Private Landownership in Egypt and the Fertile Crescent," in C. Issawi ed., *The Economic History of the Middle East, 1800–1914* (Chicago, 1966)
Balazs, E., "The Birth of Capitalism in China," *JESHO* 3 (1960), 198–216
Chinese Civilization and Bureaucracy (New Haven, 1964)
"Urban Developments," in Liu, *Change in Sung China*
Barfield, T., *The Perilous Frontier. Nomadic Empires and China* (Oxford, 1989)
Bary, T. (de) and Chafee, J.W., *Neo-Confucian Education: the Formative Stage* (Berkeley and Los Angeles, 1989)
Beasley, W.G. and Pulleyblank, P.G. eds., *Historians of China and Japan* (London, 1961)
Beeler, J., *Warfare in Feudal Europe, 730–1200* (Ithaca, 1971)
Bell, C., *Ritual Theory, Ritual Practice* (Oxford, 1992)

Berchem, M. von, "Origine de la madrasa," *Matériaux pour un corpus Inscriptionem Arabicorum*, I (Egypt: Mém, mis, arch. franç. au Caire) 19 (1894–1903), 254–65

Berkey, J., "Education and Society: Higher Religious Learning in Late Medieval Cairo (Egypt)," Ph.D. Dissertation (Princeton, 1989)

The Transmission of Knowledge in Medieval Cairo. A Social History of Islamic Education (Princeton, 1992)

Bianquis, T., *Damas et la Syrie sous la domination fatimide (359–468/969–1076). Essai d'interprétation de chroniques arabes médiévales*, 2 vols. (Damascus, 1986–9)

Bloch, M., *Feudal Society*, 2 vols., L. Manyon trans. (London, 1961)

Blum, A., *Les origines du papier, de l'imprimerie et de la gravure* (Paris, 1935)

Bosworth, C. E. et al., eds., *The Ghaznavids: Their Empire in Afghanistan and Eastern Iran* (Edinburgh, 1963)

The Medieval Islamic Underworld. The Banū Sāsān in Arabic Society and Literature (Leiden, 1976)

The Later Ghaznavids. Splendour and Decay: The Dynasty in Afghanistan and Northern India, 1040–1186 (Edinburgh, 1977)

The Islamic World from Classical to Modern Times. Essays in Honor of Bernard Lewis (Princeton, 1989)

Bourdieu, P., *Esquisse d'une thèorie de la pratique précédée de trois études d'ethnologie kabyle* (Geneva, 1972), trans. by R. Nice as *Outline of a Theory of Practice* (Cambridge, 1977)

La Distinction: Critique sociale du jugement (Paris, 1979), trans. by R. Nice as *Distinction: a Social Critique of the Judgement of Taste* (Cambridge, MA, 1984)

Homo academicus (Paris, 1984)

Choses Dites (Paris, 1987)

In Other Words: Essays towards a Reflective Sociology, M. Adamson trans. (Stanford, 1990)

Le Sens Pratique (Paris, 1980), trans. by R. Nice as *The Logic of Practice* (London and New York, 1990)

Bourdieu, P. and Passeron, J.-C., *Les Héritiers* (Paris, 1964), trans. by R. Nice as *The Inheritors: French Students and their Relation to Culture* (Chicago, 1979)

Bourin-Derruau, M., *Temps d'équilibres temps de ruptures. XIIIe siècle* (Paris, 1990)

Boyle, J. A. ed., *The Cambridge History of Iran*, vol. V: *The Saljuk and Mongol Periods* (Cambridge, 1968)

Brandenberg, D., *Die Madrasa: Ursprung, Entwicklung, Ausbreitung und künsterlische Gestaltung der islamischen Mosche-Hochschule* (Graz, 1978)

Brinner, W.M., "The Banū Ṣaṣrā: a Study on the Transmission of a Scholarly Tradition," *Arabica* 7 (May, 1960), 167–95

"The Significance of the Ḥarafīsh and their Sulṭān," *JESHO* 6 (1963), 190–215

Brown, E.A.R., "The Tyranny of a Construct: Feudalism and Historians of Medieval Europe," *American Historical Review* 79 (1974), 1063–88

Brunner, O., *Neue Wege Der Sozialgeschichte* (Göttingen, 1956)

Land und Herrschaft: Grundfragen der territorialen Verfassungsgeschichte Österreiches im Mittelalter (Vienna, 1965)

Brunschwig, R., "Métiers vils dans l'Islam," *SI* 16 (1967), 41–60

Buell, P.B., "Sino-Khitan Administration in Mongol Bukhara," *Journal of Asian History* 13 (1979), 121–47

Bulliet, R., "A Quantitative Approach to Medieval Muslim Biographical Dictionaries," *JESHO* 13 (1970), 195–211

The Patricians of Nishapur (Cambridge, MA, 1972)
Conversion to Islam in the Middle Period. An Essay in Quantitative History (Cambridge, MA, 1979)
Cahen, C., "L'évolution de l'Iqṭaᶜ du IXe au XIIIe siècle: Contribution à une histoire comparée des sociétés médiévales," *Annales ESC* 8, no. 1 (1953), 25–52
"Aḥdāth," *EI* (2)
"Mouvements populaires et autonomisme urbain dans l'Asie Musulmane du moyen âge," *Arabica* 5 (1958), 225–50; 6 (1959), 25–56, 233–65
"Réflexions sur l'usage du mot 'Féodalité'," *JESHO* 3 (1960), 7–20
"The Turkish Invasion: the Selchükids," in Setton ed., *A History of the Crusades*
Pre-Ottoman Turkey, J. Jones-Williams trans. (London, 1968)
Introduction à l'histoire du monde musulman médiéval, VIIe-XVe siècle: méthodologie et éléments de bibliographie (Paris, 1983)
Canard, M., "Le cérémonial fatimide et le cérémonial byzantin: essai de comparaison," *Byzantion* 21 (1951)
Carruthers, M., *The Book of Memory: a Study of Memory in Medieval Culture* (Cambridge, 1990)
Carter, T.F., *The Invention of Printing in China and its Spread Westward*, ed. and revised by L.C. Goodrich (New York, 1955)
Cattan, H., "The Law of Waqf," in M. Khadduri and H.J. Leibesny eds., *Law in the Middle East*, vol. I (Washington, 1955)
Chafee, J., "Education and Examinations in Sung Society," Ph.D. Dissertation (University of Chicago, 1979)
The Thorny Gates of Learning: a Social History of Examinations (Cambridge, 1985)
Chan, H.K., *Control of Publishing in China, Past and Present* (Canberra, 1983)
Chan, W., "Chu Hsi and the Academies," in Bary and Chafee, *Neo-Confucian Education*, 389–413
Chibnall, M., "Mercenaries and the *Familia Regis* under Henry I," *History* 63 (1977), 15–23
Clavel, E., *Le Wakf ou Habous*, 2 vols. (Cairo, 1896)
Cobban, A., *The Medieval English Universities* (Aldershot, 1988)
Contamine, P., *La Guerre au moyen âge* (Paris, 1980) trans. by M. Jones as *War in the Middle Ages* (Oxford, 1984)
Cottart, N. ed., *La transmission du savoir en Islam (VIIIe–XVIIIe Siècles)* (London, 1983)
Coulson, N.J., *Succession in the Muslim Family* (Cambridge, 1971)
Courtenay, W.J., *Schools and Scholars in Fourteenth-Century England* (Princeton, 1987)
Critchley, J.S., *Feudalism* (London, 1978)
Crone, P., *Slaves on Horses: the Evolution of the Islamic Polity* (Cambridge, 1980)
Pre-industrial Societies (Oxford, 1989)
Daniel, N., *Islam, Europe, and Empire* (Edinburgh, 1966)
The Arabs and Medieval Europe (London, 1975)
Denny, F., "Qurʾān Recitation: a Tradition of Oral Performance and Transmission," *Oral Tradition* 4 (1989)
Douglas, M., *Natural Symbols. Explorations in Cosmology* (New York, 1982)
Dozy, R., *Dictionnaire des vêtements arabes* (Leiden, 1881)
Supplément aux dictionnaires arabes, 2 vols. (Leiden, 1881)
Duby, G., *L'histoire continue* (Paris, 1991)

Duus, P., *Feudalism in Japan*, 2nd edn. (New York, 1976)
Eche, Y., *Les Bibliothèques arabes publiques et semi-publiques en Mésopotamie, en Syrie, et en Egypte au moyen âge* (Damascus, 1967)
Eddé, A.–M., "Une Grande Famille de Shafiites Alépins. Les Banū l-ʿAǧamī aux XIIe–XIIIe siècles," *REMMM* 62 (1991), 61–71
Eickelman, D., "The Art of Memory: Islamic Education and its Social Reproduction," in *Comparative Studies in Society and History* 20 (1978), 485–516
Knowledge and Power in Morocco (Princeton, 1985)
The Middle East: an Anthropological Approach, 2nd edn. (Englewood Cliffs, NJ, 1989)
Eisenstein, E., *The Printing Press as an Agent for Change* (Cambridge, 1979)
Elias, N., *Über den Prozess der Zivilisation*, 2 vols. (Basel, 1939; Suhrkamp, 1976); English trans. by E. Jephcott in 3 vols.: *The History of Manners* (New York, 1978); *Power and Civility* (New York, 1982); *The Court Society* (New York, 1983)
Elisséeff, N., "Les Monuments de Nur al-Din," *BEO* 13 (1949–51), 5–43
"Dimashḳ," *EI* (2)
"Ghūṭa," *EI* (2)
Nūr al-Dīn: un grand prince musulman de Syrie au temps des croisades (511–569 AH/1118–1174), 3 vols. (Damascus, 1967)
Encyclopaedia Britannica, 7th edn. (1842)
Encyclopaedia Britannica, 11th edn. (1911)
Ernst, H., *Die mamlukischen Sultansurkunden des Sinai-Klosters* (Wiesbaden, 1960)
Febvre, L., *The Coming of the Book* (New York, 1934)
Forand, P. G., "The Relation of the Slave and Client to the Master or Patron in Medieval Islam," *IJMES* 2 (1971), 59–66
Franke, H., "Some Aspects of Chinese Private Historiography in the Thirteenth and Fourteenth Centuries," in Beasley and Pulleyblank, *Historians*, 115–34
"Siege and Defense of Towns in Medieval China," in Kierman and Fairbank, *Chinese Ways of Warfare*
"Jurchen Customary Law and Chinese Law of the Chin Dynasty," in D. Eikemeir and H. Franke eds., *State and Law in East Asia* (Wiesbaden, 1981), 215–33
"The Forest Peoples of Manchuria: Kitans and Jurchens," in D. Sinor ed., *The Cambridge History of Early Inner Asia* (Cambridge, 1990)
Frye, R.N. ed., *Cambridge History of Iran*, vol. IV: *The Period from the Arab Invasion to the Saljuqs* (Cambridge, 1975)
Fu Lo-Huan, "Natpat and Ordo. A Study of the Way of Life and Military Organization of the Khitan Emperors and their People," Ph.D. Thesis (University of London, 1950)
Fustel de Coulanges, N.D., *The Ancient City*, W. Small trans. (London, 1873)
Ganshof, F.L., *Feudalism* (New York, 1951)
Gaudefroy-Demombynes, M., *La Syrie à l'époque des mamlouks* (Paris, 1923)
Geertz, C., *Negara: the Theater State in Nineteenth-century Bali* (Princeton, 1980)
Gelder (van), G.J., "The Conceit of Pen and Sword: On an Arabic Literary Debate," *JSS* 32 (1987), 329–60
Gernet, J., *A History of Chinese Civilization* (Cambridge, 1982)
Gibb, H.A.R., "Islamic Biographical Literature," in Lewis and Holt, *Historians of the Middle East*
"The Career of Nūr al-Dīn," in Setton, *A History of the Crusades*
Gibb, H.A.R., and Kramers, J.H. eds., *Shorter Encyclopedia of Islam* (Leiden, 1953)

Gibbon, E., *Decline and Fall of the Roman Empire* (New York, 1907)

Gilbert, J., "The ʿUlamaʾ of Medieval Damascus and the International World of Islamic Scholarship," Ph.D. Dissertation (University of California–Berkeley, 1977)

"Institutionalization of Muslim Scholarship and Professionalization of the ʿUlamāʾ in Medieval Damascus," *SI* 52 (1980), 105–35

Gilsenan, M., *Recognizing Islam: Religion and Society in the Arab World* (New York, 1982)

Goitein, S.D., *A Mediterranean Society: the Jewish Communities of the Arab World as Portrayed in the Documents of the Cairo Geniza*, 4 vols. (Berkeley and Los Angeles, 1967–84)

Goldziher, I., *Muslim Studies*, S.M. Stern and C.R. Barber trans. (London, 1971)

"Education – Muslim," *Encyclopedia of Religion and Ethics*, vol. V, 198–207

Goody, J., *The Interface between the Written and the Oral* (Cambridge, 1987)

ed., *Literacy in Traditional Societies* (Cambridge, 1968)

Graham,W.A., *Beyond the Written Word: Oral Aspects of Scripture in the History of Religion* (Cambridge, 1987)

Grosrichard, A., *Les Structures du sérail, la fiction du despotisme asiatique dans l'Occident classique* (Paris, 1979)

Grousset, R., *L'Empire des steppes* (Paris, 1939)

Haarmann, U., "Mamluk Endowment Deeds as a Source for the History of Education in Late Medieval Egypt," *al-Abḥāth* 28 (1980), 31–47

"Arabic in Speech, Turkish in Lineage: Mamlūks and their Sons in the Intellectual Life of Fourteenth-century Egypt and Syria," *JSS* 33 (1988), 81–114

Hafsi, I., "Recherches sur le genre 'Ṭabaqāt' dans la littérature arabe," *Arabica* 23 (1976), 228–65; 24 (1977), 1–41, 150–86

Halm, H., "Die Anfänge der madrasa," *ZDMG*, suppl. III, i, XIX (1977), 438–48

Havelock, E.A., *The Muse Learns to Write. Reflections on Orality and Literacy from Antiquity to the Present* (New Haven, 1986)

Heestermann, J.C., *India and the Inner Conflict of Tradition* (Chicago, 1988)

Heffening, W., "Waqf," *EI* (1)

Herr, F., *The Medieval World. Europe from 1100 to 1350* (London, 1963)

Herzfeld, D., "Damascus: Studies in Architecture," *Ars Islamica* 9–14 (1942–8)

Hill, D.R., "The Role of the Camel and the Horse in the Early Arab Conquests," in Parry and Yapp, *War, Technology and Society*, 32–43

Hillenbrand, R., "Madrasa," *EI* (2)

Hitti, P., *History of Syria* (London, 1957)

Hodgson, M.G.S., *The Venture of Islam. Conscience and History in a World Civilization*, vol. II: *The Expansion of Islam in the Middle Periods* (Chicago, 1974)

Hok-lam Chan, *Legitimation in Imperial China: Discussions under the Jurchen-Chin Dynasty (1125–1234)* (Seattle and London, 1984)

Holt, P. M., "Mamlūks," *EI* (2)

"The Position and Power of the Mamlūk Sultān," *BSOAS* 37, no. 2 (1975), 327

"The Structure of Government in the Mamluk Sultanate," in P.M. Holt ed., *The Eastern Mediterranean Lands in the Time of the Crusades* (Warminster, 1977)

The Age of the Crusades: the Near East from the Eleventh Century to 1517 (London and New York, 1986)

ed., *The Eastern Mediterranean Lands in the Period of the Crusades* (Warminster, 1977)

Hourani, A., *A History of the Arab Peoples* (Cambridge, MA, 1991)
Humphreys, R.S., "The Expressive Intent of Mamlūk Architecture in Cairo: a Preliminary Essay," *SI* 35 (1972), 69–119
"The Emergence of the Mamluk Army," *SI* 45 (1977), 67–99, 147–82
From Saladin to the Mongols: the Ayyubids of Damascus (Albany, 1977)
"Politics and Architectural Patronage in Ayyūbid Damascus," in Bosworth et al., *The Islamic World*, 151–74
Islamic History: a Framework for Inquiry (Princeton, 1991)
Irwin, R., "Iqṭā^c and the End of the Crusader States," in P.M. Holt ed., *The Eastern Mediterranean Lands in the Period of the Crusades* (Warminster, 1977), 62–77
The Middle East in the Middle Ages: The Early Mamluk Sultanate 1250–1382 (London, 1986)
Jing-shen Tao, *The Jürchen in Twelfth Century China: a Study of Sinicization* (Seattle, 1976)
"Liao," *Encyclopedia of Asian History*, A.T. Embree ed. (New York and London, 1988), 424–6
Jomier, J., *Le Maḥmal et la caravane des pèlerins de la Mecque XIII–XX siècles* (Cairo, 1953)
Kierman, H., and Fairbank, J.K. eds., *Chinese Ways of Warfare* (Cambridge, MA, 1974)
Kinross, J.P., *Portrait of Egypt* (London, 1966)
Kracke, E.A., Jr., *The Civil Service in Early Sung China* (Cambridge, MA, 1953)
Lambton, A.K.S., "Reflections on the Iqta^c," in G. Makdisi ed., *Arabic and Islamic Studies in Honor of Hamilton A. R. Gibb* (Leiden, 1965)
Lane, E.W., *An Arabic–English Lexicon*, 8 vols. (London, 1863–93)
Lane-Poole, S., *A History of Egypt: The Middle Ages* (London, 1901)
Lapidus, I., *Muslim Cities in the Later Middle Ages* (Cambridge, MA, 1967)
Muslim Cities in the Later Middle Ages, 2nd. edn. (Cambridge, 1984)
"Muslim Urban Society in Mamluk Syria," in Hourani and Stern, *The Islamic City* (Oxford, 1970), 195–205
"Ayyūbid Religious Policy and the Development of Schools of Law in Cairo," *Colloque international sur l'histoire du Caire* (Cairo, 1974), 279–86
Lattimore, O., *Inner Asian Frontiers of China* (Boston, 1962)
Lee, T.H.C., *Government, Education, and Examinations in Sung China* (Hong Kong, 1975)
"Life in the Schools of Sung China," *Journal of Asian Studies* 37, no. 1 (November, 1977), 45–60
"Sung Education Before Chu Hsi," in Bary and Chafee, *Neo-Confucian Education*, 105–36
Leiser, G., "The Restoration of Sunnism in Egypt: Madrasas and Mudarrisūn," Ph.D. Dissertation (University of Pennsylvania, 1976)
"The Endowment of the al-Ẓāhiriyya in Damascus," *JESHO* 27 (1983), 33–55
"The Madrasa and the Islamization of the Middle East: the Case of Egypt," *JARCE* 22 (1985)
"Notes on the Madrasa in Medieval Islamic Society," *MW* 76 (1986), 16–23
Review of S.M. Stern, *Coins in Documents from the Medieval Middle East*, in *JSS* 33 (Spring, 1988), 144–5
Lévy, J.P., *Histoire de la Propriété* (Paris, 1972)
Lewis, B. and Holt, P.M. eds., *Historians of the Middle East* (Oxford, 1962)

Little, D., "The Historical and Historiographical Significance of the Dentention of Ibn Taymiyya," *IJMES* 4 (1973), 311–27

A Catalogue of the Islamic Documents from al-Ḥaram aš-Šarīf in Jerusalem (Beirut, 1984)

Liu, J. ed., *Change in Sung China, Innovation or Reconstruction?* (Lexington, MA, 1969)

Lo, W.W., *An Introduction to the Civil Service of Sung China, with Emphasis on its Personnel Administration* (Honolulu, 1987)

Lo Jung-Pang, "The Emergence of China as a Sea Power during the Late Sung and Early Yuan Periods," *Far Eastern Quarterly* 14 (1955), 489–503

"Maritime Commerce and its Relationship to the Song Navy," *JESHO* 12 (1969), 57–107

Luṭfi, H., *Al-Quds al-Mamlukiyya: a History of Mamluk Jerusalem based on the Ḥaram documents* (Berlin, 1985)

MacDonald, D.B., "Mahommedan Institutions," *Encyclopaedia Britannica*, 11th edn.

McKnight, B., *Village and Bureaucracy in Southern Sung China* (Chicago, 1972)

"Mandarins as Legal Experts: Professional Learning in Sung China," in Bary and Chafee, *Neo-Confucian Education*, 493–516

McNeill, W., *The Pursuit of Power: Technology, Armed Force, and Society since A.D. 1000* (Chicago, 1982)

Maier, C.S., *Recasting Bourgeois Europe: Stabilization in France, Germany, and Italy in the Decade after World War I* (Princeton, 1975)

Makdisi, G., "Muslim Institutions of Learning in Eleventh-century Baghdad," *BSOAS* 24 (1961), 1–56

"The Madrasa as a Charitable Trust and the University as a Corporation in the Middle Ages," *Correspondance d'Orient*, 2 (Actes du Ve Congrès International d'Arabisants et d'Islamisants, Brussels, 1970)

"Madrasa and University in the Middle Ages," *Islamica* 32 (1970)

"Law and Traditionalism in the Institutions of Learning in Mediaeval Islam," in G. E. von Grunebaum ed., *Theology and Law in Islam* (Wiesbaden, 1971)

"The Scholastic Method in Medieval Education: an Inquiry into its Origins in Law and Theology," *Speculum* 49 (1974), 640–61

"Interaction between Islam and the West," in Makdisi and Sourdel, *Mediaeval Education*

"Ṣuḥba et riyasa dans l'enseignement médiéval" *Recherches d'Islamologie. Recueil d'articles offerts à Georges C. Anawati et Louis Gardet par leurs collègues et leurs amis* (Louvain, 1978), 207–21

"On the Origin of the College in Islam and the West," in K.I.H. Semaan ed., *Islam and the Mediaeval West: Aspects of Intercultural Relations* (Albany, 1980)

The Rise of Colleges: Institutions of Learning in Islam and the West (Edinburgh, 1981)

"La corporation à l'époque classique de l'Islam," in Bosworth et al. eds., *The Islamic World*

Makdisi, G., and Sourdel, D. eds., *Mediaeval Education in Islam and the West* (Paris, 1977)

Malamud, M., "The Development of Organized Sufism in Nishapur and Baghdad from the Eleventh to the Thirteenth Century," Ph.D. Dissertation (University of California – Berkeley, 1990)

Mann, M., *The Sources of Social Power*, vol. I (Cambridge, 1986)

Massé, H., *Islam*, H. Edib trans. (New York, 1938)
Mayer, H.E., *The Crusades*, J. Gillingham trans. (Oxford, 1972)
Mayer, L. A., *Mamluk Costume* (Geneva, 1952)
Ming-Sun Poon, "Books and Printing in Sung China, 960–1279," Ph.D. Dissertation (University of Chicago, 1979)
Moaz, A.R., "Note sur le mausolée de Saladin à Damas: son fondateur et les circonstances de sa fondation," *BEO* 39–40 (1987–8)
Moaz, K., "Le Mausolée d'Ibn al-Muqaddam," *MIFD* (1929)
Montesquieu, de, *L'Esprit des Lois* (Paris, 1867)
Motley, M., *Becoming a French Aristocrat. The Education of the Court Nobility 1580–1715* (Princeton, 1990)
Mottahedeh, R. P., *Loyalty and Leadership in an Early Islamic Society* (Princeton, 1980)
The Mantle of the Prophet: Religion and Politics in Iran (New York, 1985)
Muir, W., *The Mamluke or Slave Dynasty of Egypt* (London, 1896)
Munajjid, Ṣ. al-D., *L'acte de waqf du cadi ʿUtmān Ibn al-Munaggā* (Damascus, 1946)
Neitzen, R.W., "Hot Literacy in Cold Societies," *CSSH* 33, no. 2 (April, 1991)
Northrup, Linda, and Abul-Hājj, Amal A., "A Collection of Medieval Arabic Documents in the Islamic Museum at the Ḥaram al-Šarīf," *Arabica* 25 (1978), 282–91
Ong, Walter J., *Orality and Literacy: the Technologizing of the Word* (London, 1982)
Parry, J., "The Brahmanical Tradition and the Technology of the Intellect," in J. Overing ed., *Reason and Morality* (New York and London, 1985)
Parry, V.J., and Yapp, M.E., *War, Technology, and Society in the Middle East* (London, 1975)
Pedersen, J., "Masdjid," *EI* (1)
"Some Aspects of the History of the Madrasa," *IC* 3 (1929), 525–37
The Arabic Book, Geoffrey French trans. (Princeton, 1984)
Pedersen, J., and Makdisi, G., "Madrasa," *EI* (2)
Peters, E., *Christian Society and the Crusades, 1198–1229* (Philadelphia, 1948)
Petry, C., *The Civilian Elite of Cairo in the Later Middle Ages* (Princeton, 1981)
"A Paradox of Patronage," *MW* 73 (1983), 182–207
Piere, P., "I Saraceni di Lucera nella storia militare medievale," *Archivio Storico Pugliese* 6 (1953), 94–101
Piltz, A., *The World of Medieval Learning*, D. Jones trans. (Oxford, 1981)
Pipes, D., *Slave Soldiers and Islam: the Genesis of a Military System* (New Haven and London, 1981)
Poliak, A.N., *Feudalism in Egypt, Syria, Palestine, and the Lebanon, 1250–1900* (London, 1939)
Popper, W., *Egypt and Syria under the Circassian Sultans 1382–1468 A.D. Systematic Notes to Ibn Tughri Birdi's Chronicles of Egypt* (Berkeley and Los Angeles, 1955–8)
Pouzet, L., "Prises de position autour du samaʾ en Orient musulman au VIIe/xiiie siècle," *SI* 57 (1983), 119–34
"La descendance de l'historien ʿAli Ibn ʿAsākir et ses alliances à Damas au viie/XIIIe siècle," in *Mélanges M. Allard et P. Nwyia* (1984), 515–29
Damas au VIIe/XIIIe siècle. Vie et structures religieuses d'une métropole islamique (Beirut, 1988)

Prestwich, J.O., "The Military Household of the Norman Kings," *English Historical Review* 96 (1981)
Rabie, H., " The Size and Value of the Iqtā in Egypt 564–741 A.H./1169–1341 A.D.," in M.A. Cook ed., *Studies in the Economic History of the Middle East from the Rise of Islam to the Present Day* (London, 1970), 129–38
The Financial System of Egypt, A.H. 564–741/A.D. 1169–1341 (London, 1972)
Reischauer, E.O. and Fairbank, J.K., "China's Early Modern Society," in Liu, *Change in Sung China*, 2, 3
Risciani, N., *Documenti e firmani* (Jerusalem, 1931)
Rodinson, *Europe and the Mystique of Islam*, R. Veinus trans. (Seattle, 1987)
Rodzinski, W., *A History of China*, vol. I (Oxford, 1979)
Rosenthal, F., *Knowledge Triumphant: the Concept of Knowledge in Mediaeval Islam* (Leiden, 1970)
Runciman, S., *A History of the Crusades*, 3 vols. (Cambridge, 1951–4)
Sack, D., *Damaskus. Entwicklung und Struktur einer Orientalisch-Islamischen Stadt* (Mainz, 1989)
Salibi, K.S., "Ibn Jamāᶜa," *EI* (2)
"The Banū Jamāᶜa: A Dynasty of Shāfiᶜī Jurists in the Mamlūk Period," *SI* 9 (1958), 97–109
Sanders, P., "The Court Ceremonial of the Fatimid Caliphate in Egypt," Ph.D. Dissertation (Princeton, 1984)
"From Court Ceremony to Urban Language: Ceremonial in Fatimid Cairo and Fustāt," in Bosworth et al., *The Islamic World*, 311–21
Saunders, J. J., *The History of the Mongol Conquests* (New York, 1971)
Sauvaget, J., "Le cénotaphe de Saladin," *RAA* 6 (1929–30), 168–75
Les Monuments Historiques de Damas (Beirut, 1932)
"L'architecture musulmane en Syrie," *RAA* 8 (1934), 19–54
"Notes sur quelques monuments musulmanes de Syrie: à propos d'une étude récente," *Syria* 24 (1944–5), 211–31; 25 (1946–8), 259–67
"Décrets mamalouks de Syrie," *BEO* 2 (1932), 1–52; 3 (1933), 1–29; 12 (1947–8), 5–60
Sauvaget, J., and Ecochard, M., *Les monuments Ayyoubides de Damas*, 4 vols. (Paris, 1938–50)
Schacht, J., *An Introduction to Islamic Law* (Oxford, 1964)
Setton, K., gen. ed., *A History of the Crusades*, 2nd edn. (Madison, 1969)
Shalabi, A., *History of Muslim Education* (Beirut, 1954)
Shumaysī, H., *Madāris dimashq fī al-ᶜaṣr al-ayyūbī* (Beirut, 1983)
Sivan, E., *Interpretations of Islam, Past and Present* (Princeton, 1985)
Smith, P.J., *Taxing Heaven's Storehouse: Horses, Bureaucrats, and the Destruction of the Sichuan Tea Industry, 1074–1224* (Cambridge, MA, 1991)
Sourdel, D., "Les professeurs de madrasa à Alep aux XIIe–XIIIe siècles d'après Ibn Shaddad," *BEO* 13 (1949–51), 85–115
"Questions de cérémonial ᶜabbaside," *REI* 28 (1960), 121–48
"Réflexions sur la diffusion de la madrasa en orient du xie au xiiie siècle," *REI* 44 (1976), 165–84
Sourdel-Thomine, J., "Locaux d'enseignements et madrasas dans l'islam médiéval," *REI* 44 (1976), 185–198

Sourdel-Thomine, J., and Sourdel, D., "Nouveaux documents sur l'histoire religieuse et sociale de Damas au Moyen-Age," *REI* 32, no. 1 (1964), 1–25

Springborg, P.S., "The Contractual State. Reflections on Oriental Despotism," *History of Political Thought*, 8, no. 3 (Winter, 1987), 395–433

Western Republicanism and Oriental Despotism (Austin, TX, 1992)

Stallybrass, P., and White, A., *The Politics and Poetics of Transgression* (Cornell, 1986)

Stern, S.M., "Petitions from the Mamluk Period," *BSOAS* 27 (1964), 1–32; 29 (1966), 233–76

Documents from Islamic Chanceries (Oxford, 1965)

"Two Ayyūbid Documents from Sinai," in S.M.Stern ed., *Documents from Islamic Chanceries* (Oxford, 1965), 9–38, 207–16

Street, B.V., *The Theory and Practice of Literacy* (Cambridge, 1984)

Sublet, J., "Le séquestre sur les jardins de la Ghouta (Damas 666/1267)," *SI* 43 (1976), 81–6

Tabba, Y. (al-), "The Architectural Patronage of Nūr al-Dīn (1146–1174)," Ph.D. Dissertation (New York University, 1982)

Talas, A., *La Madrasa Nizamiyya et son histoire* (Paris, 1939)

Taylor, C., "The Cult of the Saints in Late Medieval Egypt," Ph.D. Dissertation (Princeton University, 1989)

Tibawi, A.L., "Origin and Character of the Madrasa," *BSOAS* 25 (1962), 225–38

Tribe, K., *Land, Labor, and Economic Discourse* (London, 1978)

Trimingham, J. S., *The Sufi Orders in Islam* (Oxford, 1971)

Tritton, A.S., *Materials on Muslim Education in the Middle Ages* (London, 1959)

Twitchett, D.C., "Chinese Biographical Writing," in Beasley and Pulleyblank, *Historians*, 95–114

Tyan, E., *Histoire de l'organisation judiciaire en pays d'Islam*, 2 vols. (Paris, 1938–43)

Ugur, A., *The Ottoman ᶜUlemā in the mid-17th Century: an Analysis of the Vakāʾiʿül-Fuzala of Mehmed Seyhi Ef*, in *Islamkundlische Untersuchungen*, Band 131 (Berlin, 1986)

Vajda, G., "La liste d'autorités de Manṣūr Ibn Sālim Wajīh al-Dīn al-Hamdānī," *JA* 253 (1965)

Les certificats de lecture et de la transmission dans les manuscrits arabes de la Bibliothèque Nationale de Paris (Paris: Publications de l'Institut de recherches et de l'histoire des textes, VI, 1957)

La transmission du savoir en Islam (VIIIe–XVIIIe siècles), N. Cottart ed. (London, 1983)

Valensi, L., *Venise et la Sublime Porte. La Naissance du despote* (Paris, 1987)

Veyne, P., *Bread and Circuses: Historical Sociology and Political Pluralism*, B. Pearce trans. (London, 1990)

von Glan, R., *The Country of Streams and Grottoes. Expansion, Settlement, and the Civilizing of the Sichuan Frontier in Song Times* (Harvard, 1987)

Vyronis, S., Jr., "Manpower in Byzantine and Turkish Societies," in Parry and Yapp, *War, Technology, and Society*, 125–52

Wach, J., "Master and Disciple: Two Religio-Sociological Studies," *Journal of Religion* 42 (January, 1962), 1–21

Weber, M., *Economy and Society*, G. Roth and C. Wittich eds., 2 vols. (Berkeley and Los Angeles, 1978)

"The Chinese Literati," in *From Max Weber: Essays in Sociology*, H. Gerth and C. Wright Mills eds. (New York, 1958)
Wei-Ming, T., "The Sung Confucian Idea of Education: A Background Understanding," in Bary and Chafee, *Neo-Confucian Education*, 139–50
Wensinck, A.J., *Concordance et indices de la tradition musulmane*, 2nd edn. (Leiden, 1992)
White, L., *Medieval Technology and Social Change* (Oxford, 1962)
"The Crusades and the Technological Thrust of the West," in Parry and Yapp, *War, Technology, and Society*, 97–112
Wiet, G., "La Madrasa Khaidariiya, à Damas," *Mélanges Gaudefroy-Demombynes* (Cairo, 1935–45)
L'Egypte Arabe (Paris, 1937)
"Répertoire des décrets mamlouks de Syrie," in *Mélanges René Dussaud*, 2 vols. (Paris, 1939), 521–37
Wink, A., *Al-Hind: The Making of the Indo-Islamic World* vol. I (Leiden, 1990)
Land and Sovereignty in India. Agrarian Society and Politics under the Eighteenth-century Maratha Svarājya (Cambridge, 1986)
Wittfogel, K. and Feng, Chia-Sheng, *History of Chinese Society: Liao (907–1125)* (Philadelphia, 1949)
Wüstenfeld, F., *Die Academien der Araber und ihre Lehrer* (Göttingen, 1837)
"Stammtafel der Familie Banū Asākir," in *Orientalia* (Amsterdam, 1846)
Yates, F.A., *The Art of Memory* (Chicago, 1966)
Yusuf, M.D., *Economic Survey of Syria during the Tenth and Eleventh Centuries*, in *Islamkundlische Untersuchungen*, Band 114 (Berlin, 1985)
Zilfi, M. C., *The Politics of Piety: the Ottoman Ulema in the Post Classical Age (1600–1800)* (Minneapolis, Bibliotheca Islamica, 1988)

Index